BODY IMAGE
AND PERSONALITY

BODY IMAGE
AND PERSONALITY

by

SEYMOUR FISHER

State University of New York
Upstate Medical Center, Syracuse

AND

SIDNEY E. CLEVELAND

Veterans Administration Hospital, Houston, Texas
Baylor University College of Medicine

SECOND REVISED EDITION

DOVER PUBLICATIONS, INC., NEW YORK

This Dover edition, first published in 1968, is a
revised and expanded republication of the work
originally published by D. Van Nostrand Company
in 1958. This edition contains a new Preface, a new
chapter, an additional bibliography, and new indexes
prepared by the authors.

Standard Book Number: 486-21947-X
Library of Congress Catalog Card Number: 68-19449

Manufactured in the United States of America
Dover Publications, Inc.
180 Varick Street
New York, N. Y. 10014

Preface to the Dover Edition

···

ALMOST TEN years have elapsed since this book was first published. From the very beginning it elicited strong reactions, both positive and negative. The result has been a vigorous mobilization of work dealing with the body boundary and also other related body-image dimensions. Over twenty-five dissertations and a total of about one hundred studies have issued from the hypotheses and models we originally offered in 1958. As will be described in the new supplementary chapter included in this edition, the accumulating results have not only been largely supportive of such models but, in addition, have disclosed further profitable areas to which they may be applied. It has become apparent that an individual's boundaries play a fundamental role in many aspects of his behavior. To know the state of his boundaries enables one to make meaningful predictions about his behavior at many levels, ranging diversely from the physiological to the characterological.

The growing support for the validity of boundary formulations is paralleled by a steeply accelerated interest in other body-image problems. A dramatic increase in research dealing with the body image has occurred. The body experiential framework has been shown in a range of experiments to be implicated in perceptual processes, affective attitudes and sets, patterns of physiological activation, and numerous other response realms. Clearly, the body as a psychological object has begun to assume a recognized role in the stream of modern psychology. One may anticipate that the next ten years will be marked by the application of body-image concepts and techniques to many new psychological problems. The impact should be of both theoretical and practical import.

SEYMOUR FISHER
SIDNEY E. CLEVELAND

Syracuse, New York
Houston, Texas
November, 1967

Preface to the First Edition

IN THIS book we shall concern ourselves with elaborating a point of view that emphasizes the importance of the individual's concept of his body (body image) in influencing his behavior.

There are several major objectives which we have set for ourselves in this respect. First, we shall review in considerable detail previous thought and research concerning body-image phenomena. Second, we shall describe some of our own new theoretical formulations concerning body image and the program of investigation which grew out of these formulations. This program has involved a series of research projects concerning the relationship of body image to such diverse variables as need for achievement, site of psychosomatic symptomatology, response to psychotherapy, behavior in groups, cultural patterns, and modes of physiological response. Our purpose has been to map out the areas in which body-image concepts show exploratory or predictive value. Finally, we have attempted to integrate our total findings into a generalized theory concerning the part that body image plays in personality functioning.

Many of the concepts which dominate personality theory today reflect their philosophical heritage in the fact that they deal with body phenomena only tangentially. It has been difficult for personality theorists to assimilate the individual's body as a concept into their matrix of personality concepts. This has been true whether one considers the individual's body from the point of view of its physiological characteristics or in terms of its subjective experiential significance to the individual. Personality theorists have developed relatively elaborate formulations concerning the individual's way of organizing his perceptions of the behaviors of others. But they have failed to work out any but the simplest formulations regarding how the individual organizes his perceptions of his own body and how these perceptions affect his behavior. Personality concepts like "identification," "projection," "valence," and "role" are typically presented in terms which, by and large, ignore the individual's body as a psychological variable involved in the process being defined. One finds instances in which a serious attempt is made to emphasize the importance of "body" in a given personality process. The emphasis, however, is usually a gesture that lacks documentation. There are few instances in which the concept of "body" has actually been worked into a personality scheme in the same detail and at an equivalent level with the other dimensions of such schemes. "Body" has found its way into personality theory in an irregular unsystematic fashion. Only in the sense that it is conceived of as a physiological system which produces needs and drives has it gained any sort of general interest. The main current of personality work has operationally bypassed "body" as a psychological construct.

We were aided in our work by an extremely large array of persons who are individually cited at appropriate points in the book. To an unusual degree we have been able to use materials and data collected by others and to integrate them into the broad pattern of our research. The friendly way in which various researchers have made their results available to us exceeded our most optimistic expectations and pointed up a widespread readiness in the research community to be cooperatively helpful.

Special thanks are due Dr. Robert B. Morton, Chief Psychologist, Houston VA Hospital, who encouraged and facilitated our research for many years. It is not possible to express adequately how grateful we are for the sustained help of our respective wives who not only lent their general moral support but who were frequently called upon to do such diverse jobs as administering tests, typing portions of the manuscript, and proofreading.

Dr. George Faibish, Dr. Wayne Holtzman, Dr. William Fairweather, Dr. Richard I. Evans, Dr. Daniel Sheer, Dr. Stanley King, and also numerous staff members of the Houston VA Hospital have contributed in diverse ways to the solution of many problems that we encountered.

The editor of this series, Dr. David McClelland, devoted much energy to the task of finding ways to clarify and sharpen the presentation of our findings.

Mrs. Marian Moore and Mrs. Fontaine Thorn were the typists who patiently endured the endless revising and reshaping of the manuscript.

SEYMOUR FISHER
SIDNEY E. CLEVELAND

Houston, Texas
February, 1958

Contents

Introduction

BEFORE proceeding to a review of the literature concerned with body image, it would be well to note broadly some explicit and implicit meanings which the term *body* has taken on in contemporary personality literature. One may roughly distinguish five overlapping categories of significance assigned to it.

(1) One current of work has equated *body* with *body type*. Sheldon and Stevens (280), Kretschmer (181), and others have energetically tried to demonstrate relationships between dimensions of the body structure and a variety of personality traits. They have sought, for example, to prove that such variables as bone structure and muscle distribution are significantly correlated with trait patterns. At this level, *body* is conceptualized principally as a series of measures of body structures.

(2) From another point of view, body has been equated with various measures of physiological function (e.g., blood pressure and galvanic skin reflex). Workers such as Lacey (183), Malmo and Shagass (207), and Wenger (333, 334) who take this approach seek to integrate body into personality formulations by demonstrating correlations between physiological measures and personality variables. They have been interested in developing theories concerning the manner in which the physiological occurrences in the body are linked with the behaviors which are defined as *personality*.

(3) Body concepts have also been introduced into personality theory apropos of serious body handicap or deformity. Body has been assigned importance in explaining the personality characteristics of individuals whose body structure is somehow so distorted or mutilated as to handicap them badly. Thus the absence of a body part (e.g., due to the amputation of an arm or leg) may be designated as a factor in explaining why an individual feels negatively toward himself or why he is compensatorily motivated in the direction of very high achievement. Adler (3) has probably pursued this avenue of approach farther than anyone else in its various logical alternatives. Within this framework body is a construct mainly defined relative to the defensive reactions it evokes from the personality. It is treated as if it had importance only in the extreme class of instances in which there is serious interference with its normal functioning.

ix

(4) Of course, the term *body* has acquired specific connotations in the area of psychosomatics. Those who have theorized and done research in this area, e.g., Alexander (6) and Wolff (354), have had the stated objective of demonstrating meaningful linkages between personality concepts and patterns of symptoms associated with certain types of body malfunctioning. It has been the intent to reduce the gap between personality concepts and body concepts. In actuality, most of the studies in this vein have sought to show how personality forces may distort the body physiology processes in such a way as to produce body illness. Within this framework body is primarily a symptom construct. It takes on the characteristics of a complicated screen upon which are projected symptom representations of personality patterns. There is rather limited concern in the psychosomatic literature with the body as a psychological phenomenon. For example, one finds few references to the possible role of the individual's way of perceiving his own body in the production of psychosomatic symptoms. It should also be observed that within the psychosomatic frame of reference body is treated pretty much as something noteworthy only in the extreme instances in which its normal functioning breaks down. There has been relatively little interest in the *bodies* of normal persons who do not develop clinical symptomatology.

(5) Perhaps the least known and least explored concept of body is that which has been formulated in terms of *body image*. *Body image* is a term which refers to the body as a psychological experience, and focuses on the individual's feelings and attitudes toward his own body. It is concerned with the individual's subjective experiences with his body and the manner in which he has organized these experiences. The assumption is that as each individual develops he has the difficult task of meaningfully organizing the sensations from his body—which is one of the most important and complex phenomena in his total perceptual field. It is a phenomenon relatively more complex and difficult to organize perceptually than other phenomena "out there" because of its unique simultaneous role as a participant in the perceptual process and also as the object of this same perceptual process. Those who have explored the body-image concept, e.g., Schilder (268), usually make the assumption that the manner in which the individual accomplishes this difficult organizational task becomes one of the primary dimensions in his overall system of standards for interpreting the world. The body image is literally an image of his own body which the individual has evolved through experience. The word *image* is possibly misleading because it might be interpreted as referring only to those attitudes which he holds toward himself of which he is consciously aware. Actually the term *body image* involves no assumptions regarding the availability to con-

scious knowledge of such attitudes and feelings. Indeed, it is currently a loose, generalized term with very few specific connotations.

Body image may in certain respects overlap the various usages of concepts like *ego, self,* and *self concept.* Although the term *body image* is anchored in phenomena relating to attitudes toward the body, it has wider implications which cross over into other personality areas. We shall arbitrarily postpone a detailed consideration of this overlap until we have completed a thorough analysis of a range of data pertaining to body image.

BODY IMAGE
AND PERSONALITY

PART ONE

Body Image and Body-Image Boundaries

....

CHAPTER ONE

A Survey of What Is Known about Body Image

THE BODY-IMAGE concept is difficult to trace in a historical sense because it has found application in such a diverse number of disciplines and levels of thought. It is striking over how wide a range the concept has been evaluated as a potentially useful frame of reference. As one scans the literature, one finds it referred to apropos of neurological problems, psychiatric problems, hypnotic phenomena, psychosomatic illnesses, drug effects, psychotherapy results, and so forth. In this chapter we shall review the use of the concept in these various areas and summarize the more dependable conclusions that seem to be justified on the basis of this past work.

NEUROLOGICAL CONTRIBUTIONS

It is among neurologists that one finds some of the earliest thinking about body image. They were forcefully confronted with the concept in terms of the unusual and bizarre attitudes which patients with brain damage often adopt toward their bodies. Patients with various brain lesions manifest a whole gamut of distorted body ideas. Such patients may, for example, be unable to distinguish the left side of the body from the right; they may deny the existence of various body parts; they may be unable to acknowledge the incapacitation of paralyzed body parts; they may falsely attribute new or supernumerary body parts to themselves. Following are some vivid descriptions of body-image distortions shown by neurological patients which are described by Critchley (68, p. 235) in a review of the pertinent literature.

> Examples of these more fantastic disorders of the body-image may be given. . . . A patient with an embolism of the right middle cerebral artery remembered that in the first days following his stroke he thought his paralyzed foot belonged to the man in the next bed. He also developed other corporeal fantasies—"It felt as if I were missing the left side of my body, but also too as though this dummy side were lined with iron so that it was too heavy to move. I even

3

fancied my head filled with bricks." Ehrenwald (1931) reported interesting reactions on the part of his patients toward their left-sided paralyzed limbs. Some patients regarded the left arm as "strange, ugly, disfigured, artificial, enlarged, shapeless, thickened, shortened, or snake-like." One patient insisted that a board had been inserted in place of the left side of the trunk and the left limbs.

Such distortions are clear and forceful. They indicate quite sharply that the individual is no longer thinking about his body the way he thought of it previous to his illness. In exaggerated form they point up the fact that the individual's attitudes toward his body are vulnerable to radical change. Neurologists who were exposed to the impact of such phenomena became curious about these body attitudes and feelings. They wondered how they developed, how they were organized, and under what conditions they could be disrupted.

Just before the turn of the century a French neurologist, Bonnier (42), was already making careful observations of the distortions in body attitude shown by some of his patients. He called attention to such distortions, documented them with clinical data, and offered some suggestions concerning their significance. Among some of the most interesting phenomena he noted were instances in which the individual actually felt that his whole body had completely disappeared (asche-matia). In Bonnier's work one first sees a formal explicit recognition of the fact that body image is something worth studying.

In the early 1900s the German neurologist A. Pick (235) also became interested in the body-image problem. He introduced the term *auto-topagnosia* to refer to disturbances in orientation to one's body surface (e.g., not being able to distinguish the right side from the left side). He conjectured that the individual in the course of his development evolves a "spatial image of the body." This image is an inner representation of one's own body as it appears to him consciously from information supplied by the senses. One of the special areas to which he attempted to apply body-image concepts had to do with phantom-limb phenomena. He postulated that the phantom-limb sensations experienced by amputees were a function of discrepancies between the previous body configuration and the new altered body configuration resulting from the amputation. Generally he was motivated to conceptualize and explain his clinical observations in terms of some central body-image mechanism or process. He was reaching for a model or construct which would make sense out of the diverse body distortions he encountered among his patients.

Henry Head, the British neurologist who published some of his major ideas around 1920, made body image one of the most important constructs in his system of thinking about neurological problems. Indeed,

Head was one of the first persons to construct a fairly elaborate theory concerning body image. He concluded on the basis of his observations that each individual gradually constructs a picture or model of himself which becomes a standard against which all body movements and postures are judged. Without such a model he did not see how the individual would be able to change from one posture to another in a coherent way. He indicated that each new movement we make must be evaluated relative to a continuous standard of some sort which will permit an integration of what is now occurring with what went on "before." He applied the term *schema* to this standard of comparison. It is worth while to quote one of Head's (147, p. 605) summary statements concerning the concept of schema:

> Every recognizable change enters into consciousness already charged with its relation to something that has gone before, just as on a taximeter the distance is presented to us already transformed into shillings and pence. So the final products of the tests for the appreciation of posture or passive movement rises into consciousness as a measured postural change.
>
> For this combined standard, against which all subsequent changes of posture are measured before they enter consciousness, we propose the word "schema." By means of perpetual alterations in position we are always building up a postural model of ourselves which constantly changes. Every new posture of movement is recorded on this plastic schema, and the activity of the cortex brings every fresh group of sensations evoked by altered posture into relation with it. Immediate postural recognition follows as soon as the relation is complete.

He assumed that much of the functioning of the schema was unconscious. Although he emphasized the importance of the schema mainly in terms of its guiding influence upon posture and body orientation, there was implicit in his speculations the idea that the schema was a frame of reference for evaluating a wide range of experiences. As one reads his formulations, one can see that he is implicitly proposing that some form of body image is one of the fundamental standards in any individual's judgmental system. Others (229, 16) have pointed out the limitations of Head's views. For example, he never seemed to be able to define with any specificity how a schema is organized or how it actually influences judgments. However, there is no doubt that he had a great influence on the thinking of many other neurologists. He stimulated analysis of many neurological syndromes (e.g., hemiasomatognosia and anosognosia) in body-image terms. It is less well known that he influenced important aspects of Bartlett's work (229) on selective memory. He sensitized Bartlett to the idea that our current modes of organizing new sensory data are dependent upon the models of past experience we have built up.

In Austria and in Germany the body-image approach stirred up the most long-term interest, and the foundations of a great many of our current body-image postulates were built up there. In Vienna particularly there was a group which was fascinated with body-image phenomena. Beginning in the 1920s the members of this group published a large series of papers which described pertinent neurological syndromes involving body-attitude distortions and which attempted to define the basis for such syndromes.* Paul Schilder and Otto Poetzl were outstanding members of this group. It is noteworthy that the range of data with which the members of the group concerned themselves began to expand beyond that seen in neurological patients and extended to the functional psychoses. Schilder (267, 268) was one of the leaders in generalizing beyond the neurological area. He later went on to write *The Image and Appearance of the Human Body,* which is the most detailed consideration of body-image phenomena to date and which explores the value of body-image constructs in the area of normal behavior.

In the publications of the Austrian and German group in the 1920s and early 1930s one can see that the multitude of body-image distortions observed clinically were gradually being classified and considered as clusters. One of the clusters related to symptoms which involve neglect of one side of the body. This neglect might include not moving one side of the body or even denying the existence of that side. A second cluster seemed to include all symptoms that involved the denial of impairment of any given body part. For example, a patient with a paralyzed limb might deny that there was anything wrong with it. A third cluster involved generalized feelings of depersonalization and in some circumstances of not having a body at all. A fourth roughly defined cluster embraced symptoms which involved unusual sensations from the body (e.g., deadness and heaviness). Over all, the work of these neurologists indicated that there were almost no limits to the kinds of body-image distortions individuals with brain damage might develop.

It should be parenthetically noted that there is one very unusual type of experiential distortion with body-image implications which is not easily categorized. Bonnier (42), Lhermitte (196), and others (319, 268) have described a phenomenon which involves the individual visually hallucinating a double of himself. It is referred to as *autoscopia,* and is of interest from a body-image point of view because it is such a unique irrational projection of the individual's conception of his own body. He creates a replica of his body outside of himself and it takes on reality

---

* For a detailed review of this work see Critchley (68).

for him. Autoscopia has been clinically linked with various brain lesions and epilepsy and also with schizophrenia (319).

One of the problems with which the group in Vienna was deeply concerned was determining the brain area most directly linked with body image. They wanted to show that body image was mainly the function of a circumscribed brain area. Their approach to the problem was to relate the clinical body-image distortions manifested by neurological patients during their illness to the site of their lesions as determined after death had occurred. They concluded on the basis of their work that lesions of the parietal lobe were most frequently found in patients with body-image pathology. The parietal lobe came to be considered as the body-image center. It was here that the individual constructed a picture or model of himself. Attempts were even made to correlate given types of body-image distortion with lesions in specific parts of the parietal lobe (268). Critchley (68), after reviewing all the data pertinent to this localization problem, feels that although body-image pathology is frequently associated with parietal-lobe damage, it may also be associated with damage to other brain areas.

It is noteworthy that one finds repercussions in the current literature of this interest in the brain localization of the body-image function. Freed and Paster (109) published in 1951 a study of the effects of thalamotomy on body image as measured by figure drawings. They were concerned with the specific question of whether damage to the thalamoparietal lobe radiations as the result of the operation would lead to body-image distortions. They reported no significant increase in such distortions following the operation. Bollea (41) reported in 1948 that by electrical stimulation of the posterior zones of the parietal lobes he produced sensations of elongation of the body image and disappearance of all the limbs.

Another phase of neurological work which developed in the 1920s in Germany has had considerable implications for body-image theory. In 1924 Josef Gerstmann (124) described an unusual syndrome of symptoms in a woman with brain damage. The syndrome involved an inability to recognize her own fingers, or to name them, or to point out an individual digit when so directed. There was also a right-left disorientation, particularly for parts of her own body and for the bodies of others. Furthermore, she showed difficulty in carrying out arithmetical calculations and in writing spontaneously. Gerstmann considered this syndrome to be a specific kind of disorder of the body scheme. He (124A) and others (68, 290) later found a number of cases of a similar character. The striking thing about the syndrome was that it included four kinds of dysfunction which on the surface, at least, would appear to have nothing in common. It was an intriguing question why finger agnosia, right-left disorientation, disturbance in spontaneous writing, and difficulties in arithmetical computations should all cluster together in a symptom picture. Attention was focused on the fact that finger agnosia is unique in the sense that rarely does one find an agnosia for any isolated part of the individual's body.

Speculation was aroused about the unusual significance of the hand in the body scheme. It is one of the chief tools of the individual and one of his most important means of manipulating the environment. Perhaps its particular role in the body scheme had something to do with the unique finger agnosia symptom. It was further noted that the difficulty in arithmetical computation might be explained in terms of the basic importance of the fingers in counting and arithmetical operations. That is, it is well known that among nonliterates arithmetic is a function of counting fingers. There is also evidence that the units of ten in our decimal system represent the original anatomical limits set by our ten fingers. Thus, might not the arithmetic dysfunction, which is a part of the Gerstmann syndrome, be a resultant of the breakdown of that part of the individual's body scheme which involves the hand and fingers? If this were so, the possibility also arises that the other symptoms in the cluster might be a function of the hand and finger body scheme disorganization.

The theoretical importance of this line of thought is great because it suggests the idea that various basic skills and capacities may be dependent upon a well-organized body image. It raises the question whether body image may not be a fundamental substratum which is necessary in order to build up other response systems of the individual.

It would be appropriate at this point to cite several experimental studies which grew out of this point of view. Strauss and Werner (295, 296) collected data concerning the relationship of deficient appreciation of the finger schema to arithmetic ability in subnormal boys. They found a significant correlation between these two variables. Kao and Li, as described by Critchley (68), studied a series of normal individuals and found that finger orientation was a special ability independent of level of intelligence. Benton, Hutcheon, and Seymour (29) repeated some of Strauss and Werner's work with a series of twenty-two normal children and twenty-three defectives. They did not find a significant correlation between finger-localizing ability and arithmetical skill. They did find, however, in the group of defectives that there was a moderate correlation between right-left disorientation and appreciation of the finger schema. This correlation is higher with those right-left disorientation tasks directed toward the subject's own body than with those concerned with the orientation of objects outside the subject. Benton (30) in a further study found a significant correlation in a group of defectives between ability to make right-left discriminations and finger localization facility.

Teitelbaum (311) has made some semiexperimental observations of a rather dramatic nature concerning the results of hypnotically induced body-image distortions upon certain basic skills. These observations were carried out within a framework obviously influenced by Gerstmann's work and they tend to be confirmatory of trends suggested by his findings. Teitelbaum undertook his hypnotic studies with four patients admitted to a psychiatric ward because of amnesia. In essence, he suggested to each of these patients under hypnosis, "You will forget everything about your body when you awaken." He found that they not only lost their ability to name their body parts but also manifested markedly decreased capability for doing various other things. For example, one patient found it difficult to name objects and to draw geometric figures. Another lost the ability to recognize articles of clothing, showed disturbance in two-point discrimination, and made many gross errors in evaluating the length, thickness, and parallelism of lines. But, over all, the hypnotic suggestion to forget everything about the body resulted mainly in errors of differentiation of right and left sides of the body, difficulty in arithmetical calculation, breakdown in ability to draw figures, and faulty recognition of objects. Some of these difficulties (e.g., poor arithmetical performance) are quite parallel to the symptoms which Gerstmann noted.

The most important result of the study is that it lends support to the proposition that a relatively intact body image is an anchor point or foundation necessary for the performance of certain judgments and skills. Stanton (290) has since confirmed the trend of Teitelbaum's results in an analogous intensive hypnotic study of one neurotic patient. Clearly, some of the logical implications of the Gerstmann syndrome have led to more formal studies which point up the importance of body scheme as a substratum for the development of certain skills.

As part of a review of the body-scheme work of neurologists, some emphasis should be given to their thinking about phantom-limb phenomena. It was early noted (137) that after the limb of an individual had been amputated he usually reported an illusory feeling of continued presence of the missing member. In some instances this phantom limb may have considerable reality to the individual and be the apparent source of great pain to him. He may have the feeling that he can move it and at times will unthinkingly begin a sequence of action whose completion assumes the reality of the phantom. Normally the amputee gradually adjusts to the loss of the limb and the phantom fades away; but there are also instances in which it persists for many years. In earlier speculations concerning the origin of phantom sensations a peripheral explanation was favored. It was assumed that such sensations originated from irritations by scars and neuromata of nerve endings in the stump. Similarly, it was sometimes assumed that the phantom might be caused by a pattern of neural excitation set up by the dilating and constricting blood vessels in the stump.

Neurologists became interested in this whole issue and soon took the lead in considering it. Those concerned with body-image phenomena were particularly attracted to the problem; and so the names most frequently mentioned in connection with phantom-limb studies (e.g., Head, Lhermitte, Schilder) are also those prominent in the body-image literature. These neurologists regarded the phantom limb as the manifestation of a central body-image process. They felt that when the individual continued to experience a body part which had been amputated this was the result of the persistence of a body image which had not yet adjusted to the body loss and which distorted the meaning of stimuli in order to deny the loss. In illustration of some of their work one may cite Head (145) who sought to demonstrate the central body-image nature of the phantom in his description of one case in which injury to the parietal cortex by cerebral hemorrhage abolished previously existing contralateral phantom sensations. He concluded that the stroke this patient suffered had disrupted a brain area with important body-image functions and in so doing had also disrupted the phantom-limb illusion. There were numerous case reports published after Head by others which argued pro and con regarding a central origin for phantom-limb sensations and also which debated the possible brain areas most likely involved in provoking such sensations.

More recently a few neurologists (205) have been so convinced as to the central origin and also the precise brain localization of phantom sensations that they have attempted to relieve painful phantoms by removal of specific brain areas which they conceptualize as body-image areas. Some patients have obtained relief from this type of operative procedure but the over-all results have been inconclusive. Indeed, most of the work by neurologists concerning the phantom-limb problem has been inconclusive. But once again it has focused attention on what might otherwise have been bypassed as an obscure phenomenon of little significance. It has brought to the fore some of the problems that the individual has in reorganizing his perception of his body after mutilation has occurred. Also it has emphasized the great influence which a body scheme can have upon the way the individual experiences his body. The body scheme can apparently become an unrealistic frame of reference which radically distorts the individual's perception of certain of his body parts.

One finds that a number of profitable well-designed research studies pertinent to body image have been made and are currently being further pursued, which grew out of the interest in phantom limb. These studies (139, 284) have implicitly or explicitly been inspired by curiosity concerning how the individual reorganizes his body schema after it has been radically violated by an amputation procedure. Teuber (312) and others (137) have been particularly interested in the changes occurring in tactile sensitivity in that portion of the limb remaining after amputation. Weber (326) noted long ago that tactile sensitivity is high in distal parts (finger tips and toes) and low in proximal parts (near the trunk). There is a decreasing gradient of sensitivity from distal to proximal points. Teuber and his associates were interested in whether the stump area retains a fixed position in the previous gradient or whether a reorganization process occurs. They found in a group of thirty-eight men with above-the-knee amputations that two-point discrimination was significantly better on the stump than on corresponding parts of the intact limb. They concluded that some reorganization of the gradient had occurred.

Haber (138) has carried out one of the most definitive studies apropos of this issue. He determined in a group of twenty-five male veterans the two-point threshold, point localization, and light-touch threshold on parts of the arm stump and then obtained the same data concerning homologous areas of the sound limb on the other side. He found a significant superiority applied not only to the immediate end of the stump but also to a more proximal area. One may say then with some confidence that after amputation a radical change in the sensitivity gradient does occur, and the stump takes on an increased sensitivity usually found only in more distal areas. Such results may be interpreted to mean that tactile sensitivity is not a simple function of peripheral factors. The sensitivity gradient shifts, even though the peripheral receptors have not been changed in any way that is evident. At another level, these results suggest that following the amputation of a limb there are forces mobilized to maintain a pattern of body responses as closely similar to the preamputation pattern as possible. Apparently individual body parts may be subordinate to this schema and show alterations in response pattern under the influence of the schema. The new pattern of sensitivity shown by the stump may be conceptualized as reflecting its new special position in the body schema.

Haber (139) went even further in relating the body-image concept to tactile sensitivity variables. He asked his subjects to draw a picture of how they visualized their phantom limb to look relative to the stump. About half the group visualized the phantom as existing outside the stump and half pictured it as inside the stump. The second group showed significantly better point localization and greater (though not significant) light-touch and two-point discrimination sensitivity than did the first group. Haber had no explanation for these findings. But they are striking in that they indicate a direct relationship between the way an individual pictures an area of his body and the degree of tactile sensitivity he shows in that area. We shall, at a later point, further consider these results and point up their meaningfulness relative to other body-image studies.

Simmel (284) has described some promising exploratory work concerning phantom-limb phenomena in individuals suffering from leprosy. She studied eighteen such patients. In this group there was a total of twenty amputations of leg or foot and eight of digits. There was also a total of fifteen instances in which digits were lost by absorption process associated with leprosy and in which surgical intervention was not involved. Simmel found that in all instances involving surgical amputation the patients experienced vivid phantom parts. In no instance of loss of body parts due to absorption, however, were there such phantom experiences. On the basis of these findings and others of related sort described in the literature concerning phantom-limb phenomena Simmel (p. 646) speculated:

> The body schema must constantly undergo minor changes and revisions, following the gradual changes of the body as mediated by the periphery. In patients with leprosy, peripheral anesthesia, and gradual absorption of digits the body schema can keep up with the changes in body shape and no phantom results. Under conditions of amputation or acute neurological lesion, on the other hand, the body schema is left "way behind," as shown by the presence of the phantom, whose persistence indicates how long relearning takes under these conditions.

In commenting upon some of the factors involved in the selective disappearance of specific parts of the phantom as the individual adjusts to amputation, Simmel makes another observation with important implications (p. 643):

> The sequence of disappearing parts follows, with the possible exception of the joints, the Penfield-Boldrey homunculus. Those parts which have large areas of representation on the homunculus, which are richly endowed with sensory fibers, making for high sensory acuity and fine discrimination, and, on the motor side, which have high innervation ratios and represent discrete and skilled movements rather than power are the very same parts which have the longest phantom life. By contrast, those which have minimal representation on the homunculus are relatively short-lived as phantoms.

The homunculus to which Simmel refers is the well-known cartoonlike drawing of a human figure which depicts the relative size of different areas of the body in the sensorimotor cortex. The size representations were originally determined by stimulation of various points in the sensorimotor cortex of the conscious patient and noting the specific body movements and specific areas of body sensation elicited. The relative size of the body parts in terms of their area of cortical representation are listed in descending order: head and neck, upper limb, lower limb, trunk. Simmel's observation that the rate of disappearance of phantom-limb parts is somewhat inverse to their size representation in the homunculus raises the question whether other types of body-image distortion could not be profitably viewed in such terms. If one were to tabulate the body-image distortions most frequently reported by patients with neurological defects or who are psychotic would the relative frequencies of these distortions conform to the homunculus? This possibility is at present a completely unexplored one.

Generally, the enthusiasm for the body-image concept shown by neurologists during the early 1900s has persisted in their work right up to the present. One finds a continuing series of papers in the neurological literature concerning this topic (67, 148, 197, 227, 243, 244). There tends to be a repetitive quality, however, about the observations and speculations offered. It is pointed out again and again that various brain lesions produce this or that body-scheme distortion. The theoretical constructs derived from such observations rarely go beyond the assumption of some kind of a "central" body representation or picture which aids in organizing experiences. Actually this class of body-image constructs has not added much to those first proposed by Pick and Head. But at the same time one finds new neurological concepts and techniques of investigation which are exceptions and which have provoked some novel theory construction concerning body image.

The work of Bender (22) and others (66) is a good case in point. Bender has been analyzing the reactions of individuals when they are stimulated simultaneously on two different parts of the body and asked to report what they feel. He found that there is a tendency for certain parts of the body to have dominance over others in the pattern of response to such simultaneous stimulation. The stimulus received by the dominant part is experienced and reported by the subject, whereas the stimulus to the less dominant part is not consciously perceived. This phenomenon shows up best with patients who have organic disturbances of consciousness and in children under four years of age. Normal subjects tend after a while to correct their errors and to identify both points of simultaneous stimulation correctly. The hierarchy of sensitivity which Bender found indicated that the head was most dominant, the genitals next, and the hands least dominant of all body parts.

These were the basic data which Linn (199) took as a starting point for a speculative formulation concerning a phase of body-image development. He pointed out that it was understandable that the head and genitals should be high in the dominance hierarchy. Very early both these areas are of great importance to the child, not only because they are richly endowed with receptors but also because of the vivid psychological significance assigned to them. It is puzzling, however, that the hands should be least dominant. After all, the hands are of great importance to the individual in feeding, grasping, and a vast array of manipulatory activities. One might have expected them to have been very high on the dominance hierarchy, rather than at the bottom of the scale. Linn offers the following explanation regarding this point. He suggests that very early in life the face and hands are fused in the child's perceptual field; and he does not differentiate them well, just as he has difficulty in differentiating other body areas from one another. In support of this face-hand fusion idea, Linn cites the frequency with which young children produce figure drawings in which the hand grows out of the face. He goes on to postulate that in the repeated experience of separation from mother and her breast the infant learns that others exist "out there" and that there is a boundary which delimits himself from others. In the process of being separated from mother, however, he gets frustrated and seeks a substitute for her absence. It is the hands which are assigned the task of relieving the oral tensions that build up and which mother usually relieves. But in order for the hands to become efficient helpers they must be definitely subordinated to and differentiated from the centers of oral tension localized in the face area. Linn suggests that it is the early need for the radical subordination of the hands to a helping role which accounts for Bender's findings that they are low on the continuum of sensitivity defined by the double-stimulation technique. Linn's formulation is highly speculative; but it is a refreshing attempt to integrate neurological data and psychoanalytic concepts into a fairly complex body-image proposition.

Cohen (66) has also done some interesting work apropos of the double simultaneous stimulation technique. He wanted to show that the rostral dominance which appears in the patterns of extinction obtained by simultaneous stimulation is a function of body image. He obtained drawings of a boy or girl from 200 children in the age range of three and a half through five years, and noted that the head was almost always the most prominent and clearly defined part of the total drawing. It seemed to him that this prominence of the head was a pictorial representation of the rostral dominance elicited by simultaneous stimuli and that it supported the concept of a link between body image and the actual pattern of sensitivity observed. He summarized his over-all conclusions as follows (p. 508): "It is proposed that the pattern of ipsilateral clinical extinction is intimately associated with the body image concept of the subject. In the child, clinical ipsilateral extinction represents an imprecise concept of the body image; in the case of the adult with a brain lesion, when clinical ipsilateral extinction is elicited, a regressive simplification of the body image concept into the childhood pattern is hypothesized."

PSYCHIATRIC CONTRIBUTIONS

Those who have worked with neurotic and schizophrenic patients have been forcefully impressed with the sometimes quite flamboyant body-image distortions they encounter. Schizophrenic patients have been noted (56) to show almost the same range of distortions as one may observe in neurological patients. Schilder (268), who has actively examined body-image phenomena in schizophrenics and in patients with organic brain pathology, felt that the distortions shown by both groups were on a continuum and could not be sharply distinguished. The literature abounds with descriptions of the bizarre perceptions of their own bodies that schizophrenics report. One patient may feel that a part of his body has changed shape or size; another may feel that he has lost a portion of his body; and still another may see his body as permeated with poisonous materials. At an even more elaborated level (68) patients may report that they have a radio embedded in their teeth, that they have exchanged bodies with someone else, or that their bodies are half-man and half-woman. Psychotically depressed, melancholic patients constitute another clinical group with frequent body-image distortions. They usually place much emphasis on body deterioration and body disintegration. Still another group in whom body-image distortions seem to be prominent are the conversion hysterics. Various writers (113, 92) have postulated that the hysteric's unusual sensory and motor disturbances in certain body areas are associated with unusual fantasies concerning the significance of such areas. It has been suggested that the hysterical symptom is a way of symbolically expressing a wish with a body area that is somehow magically assigned a significance relevant to the wish. Thus, an arm or a leg might be equated with the penis and be used (in terms of symptoms based on extreme hypertonus of the musculature) to act out sexual impulses.

As one reviews the range of schizophrenic body-image pathology described by various writers over the last fifty years (56, 38, 10, 21), one is struck by the variety of distortions reported, and also by the fact that these distortions roughly fall into a number of categories of greatest frequency. A rather prominent cluster of disturbed body attitudes has to do with the issue of masculinity or femininity. It includes such distortions as feeling that one has body parts of the opposite sex, that one looks like the opposite sex, or that one is half-man, half-woman. A second group of distortions refers to feelings of body disintegration and deterioration. Frequently these may involve sensations that some inner part of the body (e.g., the intestine) has been destroyed, that there has been a catastrophic decrease in the size or strength of a body part, or that some body part is being destroyed under the constant attack of some strange outside influence. A third category of pathology pertains to feelings of depersonalization. It involves a sense of unreality concerning the existence of body parts or the total body. The individual experiences his own body as if it were alien or belonged to a stranger. A fourth group of distortions revolves about a sense of loss of body boundaries. The patient feels that things happening elsewhere and to other people are happening to him. Injury to others is experienced as injury to his own body. He is not able to set up a demarcation line which will consistently distinguish his own body from that of others.

One finds in the literature only a limited organization or conceptualization of the raw clinical observations which have been published concerning schizophrenic body-scheme distortions. Schilder (268) has attempted at some length to give meaning to the schizophrenic's body attitudes, but in summarizing his efforts one finds that there is little to say. Generally he indicates that schizophrenic body-scheme pathology is a manifestation of poor socialization and a past history of poor object relations. He points out that the body image is to a considerable degree molded by our interactions with others and to the extent that these interactions are faulty the body image will be inadequately developed. Particularly he underlines the destructive effects upon body image of sado-masochistic attitudes. Hostility toward the self is reflected in sensations of disintegration and body decline. Schilder suggests that some of the schizophrenic's body-image symptoms represent an attempt to deny parts of the body symbolic of forbidden or anxiety-laden functions (e.g., genitality). Most of his descriptions of schizophrenic body attitudes are actually phrased in classical Freudian terms. He represents such attitudes as arising from deviations in the normal distribution and localization of libido in the body. His explanatory frame of reference is defined primarily in terms of such dimensions as fixation of libido, withdrawal of libido, and transposition of libido. While his theorizing does not really add much to what Freud has already said, he has instigated some direct semiexperimental work in this area.

He and a group at Bellevue Hospital in New York have published several studies concerning the body image of schizophrenics as reflected in their figure drawings. Also they have studied the changes in schizophrenic body image that accompany shock treatment. In one such study

(95) patients were asked to draw repeated pictures of a man as they awakened following either insulin or Metrazol shock treatment. Essentially what was found was that the drawings were initially vague, incoherent, and represented body parts in gross disproportion. Gradually the disproportions became less flagrant and in a fairly brief period a figure was drawn which was not much different from that produced prior to the shock treatment.

Bender and Keeler (21) have in the Schilder tradition studied the body image of schizophrenic children before and following electroshock treatment. They used behavior, verbalizations, figure drawings, and dreams as data concerning body image. One of their outstanding findings was that schizophrenic children have particular difficulty in determining the periphery of their bodies. These children seemed to be preoccupied with establishing a body boundary. Their concern was especially clear in their figure drawings in terms of heavy outlining of the body periphery. This concern could also be deduced from their use of capes, halos, and other enclosing concepts in their drawings. Nothing of much import was found concerning the effect of shock treatment upon the body image. It was simply noted that the figure drawings obtained immediately after shock were unusually confused and evidenced a considerable number of distortions, such as elongation, expansion, and multiplication of body parts. One cogent point made by Bender and Keeler was that the body-image misrepresentations of schizophrenic children seemed to be only exaggerations of similar distortions found in the dreams, art productions, and momentary fantasies of the normal individual.

It would be well to cite still another type of study which has come out of Bellevue concerning body image. This was a study of a group of very disturbed children, some of whom were schizophrenic. Owen (231) evaluated eleven such children by means of the simultaneous tactile stimulation technique which was described in an earlier part of this chapter apropos of some of Bender's work (22). Owen was interested in the relationship between errors made by the children in tactual localization and disturbances in body image as evidenced in figure drawings and overt clinical behavior. She concluded on the basis of her data that "the localization of cutaneous perception is not intrinsically related to body image and should not be used as an indicator of body-image problems in children" (p. 407). However, she also concluded that the six children who made the most localization errors "had the most immature ego structures as indicated by overt anxiety, failure to distinguish their own body boundaries, and resort to the most immature defense against anxiety—denial" (p. 407). Such findings led her to conclude that disturbances in cutaneous localization are not directly correlated with body-image distortions, but only to the degree that these distortions reflect ego immaturity. Others (3, 24) who have investigated response to double simultaneous stimulation in schizophrenics have found that schizophrenics perform about as well as do normal individuals. Although the over-all results of the double simultaneous stimulation technique have not yet contributed much to an understanding of body image, it is an interesting line of thought because it involves the use of a new method and because it seeks to establish links between body image and actual skin sensitivity. This is one of the few instances in which body image has been conceptualized as possibly having an influence upon a specific body function and in which some kind of operational attempt has been made to investigate the possibility.

Tausk (308) has put forward some interesting concepts concerning aspects of the body image in the paranoid schizophrenic. He postulated on the basis of his observations of paranoids who had delusions of being influenced or controlled by distant machines or apparatuses that the drawings they made of such machines contained elements of their body images, especially of images of their genitals and anal areas. He felt that the paranoid projected an aspect of his body image and ascribed to it various influencing powers which were symbolically wish fulfilling. This externalized representation of the body image became a central reference point in the individual's life.

The phenomenon of *depersonalization* is perhaps the most widely described and commented upon of all the body-image distortions observed among schizophrenic and neurotic patients. As indicated previously, it refers to the feeling that one's own body is strange and alien, that one's body belongs to someone else and is not a part of the self identity. In terms of clinical data, depersonalization is represented by such complaints as, "My head is dead," "My voice sounds strange to me," and "My hands seem as if they belong to someone else." As indicated by Galdston (118), this phenomenon was first noted in the literature by Krishaber in 1872, and fifteen years later was named *depersonalization* by Dugas. Schilder (269) thought of it as being a specific manifestation of disturbance in body image. Actually there has been considerable dispute concerning not only its etiology but also its frequency in various clinical populations. It has been described often in connection with full-blown schizophrenic symptomatology; but there are indications that it may be represented in its most flamboyant forms in borderline schizophrenics and very seriously disturbed neurotics who are not actively psychotic. Indeed Schilder (219) definitely refers to depersonalization as a neurotic symptom and he states "almost every neurosis has in some phase of its development symptoms of depersonalization." Mayer-Gross (209) thought that it was involved to some degree in all the psychopathies. One observer (118) goes further and points out that "lesser states of depersonalization are to be found even with normal people, either after an emotional shock or after physical exhaustion."

There has been considerable speculation concerning the etiology of the marked depersonalization seen in some patients. One viewpoint (118) has highlighted the frequency with which such patients had impersonal parents who encouraged a depersonalized attitude toward life and who also by implication suggested a similar attitude toward one's own body. A related viewpoint (118) proposes that depersonalization develops in the course of attempts to escape psychic and physical punishment by becoming like an inanimate object and thus acquiring the immunity of an inanimate object. That is, if one is like an inanimate object there is less likelihood of becoming the target of the anger of others or of various kinds of stressful demands. Galdston (118) theorizes that depersonalization represents the perception by the patient that he is functioning at a lower, less integrated level than previously. He conceptualizes this symptom as a signal from the ego that it has been damaged by disturbing conflictual demands.

Fenichel (92) defines the phenomenon as a method used by the individual to repress "overcharged feelings" which are too intense and painful to be admitted to consciousness. He takes the position that depersonalization is one of the frequent early signs of schizophrenic breakdown. Indeed, as he sees it, body-image distortions of all varieties tend to be among the earliest forerunners of schizophrenic regression. These distortions take such forms as hypochondriacal sensations, areas of decreased or intensified sensitivity, and unusual feelings of change in body size or shape. It is worth while to quote one of Fenichel's examples in this respect (p. 419):

> A schizophrenic episode began with a patient's despair over the fact that a new hat did not fit. Analysis revealed that the patient felt different when he wore this hat; he believed that the shape of his head was altered by the hat. The body image of his head was changed. The exaggerated reaction to the hat was a distorted expression of the patient's fear that something was wrong with his head.

It is striking that despite all the speculation in the literature concerning depersonalization, there is not one study which has systematically determined the frequency of the phenomenon in various clinical groups or investigated its etiology within a systematic research design. One may level the same criticism against almost all the work concerned with body-image distortions in neurotics and schizophrenics. Definitions have been vague and there has been little or no attempt to construct objective measures of body-scheme distortion. On the positive side, however, this work has called attention to intriguing phenomena and led to considerable speculation which will provide a rich matrix for future more systematic efforts.

A study of the body image of schizophrenics which was carried out recently by Reed (238) is, in terms of its relative clarity and objectivity of design, an exception to the usual undertaking in this area. Reed predicted, among other things, that schizophrenic women experience their bodies as more masculine than do normal women. Two of the main techniques he used for checking this hypothesis were the Figure Drawing Test and the Franck-Rosen Drawing Completion Test. The Drawing Completion Test consists of a series of thirty-six incomplete drawings each located in the center of a cell 2¼ inches long. The subject is simply asked to complete each drawing in any way that he would like. The drawings are scored in terms of whether the completions resemble masculine phallic symbols or feminine symbols. It is assumed that masculine body feelings result in masculine completions and feminine body feelings in feminine completions. Earlier work had indicated that scores based on such completions differentiated very significantly between men and women. When Reed compared fifty psychotic women with fifty normal controls, he found that the psychotics completed a significantly greater number of drawings in a manner indicating masculine body-image attributes. In scoring the figure drawings obtained for his subjects, Reed calculated the degree to which the drawn body proportions matched existing statistical norms regarding the male and female body. He found that "the comparative body proportions of the male and female DAP figures of the psychotic women showed inversions of actual normal criterion relationships to a significantly greater extent than did those of normal subjects" (p. 59). His results indicate a basic difference between psychotic and normal individuals in the masculinity-femininity aspect of body image.

BACKGROUND OF CONCERN WITH BODY-IMAGE PHENOMENA IN OTHER AREAS

The body-image attitudes of normal individuals and the body-image distortions produced by conditions other than neurological or psychiatric illness have attracted relatively little explicit interest because they are not as highly visible as those manifested by sick and disturbed patients. There is no doubt, however, that body-image phenomena are prominent in the normal individual's everyday experiences and that they are a matter of marked focus for the culture as a whole. Schilder (268) has impressionistically explored some of the more common body-image perceptions of normal persons. He indicates that the individual alters his picture of himself with each new posture and shift in stance. The individual perceives his body differently as patterns of muscle tonus vary. Situations which set up unusual patterns of tonus (e.g., gymnastic exercises) may stimulate feelings of body strangeness. There is also a varying pattern of stimulation of the skin surface which affects the perception of one's body. Generally the outline of the skin is not felt as a smooth and straight surface; it is blurred. But this blurred surface may suddenly be perceived as definite and distinct at points where it comes into contact with objects.

Schilder pointed out, too, the variations in the manner in which we experience the body as a mass with weight. He observes that certain areas (e.g., the abdomen) are felt as the center of gravity of the body. But the center of gravity may vary as shifts in body position occur. In situations of rapid acceleration or deceleration (e.g., in an elevator) the individual may feel strange alterations in his weight distribution. His head, feet, or other body parts may suddenly appear to be very heavy or so light as to float away. Distortions may be produced also in his perception of his body size and shape. The occurrence of pain in the body frequently has dramatic body-image repercussions. Schilder says apropos of this point (268, p. 104): "That part of the body in which the pain is felt gets all the attention . . . and the other parts of the body-image lose in importance; but at the same time the painful part of the body becomes isolated. There is a tendency to push it out of the body-image." In describing the basic framework within which the individual interprets his conscious body-image sensations and the variations in these sensations, Schilder makes this summary statement (pp. 97–98): "When we try to get an image of our own body, we first get some outstanding point, a frame, in which we fit the body image. The sole gives us the contact with the earth and the necessary basis for orientation in the adjoining space. . . . Further orientation is gained by the openings of the body and the parts of the skin that are tense over bone."

This spatial framework of the body has been referred to by others as a guide whereby the individual organizes all his spatial experiences. H. Werner (335) says:

> Primitive terms for spatial relations suggest that the body itself with its "personal dimensions" of above-below, before-behind, and right-left is the source of a psychophysical system of coordinates. Therefore it may be inferred that objective space has gradually evolved from this primitive orientation. Ernest Cassirer says: "Where the more highly developed languages, in order to designate spatial relations, normally use prepositions, particles, and post-positions, there are nominative expressions in the aboriginal languages which either stand for, or refer directly to, parts of the body: The Mande

(African) group of languages expresses 'behind' by an anthropo-
morphic substantive 'the back.'

Perhaps it would be appropriate at this point to illustrate the complexity of Schilder's speculations concerning body image by quoting
from one section of his book in which he tries to demonstrate how the
body image becomes a means whereby the individual gains control over
involuntary body processes. It was his viewpoint that the individual
could learn via his body image to produce distortions in his own body
functioning. Here is his description of the process (268, pp. 183–184):

> I would say everybody uses the small experiences of everyday
> life in organic diseases for subsequent experimenting on the body
> image and for the acquisition of the key representation for a particu-
> lar organ which is not immediately represented in the postural model
> of the body. By the term "key representation" I mean that we are
> able by specially arbitrarily chosen representations to change the
> function of intestines [or other parts]° which are otherwise beyond
> our reach. We cannot decide to increase our pulse rate, but we can
> imagine ourselves in a frightening position and can thereby provoke
> a change in the pulse rate. In every individual a continual process of
> experimenting with key representations goes on, thus gaining indirect
> influence on the inner parts of the body.

Schilder is here describing his concept of the process or model involved
in the individual's gaining control over certain involuntary functions of
his body.

One finds descriptions of all sorts of variables which may produce
body-image distortions in normal persons and which are encountered
in the course of processes involved in daily living. Thus Federn (91)
has reported in detail some of the body-image phenomena he observed
to be associated with falling asleep. As the individual gets sleepier his
body boundaries seem to become less definite; his body loses some of its
third-dimensional quality; parts of his body become vague and others
seem to disappear; and a vague sort of depersonalization occurs. Federn
noted that the head and genital region seemed to remain most distinct
and least distorted up to the point of actually falling asleep. Schilder
(268) refers to the very clear body-image distortions that the individual
may experience while asleep and dreaming. He may in his dreams see
himself as markedly elongated or short; there may be dysplastic alterations in his image of himself in the dream; there may be unusual combinations of male and female characteristics ascribed to the dream figures. Keiser (167) describes body-image changes that occur during

---

° The comment in brackets was inserted by the writers for purposes of clarification.

sexual intercourse and especially at the point of orgasm. She notes that intense patterns of localized excitation are set up which may cause the individual to experience his body as altered, strange, and out of control. This is especially true at the point of orgasm when, with momentarily decreased consciousness, there is a blurring of body boundaries. Such blurring of boundaries may be interpreted within a threatening context of disintegration or "falling apart." Indeed, Keiser feels that many neurotics do not attain orgasm in order to defend themselves against the threatening body-image changes which accompany it.

Schneider (270) has suggested that the heart plays a very fundamental role in determining the individual's image of himself. He points out that it is a unique body organ in that it produces a rhythm which is felt all over the body. He implies that this rhythm is a framework within which most important body sensations are experienced. He refers to the image of the heart as the "root of the ego." One of his most interesting formulations involves the idea that the patterns of regularity and speed shown by the heart are sometimes correlated with degree of ego integration. For example, he describes the symptoms of paroxysmal auricular tachycardia as a heart running away and symbolizing "ego dismemberment."

The importance of body image to our culture as a whole is obvious in terms of the widespread expenditure of time and effort that is given to altering the body's appearance. Individuals are constantly seeking by means of clothes, bleaches, skin preparations, cosmetics, tattooing, and even plastic surgery to change their appearance and to make themselves look more like some ideal image they have in mind. In some cultures the need to alter the body's appearance is literally expressed in a whole range of body mutilations. Body parts may be removed, shortened, lengthened, and reshaped (68). It is interesting to note how the members of a culture may radically revise their idealized body image with the passage of time or under the influential impact of another culture. For example, before World War II women in Japan adhered to a standard which deemphasized the breasts and required that they be as flat on the chest as possible. However, as the result of Western influences there was a radical shift and it is now a widespread custom for Japanese women to exaggerate breast protuberance in typical Hollywood fashion. Garma (121) and Schilder (268) have both called attention to the intimate relationship between clothes and other body decorations and psychological variables of a body-image order. Schilder refers to clothes as an extension of the body scheme and considers that the clothing being worn by an individual is incorporated into this scheme. Speculatively, Garma suggests that clothes become an outer defensive covering of the body and that they have some of the significance that one might associate with the protective fetal membrane or other maternal enwrapping symbols.

Apropos of the point that members of each culture seem intent on transforming the appearance of their bodies by means of clothes or cosmetic procedures to conform to some idealized body image, one may refer to a series of studies presented by Jourard and Secord (160). They were interested in determining how persons differ in the degree of like or dislike they express for various of their body parts. They wished to find out if these differences were related to the actual physical characteristics of the given parts and also to the kind of idealized body standards expressed by the subjects. In the course of this series of studies, subjects rated a number of their own body parts on a seven-point scale of positive-negative feeling; they estimated the size of these body parts; and indicated the size they would ideally like the parts to be. In addition, the parts were actually measured with appropriate instruments. On the basis of their findings Jourard and Secord concluded that there are shared group norms concerning the ideal dimensions for each body part, and that an individual's attitude toward his own body parts is significantly a function of the degree of deviation of these parts from the ideal norm. These findings held true for both men and women. It is incidentally interesting that the degree of dissatisfaction felt with body parts proved to be significantly related to insecurity, as measured by Maslow's test. Silverberg (282) also has collected data indicating that individuals agree considerably in their definitions of an ideal body type. Wright (359) has shown in terms of a semantic analysis of the frequency of certain body terms in the English language that there is a composite "linguistic body image" implicit in the norms of our culture.

Another indication of the importance of body image is the frequency with which transformation themes are found in folklore, myths, and popular legends. There are endless examples of such themes. There are many tales in folklore of persons who become transformed into animals (e.g., werewolves). Similarly one finds in mythology a whole array of instances in which the gods reward or punish by radically transforming the appearance of individuals. Individuals may be changed into animals, inanimate objects, plants, members of the opposite sex, and so forth. In fairy tales and children's stories characters quite frequently experience body alterations (e.g., Pinocchio and Alice in Wonderland). Hollywood movies also contain numerous body-change themes.

In more primitive societies the concern with body image is expressed in unusual ideas and superstitions which are accepted as a reality by the group. The concern about body image felt by the individuals in these groups takes direct expression rather than first being symbolically distorted within the framework of a myth or fairy tale. For example, many primitive people directly express the belief that body products and wastes (e.g., feces, hair cut off) are still representations of themselves and that harm can come to the whole body if someone exerts evil influence on these products. They may regard their shadows as part of themselves and be concerned with possible harm to the shadow. They may believe that eating certain body parts of other persons or animals with outstanding traits will impart the same traits to the person who eats them.

The various ideas and concepts concerning body image of normal individuals which have been enumerated to this point have, with but a few exceptions, been highly speculative and based on what amounts to informal anecdotal observations. However, one may also find a class of pertinent data which has been gleaned from semiexperimental and semiobjectified situations. One of the earliest sources of some fairly objective data concerning body-image distortions in normal individuals came incidentally from Stratton's studies (297) of inversion of the visual field. Stratton placed lenses over his eyes which caused his visual field to be inverted. He noted that initially the visual impressions he received concerning the position of various parts of his body were in strong conflict with his feeling about where these parts actually were. This discrepancy made him feel anxious and uneasy. Gradually, however, he revised his concept of the relationship that should exist between his visual perception of his body parts and his kinesthetic perception of these parts. He became comfortable with the new relationship. That is, he learned to make a radical change in one dimension of his body image. His ability to reintegrate his perceptions in this manner confirms the point made by both Head (146) and Schilder (268) that the body scheme is usually highly flexible and subject to constant revision. It is noteworthy that when Stratton later finally removed the lenses from his eyes he experienced feelings of nausea and strangeness. Within a matter of days he had so thoroughly altered his perception of the relation of his body to the outside world that it was disturbing to him to assume once again the usual orientation. His work highlights the plasticity of certain aspects of the body image.

There is an interesting store of data concerning body image in the mass of published reports dealing with the effects of various drugs (177, 51, 264, 95) upon subjects. One finds many informal descriptions of the strange body-image feelings produced by drugs like mescaline, marihuana, hashish, and peyote. Bromberg and Tranter (51) quote an Indian who had the following unusual body-image experiences while under the influence of peyote: ". . . I just felt as if I could throw my arms out and my arms left me, went off in the air, and I felt I was going all to pieces."

Many of the published descriptions of drug effects point up altered body feelings. One of the most detailed and carefully obtained series of descriptions of the effect of a drug upon the body scheme is contained in a paper by Savage (264). Savage was concerned with the effects of lysergic acid upon subjects. He made 300 observations on thirty-two hospitalized patients and six normal subjects. There were few basic differences between the effects noted in the hospitalized group and those observed in the normal group. Savage enumerates a wide gamut of fascinating body-image changes that occurred. He indicates that the drug very quickly increased awareness of the body. There was an increased sensitivity to all bodily feelings. There was an increased preoccupation with the body. It seemed as if the body were charged with energy, and this was experienced as either very pleasant or unpleasant. Sensations of body disruption were prominent. Parts of the body seemed dislocated. Limbs were seen as detached and floating. The body seemed to lose its symmetry and to become amazingly plastic. It might feel as light as air or as heavy as lead. It might feel large or so small that the individual would fear being stepped on. The body might seem to become separated from the individual so that he could feel himself as being at some distant point or behind himself. It might seem to come apart and there would be a sensation that the head could be removed.

Savage also observed that as the drug takes effect there is a gradual loss of sensations from various body parts. Feelings for the legs and genitals leave first, then the arms, and then the trunk. Feelings for the face and lips seem to disappear last; and finally there may be a loss of all consciousness of body and only an awareness of thoughts remains. Savage notes the fluidity of body boundaries produced by the drug. The individual finds it hard to tell where his body leaves off and the rest of the world begins. Initially the drug produces changes in the direction of enlargement of body boundaries. Everything happening in the room is experienced as within the body. The movements made by others are felt within. The individual may experience a car passing by as if it were running over him. These rich observations collected by Savage indicate the potentially wide range of body-image experiences available to the individual under varying conditions. It is interesting too that normal subjects experience patterns of body-image distortion similar to those which develop when individuals become schizophrenic or suffer certain types of organic brain pathology.

The experiences of subjects while being hypnotized constitute another semiobjectified source of data concerning body-scheme phenomena in

normal subjects. Various writers have tangentially referred to such phenomena, but Gill * (126) has noted and elaborated upon them with
great specificity. He indicates that subjects report such sensations as the
following: some subjects feel themselves changing in size, especially in
the face and extremities; they feel as if they are swelling or shrinking;
frequently they come to perceive their lower extremities as unusually
elongated. Subjects sitting in one corner of a room may feel as if their
legs extend all the way across to an opposite corner. Sensations of
swelling of the head and particularly of the mouth are common; and
subjects may say that their lips are so swollen that they cannot speak.
Gill has observed also that there are many disturbances in body equilibrium. Individuals may feel very unsteady or get the idea that they are
floating away. Other unusual body-image feelings elicited by the hypnotic situation vary over a wide range: decreasing awareness of one's
body, changes in tactile sensitivity (numbness, paresthesias, temperature
variations), and extreme blurring of body boundaries. In discussing
these body-image experiences which occur as the result of hypnotic
procedures, Gill refers to a theory developed by Kubie and Margolin
which suggests that hypnosis involves to a considerable degree an in-
corporation of an image of the hypnotist into the subject and a necessary
accompanying blurring and subsequent redefinition of ego boundaries.
Gill's viewpoint is that the intense body-image sensations of the individual being hypnotized mirror the changes in ego boundaries which
are correlated with entering into a hypnotic state. It is as if a major
change in the individual's immediate way of organizing his world were
accompanied by marked alterations in the way he experiences his body.
Klemperer (172) has reported on body-image distortions of individuals
in the course of hypnoanalysis. Most of these distortions are quite similar
to those referred to by Gill. However, there are examples of some distortions occurring during hypnoanalysis which are so unique that it is
worth while to quote descriptions of several:

> The inside of my legs, my penis, my rectum cut off. Just the out-
> side of my legs remain. . . . It is clean, like carved out in a circle.

> I am trying to cut off the tail I got. I am watching the mirror
> and I am looking funny. I feel like an animal.

> My throat feels sore all of a sudden. The right side of my
> throat. It's unbelievably sore. . . . I keep wanting to see what's in-
> side. The soreness even reaches up into my ears.

These body-image distortions are particularly interesting because they
occurred in the process of reactivating childhood sensations and emo-

---

* We are grateful to Dr. Merton Gill for making his unpublished manuscript
available to us.

tions for therapeutic purposes. Klemper suggests that "the visualizations in hypnoanalysis reproduce what the weak ego of the child once felt or thought about his own body in relationship to events which overwhelmed it" (p. 162).

A unique opportunity for observing body-image variables is of course potentially available in the day-to-day experiences of individuals who suffer severe body mutilations or injuries. Some aspects of this topic were covered at an earlier point apropos of a discussion of experiences of amputees. There are many informal descriptions (2, 47, 62) of the reactions of individuals to disfiguring burns, loss of sense organs, and operative procedures that produce radical changes in body conformations. But these descriptions are vague and rarely go beyond a statement that such body mutilations produce anxiety and are difficult for an individual to accept.

Probably one of the most interesting descriptions of reactions to an unusual body mutilation is presented in a report by Margolin (208). This report involved a Negro woman who had an artificial opening from her body exterior into her stomach as a consequence of attempting suicide by swallowing a caustic substance. She was intensively observed by a variety of techniques. The exposed lining of her stomach was studied with appropriate physiological measures. Concurrently she entered into psychotherapy and the therapist was able to note in detail her reactions to the mutilation and to the way other people responded to it. The patient displayed many special attitudes toward the artificial opening. At times she was concerned with it as a source of pain, embarrassment, and humiliation. She regarded it as a badge of calamity. At other times she was concerned with the uniqueness of her body opening and in a paradoxical fashion was pleased with the attention that it drew to her. What was most striking, however, was that the opening gradually acquired an erotic sensitivity. It took on for her some of the characteristics of a genital organ; and she experienced voluptuous feelings when it was cleaned or handled. Apparently it was integrated into the body scheme in such a way as to give a new erotic meaning to that area of the body. Margolin indicates that similar erotic reactions have been observed to occur around the artificial body openings of other patients who have had colostomies and ileostomies. The Negro patient with the opening into her stomach also interpreted the opening as a break in her body boundaries which made her particularly vulnerable to outside forces. She felt very fragile and some of her anxiety was expressed in concern about being sexually violated and penetrated. She reacted to certain physiological examinations as a violation of her body integrity. What is outstanding here from a body-image point of view is that the body opening gradually acquired a special role in her body scheme and became a center with important influence upon her perception of her body as a whole.

Having examined a sample of the kinds of data concerning body image which have been collected under rather minimally controlled conditions, it would be well to consider the kinds of data collected in more objectively oriented studies. As early as 1898 G. S. Hall (140) attempted by means of a questionnaire method to find out from children at different age levels their earliest memories relating to the parts of their bodies that first attracted their attention. He also sought to find out their early ideas about their internal organs. His results were not particularly cogent, but he certainly anticipated by many years attempts to deal with body-image phenomena in a systematic objective fashion.

A similar questionnaire type of approach was adapted by Curran and Levine (72) in their study of body image in thirty prostitutes and thirty controls who were prisoners sent for treatment to a medical ward. They developed a questionnaire with ninety-six questions derived from material in Schilder's book, *Psychotherapy.* It included such questions as, "What do you think of your own strength?", "What do you think of your beauty?", "How strongly are you sexed?" and "What is the most important part of your body?" Curran and Levine found no real differences between the prostitutes and controls in terms of their oral answers to the questionnaire. One of their most interesting findings was that subjects who were grossly ugly or unattractive tended to deny and minimize their deviations from the normal. This same tendency to deny body deviations has already been referred to in its more extreme forms apropos of patients with organic brain pathology who deny that there is anything wrong with a paralyzed limb or a paralyzed side of the body.

Werner Wolff (365) has been a pioneer in developing new techniques for analyzing expressive behavior; and much of what he has done has direct implications for the study of body image. Wolff found that if a photograph were obtained of an individual's profile or of his hands without his knowledge, afterwards the individual was not aware that they were photographs of himself when they were shown to him in the context of similar photographs taken of other individuals. If that individual were then asked to describe imaginatively the possible personality traits of the person whose profile or hands were shown in the picture, he tended to use much more extreme (usually more favorable) terms in describing the pictures of himself than of others. Similar extreme judgments were obtained with recorded voice samples and handwriting samples. When subjects were consciously aware, however, that they were evaluating pictures or other samples of themselves, they did not show the same extremeness in their judgments. Although Wolff did not use the term *body image* in connection with his results, one may easily interpret them as pertinent to the body-image construct, since they do for the most part represent the individual's unconscious reactions to aspects of his own body.

Wolff's work has provided a novel and potentially valuable means of studying body image. It has also made it clear that samples of an individual's attitudes toward his body will vary considerably as a function of how they are obtained from him. If he is simply asked to describe representations of his body, he takes a controlled, censoring attitude and reveals little that is either strongly positive or negative. But if his judgments are obtained in such a manner that he is not conscious that he is describing areas of his own body, his censorship is evaded and he reveals his more extreme emotional attitudes.

Erik Erikson (884) has attempted to apply body-image interpretations to the constructions produced by adolescents with play materials. As part of a long-term developmental study in California, he arranged for children to build scenes with various play materials on their eleventh, twelfth, and thirteenth birthdays. He placed each child in a room with numerous toys, blocks, and dolls, and then photographed the situations they constructed. He evaluated the photographs particularly in terms of spatial and architectural categories. For example, he tabulated frequency of enclosing walls, types of enclosures, use of towers, number of tunnels, and use of ornamentation. His results indicated rather clear differences between boys and girls in the patterns of their constructions. For instance, boys erect towers and build streets more often than girls. Significantly more boys build enclosures only in conjunction with elaborate structures or traffic lanes; whereas more girls are satisfied with an unelaborated enclosure. Boys show greater concern with representations of up-down. Girls more frequently build houses with interiors that are open to the outside and which are in a context of action involving intrusion from the outside. Erikson conceptualizes such variations as being analogous to the differences in morphology of the male and female sex organs. In the male the external organs are erectile, intrusive, and mobile. In the female the external organs represent an opening, a place of access. Consequently the boys produce more constructions with towers and traffic lanes (areas of mobility); girls build more configurations which are open, less elaborately enclosed, and easier to enter. Erikson is suggesting then, that play constructions mirror an aspect of body image and may be used as a type of body-image measure. He incidentally mentions that Freud anticipated the body-image implications of house representations; and he quotes him as follows: "The only typical, that is to say, regularly-occurring representation of the human form as a whole is that of a house."

Katcher and Levin (166) have taken a very direct approach to body-image measurement. They were interested in children's conceptions of their body size. The technique they used for dealing with this problem is quite unique. Each child was individually presented with a series of triads of schematic body parts depicting heads, torsos, arms, and legs. Each triad consisted of three sizes of each part. For each trial three different-sized pieces were placed in front of the child, with equal spaces between them. The child was asked to tell which part looked like mother's, then which looked like father's, and which looked like himself. The procedure was administered to sixty-nine children from a nursery school who ranged in age from two years and nine months to five years and four months. The most interesting findings revolved about a comparison of the judgments of the older girls with the other subgroups. Of all the subgroups (younger boys, older boys, younger girls), the older girls tended most consistently to identify as their own body parts those which were the smallest and they were significantly different from the younger girls in this respect. Such a differentiation did not occur in the boys' group. Katcher and Levin think that these results might mean that girls learn to assign definite sex role characteristics to their bodies earlier than boys do. That is, since body smallness is a characteristic associated with femininity in our culture, the greater consistency of the older girls in assigning this characteristic to themselves might mean that they are ahead of the boys in developing a sexually differentiated concept of their bodies. Katcher and Levin also suggest that this might be due to the fact that both boys and girls have their early primary relationships mainly with the mother. Thus the girls would have an immediate and direct sex-role body model, whereas the boys would be delayed in finding a suitable model until they later could establish a more intense relationship with father.

Machover (203) takes the position in her book, *Personality Projection in the Drawing of the Human Figure*, that an individual's spontaneous drawing of the human figure represents in many ways a projection of his own body image. If this were so, then all studies which have used figure drawings would have pertinence to the body-image issue. As one reviews the range of studies involving figure drawings, however, one is struck by the fact that a large number of them are concerned with issues rather far afield from body image. Many (128, 289, 203) are focused on the figure drawings as an indicator of personality pathology, as a means of differentiating given diagnostic groups, and as an indicator of specific types of personality conflicts. Such studies usually involve a search for empirical signs that will detect this or that syndrome. Many studies of children's figure drawings have been concerned with the effectiveness of figure drawing as a measure of intelligence (128, 31). A number of analyses have been made of the developmental shifts shown by children in the way they represent the body with increasing chronological age (125, 129). But the findings in general simply indicate that the child begins with a confused concept in which various body parts are illogically fused and gradually progresses to a more realistically differentiated concept. There is evidence also that the child earlier shows facility in drawing the head region than any other body area. Over all there is little relative to the total volume of the figure-drawing literature which is a direct important contribution to our knowledge of body image. We have already reviewed several of the more relevant studies in our historical summary. A review of a number of other pertinent studies follows.

Goitein (128) and Brown and Goitein (52) sought to obtain a measure of body image by having subjects draw blindfolded "a mental picture of yourself (your figure, your body) in space and draw it in outline as if viewed from behind, feeling your way around this image with both hands. . . . Do the same for side-view (yourself in profile) and your body in lying down position." They administered this test to a group of over 400 subjects which included such subgroups as students in a psychology class, asthmatics, patients with allergies, and assaultive psychopaths. They attempted to analyze their data in a semiquantitative fashion by a consideration of such variables as size, placement in space, and treatment of the head. Their statistical procedures were very vague; and although they indicate some success in differentiating various groups, it is difficult to see that they actually found anything significant. What is most interesting is their use of a blindfolded technique for obtaining the drawings. This was done to minimize the effects of artistic skill upon the drawings.

Tait and Ascher (306) have experimented with a version of the figure drawing which they call "Inside-of-the-Body Test." The subject is asked to "Draw the inside of the body, including the organs." Three minutes are allowed for the drawing and one additional minute is given to "draw a line from each organ to the outside and label the organ on or next to the line." Tait and Ascher indicate that they intend by this procedure to find out the concept the individual has of the inside of his body. They administered the test to over 200 subjects. Their group included hospitalized psychiatric patients, candidates for admission to the Naval Academy, patients on a medical ward, and children in the sixth grade. Most of their findings which are of interest in a body-image sense were of a qualitative order. They found that among adults the heart is the most frequently labeled organ and the cardiovascular and gastrointestinal systems the most frequently represented. There was a trend for patients with psychosomatic problems to emphasize the organ or system involved in the illness. Among the children the skeletomuscular responses were most popular. It was noted that children more often omitted any reference to the reproductive system than did adult subjects. The authors stated that they were in the process of further standardizing the test and discovering some of its significant correlates.

Abel (1) obtained figure drawings from a group of seventy-four patients with various types of facial disfigurement. Drawings were obtained from them at the time that they came seeking plastic surgery for improvement of their defects. When the patients were divided into a mild to moderately disfigured group and a severely disfigured group, it was found that very few of the moderately disfigured projected their disfigurement into the like-sexed drawing; whereas eleven of nineteen seriously disfigured did evidence such projection. Abel reports that following plastic surgery there was great variation in the degree of change shown in the repeat drawings of patients. After describing some patients whose appearance was much improved by surgery and who reflected this improvement by elimination of disfigurement in their repeat drawings, she goes on to say (p. 259), "In some other cases, there is little or no shift in the figure drawings, although dramatic changes have taken place in the actual physical appearance of the patient's face due to corrective surgery. In other instances, dramatic changes take place in a second set of drawings although no surgery has been performed."

Silverstein and Robinson (283) obtained same-sex, opposite-sex, and self figure drawings from a group of twenty-two children who had had poliomyelitis and who manifested paralytic residuals of the lower extremities. The same set of drawings was obtained from a matched group of forty-four normal children. Judges were unable to distinguish the drawings of the paralytic children from those of the normal either by use of individual signs or global judgments. Silverstein and Robinson concluded that there was no one-to-one basis between body disfigurement and figure-drawing configuration. They state (p. 340), "The present study and other similar investigations have rested on the assumption that the physical body, the body image, and the drawn figure are in isomorphic relation. Given careful exploration, this one-to-one relationship does not seem to exist."

In Witkin's book, *Personality Through Perception*, Machover (348) has recently described some intriguing data concerning the relationships of figure-drawing indices to certain types of perceptual performances. She worked with the figure drawings of college students who had taken a whole battery of perceptual tasks devised by Witkin. These tasks were intended to evaluate the subject's ability to maintain spatial orientation in a variety of situations in which cues regarding spatial position had been removed or distorted. Witkin found that one of the main sources of difference in the way individuals dealt with situations that were spatially confusing had to do with the degree to which they based their orientation on kinesthetic cues or cues supplied by the immediate field situation. Those who relied most on kinesthetic cues were best able to maintain a realistic orientation in a situation designed to be spatially misleading. Machover was able to devise a technique for rating figure drawings which correlated very significantly with the degree of field dependence versus independence of field shown by the subjects. She observed that persons who are field-dependent produce figures reflecting a low evaluation of their bodies ("low body confidence"). Those subjects who are relatively less field-dependent produce drawings which reflect a "high degree of narcissistic investment in the body," effective body integration, and mature body sexual features. Machover concluded on the basis of her data that an individual's attitude toward his body has a significant influence upon his ability to deal with unstructured spatial situations. Machover noted that the field-independent subjects freely included a range of both male and female features in their drawings, as contrasted to an emphasis on like sex traits in the more field-dependent subjects. She postulated that the less field-dependent person in his drive for narcissistic independence may "overlook or ignore the barrier between sexual differential, and incorporate into his own self-image enhancing traits from both sexes" (p. 241). This study is one of the most clear-cut and definitive in the whole body-image literature. It demonstrates in a convincing fashion that body image is an important variable in a primary area of perceptual functioning. It tangentially adds support to the clinical and semiexperimental (311) data earlier cited which suggested that ability to grasp certain types of spatial relationships is affected by body-image distortions.

It should be parenthetically noted, apropos of Witkin's over-all results concerning spatial perception, that he found that men use kinesthetic body cues in orienting themselves to a significantly greater extent than do women. Witkin found further that there is a greater degree of correlation between personality characteristics and attitudes toward one's body in male subjects than in female subjects. He speculated that there is a "greater identity between body and 'self' in men than in women"; and he concluded that men have a somewhat self-contained sensitivity to their own body sensations which contrasts with the attitude of women who are more concerned with the relation of their bodies to the outside world.

A number of other figure drawing studies should also be briefly cited. Elkish (84) has referred to the frequency with which machines appear in the spontaneous drawings of boys. She feels that the machine may be used symbolically as a representation of the body. The machine may be a disguised model of the body. When boys draw machines, they may be attempting to work out the relationships of their bodies to reality.

Berman and Laffal (32) found in a group of psychiatric patients that there was a significant correlation of +.35 between the patient's actual body type and the body type of his figure drawing. This result opens into a whole area of possible investigation of the relationship between the individual's body image and his actual physical structure.

Fisher and Fisher (98) reported that in a group of women in a state hospital there was a borderline significant relationship between the degree of femininity of their figure drawings and their style of past sexual behavior. Those at the extremes, whose drawings had the appearance of either very marked femininity or very little femininity, tended to have been most maladjusted in their sexual relationships. It was particularly noteworthy that physical dysfunction of the reproductive system was linked with low femininity in the drawings.

Swensen (303) described a scale for sexual differentiation on the Draw-A-Person. This scale demonstrated a significantly poorer sexual differentiation for hospitalized mental patients than for patients being treated in an outpatient clinic.

The results obtained by Fisher and Fisher (98) and by Swensen (303) suggest that the sexual differentiation dimension in the figure drawing is a meaningful one with predictive value relative to sexual adjustment and general personality integration. The results of some work by Woods and Cook (357) indicate that it would be wise to take a cautious attitude about the degree to which a figure drawing is actually a representation of body image. They found in a group of 138 eighth-graders that the manner of representing the hands was significantly a function of proficiency in drawing. That is, a factor extraneous to body image had a determining effect upon an important aspect of the figure drawn.

By and large, one gets the impression that although the figure drawing may be a potentially valuable method for studying body image, it has as yet not added much to our knowledge in this area. It is still mainly used in a vague impressionistic manner and there has been limited success in differentiating which aspects of the drawing are linked with body image, which with drawing skill, and which are due to the manner in which the drawing is obtained. Perhaps one of these important difficulties could be surmounted by utilizing variations of the figure-drawing test which minimize artistic skill. For example, the blindfolded drawing method used by Brown and Goitein (52) might prove of value in this respect.

Another technique for measuring body-image variables is exemplified in the work of Secord (276) who developed a word-association method.

He was interested in measuring objectively the degree of concern an individual has about his body and he assumed this could be done by eliciting associations to certain selected words. He built up a list of homonyms "which had meanings pertaining either to bodily parts or processes, and which had in addition common non-bodily meanings." Words like *colon* and *graft* are examples. Body responses to these words might be: colon-intestine, graft-skin, whereas non-bodily responses might be colon-comma, graft-politics. A list of such words was read to subjects at the rate of one every five seconds and the subjects were asked to write down the "first word occurring to them as each homonym was read." It was postulated that the greater the number of bodily associations given the greater the implied concern with one's body. Secord says (p. 483), "High scoring individuals are considered to fall into two exclusive categories: (a) narcissistic, (b) anxious. Narcissistic individuals, who are believed to constitute a small minority of the high scorers, overvalue and overprotect their body because of its great worth. Anxious individuals, on the other hand, are abnormally concerned with their body parts or processes, they fear pain, injury, or disease or they feel that their bodies are ugly and shameful. Low-scoring individuals are believed to be overcontrollers, i.e., they rid themselves of anxious feelings by means of a self-denial mechanism, and thus avoid giving bodily responses." It was demonstrated by Secord that high scorers and low scorers could be significantly differentiated on the basis of this formulation when their Rorschach records were evaluated on a blind basis. It was further shown in a group of fifty-six females that those who scored high on the homonym word associations were significantly less satisfied with the appearance of their bodies than those scoring lower. The fact that meaningful data about body attitudes could be obtained by means of word associations extends further the array of procedures available in this area.

The use of distorting lenses to study body image has in more recent times (subsequent to Stratton's work) been carried forward by Wittreich (352) and by Gilder, et al., as described by Wittreich (353). Gilder and his associates indicate that when an observer views an amputee and a person without body deformity under conditions of induced optical distortion he reports significantly less distortion in the appearance of the amputee. Optical distortion was induced by means of aniseikonic lenses. Wittreich and Radcliffe, Jr. (353) confirmed these results by reduplicating them with a group of twelve subjects. It was difficult to formulate any kind of satisfactory explanation for such results, but the mere fact of their occurrence suggested that aniseikonic-lens distortions might be a fruitful means of exploring body-image phenomena. Wittreich and Grace (351) went on to find, in further studies of body image by means of optical-distortion techniques, that normal individuals reported a different pattern of changes in their own optically distorted mirror images than they did in viewing the mirror images of a stranger. In describing distortions of one's own image the emphasis was upon minor details, with relatively little attention shown to over-all size change or body tilt. In describing other individuals under such distorting conditions, however, the pattern was reversed, with emphasis upon over-all size changes and less emphasis on detail.

Wittreich (352) extended this line of investigation to a group of twenty-one neuropsychiatric patients. Each subject was asked to stand 4 feet from a large mirror and to describe himself when not wearing aniseikonic lenses, when wearing blank lenses, and when wearing aniseikonic lenses. Subjects first described themselves freely and spontaneously and then were asked specifically about various parts of their bodies. Generally it was shown that the neuropsychiatric patients differed from normal subjects in that their reported distortions in self-image mainly involved over-all size, whereas in the normal group the reported distortions focused on specific body parts. This difference was statistically significant. Wittreich, in speculating about these results, suggested that the normal individual tends to have a more differentiated "detailed" body image which "functions differently in different environments and roles." He goes on to say (p. 3). "The 'sick' person is often characterized by an inflexibility of behavior which results in bizarre actions inappropriate to the particular situation. Our results indicate that this may be due at least in part to the undifferentiated body image. The patient may very well be operating in terms of a global, homogenous image of himself which fails to meet the varying demands of a shifting social environment."

Wittreich and Grace (351) proceeded further to explore the potentialities of the aniseikonic technique by studying a group of 140 school children, seventy boys and seventy girls, who represented an age range from four to seventeen years. Each child, while wearing aniseikonic lenses, viewed himself and then also a contemporary in a large mirror and was asked if any of the following parts of the body image appeared to be changed: feet, legs, hands, arms, shoulders, face, nose, and finally the over-all image itself. Previous to this procedure each child had viewed the same mirror images through "control lenses" which consisted of a pair of frames with no lenses in them. Thus the changes experienced as occurring while actually wearing lenses could be compared with those occurring while real lenses were not being worn.

Subsequent to these procedures, the Draw-A-Person test was administered. Each child drew two pictures: one of a person of the same sex and one of the opposite sex. The drawings were scored in terms of one index (Body Maturity Rating) which is a modification of scoring keys used by Goodenough. This index gives increasing credit to increasing recognizability and differentiability of important parts of the body as well as increasing correctness in the proportions of these parts. A second index, entitled "Sexual Differentiation Rating," gives increasing credit to increasing indications in the two drawings of an awareness of those parts of the body which differentiate male from female. Finally, each child was rated by his teachers on each of seven personality characteristics assumed to be related to body-image concept, e.g., "ability to verbalize spontaneously" and "gracefulness and coordination in large movements such as walking and running." The results of the total study indicated that under aniseikonic conditions subjects report significantly more body distortions than under control conditions. Certain parts of the body are reported as changing more frequently than other parts. The eight body parts that were evaluated are listed in order from those most subject to distortion to those most resistive to distortion:

Legs	Hands
Over-all	Nose
Arms	Face
Feet	Shoulder

Further analysis of the data established that with increasing age there is a significant increase in the difference between the amount of distortion occurring in the four body aspects most subject to change and the four least subject to change. It was also true that for the four parts which distort most readily, the boys report change significantly more often than do the girls. The two figure-drawing indices obtained both proved to be significantly positively correlated with the degree to which subjects experienced aniseikonic distortions in the four body parts easily distorted versus the four resistive to distortion. None of the personality ratings obtained from the teachers, however, proved to be related either to aniseikonic distortion scores or the Draw-A-Person indices.

Wittreich and Grace (351) speculate on the basis of their data and cues from their previous work that the individual is most able to experience distortions of those body parts about which he has the greatest degree of security and is least able to accept change of those body parts about which he is insecure. They indicate (p. 17), "Anything with which we have had very little experience, which is in any way threatening or anxiety provoking, in short which makes us highly uncertain as to the reliability of our future action in relation to it, is very unlikely to change under conditions of optical distortion." Thus, they explain the resistance of the face to distortion on the basis of the idea that "looks" and "good looks" are very much a function of how others appraise us and we have no self-contained way of establishing with confidence the kind of "looks" we have. On the other hand, they point out, the legs which are very subject to aniseikonic distortion represent a part of the body which "must function basically as a means of effective locomotion. For this fundamental purpose a constant overt testing-out process occurs. As a result of this process a very solid and secure set of expectancies is built up which has little or nothing to do with the reflected appraisals of others." Wittreich and Grace hypothesize that the significantly greater distortions reported by boys represent the fact that girls are more dependent upon the reflected opinions of others than are boys for an evaluation of their body parts. The body parts of a girl are more often evaluated in terms of their aesthetic appeal to other people. Thus girls are more insecure about their body areas and less able to experience them as distorted.

The whole train of work involving aniseikonic lenses gives promise of demonstrating meaningful body-image differences between sex groups and groups varying in degree of personality disturbance. But most of all, this work has developed a relatively objective and direct means for studying body-image phenomena in a variety of contexts.

FORMULATIONS CONCERNING BODY IMAGE IN VARIOUS THEORETICAL SYSTEMS

"CLASSICAL" PSYCHOLOGY

Few psychologists within the main current of "classical" psychology have given systematic attention to the body-image concept specifically. None of the more classical "schools" within psychology have shown significant interest in the concept. It is a construct which is not seriously treated in any standard textbooks in general psychology. As one looks back, however, over the development of psychology it is apparent that concepts with body-image implications have at times been proposed and treated as significant.

One of the first examples of a theory with body-image implications that one encounters in the past psychological literature is Lotze's theory of space-perception. Lotze, wrestling with the perennial problem of how the individual develops spatial perceptions, took the position that the spatial characteristics of sensations are acquired by experience. Allport (7, p. 88) gives a neat summary of Lotze's viewpoint:

> The process of acquisition involved muscular sensations and the associative combination or fusion of sensory components. Every tactual or retinal point had its local label. The experienced laws of the former depended upon its proximity to tendons, fatty tissue, or

other conformation that affected the stimulation pattern of the spot touched. The aspect of sensory experience which carried the spatial quality was, for Lotze, the attribute of intensity of *muscular* sensations, an intensity pattern *specific for the spot touched.* For retinal points the local sign was given by the tendency of the muscles that rotate the eyeball to contract in such a way as to bring the image of an object falling on that point to bear upon the fovea. Every retinal point thus had associated with it an intensity of the muscular sensation involved in this specific eye movement. With the continuous movement of a receptor in relation to a surface the successive local signs are experienced in proper sequence. Continuity and order in space, the basis of the perception of linear and surface dimensions, therefore resulted from this process.

Lotze's theory could not be more explicit in its focus upon the body as a standard or "map" which imposes a certain type of order upon the individual's experiences. One might paraphrase his theory by saying that the individual builds up a complicated series of body "landmarks" which become reference points in interpreting spatial relationships.

It was with the rise of the method of introspection that the possibility of observing body-image phenomena was maximized. That is, if the introspectionist focuses on his inner sensations and feelings and analyzes them in great detail, it becomes only a matter of time before he notes that there are certain body experiences which are almost a constant background to perceptions of the world. It is soon noted, too, that such body experiences affect the intensity and meaning of sensations. Thus, the individual's perceptions of his body become a significant psychological dimension. Wundt placed great emphasis on kinesthetic sensations (both from the eyes and the body) in explaining the experience of spatial continuity.

The Wurzberg group (Kulpe, Marbe, Ach, Watt) showed in the course of its work that kinesthetic sensations from the body played an important role in judgments relating to various psychophysical tasks. The concept of "determining tendency" or set grew into prominence as the result of the Wurzberg research. This concept referred to the idea that judgments were affected by certain attitudes or expectations which the subject brought to the judgment task. Such attitudes could exert a constant directionality upon response. What is significant from our point of view is that there seemed to be a link between "determining tendency" phenomena and certain kinds of kinesthetic body experiences. Titchener assigned considerable importance to body sensations in the total process of perception. Allport (7, pp. 75–79) says of Titchener in this respect:

In Titchener's view there is one special type of sensation that is paramount as a contextual, meaning-providing process, namely, kinaesthesis. As the organism faces the situation it adopts an attitude toward it, and the kinaesthetic sensations resulting from this attitude (assuming it to be a muscular tension or reaction) give the context and meaning of the object to which the organism is reacting.

Implicit in this viewpoint is the idea that patterns of body sensation are involved in the meaning attributed to perceptual phenomena. One gets the impression that similar ideas are implicit in motor theories of perception (e.g., Washburn's) which basically conceive of perception as an active process arising out of an influential context of feelings and kinesthetic sensations.

It is perhaps a distortion to read such body-image implications into motor theories of perception. However, Werner and Wapner (336), have relatively recently proposed a sensory tonic theory of perception in which the motor aspects of perception are highlighted and in which the body is fairly explicitly assigned important reference-point functions. They have shown in a whole series of studies that changes in an individual's perceptions can be produced by subjecting that individual to experiences which alter his pattern of proprioceptive sensations. For example, the individual's judgment concerning the true vertical for a luminescent rod in a darkroom was demonstrated to tilt in a direction opposite to that of the side of his body which had been subjected to electric stimulation intended to produce increased muscular tonus on that side. Similarly it was shown that the apparent vertical was tilted, relative to objective vertical, in a direction opposite to the actual body tilt of the subject. Werner and Wapner interpret such experimental findings to mean that perception is the outcome of an equilibrium process involving both the effects of stimulation from an object and the existing distribution of body tonus. They state that perceptions are shaped in the direction of minimally disturbing the existing tonus pattern in the body. They are quite specific in their contention that the body, as a field of sensation and experience, must be taken into account in understanding perception. The role they assign to "body" has familiar connotations, because many of the studies already outlined ascribe the same role to "body image." There is clearly some overlap between the sensoritonic conceptualization of body and the concept of body image. It would be an intriguing undertaking to determine if many of the phenomena described in the body-image literature could be captured and understood within the framework of the body tonus patterns which Werner and Wapner consider to be so important.

The brief review just presented indicates that there has indeed been only limited explicit interest in body image in "classical" psychology. There has been more interest in this topic, however, than one might presume from merely scanning the topics which have occupied the major attention of psychologists. In the background of such topics as introspection, spatial localization, set, and perception there has been some recognition of the importance of the body as a frame of reference. But this recognition has been tangential and heavily covered over with terms which make it difficult to tease out the body-image implications.

FREUDIAN POSITION

Freud and others in the psychoanalytic tradition have put forth considerable effort to integrate body-image constructs into their theoretical system. We shall now consider some of the principal psychoanalytic body-image formulations and then proceed to an analysis of related formulations found in the thinking of Adler, Jung, Reich, and Rank.

In his writings Freud placed great emphasis on body image, both explicitly and implicitly. His interest in this concept became clear in his later writings, when he shifted his focus from instinctual variables to organizational variables (e.g., ego controls). Body image was for him another means of describing how the initially undifferentiated organism develops an organizational structure. He saw the body image as fundamental to the development of an ego. In his book, *The Ego and the Id*, he states (111, p. 31): "The ego is first and foremost a body ego; it is not merely a surface entity but it is itself the projection of a surface." The authorized translator of this book (Joan Riviere) appended the following note in clarification of Freud's statement: "That is, the ego is ultimately derived from bodily sensations, chiefly from those springing from the surface of the body. It may thus be regarded as a mental projection of the surface of the body. . . ."

Freud conceived of the earliest ego development as proceeding in terms of the child's learning to integrate sensations from his body surface and using these sensations as a basis for discriminating between the outer world and his own body. Fenichel (89) provides an excellent brief summary of the process: "In the development of reality the conception of one's own body plays a very special role. At first there is only the perception of tension, that is, of an 'inside something.' Later, with the awareness that an object exists to quiet this tension, we have an 'outside something.' One's own body becomes something apart from the rest of the world and thus the discerning of self from nonself is made possible. The sum of the mental representations of the body and its organs, the so-called body image, constitutes the idea of I and is of basic importance for the further formation of the ego."

Various psychoanalysts (113, 151, 92) suggest that initially the child does not discriminate his own body from that of his mother. They postulate that the child does not perceive the mother's breast as distinct from his own body and that he begins to make this distinction only gradually as he discovers that the breast is not available whenever he wants it. Repeated traumatic separations from the breast reinforce the distinction. Hoffer (151) and Linn (199) have theorized that as the child experiences the frustration of not being able to get oral gratification whenever he wants it, he looks for other modes of gratification and discovers that his fingers have a certain substitute value. Sucking the fingers can diminish his oral tensions. Both Hoffer and Linn indicate that in the child's discovery that a part of his own body can relieve tension, he gets a first vivid impression of identity and partial autonomy. Hoffer says (151, p. 50), "In general psychology the function of the hand has mainly been studied as that of an organ which grasps. I am not suggesting that before this grasping function manifests itself, the hand is merely an attachment to the mouth, but that from intrauterine life onward it becomes closely allied to the mouth for the sake of relieving tension and within this alliance leads to the first achievement of the primitive ego." Nacht (226) has made a very specific statement concerning one of the variables involved in the initial development of the body image (p. 56):

> The body image probably begins to take shape in its unity from the sixth month on. . . . By unity, I mean that it is then perceived as being at the same time *one* (synthesis) and *separate* from the environment.
>
> Now, this corresponds exactly to the age at which the maturation of the pyramidal system as well as the myelinization of the fibers of coordination begin to take place: i.e., to the start of voluntary motility. Thus, it seems that the originally diffuse, incoherent, internal bodily perceptions must first become capable of being consolidated and projected outward in action conducive to the gratification of instinctual needs, before such feeling of the unity of the ego can be established.

It is clear that in Freud's thinking and in the thinking of various Freudian psychoanalysts the body image is basic to the development of the total ego structure and becomes a substantial nucleus of later ego elaborations.

Freud's conception of the development of sexuality is in many ways a body-image-oriented theory. In his *Three Contributions to the Theory of Sex,* he suggested that the infant is initially "polymorphous perverse" and does not experience any of his body zones as primary sources of erogenous stimulation. All kinds of stimuli can become a source of excitement; and there are really no well localized body landmarks. Freud proposed, however, in terms of his well-known three-stage libido organization theory (113), that in the course of the child's development certain body areas take on in sequence special importance as sources of erogenous stimulation and as "scenes" for learning to master specific types of impulses. The first postulated phase in the sequence is the "oral stage." In this phase the mouth and oral mucous membranes are considered to manifest the greatest sensitivity to stimulation. The aims of the child are described as focusing on pleasurable stimulation of this area. The child makes great use of its oral sensitivity as a means for exploring and sampling things. He tends to put objects into his mouth in his attempts to fully experience them. Mouth experiences are at this point at the top of the total experience hierarchy. The mouth region is then dominant in the body scheme.

In the second year, however, the mouth begins to lose its primacy and the anal area of the body tends to gain dominance. The child becomes unusually concerned with stimuli in the anal region and much of his erogenous excitement focuses in this region. His toilet-training experiences about this time cause him to be unusually interested in matters of anal retention and expulsion. Freud pointed out that the child at this stage expresses his feelings toward his parents, particularly their attempts to control him, in terms of well-timed or poorly-timed retention and expulsion of feces. Thus, anal function acquires special connotations relative to the expression of aggression. The child learns to associate an area of its body with hostile impulses. At this point also the child is exposed to the phenomenon that in the process of defecating a part of his own body substance is detached. He has to integrate this observation of self-loss with his on-going attempts to build up a satisfactory image of his body. During the anal stage of libidinal organization the anal part of the body is perceived with a prominence many times its actual size representation in the body.

The third libidinal phase is described as coming into prominence during the fourth and fifth years of life. Now the genital region is dominant in the body scheme. Sensations from this region become of greatest importance and the child builds many fantasies about these sensations. He begins to masturbate more because of his increased enjoyment of genital sensations. Freud indicates that at this point the boy is unusually identified with his penis and places more value upon it than any other part of his body. Because of the importance he assigns to it, he is concerned about its safety and is quick to interpret threatening situations as a possible source of mutilation of his penis (castration anxiety). His fear of genital mutilation may be reinforced by the observation that girls do not have a penis and his assumption that this is due to castration. Freud suggested that many of the child's problems of sexual identification were manifested in terms of feelings about the genitals. Thus, the boy with an insecure or threatened male identification would tend to have insecure feelings about his penis. Freud assumed that the zone of greatest genital sensitivity in the girl during this phase is the clitoris and that only later during puberty does the vagina acquire erogenous dominance. He postulated that girls interpret the clitoris as the remnant of a penis and feel that they have been castrated. This carries with it the concept that women come to look upon their bodies as inferior because they do not have a penis.

Freud perceived the genital region as dominant over the anal and oral regions in the mature individual. Maturity could come only as the individual experienced a sequence of phases of varying body-area dominance and then finally the genital zone became most important in the hierarchy. One of Freud's most significant related formulations with body-image implications has to do with the concepts of regression and fixation. He indicated that various factors in the individual's life experiences could cause him to remain fixed in a given libidinal phase or force him to retreat to an earlier phase after having attempted mastery of a later step in the sequence. Thus an individual might enter into a phase of genital primacy but find the problems of reorganizing himself in terms of this new hierarchy of sensitivity and response so difficult that he would find it necessary to fall back upon the pattern of organization characteristic of the anal period. If the individual is fixated at an earlier phase, he has to deal with adult experiences in terms of a body context more appropriate to simpler, less complicated childhood experiences.

Freud, Schilder (268), and others (91, 92) have seen this fixation process and the stage at which it occurs as prime determinants of the specific pattern of body-image distortions (e.g., in states of disturbance or excessive fatigue). Fixation at an earlier pattern of erogenous dominance may eventually lead to a rigid misinterpretation of all stimuli in terms of the tremendously exaggerated importance assigned to the earlier erogenous zone. Thus, a woman who is orally fixated may generalize the sensitivity and dominant role of the mouth to all body openings. She may equate her vagina with the mouth and react to sexual stimulation as if it were something with nutritive qualities that should be incorporated. Similarly she may equate her eyes with a mouth and derive incorporative experiences from looking.

In the process of categorizing the various body-image distortions that may occur as the result of regression and fixation, Freud formulated some generalizations about their mode of appearance. He noted that the individual tends to equate the various openings in the body. They are alike in that they are openings; and so wishes for certain types of forbidden gratification that involve one opening may be displaced in a disguised fashion to another opening. There are many descriptions in the psychoanalytic literature which involve the equation of such openings as mouth with anus, anus with ear, and even of operatively produced body openings (e.g., colostomy opening) with vagina. Freud indicated, too, that parts of the body which project *out* tend to be equated. Thus, the nose and the hands seem frequently to be symbolically linked with the penis. He further observed a tendency for erogenous sensations occurring in the genital region (lower part of the body) which were unacceptable and repressed to reappear in a disguised fashion in displacement upwards. The genital sensations may be translated upward into headaches or pain in some part of the face. By being displaced upwards the "lower" sexual significance of the sensation is doubly denied. The sensation is localized above and certainly does not emanate from "below." Freud has in such terms proposed that body-image distortions are governed by a certain kind of archaic logic and he has defined some aspects of this logic.

This brief summary of some of the body-image implications of Freud's theoretical system indicates that body-image concepts are one of the cornerstones of the system. Freud conceived of the body image as the original framework for the development of the whole ego structure. His theory of libido and of erogenous zones is stated almost entirely in terms of body zones and areas of body sensitivity. Many of his descriptions of personality development revolve about sequences of body-sensitivity dominance. Most of the ideas about body image in the current literature stem at least in part from Freud's theorizing about body experiences.

OTHER PSYCHOANALYTIC POSITIONS

One finds some concern with body-image phenomena in the theory constructions of almost all the subgroups of analytic thought that branched off from Freud. Thus, although Adler (3) was not explicitly concerned with body image as such, many of his descriptions of personality dynamics are rich with implicit body-image references. His theory that neurosis and other manifestations of maladjustment are elaborate stratagems designed to compensate for organ inferiority has body-image connotations. He indicated that when an individual has a morphologically inferior organ or an organ which is below par for functional reasons that individual develops generalized feelings of inferiority and tries to compensate for the "defect" by use of another organ or by intensified use of the inferior organ itself. Is Adler not really saying that when an individual perceives an aspect of his body as inferior, he generalizes this inferiority to his total concept of himself? One organ in the total body scheme takes on exaggerated importance and size relative to the rest of the body scheme and exerts a generalized distorting effect. Basically this conceptualization has much in common with the body-image formulation implicit in Freud's description of libidinal fixation. In parallel fashion, libidinal fixation in a given erogenous zone results in that zone taking on a disproportionate influence in the total body scheme and producing distortions of various sorts.

Jung's theories (161, 162, 163) are less focused on body-image phenomena than are Freud's. But in so far as he postulates a libido which shifts as the child develops from the nutritive to the sexual areas of the body, he does show an interest in body scheme. He does assign significance to the idea that different areas of the body have a shifting hierarchical pattern of importance to the individual and that this existing hierarchy has definite effects upon behavior. The principal concept in Jung's work which involves body image is that of the *mandala,* or containing protective container. He early showed great interest in the idea that the mother figure is represented in various symbolic contexts as an enclosing protective form (161, 162). He felt that in mythology, in folklore, and in dreams mother was symbolized by such images as "cask," "basket," "womb," "cave," and "valley." It was his postulation that when individuals felt troubled because of some stress they developed wishes to retreat into some mother representation. They wished to find refuge in an enclosed protective place. In his book, *Psychology of the Unconscious,* Jung referred to the idea that the troubled person may become very introverted in order to seek refuge and protection within himself. He thought of this process as a way of reanimating the mother figure and obtaining her protection. That is, introversion could at one level be thought of as an attempt to convert one's own body and personality into a container analogous to the mother container. Jung did not explicitly indicate that the individual came to think of his body as a container. One must rather arbitrarily impose such a body-image interpretation on his early thinking regarding this point. But it will become clear that such a body-image interpretation is not far-fetched in terms of later developments in the Jungian tradition that will be cited.

Jung continued to show his interest in the protective-container idea in terms of a very elaborate study of the mandala. The mandala is a symbol which usually takes the form of a round or square enclosure and is found in the symbol productions of many cultures. Its basic form is the circle or circle and square, but it may have many elaborations. It may be illustrated by such representations as a Christ child surrounded by a circle, a globe, and the zodiac. These enclosures are considered to have magical value to those who create them as a symbolization of the need for protective walls that will prevent breakdown and disintegration. Jung feels that these symbols originated in dreams and visions and are among the oldest religious symbols of humanity. He indicates that in the East mandalas, which consist frequently of a circle with a figure of high religious value in the center (e.g., Buddha), become objects of intense contemplation for persons seeking solutions to their difficulties in a religious experience.

But from our point of view what is of special importance about this concept is that some of Jung's followers have explicitly given it a body-image reference. The idea has evolved that the individual seeks to make a mandala of his own body. He seeks protection in the idea of his body as an enclosing container. The following quotation from a paper by G. Adler (4) illustrates this point of view:

> An intuitive interpretation may say that the first ego experience of the baby is bound up with its skin, and that playing with its own body, it learns its demarcation from the surrounding world. It is as though the skin, the "four walls" or "circle" of the body formed a magic circle, a sort of "primordial mandala," marking off an "ego" sphere, and a "non-ego" sphere, and within which the ego experiences itself sensorially.

Perry (234), Fordham (107), and Adler (4) all refer to drawings they have collected from disturbed children and adults in which mandala symbols are prominent. Perry (234) describes a schizophrenic woman who pictured herself as a "quadrated circle." Adler (4) describes a disturbed child who in his drawings represents himself as surrounded by a magic circle.

These Jungian formulations with body-image connotations have been described here in some detail because they are novel. The aura of semi-mystical data in whose context they are usually presented tends to discourage investigators with even a moderately objective research orientation from taking a look at them. However, underneath the associated speculative thinking, there is a postulated body-image dimension which could perhaps be studied profitably by means of objective procedures. It is incidentally interesting that Machover (203) and others (129, 179), who are not oriented in a Jungian fashion, have in some of their discussions of figure drawing interpretation referred to the body walls as protection from outside danger and a means of holding in disturbing impulses.

Otto Rank (237) was quite fascinated with what he called *maternal symbols* and he emphasized their containing protective properties. Within his theoretical system the separation from the mother's womb at birth is a tremendous trauma. He postulated that many of the later struggles and symptoms of the individual can be interpreted as attempts to regain the security of the womb. The body-image implications of his theorizing are observable mainly in his references to the idea that individuals may seek to convert their own bodies into a kind of womb or protective container. That is, individuals may seek security in visualizing their bodies as having invulnerable walls. They may actually take measures to reinforce their body walls with devices which will facilitate picturing the body as a container that provides refuge. For example, they may wear armor or protective clothing of various sorts. At a more imaginative level, this aim is represented in myths about heroic figures who are invulnerable because of a magic hood or impenetrable cloak.

Rank is so convinced of the significance of the protective container in this respect that he assumes that drawings of the human figure in art work evolved originally from crude drawings of a vessel (maternal symbol). He suggests that the original drawings of vessels were gradually modified into representing a child or its head and then in later art were transformed into a representation of a complete human being. He implies that the vessel or container is a basic prototype of the individual's conception of his body.

Wilhelm Reich (239) has assigned importance to body-image ideas throughout his work. He has assiduously noted a complex interaction between the individual's personality conflicts, the individual's expressions of these conflicts in patterns of muscle tonus, and the repercussions of these tonus patterns upon the individual's way of experiencing himself and others. He has expressed the view that certain kinds of conflicts result in the individual's "armoring" himself and trying to model his body after something with hard rigid surfaces. In his published work he cites many clinical examples of patients whom he describes as manifesting such armoring phenomena. More recently in the extreme and rather disorganized extensions of his theories, he has built a whole system of psychotherapy which has as one of its major aims the loosening and dissolving of "body armor." Some of his earlier formulations concerning the factors involved in armoring are worth mentioning. It should be incidentally noted that sometimes it is difficult to determine, in his discussions of armoring, whether he is applying the concept to ego-structure phenomena or body-concept variables. In any case, he has outlined a number of factors which directly or indirectly would bear upon the degree to which the individual modeled his body after something hard and rigid.

Reich suggests first of all that the more an individual identifies with a frustrating reality (e.g., a parent who emphasized inhibition and self-control) the more will he tend toward armored hardness. He assigns the same hardening significance to factors which cause the individual to turn aggression against himself and inhibit its motor expression outwardly. Further, he attributes a similar influence to conditions which build up reactive attitudes toward sex and arouse fear of punishment for sexual wishes. It is his view that everyone is armored to some extent, but that it is the degree of rigidity of the armor which distinguishes the disturbed person from the well person. His concern with the body-image aspects of his theory constructs is apparent in the fact that he devotes considerable discussion to how individuals with different degrees of armoring experience their bodies and the measures they may take to make these experiences more pleasurable. Thus, in referring to the masochist who may be thought of as rather heavily armored, Reich says (p. 227):

> The masochist has . . . some kind of wish for activity at the skin or at least phantasies of it—to be pinched, brushed, whipped. . . . All these wishes have in common that the patient wants to feel the warmth of the skin, not pain. If a patient wants to be whipped, it is not because he wants to feel pain; the pain is taken in the bargain because of the "burning"—the sensation of skin warmth which is based on dilation of the peripheral vessels—is a specific part of the pleasure syndrome.

It is obvious that there are certain similarities between Reich's armor concept, Jung's mandala formulation, and Rank's containing-vessel idea. They all imply that the individual seeks to surround his body with protective boundaries and that he may implement such wishes in terms of muscle tonus, body embellishment, and other measures.

SUMMARY OF PAST TRENDS

We have at this point completed a survey of a mixed array of facts, speculations, and theories concerning body image. It would be well to pull this material together more tightly and consider what main points emerge. The following is an impressionistic summary of what appear to be the most prominent trends and justified generalizations:

(1) There is some evidence that the body scheme may function as a basic standard or frame of reference which influences some of the individual's modes of perception and also his ability to perform certain skills. The observations of Tausk (308), Gerstmann (124A), and Teitelbaum (311) and some of the research they have stimulated (290, 295, 296) suggests that body-image variables may have such diverse effects as shaping a schizophrenic's concept of the type of machine which he feels is magically controlling him from a distance, determining an individual's ability to do specific kinds of arithmetical calculations, and influencing

his grasp of certain types of spatial relationships. At present there are few substantiated facts in this area; and the whole problem awaits systematic exploration.

(2) By and large, body image has been defined as a psychological variable. That is, it is usually described as evolving gradually in the course of a learning process in which the individual experiences his body in manifold situations and also notes the varied reactions of others to it. Apparently as he grows he explores his body in many ways and comes to assign a hierarchy of values to its principal areas. Some of the speculations concerning the development of body image assume that the earliest crystallizations of body image represent the nucleus about which the individual first tries to build an ego structure.

(3) There have been numerous attempts to give further meaning to the concept of body image by theorizing concerning its mode of representation in the individual and also concerning the mechanisms involved in its functioning. Head (147), Schilder (268), and others (21) have directly or indirectly postulated that body image is a *central model* against which the individual somehow measures a good many of his perceptions. Some (268, 68) have taken the position that this central model is mainly linked in its functioning with the parietal area of the brain.

The most complicated body-image constructs in the literature have been formulated by Freud and others who are psychoanalytically oriented. Within Freud's system of thought the body image is primarily demarcated relative to three main body areas which are, over a period of time, successively of unusual sensitivity and erogenous significance. The adult's body image is considered to be a final product of his success and failures in integrating his life experiences to cope with the changing demands of each new area of erogenous dominance. One of the most original aspects of this theory is that it concerns itself with the consequences of an individual's inability to integrate the functioning of given body zones into his total body scheme. It is assumed that this results in the carry-over into adulthood of a childlike body scheme in which early dominant erogenous zones (e.g., mouth) have an overgeneralized importance. It is further assumed that such a childlike body image interferes seriously with gaining satisfactions from adult experiences and therefore becomes a source of personality disturbance.

Brief but novel body-image formulations may be found in the theories of Jung and Rank. Within both the Jungian and Rankian traditions there are concepts which propose that the individual has strong needs to conceive of his body as a container with defensive walls into which he can retire for protection at times of danger. Detailed clinical descriptions

(162, 163) have been offered regarding how he goes about maximizing the enclosing, protective aspects of his body and reassuring himself of its sheltering value.

(4) There is an imposing amount of observation which indicates that individuals are subject to a wide gamut of body-image distortions (268, 92, 91, 147). These distortions range from the mildly unusual sensations of the normal person while riding in a high-speed elevator to the gross misconceptions of the patient with organic brain pathology who cannot distinguish the right side of his body from the left side. The range of observed distortions seem to lie on a common continuum. Thus, even some of the extreme forms manifested by organic patients are at times experienced by normal persons in situations of unusual stress. Despite the manifold variations in reported body-image deviations, they do seem to fall into certain broad categories of greatest frequency. These categories may be roughly defined as follows:

   a. Feelings of loss of body boundaries which involve a sense of blurring of the demarcation line between one's own body and that which is outside one's body.
   b. Sensations of depersonalization which revolve about a perception of one's body as strange, alien, and perhaps even as belonging to someone else.
   c. The attributing to one's body of unrealistic qualities and extra parts (e.g., phantom limb).
   d. Confusion regarding the distinction between the right versus the left side of the body; or the attributing of contrasting characteristics to the right versus the left side.

(5) It is clear that when the individual suffers radical body mutilation (e.g., loss of limb) he resists accepting its reality and tends to persist in viewing his body in terms of the previous intact body image (139, 284). Once he begins to integrate the mutilation into his current body scheme, however, this may result in both quantitative and qualitative changes in sensitivity in the altered body area (137, 138). These changes are apparently of such a character as to correspond to the new value assigned to the altered body area in the revised body scheme.

(6) Clinical data indicate the possibility that body image is also a force in determining the locus of body incapacitation in specific syndromes in which body dysfunction is the main response to psychological stress. Illustratively, some of the work which has been done with conversion hysterics (113, 92, 6) suggests that they have assigned exaggerated symbolic qualities to those parts of their bodies which develop paralysis or hypersensitivity. It is as if the symbolic meaning they have

assigned to a body part makes it vulnerable to be used as a distorted means for finding outlet for certain tensions.

(7) Quite a repertoire of techniques for studying body image may now be found in the literature. A considerable quantity of information has accumulated simply on the basis of introspection and informal observation of individuals with body-image distortions caused by such factors as drugs, the induction of hypnotic states, body mutilation, and psychotic regression. More controlled and quantitative techniques have also been used for evaluating body-image phenomena. The questionnaire (140), drawing of a person (1, 203, 21), drawing of the inside of the body (306), and self-ratings (72) are examples of such techniques. Among the most novel potentially valuable means for obtaining body-image data are the methods of unconscious self-confrontation developed by Wolff (356); the double simultaneous stimulation procedures utilized by Bender (22) and others (66, 231); the procedures involving schematic representation of body parts described by Katcher and Levin (166); the aniseikonic-lens technique so successfully developed by Wittreich (351); and the word-association methods worked out by Secord (276).

Generally, it is apparent that what we know about body image today is difficult to condense or systematize. There are many individual items of information which have been noted and gathered. Most of these items are based on half anecdotal observation; and there are only a limited number of things that have been said about body image which one can point to as examples of scientifically verified fact. Our existing pool of data should be considered primarily as a place to fish out hunches and hypotheses that will be worth more systematic testing.

....

CHAPTER TWO

The Body-Image Boundary Dimension

INITIAL SPECULATIONS

THE PRECEDING review of the literature concerned with body image provides a contextual background against which to present our own findings and formulations. The remaining portion of this book will be devoted to an account of a body-image frame of reference which we have developed and which we consider to have considerable value in clarifying a variety of personality phenomena. Our body-image constructs have evolved out of a series of studies which were undertaken over a period of several years. We have sought to apply these constructs to a wide range of problems and thus to map out the areas in which they have clarifying, predictive value and those to which they make little contribution. Our intent has been to determine the value of systematically attacking a variety of problems in terms of a body-image frame of reference. We have limited ourselves to one dimension of body image out of many other possibilities because a thorough analysis of just this one dimension has proved to be a very demanding undertaking. In considering the clearest way in which to present our work, it seems best to begin with a somewhat sequential description of how our thinking and concepts emerged.

Although the greater part of our work has been done with normal subjects, our initial interest in body image was stimulated by observations of various types of patients who manifested symptoms frequently considered to have marked psychosomatic determinants. In one of our first projects we attempted in an exploratory fashion to find out if there are patterns of behavior or fantasy which particularly characterize patients with rheumatoid arthritis. We studied this group by means of intensive interviews, the Rorschach test, the Thematic Apperception Test, and Figure Drawings (62). The group consisted of twenty-five male patients in a Veterans Administration hospital.

In the course of our analysis of the data obtained we were struck by how much concern the arthritic has about his body. A good part of his energy seemed to be tied up in certain wishes and expectations concerning his body. His body appeared to be the most important thing in his immediate field of experience and his fantasies were saturated with body references. When, therefore, we noted that the arthritic gave an unusual number of rather unique Rorschach responses, we were inclined to speculate whether or not these responses had something to do with his way of perceiving his body. These Rorschach responses were unusual in that they involved a special emphasis on the containing, protective, and boundary-defining qualities of the periphery of percepts. The following are examples: "cave with rocky walls," "flower pot," "knight in armor," "something with a wall around it," "turtle with a shell," "cocoon," and "mummy wrapped up." In each of these percepts either the hardness or protective insulation value of the periphery is prominent. The hypothesis suggested itself that the arthritic was projecting into such responses his feeling that his body periphery is a hard defensive wall which affords him special protection. We were also impressed by the fact that the arthritic actually does show, as part of his total symptomatology, a stiffness of body musculature which imparts a certain hardness and exterior stiffness to his appearance. Thus, there seemed to be a possible link between an aspect of the arthritic's literal body symptomatology and the unique Rorschach percepts he produced. In further exploring our data, we found that the tendency to emphasize the periphery of percepts could be detected even in the arthritic's TAT stories. There were many unusual references to the protective-covering function of the clothes of the story characters. In addition, there were a number of plots which involved figures who were enclosed "in a well" or "surrounded by walls." It seemed as if the arthritic had such a marked need to feel enclosed by protective barriers that he projected such barriers, sometimes inappropriately, into the TAT pictures.

In the process of analyzing the interview information, we were struck by how much difficulty arthritics had in expressing anger. They rarely lost their tempers and even in situations of considerable frustration maintained an affable attitude. It seemed as if they were afraid to express anger and felt it necessary to contain it inwardly in a tightly controlled fashion. This led to the speculation that their emphasis on definite enclosing peripheries in the Rorschach and also their focus on symptoms which involve muscle stiffness and rigidity might both represent, at different levels, the attempt to defend against feelings which are felt to have catastrophic implications unless held in check. That is, one could conceive of the arthritic as a person who has certain unacceptable impulses over which he is so fearful of losing control that he has found it necessary to convert his body into a containing vessel whose walls would prevent the outbreak of these impulses. We were especially intrigued by the idea that he was selectively utilizing a particular layer of his body (striate musculature) to achieve a protective wall about himself. His muscle stiffness seemed to be equated with inhibition and making the body exterior tough and resistant.

The data from the arthritic group suggested to us the idea that one significant dimension of body image might be the manner in which individuals perceive their body boundaries. Perhaps people show wide differences in the degree to which they experience their body boundaries as definite and firm versus indefinite and vague. One could conceive of each individual as equating his body with a "base of operations," a segment of the world that is specially his. His body would encompass his private domain and be the cumulative site for all of his past integrated experiences. It could be regarded as bounding and containing a complex system which has been developed to deal with the world. It would encompass a structure which the individual has built up in his attempts to make life satisfying for himself. Therefore, would one not expect that the sort of boundaries which the individual attributes to his body would tell a good deal about his over-all life-building operations? Would one not assume that the person who sees his body as an area highly differentiated from the rest of the world and girded by definite boundaries had constructed a different type of "base of operations" from that of the person who regards his body as an area with indefinite boundaries? There are, of course, many precedents in the past literature for considering body-boundary phenomena to have importance for the individual's behavior.

Much of the pertinent literature has already been reviewed in the previous chapter. It was, for example, pointed out that Freud (111) showed great interest in body-boundary phenomena and that he explored them in considerable detail in terms of the attitudes that patients take toward their body openings (particularly mouth and anus). It was further described how important Reich (239) considered this area of study to be and how he examined its implications by means of the concept of "character armor." Jung (163) and various others (4, 237, 107) were also cited for their interest in issues having body-boundary implications. One can actually find a large accumulation of clinical data in the literature which supports the notion that individuals do differ in the degree of openness and penetrability they ascribe to their bodies. This accumulation of past observation coupled with our own findings regarding patients with rheumatoid arthritis affirmed the potential value of undertaking a systematic study of body-boundary phenomena.

The first logical step in such an undertaking would appear to be to develop a method for objectively measuring the degree of definiteness the individual assigns to his body boundaries. From our study of the arthritic group we had Rorschach, TAT, Draw-A-Person, and interview data available which presumably tapped in varying ways the boundary definiteness dimension. We evaluated each of these sources in terms of the richness of the information that each provided concerning this variable. It was immediately apparent that the individual had little conscious information about his attitudes toward his body boundaries and that such attitudes could only with difficulty be deduced from information obtained from a depth interview. Furthermore, such interview material was extremely difficult to quantify. The projective tests seemed to be the best potential source of the sort of data we wished to obtain.

In comparing the Rorschach, TAT, and Draw-A-Person tests in this respect, it was noted that the Rorschach elicited considerably more information that was pertinent and subject to quantification. The ink-blot stimulus seemed to afford the subjects a particularly good opportunity to project images which differed in boundary attributes. Of course, there is quite a gap to bridge in assuming that the differences in boundary attributes of images elicited by ink blots are correlated with differences in the manner in which individuals perceive their body boundaries. At the outset of our work the only rationale for this assumption was the observed analogy between the symptoms, body attitudes, and projective fantasies of the arthritics. Only in a later phase of our work (described in Chapter 3) did we explore the reasonableness of the assumption by means of systematic studies. Having chosen ink-blot stimuli as the method for eliciting data concerning the individual's concept of his body boundaries, there still remained the further choice of constructing a special group of ink blots or of using the conventional Rorschach as a measuring instrument. One could conceivably develop a series of blots which would maximize associations or images having to do with boundary properties. It was decided, however, to use the conventional Rorschach as a measuring instrument for several reasons. First of all, it was an instrument which had already shown some initial promise in terms of the arthritic data. Second, there seemed to be an advantage in the fact that it was in wide standardized use and thus would make it easier for others who might want to duplicate any results we obtained. Third, we were struck by the idea that if a boundary measure derived from the Rorschach proved to have value, it would be possible to take a short cut to exploring many problem areas by reevaluating large stores of Rorschach records which have in the past been collected for other purposes.

FORMULATION OF EMPIRICAL SCORING SYSTEM

In order to devise a scoring system for evaluating the boundary dimension in terms of Rorschach responses, it was necessary to build upon and elaborate from the clues supplied by the records of the arthritics. We intensively studied these records for their unique characteristics and also for their commonality with other sorts of records. We tabulated and categorized all responses which even remotely referred to special qualities of the boundaries or peripheries of things. References to surfaces in terms of hardness, softness, unusual texture, unusual coloration, and any other special attributes were noted. We soon found that such references fell into two broad classes which became the basis for two separate scores. One group of references had to do with assigning definite structure, definite substance, and definite surface qualities to the bounding peripheries of things. These references took such diverse forms as noting the unusual fuzziness of the skin of an animal, emphasizing the decorative pattern of a surface, or elaborating upon the clothing worn by a person. The emphasis here was upon the positiveness and definiteness of boundaries. Percepts containing such references were labeled "Barrier responses." * A second group of references, which was the basis for another boundary score, had to do with boundary peripheries only in the negative sense of emphasizing their weakness, lack of substance, and penetrability. Responses of this sort concerned surfaces being broken, destroyed, or absent. They were labeled "Penetration of Boundary responses."

It was considered that a score based on Barrier responses would tap the boundary dimension at a level of positive assertion of boundary definiteness. A score derived from Penetration of Boundary responses was perceived as getting at sensations of boundary breakdown and fragility. It appeared likely that the occurrence of Penetration of Boundary responses would be indicative of a greater sense of boundary fragility than simply the lack of occurrence of Barrier responses. There seemed to be an especially explicit note of boundary weakness and openness in the Penetration of Boundary images. We anticipated that the Barrier score and the Penetration of Boundary score would tend to be negatively correlated. These were pretty much guesses. The actual data we later collected turned out rather different than we expected. But in any case, we first set up two separate body-image boundary scores because we felt that although both scores were in their own ways tapping aspects of a boundary-definiteness dimension, we were still un-

---

* The term *barrier* is not intended by us to refer to an obstacle or obstruction. We are using it in the sense of "any limit or boundary" (Webster definition).

certain whether these aspects were sufficiently overlapping to permit them to be combined meaningfully into one score.

BARRIER SCORE

There will be presented now a specific breakdown and categorization of the various types of responses that were considered to be indicative of Barrier attributes. It should be emphasized that the categorizations were based on empirical inspection of the arthritics' Rorschachs and sometimes represent speculative elaborations of hints supplied by such inspection. The scoring categories° which were designed are as follows:

(1) All separate articles of clothing are scored Barrier. This is true also of all articles of clothing worn by animals and birds. If the clothing is being worn by a person, however, it is scored only if it is unusual in its covering or decorative function.† Note -these examples of clothing being worn by someone that are scored as Barrier responses:

woman in a high-necked dress	imp with a cap that has a tassel on it
person in a fancy costume	people with mittens or gloves
woman in a long nightdress	people with hoods
man with a crown	feet with fancy red socks
man in coat with a lace collar	man with a cook's hat
man in a robe	man with chaps
man with high collar	

The popular boots on card IV, and the bowtie on III are not scored as clothing because of the frequency with which they are given.

Examples of clothing being worn which are *not* scored:

woman in a dress   man with a coat on   man with a hat

(2) Animals or creatures whose skins‡ are distinctive or unusual are scored only if more than the head of the animal is given. The following is a complete list of such animals:

alligator	fox	lynx	prairie dog	skunk
badger	goat	mink	rhinoceros	tiger
beaver	hippo	mole	scorpion	walrus
bobcat	hyena	mountain goat	sea lion	weasel
chameleon	leopard	peacock	seal	wildcat
coyote	lion	penguin	sheep or lamb	wolverine
crocodile	lizard	porcupine	Siamese cat	zebra

° The practical application of the scoring categories is illustrated in terms of several Rorschach records which are presented in the Appendix.

† This scoring rule has been changed since 1958. Now *all* references to clothing are scored Barrier.

‡ This category of responses was included on the assumption that concern with animals having unusual, valued, specially marked, or specially protective skins represents a focus on some aspect of the substantiality of covering surfaces.

Any animal skin (except bearskin on card IV) may be considered Barrier if unusual emphasis is placed on the textured, fuzzy, mottled, or striped character of the surface. Examples:

> fuzzy skin   skin with spots
> skin with stripes

Included in this general covering category are all shelled creatures except crabs and lobsters. Crabs and lobsters are excluded because of their frequency of occurrence. Lobsters and crabs are scored only in the unusual instances in which the shell alone is seen. Examples of shelled creatures:

> snail   shrimp
> mussel   clam
> turtle

(3) Score references to enclosed openings in the earth. Examples:

> valley   mine shaft
> ravine   well
> canal

(4) Score references to unusual animal containers. Examples:

> bloated cat   kangaroo
> pregnant woman   udder

(5) Score references to overhanging or protective surfaces. Examples:

> umbrella   dome
> awning   shield

(6) Score references to things that are armored or much dependent on their own containing walls for protection. Examples:

> tank   rocket ship in space
> battleship   armored car
> man in armor

(7) Score references to things being covered, surrounded, or concealed. Examples:

> bowl overgrown by a plant   man covered with a blanket
> house surrounded by smoke   person hidden by something
> log covered by moss   someone peeking out from behind a stone
> person behind a tree   donkey with load covering his back
> person caught between two stones

(8) Score references to things with unusual containerlike shapes or properties. Examples:

bagpipes   ferris wheel
throne   chair

(9) Do not score masks or buildings.* There are, however, a few exceptional instances in which unique structures are scored. The following are the exceptions:

tent   fort   igloo   quonset hut   arch

(10) Do *not* score instruments which grasp or hold. Examples:

pliers   tweezers   tongs

Additional *general* examples of Barrier responses:

basket	cove	mountain covered
bay	curtain	with snow
bell	dancer with veil	net
book	frosting on cake	pot
book ends	fuzzy poodle	river
bottle	globe	screen
bubble	harbor	spoon
cage	headdress	urn
candleholder	hedge along a walk	wall
cave	helmet	wallpaper
cocoon	inlet	wig
	lake surrounded	
	by land	
	land surrounded	
	by water	

In scoring any given Rorschach record, the total number of responses falling into the above categories is compiled. Each response is given a value of 1. The final score is simply equal to the total number of Barrier responses.

PENETRATION OF BOUNDARY SCORE

An individual's feeling that his body exterior is of little protective value and could be easily penetrated was considered to be expressed in his Rorschach responses in three different ways:

(1) In terms of images that involve the penetration, disruption, or wearing away of the outer surfaces of things. The following Rorschach responses are illustrations of such images: "bullet penetrating flesh,"

---

* Since 1958 the scoring rules have been altered and now *all* references to buildings and vehicles with containing attributes (e.g., automobile, airplane, rocket) are scored Barrier.

"shell of a turtle that has been broken open," "squashed bug," "badly worn away animal skin."

(2) In terms of images that emphasize modes or channels for getting into the interior of things or for passing from the interior outward to the exterior. Here are some examples: "vagina," "anus," "open mouth," "an entrance," "doorway."

(3) In terms of images that involve the surfaces of things as being easily permeable or fragile. The following are examples: "soft ball of cotton candy," "fleecy fluffy cloud," "mud that you can step through."

The following is an enumeration of the specific subcategories of Penetration of Boundary response.

(1) Score all references to the mouth being opened or being used for intake or expulsion. Examples:

dog eating	man vomiting
dog yawning	boy spitting
man sticking tongue out	person with mouth open
animal drinking	

Do *not* score references to use of the mouth for singing or talking.

(2) Score all references to evading, bypassing, or penetrating through the exterior of an object and getting to the interior. Examples:

X-ray picture	body cut open
body as seen through a fluoroscope	inside of the body
cross section of an organ	autopsy

(3) Score references to the body wall being broken, fractured, injured, and damaged. Examples:

mashed bug	wound
wounded man	man stabbed
person bleeding	man's skin stripped off

Do *not* score instances in which simple loss of a body member has occurred (e.g., amputation, head cut off) unless there is a description of concomitant bleeding.*

Another subvariety of this category includes responses involving some kind of degeneration of surfaces. Examples:

diseased skin   withering skin   withered leaf   deteriorating flesh

(4) Score examples of openings in the earth that have no set boundaries or from which things are being expelled:

bottomless abyss	geyser spurting out of ground
fountain shooting up	oil gusher coming in

---

* Since 1958 *all* references to loss of a body member are scored Penetration.

(5) Score all openings. Examples:

anus	looking into the throat
birth canal	nostril
doorway	rectum
entrance	vagina
window	

(6) Score references to things which are insubstantial and without palpable boundaries. Examples:

cotton candy	shadow
ghost	soft mud

(7) Score all references to transparency. Examples:

can see through the dress
transparent window

Further general examples of Penetration of Boundary responses:

animal chewing on a tree	bat with holes
broken-up butterfly	torn fur coat
jigsaw not put together	frayed wings
doorway	deteriorated wings
fish with meat taken off	grasshopper pecking at something
broken body	harbor entrance
man defecating	

In scoring any given Rorschach record, the total number of responses falling into the above categories was compiled. Each response was given a value of 1.

We discovered that there are instances in which a response has both Barrier and Penetration of Boundary characteristics. For example, such responses as "man with broken armor," "bombed battleship," and "broken vase" have simultaneous connotations of unusual protective or containing properties and also disrupted boundaries. These responses are scored both as Barrier and Penetration of Boundary. Although such scoring may appear to be paradoxical, we decided to adhere to it empirically if it followed from our basic scoring scheme.

The interscorer reliability of the scoring system has in general been found to be rather high when the scorers are trained regarding the various judgmental standards involved. Thus, the authors individually scored one series of twenty records; and when the sets of scorings were compared the rho correlation for Barrier scores was +.82 and the rho for Penetration of Boundary scores was .94. The writers individually scored a second series of twenty records. For this series the Barrier scores correlated .97 and the Penetration of Boundary scores correlated .99. In addition, three other individual clinical psychologists were asked to score the second series of twenty records. Their scoring was compared with the scoring of one of the writers, which was arbitrarily chosen as

TABLE 2:1   INTERSCORER RELIABILITY FOR THE TWO BODY-IMAGE MEASURES

Raters	Barrier Score Correlations	Penetration of Boundary Correlations
Rater A vs. rater B (Group 1)[a]	.82[c]	.94
Rater A vs. rater B (Group 2)[b]	.97	.99
Rater C vs. criterion	.91	.91
Rater D vs. criterion	.97	.87
Rater E vs. criterion	.82	.83

[a] Group 1—One group of 20 Rorschachs.
[b] Group 2—A second group of 20 Rorschachs.
[c] All coefficients are of the rank-order type.

a criterion standard. Two of the scorers correlated with this criterion Barrier scoring in the .90s (.91 and .97). The third scorer correlated with the Barrier criterion .82. Relative to the Penetration of Boundary score, one judge correlated .91 with the Penetration criterion and the other two correlated in the .80s (.87 and .83). The over-all average of the five Barrier score correlations is .92; and the average of the five Penetration of Boundary correlations is .91. These results indicate that, if well trained, scorers can learn to agree with regard to both the Barrier and Penetration of Boundary indices at a level somewhere in the .90s. Individuals do show differential ability to learn the scoring schemes, as witness correlations which range from .82 to .97 for the Barrier index and .83 to .99 for the Penetration of Boundary variable. But carefully trained and well-motivated judges can generally agree somewhere in the .90s.

RORSCHACH CORRELATES OF THE BODY-IMAGE SCORES

We were, of course, immediately aware of the probability that both the body-image boundary scores would to some degree be a function of the response totals of the Rorschach records from which they were derived. If an individual produces a short record, it is likely that his chances of giving the sorts of percepts that are considered to have body-image connotations would be less than would the chances of an individual producing a long record. We examined the relationship of response total to each of the body-image scores in a number of different subject groups. These groups were used in a series of studies to be described at a later point.

TABLE 2:2   RHO CORRELATIONS OF THE TWO BODY-IMAGE MEASURES
WITH RORSCHACH RESPONSE TOTAL

Group	Barrier vs. R	Level of Significance	Penetration of Boundary vs. R	Level of Significance
Dermatitis (N = 25)	.53	.01	.60	.01
Arthritis (N = 25)	.55	.01	.37	Not significant
Burns (N = 22)	.41	.05	.29	Not significant
Ulcerative colitis (N = 20)	.66	.01	.52	.05
Student nurses (N = 30)	.60	.01	.63	.01

Table 2:2 indicates that in a variety of groups with psychosomatic symptoms and in a normal group of student nurses, Rorschach response total is correlated significantly with both the Barrier score and the Penetration of Boundary score. The degree of correlation fluctuates from group to group, but is sufficiently generalized as to leave no doubt concerning the necessity for controlling response total when body-image scores from different individuals are to be compared. Several different methods were developed for dealing with the response total problem:

(1) In many of the studies to be described, subjects were asked to give a fixed number of responses to each card. Therefore, each subject completed the ten blots with exactly the same number of responses. Details of this method of administration will be presented at a later point.

(2) In a considerable number of studies, response total variance was controlled by eliminating all Rorschach records with less than 15 responses and reducing all records with more than 25 responses to 25. A set method for reducing response total was developed which will be described elsewhere.

(3) There were several instances in which neither of these two methods for controlling response total was applied; but conclusions concerning differences between groups in body-image scores were contingent upon

demonstrating that the groups did not differ significantly in total response.

In order to clarify in detail the relationships of the body-image scores to the usually measured attributes of Rorschach protocals, an intensive analysis was undertaken of individual records of fifty college students which had been collected by Westrope (338).* There were twenty-five men and twenty-five women in the group. Two types of analyses of the data were undertaken. In one instance the body-image scores based on the entire unlimited record were compared to a number of the conventional Rorschach determinant scores which were tabulated on the basis of the entire record. In another type of analysis the body-image scores derived from an arbitrarily limited portion of each record were related to the conventional determinants based on the entire record. This second mode of analysis permits an evaluation of how the body-image scores are related, somewhat independent of response total, to the determinant scores derived from the over-all record.

TABLE 2:3   CHI-SQUARE TESTS OF DIFFERENCES IN VARIOUS RORSCHACH FACTORS BETWEEN SUBJECTS ABOVE AND BELOW THE UNCONTROLLED BARRIER SCORE MEDIAN AND SUBJECTS ABOVE AND BELOW THE UNCONTROLLED PENETRATION OF BOUNDARY MEDIAN

Rorschach Factor	Barrier Group Obtaining Higher Score	Significance Level	Penetration of Boundary Group Obtaining Higher Score	Significance Level
Response total[a]	H.B.[b]	.001	H.P.[b]	.001
No. of W. responses	N.D.	—	N.D.	—
F + %	L.B.	.001	N.D.	—
Color total	N.D.	—	N.D.	—
Shading total	H.B.	.001	N.D.	—
Human movement	H.B.	—	N.D.	—

[a] All the Rorschach factors enumerated are defined and scored in terms of Beck's criteria.
[b] H.B.—High Barrier. L.B.—Low Barrier. N.D.—No difference. H.P.—High Penetration.

Table 2:3 indicates that when the Barrier score is based on the total Rorschach record of each subject, those with the highest Barrier scores give a significantly higher response total and make significantly more use of shading determinants. But those with low Barrier scores obtain

---

* We are grateful to Dr. Martha Westrope for permitting us to use her data.

significantly higher F+ per cents. There is no difference between high and low Barrier scorers for number of whole responses, the degree to which chromatic color determinants are utilized, or for number of human movement responses. The high Penetration of Boundary subjects show up as having significantly higher response totals than the low Penetration subjects, but otherwise the two Penetration groups do not differ.

TABLE 2:4   CHI-SQUARE TESTS OF DIFFERENCES IN VARIOUS RORSCHACH FACTORS BETWEEN SUBJECTS ABOVE AND BELOW THE CONTROLLED BARRIER SCORE MEDIAN AND SUBJECTS ABOVE AND BELOW THE CONTROLLED PENETRATION OF BOUNDARY MEDIAN

Rorschach Factor	Barrier Group Obtaining Higher Score	Significance Level	Penetration of Boundary Group Obtaining Higher Score	Significance Level
Response total[a]	N.D.[b]	—	N.D.[b]	—
No. of W. responses	H.B.	.05–.02	N.D.	—
F + %	L.B.	.02	N.D.	—
Color total	N.D.	—	N.D.	—
Shading total	N.D.	—	N.D.	—
Human movement	N.D.	—	N.D.	—

[a] All the Rorschach factors enumerated are defined and scored in terms of Beck's criteria.
[b] H.B.—High Barrier. L.B.—Low Barrier. N.D.—No difference.

Table 2:4 shows the changed relationships which appear when the Barrier scores are obtained from arbitrarily limited records. The limits imposed on the records were such that all responses over 25 were eliminated from consideration. Responses were eliminated according to a fixed procedure which involves selection of the first three responses on the first five cards and the first two responses on the last five cards. Where such selection was not possible on any given card because of too few responses present, additional responses were selected on the next card in the sequence which had more than the number of responses necessary for that card. In this way, no Barrier score is based on a total larger than 25 responses. However, one record initially had as few as 16 responses; five had as few as 19 responses; and eight fell in the range 20–23. By and large, then, the controlled Barrier scores in this group were derived from response totals clustering in the range 20–25. Those subjects with high controlled Barrier scores do not significantly exceed the low Barrier scorers in response total or use of shading determinants. Likewise, the high scorers continue not to exceed the low Barrier group in use of chromatic color determinants or in number of human movement responses.

The significantly higher F+ per cent found for those subjects with low Barrier scores based on an uncontrolled response total is present also in terms of the controlled Barrier scores. Further, those with high Barrier scores give a significantly greater number of whole responses than do those with low scores. The controlled Barrier scores seem to be significantly linked with only two of the usual Rorschach determinants, viz., F + per cent and number of whole responses. It is not at present clear to us why the relationship with F + per cent occurs. However, the fact that high Barrier scorers give a larger number of whole responses than low scorers may be meaningfully interpreted if one accepts the conventional Rorschach assumption that production of whole responses reflects striving and efforts to attain. We found in a number of studies (to be later described) that high Barrier individuals show a higher aspiration level than low Barrier individuals. Thus, the larger number of whole responses given by the high Barrier individuals could be considered as a reflection of their relatively greater orientation toward high achievement.

Table 2:4 establishes that when response total is controlled the Penetration of Boundary score is not significantly related to any of the usual Rorschach determinants.

It may be said, then, that the two body-image scores tend to have limited relationships with any of the usual Rorschach determinants. The controlled Barrier score is somewhat more linked with these determinants than the controlled Penetration score, but still with only two of the six major determinant categories.

THE BODY-IMAGE SCORES AND VERBAL PRODUCTIVITY

It was brought to our attention as the result of a study carried out by Appleby (11) that verbal productivity might have a significant influence upon the body-image scores, even when Rorschach response total was held constant. Appleby found in a group of sixty college undergraduates that there was a phi coefficient of .46 between Barrier scores and number of words in total Rorschach protocols equated for Rorschach response total. This finding, however, seems to have been peculiarly a function of the sample he studied. In two subsequent studies, each involving samples of forty subjects, we found only a chance relationship between the Barrier score and Rorschach protocol word count and also between the Penetration of Boundary score and word count. Furthermore, we established in one sample that 69 per cent of all Barrier scores were based on single words, 75 per cent on two words or less, 93 per cent on three words or less, and 99 per cent on four words or less. Only 1 per cent of the scores involved phrases of over four words. In this sample 30 per cent of all Penetration of Boundary responses were one word; 82 per cent were two words or less, 95 per cent three words or less, and 100 per cent four words or less. We found in this same sample that the average number of words per Rorschach response of subjects in the below median Barrier group and also in the below median Penetration of Boundary group was about five words. Thus, it was apparent that the subjects with the lowest Barrier scores or lowest Penetration of Boundary scores were potentially able, as far as simple verbal productivity is concerned, to have obtained a Barrier or Penetration scoring for each response they produced.

Further definition of the relationship between the two body-image scores and verbal fluency was provided by data collected from a group of twenty-four subjects participating in a workshop on group behavior. This group consisted of psychologists, psychiatrists, social workers, and others in related areas. There were twelve men and twelve women. The group Rorschach was administered and body-image scores were determined. In addition, a very difficult language-facility test was administered. This test was devised by Blake (37) from items which have appeared in the *Reader's Digest*. It consists of a series of forty difficult words, each followed by four words from which the subject selects one which he considers closest in meaning to the first word. The words in each multiple choice grouping were chosen to represent different degrees of synonymy relative to a given word; and the discrimination of the correct choice involved very fine distinctions. It was found that neither of the body-image scores was significantly correlated with the total number of correct choices made by the subjects in the language-facility test.

THE BODY-IMAGE SCORES AND INTELLIGENCE

Several groups of subjects were evaluated to determine if the body-image scores were in any way linked with intelligence level. Since the scores are derived from verbal content, the possibility presented itself that more intelligent individuals might, in terms of their greater productive complexity, give a relative greater range of responses that would increase the odds of finding scorable body-image concepts in their protocols. The data from three separate studies, however, indicate only a chance relationship between intelligence and the body-image scores. Appleby (11) found in a group consisting of thirty men and thirty women who were undergraduate college students that the Barrier score was not significantly related to the Wonderlic Personnel Test, which is basically a verbal intelligence test. The writers analyzed the relationships of the two body-image scores to Miller Analogies scores in a group of 123 graduate students who were studied by Kelly* and Fiske as part of an over-all investigation of the factors that make for success in clinical psychology. The relationships were of a chance order. In a third study Ware and the writers (324) determined the relationships of the body-image scores to Wechsler-Bellevue Verbal Scale scores in a group of 52 patients who were recovering from poliomyelitis. The median IQ of this group was 113, with a range from 70–140. The relationships were not significant. One may say with fair assurance that the body-image scores are not appreciably influenced by intelligence, at least not within the range of intelligence represented in the three studies just enumerated.

BODY-IMAGE NORMS

When Rorschach response total is controlled, the Barrier and Penetration of Boundary norms are quite stable in various comparable samples of subjects. In three successive groups of college students ranging from forty to eighty individuals and in which the group Rorschach (set at 24 responses) had been administered, the median Barrier score was consistently 4 and the median Penetration score was 2. The median Barrier score for a total group of 200 subjects with approximately equal sex representation was 4 and the median Penetration score 2. Barrier scores in the total group ranged from 0–12 and Penetration scores from 0–8. The mean Barrier score was 4.1 with a standard deviation of 2.1; and the mean Penetration score was 2.2 with a standard deviation of 1.6. It can be seen from the proximity of the mean and median values that the distribution of the Barrier scores tends to be normal in character. Likewise, the distribution of Penetration scores definitely tends toward normality, but is more positively skewed. There were no significant sex differences for either of the boundary scores in any of these subject groups.

The body-boundary norms obtained from individually administered Rorschachs (reduced to 25 responses) are just about identical with those obtained from the group administered Rorschachs. Thus, in one sample of fifty subjects made up equally of men and women, the median Barrier score was 4 and the median Penetration score was 2. Apparently,

* We acknowledge Dr. Lowell Kelly's kindness in making these data available to us. We also acknowledge with gratitude the financial assistance of the Hogg Foundation which made it possible for us to study the data Dr. Kelly has made available.

as long as response total is controlled, the boundary scores are not influenced by the fact of whether the Rorschach records from which they are determined were secured individually or on a group basis.

There are Barrier and Penetration of Boundary norms available for many other special groups; but they will be described in various sections of the book which are concerned with specific problem areas.

CHAPTER THREE

....

Initial Studies of Psychosomatic and Other Correlates of the Body-Image Boundary Dimension

T H E   T W O body-image boundary measures we formulated were initially based on the slim leads supplied by data from the rheumatoid arthritic group we had studied. These measures were almost entirely speculative. There was no evidence that they actually had anything to do with body image or that they would relate meaningfully to any other phenomena. It would perhaps have been the logical thing to conduct a series of studies aimed at demonstrating that the measures were meaningfully linked with body-image phenomena. However, we chose to assume the body-image implications of the measures and to go ahead with a number of broad exploratory projects. Only after the relative success of these initial studies were attempts made to establish the body-image basis of the boundary definiteness concept.

EXPLORATION OF PSYCHOSOMATIC PHENOMENA

HYPOTHESES

Since the body-image boundary concept had first presented itself in a study of a psychosomatic group, it seemed logical to pursue our initial exploratory investigations of it in terms of other psychosomatic groups. The specific direction of our investigations was determined by our preliminary findings from the rheumatoid arthritic subjects. Foremost in our perception of the arthritics was the fact that they produced fantasies which suggested that there was a link between the way they perceived their bodies and the character of their psychosomatic symptomatology. That is, we had associated the protective enclosing attributes they assigned to the peripheries of their Rorschach percepts with the characteristic symptomatic stiffening of muscles in the outer body layers; and we had concluded that such attributes somehow represented the way in which they perceived their body boundaries. We were thus postulating a link between certain aspects of the individual's way of perceiving his

72

body (body image) and the geography or site of his psychosomatic symptomatology. We noted further that psychosomatic symptomatology could be roughly conceptualized as falling on a continuum in terms of whether it involved the exterior body layers at one extreme or the internal viscera at the other extreme. The intriguing possibility then presented itself that there might be a relationship between the individual's manner of picturing his body boundaries and the site of his psychosomatic symptoms relative to the body-exterior–body-interior continuum.

Guided by our findings in the arthritic group, we proposed the specific hypothesis that those persons whose psychosomatic symptoms involve the body exterior would conceive of their bodies as surrounded by a protective, defensive wall, whereas those with symptoms involving the body interior would conceive of their bodies as lacking a defensive wall and being easily penetrated. That is, persons with body exterior symptoms should obtain high Barrier scores and low Penetration of Boundary scores. The converse should be true of individuals with interior symptoms. It was further hypothesized that such differences in body image between those with interior symptoms and those with exterior symptoms would not be merely a reaction to having lived with interior versus exterior symptoms, but that the body-image differences themselves played some etiological role in the choice of an internal versus exterior symptom site. We assigned the body-image boundary dimension some determining part in the total process of psychosomatic symptom formation.

These are the hypotheses we set out to examine in our initial body-image investigations. The first of these hypotheses will be referred to as Hypothesis I and the second as Hypothesis II.° Over all, these hypotheses imply that one of the important dimensions of an individual's body image is the way in which he fantasies his body interior to be differentiated from his body exterior. These hypotheses further suggest that this mode of body-image differentiation is correlated etiologically with the appearance of psychosomatic symptoms in given types of body sites.

METHODS AND SUBJECTS INVOLVED IN
TESTING HYPOTHESIS I

In order to test operationally the hypothesis that individuals with outer and those with inner psychosomatic symptoms differ in the emphasis they place upon the defensive value of the body exterior in their body image, it was necessary to compare body-image data from various symptom groups.

° A large part of this work describing psychosomatic groups appeared in an earlier monograph (99) published by the writers.

Table 3:1 indicates the groups that were utilized in this comparison.

TABLE 3:1   CHARACTERISTICS OF SUBJECTS WITH SYMPTOMS INVOLVING
THE BODY INTERIOR AND OF SUBJECTS WITH SYMPTOMS INVOLVING THE
BODY EXTERIOR

Diagnostic Category	Number	Mean Age	Sex	Mean Education, Years	Median Duration of Symptoms, Years
Interior Symptom Group					
Stomach disturbance	25	31.7	All men	11.6	2.0
Ulcerative colitis	20	33.5	All women	11.4	10.0
Exterior Symptom Group					
Rheumatoid arthritis	25	31.8	All men	11.0	5.5
Neurodermatitis	25	34.0	All men	10.4	9.5
Conversion hysteria	20	30.0	14 men	10.00	3.5
			6 women		

The interior group consisted of two diagnostic subgroups: a subgroup of patients with stomach difficulties and a subgroup of patients with ulcerative colitis. Clearly the patients in both these subgroups had symptoms which focus on the body interior. The group with stomach difficulties was obtained at the Houston VA Hospital. It consisted of eighteen patients with stomach ulcers and seven patients with such symptoms as chronic stomach pains and vomiting. The ulcerative colitis group consisted of twenty women who were.patients at Mt. Sinai Hospital in New York and who were tested by Sheldon Waxenberg.°

A more detailed explanation is required for the three diagnostic subgroups included in the body-exterior category. The term *body exterior* is used here in a broad sense to include all the tissue (viz., skin and musculature) which constitutes the sheath of the body and its appendages. Thus, one of the subgroups consisted of twenty-five rheumatoid arthritics. These individuals all had symptoms which involved, among other symptoms, a stiffening and limitation in movement of various parts of the musculature. They were all veterans who were patients at the Houston VA Hospital. A second group consisted of twenty-five patients with symptoms in the category of the neurodermatoses. This group contained subjects who had a variety of symptoms

---

° We are grateful to Dr. Waxenberg for having made the Rorschach records of the ulcerative colitis group available to us.

involving irritation or inflammation of the skin. These symptoms could not be ascribed to a specific external etiological factor (e.g., chemical irritant or particular infectious agent) and were diagnosed as falling in the neurodermatoses category because they were considered to be psychosomatic in origin. All the subjects in this group were veterans at the Houston VA Hospital.

The third subgroup in the exterior-symptom category consisted of twenty conversion hysterics with symptoms that involved either paralysis or ticlike hyperactivity of portions of the musculature. Five were seen at the Illinois Neuropsychiatric Institute and fifteen were seen at the Houston VA Hospital. The group included nine patients with limb paralysis, three with disturbance of neck muscles manifested in a torticollis type of twisting of the neck, and eight miscellaneous patients with marked widespread tics or unusual muscle spasms that interfered seriously in daily living. All the patients in the group were using malfunctioning of their musculature as their chief mode of symptom expression. Such conversion symptoms have not been customarily classified as psychosomatic, but of course the dividing line between the terms *conversion* and *psychosomatic* is vague and much disputed. In any case, the symptomatology of the group involved disturbance in the functioning of the musculature (which is a part of the outer body layers) as a reaction to psychological stress, and thus provided data for testing Hypothesis I as it was formulated.

RESULTS RELATING TO HYPOTHESIS I

The testing of Hypothesis I requires a comparison of the various body-image scores of the interior-symptom groups with those of the exterior-symptom groups. If the hypothesis holds true, those scores which indicate emphasis on the barrier value of the body exterior should be significantly higher in the exterior-symptom group than in the interior-symptom group. Furthermore, the score which indicates a concept of the body as being easily penetrated should be significantly higher in the interior-symptom group than in the exterior-symptom group.

Before proceeding to test these differences, it was necessary to determine if the various groups differed significantly in the number of Rorschach responses they had produced. If such were the case, any differences among them in body-image scores might be a function of total number of responses rather than of real differences in body-image scores. The median R of the arthritis group was seventeen, of the dermatitis group twenty-one, of the conversion group twenty, of the stomach difficulty group twenty-two, and of the colitis group sixteen. An analysis of variance technique for groups of unequal size was used to test whether the variance between groups for number of Rorschach responses was significant. An F of 2.37 was obtained, which falls below the 5 per cent level of significance. Thus, one may assume that any differences in body-image scores among the group would not be a function of number of Rorschach responses. It may also be noted that one of the groups (stomach difficulty) which has the lowest Barrier score median has the highest response total median.

TABLE 3:2   MEDIAN AND RANGE OF SCORES IN THE EXPERIMENTAL GROUPS

Group	Barrier Scores		Penetration of Boundary Scores	
	Median	Range	Median	Range
Arthritis	4	0–8	1	0–6
Neurodermatitis	4	0–15	2	0–7
Conversion	5	1–15	2	0–7
Stomach disturbance	1	0–3	5	1–9
Colitis	1	0–5	3	0–11

Table 3:2 indicates that all the median Barrier scores fall in the direction predicted by Hypothesis I. Thus, the median Barrier score of each of the interior-symptom groups is exceeded by the medians of the exterior-symptom groups.[*] Furthermore, the upper range of Barrier scores is higher in each of the exterior groups than in the interior groups. The Penetration of Boundary medians, shown in Table 3:2 likewise fall into a pattern congruent with Hypothesis I. The two interior-symptom groups both have higher Penetration of Boundary medians than do any of the exterior-symptom groups. In addition, the upper range of scores in the interior groups is higher than in the exterior groups.

Because the distributions of Barrier and Penetration of Boundary scores were seriously skewed, it was decided to test for the significance of differences between groups by means of chi square.[†] As shown in Table 3:3, almost all the exterior groups are differentiated in the direction of having higher Barrier scores than each of the interior groups at

---

[*] The practice has been adopted throughout of applying Yates correction only when expected frequencies in any cell fall below 5. Snedecor's (287) rather liberal view in this respect has been adopted because the prime goals of the present studies are exploratory rather than the determination of exact relationship.

[†] It may be added at this point that the finding of a median Barrier score of 4 and a median Penetration of Boundary score of 1 in the arthritic group has been duplicated in a group of 28 male arthritics studied by Mueller (224). Dr. Mueller was kind enough to lend us his data and we found that when his Rorschach records were equated with ours for response total, equivalent results were obtained.

TABLE 3:3 CHI-SQUARE ANALYSIS OF THE DIFFERENCES IN BARRIER
SCORES BETWEEN EXTERIOR- AND INTERIOR-SYMPTOM GROUPS

Groups	χ^2 Value[a]	Significance Level	Group with Larger Score
Arthritis vs. stomach disturbance	19.1	.001	Arthritis
Dermatitis vs. stomach disturbance	19.4	.001	Dermatitis
Conversion vs. stomach disturbance	32.0	.001	Conversion
Arthritis vs. colitis	6.4	.01	Arthritis
Dermatitis vs. colitis	5.2	.02	Dermatitis
Conversion vs. colitis	15.7	.001	Conversion
Total exterior group vs. total interior group	36.5	.001	Exterior

[a] Scores were categorized into 0–2 Barrier responses and 3 or more. This cutting point was arbitrarily established by inspection of scores in the arthritis group.

the .001 level. The total exterior group is differentiated from the total interior group at the .001 level. The only differences which fall below the .001 level are those involving arthritis versus colitis and neurodermatoses versus colitis. The arthritis versus colitis difference is at the .01 level; and the dermatoses versus colitis difference is at the .02 level.

TABLE 3:4 CHI-SQUARE ANALYSIS OF THE DIFFERENCE IN PENETRA-
TION OF BOUNDARY SCORES BETWEEN EXTERIOR- AND INTERIOR-
SYMPTOM GROUPS

Group	χ^2 Value[a]	Significance Level	Group with Larger Score
Arthritis vs. stomach disturbance	11.7	.001	Stomach
Dermatitis vs. stomach disturbance	8.0	.01	Stomach
Conversion vs. stomach disturbance	3.6	.05–.10	Stomach
Arthritis vs. colitis	.00	—	—
Dermatitis vs. colitis	.23	—	—
Conversion vs. colitis	.00	—	—
Total exterior group vs. total interior group	5.3	.02	Interior

[a] Scores were categorized into 0–2 Penetration of Boundary responses and 3 or more. This cutting point was arbitrarily established by inspection of scores in the arthritis group.

Table 3:4 indicates that, by and large, Hypothesis I is also confirmed in terms of Penetration of Boundary responses. The Penetration of Boundary responses of the total interior group exceed those of the total exterior groups at the .02 level. Two of the exterior groups are differentiated from the stomach-disturbance group at the .01 level or better, and a third exterior group is differentiated from the stomach-disturbance group at a .05–.10 level. None of the exterior groups are significantly exceeded by the colitis group in Penetration of Boundary responses. But as Table 3:2 indicates, the median Penetration score of the colitis group is in the predicted direction of being higher than the corresponding score of each of the exterior groups.

Another test of the basic difference in body-image responses between the interior-symptom and exterior-symptom groups was undertaken by means of a sorting procedure. The Rorschach records of five arthritic patients (exterior) and of five stomach-difficulty patients (interior) were submitted without identification to three different clinical psychologists. Each sorter was told that five of the records were obtained from arthritics and five from patients with stomach difficulties, and he was instructed to sort them into the two groups. Before undertaking the sorting, each psychologist was thoroughly instructed in the body-image criteria used to distinguish the exterior group from the interior group. Two of the sorters were able to make the distinction required without error. One sorter misplaced two records. These results further confirm the fact that the distinction between interior-symptom and exterior-symptom records can be made with a good deal of accuracy. This also, incidentally, represents an additional demonstration, in a global manner, of the objectivity and reliability of the variables involved in scoring of Barrier and Penetration responses.

In general, then, the results of the over-all analysis indicate that the subjects with exterior body symptoms significantly exceeded subjects with interior body symptoms in the degree to which they conceived of their bodies as surrounded by a well-differentiated boundary. Conversely, subjects with interior symptoms exceeded those with exterior symptoms in the degree to which they regarded their bodies as easily penetrated.

TESTING OF HYPOTHESIS II

The results described up to this point indicate that patients with interior body symptoms can be significantly differentiated from patients with exterior symptoms in terms of specific body-image criteria. But the question arises as to the origin of this difference. Is the difference in body concept a long-standing characteristic which perhaps is of etiological significance in determining the site of body disturbance? Or is the difference simply a reflection of the fact that when an area of an individual's body becomes disturbed, the disturbance causes a distortion in some aspect of the body image which is correlated with the area of body disturbance? That is, if individuals with exterior body symptoms differ in body image from those with interior symptoms, may this body-image difference perhaps be attributed to the impact of experiencing unusual sensations from disturbed body sites that are differently located? Of course, Hypothesis II states that such is not the case and that the body image plays an etiological role in choice of psychosomatic symptom site.

It was felt that one way to test the hypothesis would be to use control subjects with symptoms that were subjectively equivalent to given psychosomatic symptoms, but which are determined by factors known to be nonpsychosomatic in character. Thus, if an individual were experiencing symptoms similar to those of a rheumatoid arthritic but it was known that these symptoms were the result of a specific mechanical injury, it would then be possible to observe whether or not the individual's body image was like that of the arthritic. If it were like that of the arthritic, despite the very different origin of the symptom, this fact would lend support to the idea that it is the subjective experiencing of the symptom itself which distorts the body image in a given fashion. But if, even in the face of the similarity in symptoms, the individual with the mechanical injury did not have a body image similar to the arthritic, this condition would lend support to the concept of the body image as having a determining influence on the arthritic symptom, rather than being a reaction to the symptom.

Two groups of subjects were used to test Hypothesis II in terms of the logic just described.

TABLE 3:5   COMPARISON OF THE TWO SYMPTOM ORIGIN CONTROL GROUPS

	Back Pain Group	Skin Damage Group
Number	20	22
Mean age	31.7	32.8
Sex	All men	All men
Mean education, years	10.1	12.1
Median duration of symptoms, years	4.5	.5

One group of twenty subjects consisted of patients at the Houston VA Hospital who had suffered injuries to the back or spine as the result of accidents and whose symptoms involved mainly pain in the muscles, difficulty in moving, and stiffness. It should be indicated that in several cases the specific cause of the pain and stiffness was not known, but was suspected to be due to mechanical trauma. The over-all group was chosen to duplicate as far as possible the symptomatology of the rheumatoid arthritics. A second group of twenty-two subjects was utilized which consisted of sixteen patients with burns of the skin and six patients with dermatitis due directly to contact with specific chemical substances. This group was chosen to duplicate the symptoms of the neurodermatoses group. There was a similar blemishing and irritation of the skin, but the origin could be traced to a specific nonpsychosomatic factor. Ruth Levy° had used this control group in a previous study (192). She obtained the subjects in the group from among employees at an industrial plant.

It should be acknowledged that the two control groups are partially lacking in the respect that the duration of symptoms is not equal to that of the given groups with which they are intended to be matched. Thus at the time the Rorschach was administered, the median duration of symptoms in the skin-damage group was six months. But the median duration in the neurodermatoses group was nine and one-half years. The disparity is marked, but could not be avoided because of the difficulty of obtaining a group of subjects with injuries to the skin due to known external agents. However, such a disparity was to a large degree avoided in the instance of the back-pain group versus the arthritic group. In the back-pain group the median duration of symptoms was four and one-half years, and the median in the arthritic group was five and one-half years. This difference of one year would not appear to be of much psychological significance relative to the total period of time involved. One cannot be certain, however, and a further analysis of this problem of difference in symptom duration between the groups is described at a later point.

Before determining the differences in body-image scores between each control group and the given group to which it was matched, the data were tested to ascertain if significant differences in number of Rorschach responses existed between the groups. Such differences might produce body-image score differentiations which were a function of total number of Rorschach responses rather than of real body-image differences. A chi-square analysis, based on a threefold breakdown of each group into records of 1–10 responses, 11–20 responses, and over 20 responses, indicated that the arthritic and back-pain groups were not significantly different, and likewise indicated that the neurodermatoses and skin-damage groups were not significantly different in this respect.

A chi-square analysis was made of the difference in Barrier scores between each experimental group and its given control group. It was found that the arthritic group gives significantly higher Barrier scores than the back-pain group. The difference is significant at the .001 level. Furthermore, the neurodermatoses group gives significantly higher Barrier scores than the skin-damage group. Here, too, the difference is sig-

---

° We are grateful to Dr. Levy for making the Rorschach data of the group available to us.

nificant at the .001 level. These differences agree with the predictions of Hypothesis II. It may also be noted at this point that in order to check on how well each control group could be distinguished from the given group to which it was matched, a sorting technique was attempted. Five Rorschach records from the arthritic group and five from the back-pain group were given without any identifying data to three individual clinical psychologists. The barrier characteristic of the arthritic body image was explained, and each sorter was asked to select the five arthritic records from the total group of ten records. Two raters accomplished this without error and one rater made two errors. The same procedure was followed with five neurodermatoses records and five skin-damage Rorschachs. These records were submitted to six clinical psychologists for evaluation. Four sorters were able to make the distinction required without any errors. One sorter misplaced two records, and one sorter misplaced four records.

Thus, although the two control groups are each characterized by symptoms subjectively like those of the exterior groups, they are definitely distinguishable in terms of body-image criteria from the psychosomatic group to which each is matched. Apparently it is not the external symptom itself which gives rise to the body image with barrier boundaries. Of course, the fact that the two psychosomatic groups had experienced their symptoms for a longer period than the two control groups makes it possible to raise some doubts about the meaning of the higher Barrier scores in the two psychosomatic groups. Perhaps they are simply the result of the longer duration of symptoms.

In order to check on this possibility, a division was made of each of these psychosomatic groups into that half with the longest duration of symptoms and that half with the shortest symptom duration. Where there was an odd number of cases, the middle case was dropped from the analysis. Using a nonparametric technique (341) to test for significance of difference, it was found that in neither of the two exterior groups did the subgroup with symptoms of longest duration significantly exceed the subgroup of shortest symptom duration in Barrier scores. The long and short duration subgroups within the conversion group were also compared, and here too the Barrier score differences were not significant. Over all, these results strongly suggest that the Barrier scores are not a function of duration of an exterior symptom. Thus, the difference in Barrier score between the arthritics and the back-pain group and between the neurodermatoses patients and the skin-damage patients would seem to be a meaningful one that has strong confirmatory value for Hypothesis II.

A still further analysis of the Barrier scores of the two control groups was undertaken by comparing these scores with those of the two internal-symptom groups. This analysis was carried out to determine if the Barrier scores of the control groups would significantly exceed the Barrier scores of the internal-symptom groups. If the body-image boundaries of the subjects in the control groups have been even perceptibly affected by their symptoms, which are subjectively similar to body-exterior symptoms, one would assume that the Barrier scores of these subjects would be significantly greater than those subjects in the interior-symptom groups. Results of a chi-square analysis, however, indicated that the Barrier scores of the control groups were not significantly greater than those of the interior-symptom groups. This is additional confirmation that the mere experiencing of a symptom on the exterior of the body does not determine the barrier characteristics of the body image. Here also is a further indirect confirmation of Hypothesis II.

DISCUSSION OF RESULTS

These initial results indicated that the body-image boundary dimension we had conceptualized did have some significant value in clarifying the problem of why the individual develops psychosomatic symptoms at one body site rather than another. Looking back over the literature concerning psychosomatic symptomatology, we found that the results were congruent with hypotheses and results presented by others interested in this area. One does find that the concept of inner symptoms versus outer symptoms has played a part in the thinking of others. In a general way, both Schilder (268) and Reich (239) recognized the unusual significance of the body exterior to the individual. Reich was especially impressed with what he called the "body armor"; and he felt that people used rigidity of the musculature in various parts of their bodies to impose restrictions upon disturbing influences within themselves. More recently, Seitz (277) and Kepecs (169) have suggested on the basis of clinical data that psychosomatic symptoms tend to fall into interior and peripheral groupings; and they have particularly emphasized the value of this concept in explaining the sequence of symptoms when an individual loses one symptom and develops a new one. Thus Seitz (277) has shown that if an individual is induced by means of hypnotic techniques to give up a symptom which involves the exterior of the body, this symptom will tend to be replaced spontaneously by still another exterior symptom. A particular publication pertinent to the body-image boundary results should be cited. Lorr (201) obtained ratings from individual therapists of the symptoms and behavior of patients in psychotherapeutic treatment. Upon analyzing the results, Lorr found three factors which he felt roughly corresponded to the three embryonic germinal layers of the body and which seemed to correspond, at one level, to different groupings of psychosomatic symptoms. He linked given groupings of psychosomatic symptoms with given layers of the body.

The question does arise as to why the distinction between body interior and exterior should play a significant role in the individual's way of defending himself against psychological stress. Why is it that some individuals come to give so much positive or negative importance to the body exterior as a line of defense? Those who have speculated about this problem in the past (92, 182, 111) have had a number of explanations to offer:

(1) It has been pointed out, first of all, that the body exterior is that part of the individual which literally serves as the contact point between the individual and his environment. The body exterior is the most immediately exposed to the impact of new or threatening situations. In this sense, the body exterior does actually occupy the position of a line of defense, a boundary line.

(2) It has been indicated that the individual can better visualize the exterior of his body than he can the interior of his body. He does have a detailed image of his outer aspects, whereas the interior of his body remains hazy and ill defined. Consequently, the body exterior may be thought of as having more substance and material reality to the individual than does his body interior.

(3) It is also true that the activities of the exterior layers of the body are much more subject to voluntary control than are those of the body interior. The individual can embellish, cover up, or change the appearance of his skin, and he exerts controlling force over his striated musculature. But his body interior is, by and large, subject to the influence of involuntary autonomic centers. Consequently the individual is probably left with the feeling that his body exterior is something which he commands and can actively use in his own defense. This is a feeling which he lacks about his body interior.

It is parenthetically interesting to speculate concerning the subjects in the interior-symptom group. Their body images are characterized by boundaries which are pictured as being easily penetrated. In this group the body-image boundaries are fluid and vague rather than definite and explicit. It is as if the individuals feel stripped of their body exterior and experience the body interior as directly exposed to whatever impinges upon them. They experience their bodies as being open rather than closed. One wonders whether the symptoms of individuals in this group do not represent an earlier form of body defense than do the symptoms of those in the exterior-symptom group. Is it possible that the typical individual in the interior-symptom group was exposed to stresses which required defensive body reactions at a period early in life before he had mastery over, or a body-image concept of, his body exterior? At such an early period the workings of the internal organs (e.g., stomach and lower intestines) might perhaps represent the most articulated aspect of a hazy and just-developing body image. Thus, tension and disturbance requiring body reactions might more meaningfully be expressed through the response of internal organs than through response of the body exterior. In this way a primary pattern might be laid down which would interfere with the development of a body image with barrier boundaries. The individual's attitudes about his body would have been somewhat fixed at a point where the concept of defensive mastery of the body exterior had not yet developed. A body concept of this sort might later prevent free experimentation with the potentialities of the body exterior as a channel of expression and defense.

THE BODY-IMAGE BOUNDARY DIMENSION APPLIED TO NORMAL SUBJECTS

The relative success of the body-image boundary concept in predicting site of psychosomatic symptomatology led us to explore further with it. We wondered about its usefulness in clarifying the behavior of normal persons. Would this concept, derived from observations of extreme groups containing individuals who had broken down under stress, have meaningful applicability to normal subjects? We were interested in determining how the Barrier score and Penetration of Boundary score would be related to various indices of normal behavior and also whether these scores would each show a differential pattern of relationship.

METHOD AND EMPIRICAL PREDICTIONS

The subjects consisted of eighty-seven undergraduate students[*] enrolled in two different introductory psychology courses at the University of Houston. There were twenty-five women and fifty-eight men.

Rorschach records were obtained from subjects on a group basis in order to evaluate their body-image boundary characteristics. Subjects were asked to give a definite number of responses to each card. This equalized response total throughout the group. Three responses were obtained for four cards (I, II, III, VIII) and two responses for the other six.

The kind of information that it was decided to collect from each subject, aside from the Rorschach body-image indices, was a function of certain leads suggested by the previous results obtained from the

---

[*] This study was previously published by the writers in the *Journal of Abnormal and Social Psychology,* 52:373–379 (1956).

psychosomatic patients. A review of the other measures obtained follows:

(1) Since exterior versus interior body symptoms had been one of the chief dimensions distinguishing patients with different body-image indices, it was planned to inventory the range of the body symptoms that had already been experienced by the normal subjects. It was predicted that high Barrier scores would be associated with exterior body complaints and high Penetration scores with interior body complaints. Each subject was asked to indicate on a check list whether he had had symptoms involving any of seven different exterior and interior areas of the body.

(2) As previously mentioned, in the course of our investigation of the arthritics (exterior group) we had found that they tended to engage in much strenuous muscular activity, particularly in sports. We had also found that they showed an unusual interest in cooking and that patients with neurodermatoses (exterior group) were outstanding for their concern with political and law issues. Details of these findings are available elsewhere (63). Such special kinds of focused interest seemed to be representative of predilections for certain ways of living or certain modes of self-expression. Therefore, subjects in the normal group were asked to fill out a questionnaire which required them to describe in detail their activities in these specific areas. The prediction was made that subjects with more definite (high Barrier) body-image boundaries would, like the arthritics and patients with neurodermatoses, show more interest in athletics, law, and cooking than subjects with less definite boundaries. These were arbitrary empirical predictions based on the previous findings.

(3) The F-scale was included in the battery for exploratory purposes to determine if there were broad differences in ideological orientation between those with different body-image concepts.

(4) Each subject was asked to write a story based on five different TAT cards (1, 2, 7BM, 6GF, 6BM) projected on a screen. It was intended to use the TAT data in a semiexploratory fashion to find out if differences in body-image concept might be associated with three TAT variables, level of aspiration, attitudes toward parents, and deceptiveness.

Level of aspiration was chosen as one TAT variable simply on the basis of hints from earlier work (62) that emphasis on the exterior (skin-muscle) layers of the body might be correlated with an active, "muscular," achieving attitude toward the world. In order to evaluate the level of aspiration, two indices were derived from each subject's TAT stories. One index (High Aspiration) was simply a count of all statements which referred to a story character's hoping for high achievement, working hard, or having attained high goals. A second index (Inactivity) involved counting all statements in which a story character was described as asleep, daydreaming, bored, or resting. It was hypothesized that subjects with more definite boundaries would obtain higher aspiration scores and lower inactivity scores than subjects with less definite boundaries.

A second TAT area had to do with attitudes toward parental figures. Two raters working together and on a blind basis evaluated for each subject all stories involving mother figures and all those involving father figures. The role assigned to each parental figure was categorized as predominantly friendly and helpful or predominantly negative and hostile. When the data were too vague to make such specific positive or negative categorizations, a category of "insufficient information" was noted. The question asked here was whether the body-image indices were in any way significantly linked with the positive friendliness or negative hostility of the role assigned in fantasy to the parental figures. No prediction was made concerning the hostility score.

Fantasies about parental figures were also evaluated on a continuum of Weak-Vague as against Definite-Forceful. The concern here was not with direction of attitude toward parents, but rather with the definiteness of the image of the parents. This variable was evaluated by considering TAT cards 2, 7BM, and 6BM as evoking relatively more associations concerning parental figures than any of the other cards used in the study (viz., 1 and 6GF). It was then assumed that individuals with definite attitudes toward the parental figures should make specific positive or negative statements about both mother and father on card 2, about father on 7BM, and about mother on 6BM. If an individual made a definite statement about both parents on card 2 he was given a credit of +1 for each of these statements and was likewise given a credit of +1 for a definite positive or negative characterization of father on 7BM and another +1 for such a characterization of mother on 6BM. Thus, a maximum of +4 could be attained for the highest degree of definiteness. If a subject gave a weak or not definitely positive or negative description of one parent on card 2 he was given a penalty score of −1. An unclear description of both parents on this card resulted in a penalty of −2. Another penalty unit could be obtained for card 7BM and also one for 6BM. The maximum penalty score was −4. An individual's final definiteness score was equal to the difference between the total number of plus and minus units. The most definite image of the parents would result in a score of +4 and the least definite image would be represented by a score of −4. Determinations of plus or minus values for each card were made by two raters working together on a blind basis. It was predicted that individuals who emphasize the definiteness of the body exterior would see the parental figures in relatively definite terms.

Another TAT index is referred to as Exterior Deception. This measure is a count of all instances in which a story character is described as overtly acting or appearing in a certain way but as having internal motives quite different from the surface appearance. An example of this measure is provided by a story in which a man smiles in a friendly way at a woman but all the while intends to hurt her. It was argued that individuals emphasizing the barrier aspects of the bodily surface tend to think of the body exterior as a screen or shield concealing one's true inner state. Consequently it was predicted that such persons would score relatively high on this variable.

RESULTS

The chi square was employed to determine if there were any sex differences in the distributions of the two body-image indices. No significant differences were found. The same test was then used to evaluate the significance of the various score differences between the two halves of the Barrier index distribution. As indicated by Table 3:6 those subjects with the higher Barrier scores manifest significantly more exterior bodily symptoms than do those with lower Barrier scores. They report a significantly greater number of symptoms involving the skin and

TABLE 3:6   CHI-SQUARE TESTS OF DIFFERENCES BETWEEN THE UPPER AND LOWER HALF OF THE BARRIER SCORE DISTRIBUTION OF THE EXPERIMENTAL GROUP

Score	Barrier Group with Larger Score	Significance Level
Exterior body symptoms	H.B.[a]	.02
Interior body symptoms	L.B.	N.S.[a]
TAT high aspiration	H.B.	.01
TAT inactivity	L.B.	.05–.10
TAT exterior deception	H.B.	.01–.02
F-scale	L.B.	N.S.
Participation in athletics	H.B.	.02–.05
Participation in cooking	N.D.	—
Interest in law and politics	N.D.	—
Degree of TAT hostility toward mother	N.D.	—
Degree of TAT hostility toward father	N.D.	—
Definiteness of TAT attitude toward both parents	H.B.	.01

[a] H.B.—High Barrier group. L.B.—Low Barrier group. N.D.—No difference. N.S.—Not significant.

musculature. The high Barrier group is significantly more active in athletics, more productive on TAT themes with High Aspiration implications, and more likely to give TAT stories in which there is Exterior Deception. The high Barrier group produces fewer TAT themes of inactivity, but the difference is not significant (.05–.10).

The high Barrier group, although not differing from the low Barrier group with respect to the *direction* of feeling toward the parental figures in their TAT stories, was significantly more definite in attitude toward these figures. At the .01 level of significance, the high Barrier group more frequently gave TAT descriptions of the parents which could be classified as definitely positive or negative.

The high Barrier group reported fewer body-interior symptoms than the low Barrier group, but this difference was not statistically significant. Differences between the groups in terms of interest in cooking, interest in law, and F-scale scores were likewise not significant.

Chi-square tests were also utilized to ascertain the significance of the score differences between the upper and lower halves of the Penetration of Boundary distribution. As indicated by Table 3:7 the only difference

TABLE 3:7   CHI-SQUARE TESTS OF DIFFERENCES BETWEEN THE UPPER AND LOWER HALF OF THE PENETRATION OF BOUNDARY SCORE DISTRIBUTION OF THE EXPERIMENTAL GROUP

Score	Penetration Group with Larger Score	Significance Level
Exterior body symptoms	N.D.	—
Interior body symptoms	L.P.[a]	.05–.10
TAT high aspiration	H.P.	.02–.05
TAT inactivity	N.D.	—
TAT exterior deception	N.D.	—
F-scale	N.D.	--
Participation in athletics	N.D.	—
Participation in cooking	N.D.	—
Interest in law and politics	N.D.	—
Degree of TAT hostility toward mother	N.D.	—
Degree of TAT hostility toward father	N.D.	—
Definiteness of TAT attitude toward both parents	N.D.	—

[a] H.P.—High Penetration group. L.P.—Low Penetration group. N.D.—No difference.

attaining significance was that involving High Aspiration. Those subjects with higher Penetration of Boundary scores gave a significantly greater number of high-aspiration TAT themes than did those with lower Penetration scores.

In a total overview of the results, one can see that the Barrier score is successfully differentiating in five out of twelve tests of significance. The Penetration of Boundary score, however, proves to be significantly differentiating in only one of twelve tests. A tetrachoric correlation of −.12, which is not significant, was found between the Barrier score distribution and the Penetration of Boundary score distribution. The two scores may therefore be treated as independent variables. It is clear that the one significant difference obtained with the Penetration score is of a chance order. But the five significant differentiations associated with the Barrier score tend to cluster at the .01 level, and they exceed the number of significant differences one would expect by chance to obtain in twelve tests of significance (.01 level). The Barrier index results were further analyzed by intercorrelating the three TAT scores which are significantly related to the Barrier score. If these three TAT scores were fairly highly intercorrelated and actually represented just one broad TAT dimension, it would reduce the five significant tests obtained to three and detract considerably from the possible value of the results.

Tetrachoric correlations were used to test the interrelationships among these TAT measures, since the distributions seemed to fulfill the assumptions of continuity and normality. The three correlations obtained were .04 (High Aspirations versus Parental Definiteness), .23 (Exterior Deception versus Parental Definiteness), and .37 (High Aspiration versus Exterior Deception). None of these coefficients are significant. It may be incidentally noted that when the intercorrelations of all the dependent variables were computed, it was found that they also were not significant and may be regarded as essentially independent.

In order to check on the stability of the significant results obtained with the TAT measures, it was decided to do a cross-validation study on a new group. Thirty-eight women enrolled in a graduate psychology course at the University of Houston were used as subjects. The TAT and Rorschach were administered on the same basis as has already been described for the first experimental group. Scores were computed for only those variables which had been significant or close to significance in the first study. Thus only the Barrier score was determined from the Rorschach, since the Penetration of Boundary score had given almost completely negative results. The High Aspiration score, the Inactivity score, and Parental Definiteness score were determined from the TAT data. It was not possible to test the Exterior Deception score because less than a fifth of the thirty eight subjects gave responses that were scorable in this respect.

The results in Table 3:8 suggest a high degree of stability in the findings involving the TAT reported for the first experimental group.

TABLE 3:8 CHI-SQUARE ANALYSIS OF DIFFERENCES IN TAT SCORES BETWEEN THE UPPER AND LOWER HALF OF THE BARRIER SCORE DISTRIBUTION OF THE CROSS-VALIDATION GROUP

Score	Barrier Group with Larger Score	Significance Level
TAT high aspiration	High Barrier	.02–.05
TAT inactivity	Low Barrier	.05–.10
Definiteness of TAT attitude toward both parents	High Barrier	.05

Once more, the high Barrier group was significantly higher in Aspiration and also in Definiteness of attitude toward both parents than the low Barrier group. The TAT Inactivity score indicated that the low Barrier group produces more themes of inactivity than the high Barrier group. This difference falls at the .05–.10 level of significance and is at the same borderline level as found for the first group. It cannot be considered as strictly significant. The tetrachoric intercorrelations of the three TAT measures were determined. They ranged from .01 (High Aspiration versus Parental Definiteness) and .23 (Exterior Deception versus Parental Definiteness) to .39 (High Aspiration versus Exterior Deception). None of these coefficients even approached significance.

DISCUSSION

It is interesting to note that the results obtained confirm, within a normal group, a basic relationship that was previously shown (99) to exist between body image and site of symptomatology in individuals with serious psychosomatic symptoms. The results indicate that normal subjects who dramatize the definiteness or barrier value of their body-image boundaries report experiencing significantly more physical difficulties involving exterior body layers than do those not emphasizing exterior boundaries in the body image. Thus the relationship holds true even within a normal group where the physical difficulties reported are very minor and have, by and large, not yet reached the status of formal illness.

The most important results emerging from the study have to do with the high level of activity and aspiration manifested by those with high Barrier scores as contrasted to those with low Barrier scores. The high Barrier scorers are significantly higher in degree of participation in athletics and also higher in the number of TAT themes they produced involving hard work and pursuit of high goals. These differences suggest that those who stress the defense value of the body exterior are more likely than those who do not so dramatize their exteriors to take an active "muscular" attitude toward life. The high Barrier group seems more likely to seek muscular expression in athletic activity. It seems more dedicated to values having to do with getting to the top. The low Barrier group is more flaccid in its orientation. It is intriguing to speculate as to the basis for this broad difference in life style.

As was pointed out earlier, an emphasis on the exterior body layers means emphasis on the skin and the striated musculature. These tissues constitute the part of the individual most directly in contact with reality. Skin and musculature contrast with the interior of the body which is relatively less available as a voluntary means for setting up relationships to the external world. It could easily follow that emphasis on the body-image boundary is a reflection of a style of life based on an unusually strong definition of self-identity and on active self-expression aimed at setting up a stable, controlling relationship with the environment.

The basic difference in life orientation between those with high and those with low Barrier scores is further pointed up by the fact that the high Barrier group produced significantly more TAT Exterior Deception themes. That is, high Barrier people are more likely than low Barrier people to regard life as full of potential deception. They are more likely to see people as cloaked and masked and concealing their real intentions. This raises a question, which will be considered later, whether under conditions of severe personality regression (e.g., schizophrenic breakdown) they would have a greater tendency to show paranoid symptoms than would low Barrier people.

The finding that those with high Barrier scores in both the original experimental group and the cross-validation group gave significantly more definite and forceful TAT descriptions of parental figures than did those with low Barrier scores suggests that each may have had a different pattern of relationship with the parents. Perhaps this variation in pattern of relationship is an important factor in determining body-image differences. It would appear that the more definite body boundaries of those with high Barrier scores represent an identification with parents who provided a well-defined model, whether the model be positive or negative. That is, subjects whose parents stood for certain definite values and ways of doing things would have more definite models after which they could fashion an image of self. But subjects whose parents appeared weak and indefinite would have only hazy models after which to fashion an image of self.

Quite in contrast to the results with the Barrier score, the Penetration of Boundary score proved to have no significance in the normal group. We were puzzled by this result because over a range of psychosomatic groups the Penetration of Boundary score had shown itself to have meaningful value. In the course of exploring this issue, we found that in groups where the number of Rorschach responses obtained from individuals was not somehow limited or equated, the two scores tended to correlate positively and significantly. This was due, as indicated earlier, to the fact that they were both to some degree a function of response total.

TABLE 3:9 CORRELATIONS BETWEEN BARRIER SCORES AND PENETRATION OF BOUNDARY SCORES

Group	Correlations[a]	Level of Significance
Dermatitis (N = 25)	.52	.01
Arthritis (N = 25)	.25	—
Burns (N = 22)	.33	—
Ulcerative colitis (N = 20)	.58	.01
Student nurses (N = 30)	.51	.01
University students[b] (N = 86)	−.12	—
University students (N = 60)	.02	—

[a] All the correlations are Rho's except that for the university students, which is tetrachoric.

[b] The subjects in the student groups were all instructed to give exactly the same number of responses to the Rorschach. Thus, response total in these groups was controlled, which contrasts with the uncontrolled response range in the other groups enumerated in the table.

Table 3:9 shows the range of relatively high positive correlations of the Barrier score with the Penetration of Boundary score in a variety of the groups in which response total was uncontrolled. However, one can also see in Table 3:9 that when response total was controlled, there was an absence of significant relationship between the two scores.

Theoretically, if one assumes that the Barrier score measures definiteness and firmness of boundaries and the Penetration score measures penetrability of boundaries, one would expect the two scores to be negatively correlated. The fact that such is not the case and the further fact that the Penetration score did not appear to have predictive significance in a normal group led us to conclude that the Penetration score does not neatly represent the opposite equivalent of the Barrier score. It apparently did not have the scope of the Barrier score and we were less sure of its significance. We felt in reviewing our data that it gave valid results only in abnormal or extreme groups and that it was not differentiating within the normal adult range. We decided, therefore, to restrict our measure of body-image boundary definiteness in the normal range entirely to the Barrier score. In later chapters it will be shown that the Penetration of Boundary score does have meaningful application to certain special groups. The reasons for its narrow area of application will be discussed at that time.

ATTEMPTS TO EXPLORE AND VALIDATE THE BODY-IMAGE BASIS OF THE BARRIER SCORE

PRELIMINARY CONSIDERATIONS

Our preliminary investigations up to this point had established that the Barrier score did pretty well predict the sorts of things we had assumed it would. It predicted a variety of phenomena concerning site of psychosomatic symptoms and also it significantly anticipated some important aspects of normal behavior. We had operationally assumed that its predictive value was a function of the fact that it measured a basic dimension of the individual's way of picturing or perceiving his body. We had assumed that the Barrier score was getting at something closely tied to body experiences and body sensations. The problem of demonstrating that this is the case is a complicated and difficult one. There are no direct well-validated ways of obtaining samples of how an individual experiences his body which could be used as criteria against which to check such an indirect and considerably conceptualized measure as the Barrier score. It is especially true that valid criteria concerning body-boundary experiences are not available. Our strategy in dealing with this problem has been to devise situations in which the Barrier score could be related to other measures which get at body-experience phenomena in a manner which is less indirect and less an artifact of complex abstraction than the Barrier score. We have sought to relate the Barrier score to measures which are more literally phrased in body terms and in the language of body sensation.

As indicated at an earlier point, some element of support for the idea that the Barrier score is founded on body experiences is implicitly provided by the fact that it was developed with the body and body experiences as a principal frame of reference. The score was derived in terms of qualitative observations concerning the body attitudes and body feelings of individuals who seemed to be expressing various psychological conflicts in the form of psychosomatic symptomatology. The train of logic underlying the formulation of the Barrier score was heavily loaded with analogies relating to fantasies about the body. One should consider that there is, after all, something rather striking about the literal analogy involved in the fact that individuals who focus their interests on the exterior body layers and who express tensions through symptoms involving these layers produce Rorschach percepts whose exterior peripheries are assigned unusual qualities. This does constitute one level of connection between the Barrier score and a class of phenomena which apparently involve the assigning of certain hierarchies of value to given body areas.

The first line of confirmation of the body-image basis of the Barrier scores (aside from that implicit in the data from the psychosomatic groups) was obtained from the initial normal group that was studied. It will be recalled that the subjects in that group were asked to indicate on a check list whether they had had uncomfortable sensations or symptoms involving any of seven different exterior and interior areas of the body. It was found that subjects with above-median Barrier scores experienced a significantly (.02 level) greater number of sensations and symptoms in the exterior body layers (muscle and skin) than did the below-median Barrier subjects. This was the result that had been predicted. It should be considered that none of the subjects in the group had real full-blown psychosomatic illnesses. They were mainly reporting by means of the check list the areas of their bodies which were outstanding to them because of the presence of uncomfortable sensations. They were, by and large, identifying certain body sensations which were prominent in their total field of body experiences. Such identification of body sensation landmarks parallels the introspective reports of body experiences which have in the past (67) (268) been considered to be the basic source of information concerning body image. The fact that the Barrier score was able to predict rather well the body areas which were relatively outstanding to the individual would seem to add strong support to the idea that it is a measure which is a function of the body schema.

BODY ASSOCIATIONS

The relative success attained in relating the Barrier score to the symptom check list scores, which may be considered indirect measures of the relative prominence of outer-layer body sensations versus interior sensations, encouraged further exploration along this path. The question arose whether it would be possible to relate the Barrier score to the pattern of an individual's perceptions of his body when he was asked to introspect and to report as systematically as possible the sorts of body sensations he experienced over a sequence of time. If a meaningful relationship could be detected, it would represent one of the most direct possible demonstrations of the body-image *anlage* of the Barrier score. It was specifically predicted that in his reports concerning his stream of body sensations, the high Barrier person would show a predominance of exterior sensations over those from the interior. That is, he would report a greater proportion of sensations from the skin and musculature than from the viscera (e.g., heart and stomach). Conversely it was predicted that the low Barrier person would report a predominance of interior body sensations over exterior body sensations.

In order to test this hypothesis the following procedure was followed. The group Rorschach requiring a fixed number of responses per card was administered to a total of seventy-five college students in two introductory psychology classes. Following the administration of the Rorschach, it was explained to the subjects that they were about to participate in an experiment which was concerned with the individual's ability to make observations about his own body. They were told to list in order on a blank sheet of paper four words: heart, muscle, stomach, skin. They were further told that at a given signal each person was to turn his attention fully upon his own body for a period and that every time he noticed a sensation in any of the four areas designated by the words on the blank sheet, he was to place a check after the appropriate word. The subjects made these observations for a period of three minutes. The room in which they were seated was kept dimly lighted in order to minimize extraneous stimuli from outside of the body.

It was necessary to eliminate ten subjects from the study because it was found that some had given considerably less than the expected twenty-four Rorschach responses and some had failed to report any body sensations at all. The sixty-five subjects remaining consisted of forty men and twenty-five women. Inspection of the data indicated that the ratio of reported skin sensations to the body-interior sensations was completely nondifferentiating between the high and low Barrier groups. However, the ratio of muscle sensations to interior sensations did show promise relative to the hypotheses that had been proposed. It was found that for 42 per cent of the high Barrier subjects the muscle sensations exceeded the sum of heart and stomach reports. But in the low Barrier group this was true for only 27 per cent of the subjects. In the same vein, it was found that for 63 per cent of the low Barrier subjects the sum of heart and stomach sensations exceeded the muscle reports. However, the analogous percentage in the high Barrier group was 46 per cent. None of these differences are statistically significant but they are consistently in the predicted direction.

Mean values were computed for reported muscle sensations on the one hand and heart plus stomach sensations on the other in the two Barrier groups. In the high Barrier group the muscle mean was 3.9, and the mean of the combined interior reports was exactly the same. But in the low Barrier group the muscle mean of 3.5 was exceeded by the combined interior reports mean of 5.2. This difference falls at the 10 per cent level of significance. The over-all results are far from clear-cut in their substantiation of the hypotheses that were proposed. But they do tend to be supportive. Indeed, when one considers the rather crude manner in which the introspective reports of body sensations were collected, the consistent trends that did emerge would seem to have substantial import.

PROJECTIVE MOVEMENT SEQUENCE

Another method used to evaluate the relationship of the Barrier score to images and fantasies phrased in body terms involved the Projection Movement Sequence technique developed by William H. Lundin (202). This technique makes use of motion pictures to present moving unstructured stimuli to subjects. It consists of eight scenes or sequences, each projected for approximately thirty seconds at silent speed. Subjects are asked to develop a story for each sequence based on their impressions of the movement they see on the screen. The movie projector is stopped after each sequence. In the present study subjects related their stories and they were written down by the experimenter. The sequences of movement presented on the screen were originally made by photographing the movement of powdered, black iron filings controlled by two hand magnets.

This technique was adapted to the present study because in some preliminary investigations we found that it frequently evoked associations about the dissolution or breaking up of animal and human bodies. It tended to elicit such associations because many of the figures projected on the screen have animal and human shapes which at some stage in the moving sequences actually break up or change to form new figures. That is, the very structure of the film patterns emphasizes the instability of the figures. It seemed logical to assume that if an individual experienced his own body boundaries as firm and definite, he would be less likely to be concerned with themes of body dissolution in the Projective Movement Sequence than would the individual who perceived his body boundaries as indefinite and insecure. It is important to note that in evaluating the dissolution fantasies projected by subjects, only those fantasies were considered which referred to an animal or human body. Dissolution of inanimate objects was excluded from consideration. Thus the focus was kept entirely on fantasies having body implications.

A scoring system was set up for evaluating concern with body dissolution in the Projective Movement Sequence. The degree of prominence of body dissolution imagery was considered to be equal to the total number of human and animal bodies which were described by a subject as spontaneously breaking up or falling apart. It should be noted that only body disintegration occurring spontaneously (e.g., body falling apart) was scored. If the disintegration was due to the impact of some outside force (e.g., a blow or a collision) it was not counted. This mode of scoring was chosen in order to restrict the data to the more extreme fantasies of body breakdown occurring even in the absence of an identifiable outside threat. It was assumed that the individual who perceives body dissolution in a setting where he does not even attempt to assign the cause of breakdown to an outside agent is one who has maximum doubts about his body integrity.

The group of subjects used for this study consisted of sixteen alcoholics, four patients with stomach difficulties, seven patients with anxiety symptoms, and three schizophrenics. This diverse group was chosen simply on the basis of opportunities for administering the Projective Movement Sequence within a hospital setting. The Projective Movement Sequence was shown individually to each subject; and in addition an individual Rorschach was administered. The Rorschach was scored blindly for the Barrier score and the Projective Movement Sequence was scored blindly for number of body-disintegration fantasies.

When the Barrier scores were ranked so that the highest score was rank 1 and the Projective Movement body-dissolution scores arrayed so that the lowest score was 1, a rho correlation of .45 between the sets of ranks was found. This correlation is significant at about the .02 level. Those subjects who obtain high Barrier scores perceive the smallest number of body-disintegration themes in the Projective Movement sequences. Subjects with low Barrier scores focus on themes of body dissolution. This is the result that was predicted. The fact that fantasies of dissolution directly phrased in body terms are significantly linked with the Barrier score dimension lends support to the idea that it is a body-image dimension. One might logically take the position that the greater number of body-dissolution themes seen by persons with low Barrier scores reflects not a greater concern about body dissolution, but simply a special sensitivity to the instability of the projected figures. Thus, the higher body-dissolution scores would be a function not of a body-image variable but of a greater concern with figural instability in general. This possibility was checked by computing for each subject the total number of inanimate objects and things which he perceived as disintegrating. Such scores based on inanimate dissolution were not significantly correlated with the Barrier scores. Apparently, then, the Barrier score shows a meaningful relationship only to disintegration involving living bodies.

PHANTOM LIMB

A fourth method that was utilized to show the linkage between the Barrier score and body-image phenomena involved a study of amputees. It has been widely observed (137, 284) that when an individual loses a limb as the result of amputation he frequently continues to experience sensations from the stump which create the feeling that the limb is still intact. The individual has the illusion that he is experiencing sensations from the part of the limb that has been amputated. This illusory member is referred to as the "phantom limb." After experiencing an amputation, most persons do have varying degrees of phantom-limb sensations. But with time the phantom limb usually shrinks and finally pretty much disappears. The phantom limb is usually felt initially to be outside the stump and then it gradually decreases in size and retracts and may in later phases, before it completely vanishes, be experienced as inside the stump. Individuals show considerable variation in the length of time that they require to go through the various phantom limb-phases preceding the ultimate dissolution of the illusion. Here, then, is a phenomenon which obviously involves images or fantasies which the individual has about his body. The amputee somehow resists picturing his mutilated limb as it really is and persists in holding on to a picture of his limb as it previously was. The fact that there are wide individual differences in the manner in which the phantom limb is experienced and later dissolved suggested that this might be a fertile area in which to explore with the body-image boundary concept.

The opportunity for such exploration was provided by Dr. William B. Haber* who made available to us a variety of data he had collected concerning a group of amputees (138, 139). Haber studied an amputee population consisting of twenty-four male World War II veterans with unilateral above-elbow amputations. Among a number of other measures, he obtained from each subject a drawing showing how that subject perceived his phantom limb relative to his stump. Haber also secured a Rorschach record from each subject. In evaluating the drawings of the phantom limbs he found that twelve of his subjects pictured the phantom as outside of or even detached from the stump. The other twelve subjects drew the phantom limb as being completely inside the stump or with only the fingers protruding from the stump.

This difference in the manner of representation of the phantom limb appeared to us as one which could be meaningfully conceptualized in terms of body-image boundaries. It may, first of all, be assumed that the individual with firm protective boundaries is one who is more likely than the individual with poorly articulated boundaries to adjust realistically to a breach in his boundaries produced by body mutilation. One would conjecture that when a body mutilation is inflicted upon an individual he is faced with the task of reorganizing his body boundaries in order to take into account the body loss incurred. If his boundaries are

---

* We are much indebted to Dr. Haber for his assistance.

vaguely organized to begin with, the process of reestablishing a new boundary would be especially difficult. Therefore, one would hypothesize that amputees who are slowest to retract the phantom into the stump, which is the stage usually just prior to phantom disappearance, would be those with the less definite body-image boundaries. That is, firmness and good articulation of body-image boundaries is being equated with ability to rebuild a realistic body boundary which has been disrupted by actual body destruction.

If one translates these assumptions into operational terms, it would follow that amputees who picture their phantoms as extended outside the stump should obtain significantly lower Barrier scores than subjects who picture their phantoms as within the stump. This hypothesis was confirmed when the Rorschach records of the amputees were blindly scored for the Barrier variable and these scores were compared to the outside-stump versus inside-stump position of each phantom. A chi-square test indicated that the group with outside-stump phantoms were significantly lower in Barrier scores (.01 level) than the inside-stump phantom group.

This result further documents the body-image foundation of the Barrier score. It indicates that the score does meaningfully relate to a variable which is about as pure a body-image phenomenon as one can find.

SENTENCE COMPLETION

One of the relatively more direct methods which was used to relate the Barrier score to body concepts involved a sentence completion technique. A series of incomplete sentences were constructed which introduced themes concerning the skin. The following are examples of such incomplete sentences:

The skin is easily . . . .
The skin can start to . . . .
The skin often . . . .
If you look carefully at a person's skin . . . .
Most people think their skin will . . . .

It was postulated that individuals who felt least secure about their body boundaries and who were most concerned about the low barrier value of these boundaries would complete the skin themes with a greater number of statements involving body vulnerability than would individuals who felt more secure about their body boundaries. That is, it was assumed that the incomplete sentences would evoke a greater number of responses of body breakdown from those with low Barrier scores than from those with high Barrier scores.

A preliminary series of twenty incomplete sentences was administered to a group of twelve women who were in training as dietitians at a Veterans Administration hospital and also to thirteen college seniors. Group Rorschachs were administered to these subjects in the same manner as earlier described for other subject groups. A rough exploratory analysis of the data was made in order to set up a scoring procedure which would maximize differences between high and low Barrier groups and also to eliminate items which seemed to have little discrimination value. The scoring method which was developed assigned body-vulnerability significance to any sentence completion with the following characteristics:

(1) Reference to the skin in terms of opening, cutting, peeling, burning, being diseased.

(2) Reference to the skin's appearance as indicating illness or weakness of the body in general.

During the course of this exploratory phase six of the original items were eliminated and the final form of the measure contained fourteen incomplete sentences.

The incomplete sentences and group Rorschach were then administered to a group of thirty-nine students in an introductory psychology class. All scoring of the incomplete sentences was done blindly without any knowledge of the Barrier scores of the individuals involved. Analysis of the data confirmed the hypothesis being tested. A chi-square test indicated that those subjects with high Barrier scores gave a significantly smaller number of sentence completions with body vulnerability connotations than did those subjects with low Barrier scores. The chi square was 5.2 which is significant at the .05–.02 level.

SECORD WORD ASSOCIATIONS

The process of exploring the relationship of the Barrier score to more direct indices of body attitudes was rounded out by means of a word-association procedure. As earlier described (Chapter 1), Secord (276) has developed a word-association technique (Body Cathexis Test) for measuring the degree of concern an individual has about his body. His technique involves eliciting associations to a word list consisting of homonyms "which had meanings pertaining either to bodily parts or processes, and which had in addition common nonbodily meanings." Words like *colon* and *graft* are examples. Body responses to these words might be: colon—intestine, graft—skin; whereas nonbodily responses might be colon—comma, graft—politics.

There are seventy-five homonyms in the association list and twenty-five neutral words which are included for camouflage or "buffer" purposes. Secord concluded on the basis of his work with the homonym list that individuals giving a large number of bodily associations were abnormally concerned with their body parts or processes, were fearful of body injury, and tended to view their bodies as ugly and shameful. He demonstrated in a group of fifty-six females that those who scored high in number of body associations to the homonyms were significantly less satisfied with the appearance of their bodies than those who scored lower.

It was assumed that the individual with definite boundaries would reflect the fact that he felt relatively more secure about his body than the indefinite boundary individual by giving relatively fewer body associations to the homonyms. In order to test this assumption a group of sixty-two college students (thirty-three women and twenty-nine men) in an introductory psychology class were studied. The group Rorschach was administered and scored for the Barrier variable. In addition, the Secord homonyms were read to the group at the rate of one every five seconds, and the subjects were asked to write down the "first word occurring to them as each homonym was read." When the results were tabulated, it was found that the subjects with above median Barrier scores gave a median of sixteen bodily associations. The low Barrier subjects gave a median of twenty such associations. It should be incidentally indicated that the sex distribution in the high and low Barrier groups was proportionally equal. A chi-square test of the difference in number of bodily associations between the high and low Barrier subjects was significant at the .001 level. Thus the outcome was well in the predicted direction.

This result, when considered in conjunction with the body-symptom data, the Projective Movement Sequence data, the phantom-limb data, the body-association data, and the incomplete-sentence data lends support to the idea that the Barrier score is basically a function of attitude toward, and feelings about, one's body. It has been shown that the Barrier score is significantly linked with measures of body attitudes obtained in widely different settings. Thus, it significantly predicts fantasies of body dissolution evoked in the course of reaction to a projective motion picture. It predicts an important aspect of the individual's adjustment to a loss of part of his body. It predicts a degree of concern about body vulnerability that is elicited by incomplete sentences which are phrased in body terms. The predictions hold not only in terms of overt behavior and fantasy, but also in terms of fantasy tapped in several different ways.

Despite the fairly significant results obtained in this attempt to relate the Barrier score to less devious and circuitous indices of body-image phenomena, it appeared more and more to us that one could not directly validate the body-image basis of the Barrier score by means of any one or two or three studies. Rather it seemed that what was required was an

elaborate pattern of interlocking studies which would tap many levels
of behavior that might be considered to have a relationship to body-
image boundaries. The results from such a pattern of studies could then
be evaluated to see if they held together in a manner consistent with the
body-image assumptions underlying the Barrier score. Just such a broad
pattern of studies was undertaken; and an over-all analysis of the results
which were relevant to the body-image question will be presented in
later chapters.

OTHER CONSIDERATIONS CONCERNING THE BARRIER SCORE

DRAWING OF A HOUSE

One question in which we were particularly interested regarding the
Barrier score was whether the underlying variable which it represented
would manifest itself in some other form of expression besides Rorschach
productions. Would the Barrier variable show up in such a task as
drawing, which, in contrast to the perceptual emphasis of the Rorschach, involves considerable motor behavior? Exploratory attempts to
find a relationship between the Barrier score and drawings of the human
figure led to entirely negative results. A variety of figure drawing indices (e.g., firmness of lines and character of clothing) proved to have
little value relative to the body-image boundary dimension. Exploratory
work with the drawing of a house, however, proved to be considerably
more successful in this respect. Initial observations suggested that the
degree to which an individual sketched in an elaborated façade on his
drawing of a house and the degree to which he surrounded the house
with ornamental, landscape, and decorative details was significantly
linked with the Barrier score. The high Barrier person seemed to reflect
his firm body-image boundaries in the elaborated treatment he gave to
the surroundings and bounding aspects of the house. The first opportunity to validate this formulation was provided by drawings of a house
obtained from thirty-eight women schoolteachers who were enrolled in a
summer workshop class, and from whom group Rorschachs had also been
obtained. These subjects were simply instructed, "Draw a picture of a
house." The two writers jointly and blindly rated each drawing as being
either above average in the elaborateness of its façade or below average.
Where there was considerable doubt about the classification of a drawing, it was excluded from consideration. Six drawings were not used
for this reason. When the dichotomous grouping (elaborated façade
versus unelaborated façade) of the drawings was compared with the
Barrier score distribution by means of a chi-square test, it was found
that the above median Barrier scores were associated significantly with

elaborated house façades and the below median Barrier scores with relatively unelaborated house façades (.001 level). It should also be reported that when the two writers independently scored a sample of forty house drawings obtained from another group (11), the two sets of scores correlated .97.

A check on the findings in the teacher group was attempted by comparing the Barrier scores and the drawings obtained on a group basis from eighteen college seniors and another group of twelve student dietitians in training at a Veterans Administration Hospital. Of these thirty subjects only five were men. A chi-square test indicated a chance relationship between the Barrier scores and the house drawings. We were puzzled about the shift from results significant at the .001 level in the teacher group to results of a purely chance order in this group.

Therefore, we proceeded to analyze additional pertinent data which were collected by Appleby (11). In the course of his own study of the Barrier variable, Appleby obtained Barrier scores and drawings of a house from two different groups of college students: one group of fifteen men and forty-six women, the other of fifty-four men and twelve women. The drawings were scored jointly on a blind basis by the writers. In the process of scoring and analyzing some of the house drawings, we noted that the men and women differed in that the men tended to use more constantly façades which had been considerably elaborated. If the women were judged within the same frame of reference as the men, their scores tended to fall, by and large, into the low façade-elaboration category. We also noted that the subjects in one of the groups had apparently been less motivated than those in the other group and had generally done very hasty incomplete sketches in which they showed little ego involvement. This was particularly true of twelve women subjects in this group.

On the basis of these observations we decided to analyze the men separately and to drop from the study the twelve women in one class who had shown such minimum ego involvement. When this was done, it was found that in both the male group and the female group the above median Barrier scorers were significantly higher in elaborateness of house façade than the below median Barrier scorers, as indicated by a chi-square test. The difference in the male group was significant at the .05 level and in the female group it was significant at the .05–.02 level. We are not clear as to why it was necessary to use different standards in rating the drawings of the men and women. We do not know whether this was the result of differential situational motivation on the part of the men and women or whether it was a function of a more basic difference in what a house represents to a man as compared to a woman.

The results, however, do support the idea that whatever underlies the Barrier score can manifest itself in other forms of expression besides Rorschach responses. It is not simply a Rorschach variable; and as will be shown later, it may be observed in many different kinds of response patterns. The Rorschach has been here most systematically adopted for the measurement of the Barrier dimension because it has proved easiest to quantify and easiest to administer on a large scale. Furthermore, we have found it much less subject to the sort of erratic motivational effects which showed up in the house drawing data.

An interesting sidelight on the significant association of the Barrier score with the façade aspect of the house drawings is the fact that there are many references in the psychoanalytic literature to the house as a symbol of the body. Freud (113) once stated, "The only typical, that is to say, regularly occurring representation of the human form as a whole is that of a house." Others (92, 213, 268) also have assigned a body significance to house symbols in dreams, drawings, and free associations. As described in Chapter 1, Erikson found in a rather well-controlled study that when adolescent boys and girls construct houses with play materials they show differences in pattern which he considers analogous to the differences in male and female configurations.

DREAM IMAGERY

We pursued further the question of whether the variable underlying the Barrier score would manifest itself in other forms of expression besides Rorschach responses. We extended our exploration into the area of dream imagery. The question was: were there definable aspects of an individual's dreams which were significantly related to his Barrier score? Would the dream imagery of a high Barrier person differ significantly from the imagery of a low Barrier person?

In order to answer this question twenty subjects were each asked to write a description of any dream he could recall. These subjects were all students in a course in general psychology. There were six women and fourteen men. The group Rorschach was administered to them by the method which involves requesting fixed numbers of responses for each card. Preliminary qualitative analysis of a number of dreams earlier obtained from other individuals had suggested that the boundary definiteness dimension could be conceptualized as manifesting itself in dream content at two different levels:

(1) One could consider whether the physical boundaries of persons and things were described as intact and unbroken or violated and penetrated. If there were references to things being opened up, burned, or destroyed, one could consider the boundaries of the dream content to be indefinite and like those of a low Barrier individual.

(2) One could consider the boundaries of any behavior sequence in the dream. If an individual in a dream were described as undertaking a course of action and then completing it by virtue of his own effort, his behavior would exemplify an independently segregated and independently bounded phenomenon. However, if an individual in a dream were described as doing various things without any volition of his own and as being at the mercy of various accidental forces, this would exemplify a behavior pattern that lacks independent boundedness. With these two broad concepts in mind, the following specific plan was set up for roughly dichotomizing dreams into those with definite boundaries and those with vague boundaries.

a. The occurrence of physical penetration of any human figure or any structure (e.g., house, car, bus) in a dream automatically classifies it in the vague-boundary category. Penetration refers to such phenomena as stabbing, crushing, burning, breaking, and cutting.

b. In the absence of any references to penetration, the second determinant of classification is the boundedness of the behavior sequence. Descriptions of dream figures as doing things without purpose, without conscious control, and without awareness indicate a vague-boundary dream.

c. Finally, in the absence of penetration themes or of vague-boundary behavior sequences, a dream is considered to fall into the definite-boundary category. Generally, this system of dream classification is based mainly on the presence or absence of indications of vague-weak boundaries, rather than upon explicit definition of firm boundaries.

Four clinical psychologists were each asked to categorize the twenty collected dreams on the basis of this classification scheme.

Table 3:10 presents the results obtained. The ratings of all the raters were in the predicted direction. That is, the dreams of high Barrier people are judged to be more firmly bounded than are the dreams of low Barrier people. Three of the four distributions of ratings give uncorrected chi squares that range from the .01–.05 level to the .01 level. When corrected for discontinuity, these three chi squares fall to 2.2 (.15–.10 level), 3.1 (.10–.05 level), and 5.7 (.02–.01 level). A percentage analysis of the correctness of the ratings of the dreams (with Barrier score taken as the criterion of correctness) indicates that in the case of all four raters the percentage of correct ratings exceeds the percentage of incorrect ratings. The range of correctness varies from 80 per cent to 60 per cent. The three raters who were most successful were especially accurate in their classification of dreams given by low Barrier individuals. Of eleven dreams given by low Barrier subjects, they identified

TABLE 3:10   DIFFERENCES BETWEEN HIGH AND LOW BARRIER SUBJECTS
WITH REGARD TO BOUNDARY FIRMNESS IN DREAM IMAGERY

Raters	Group with Most Firm Boundary Dreams	χ^2	Signifi-cance	With Yates[a] Correction	Signifi-cance	% Correct and Incorrect Ratings	
						Cor-rect	Incor-rect
A	High Barrier	3.6	.10–.05	2.2[b]	.15–.10	71	29
B	High Barrier	4.9	.05–.02	3.1	.10–.05	75	25
C	High Barrier	8.1	.01	5.7	.02–.01	80	20
D	High Barrier	.8	.50–.30	.2	.70–.50	60	40

[a] Yates correction was used because there are expected frequencies in some cells of less than 5.
[b] With full awareness of the limitations of the procedure in this instance, the four corrected chi squares were added. This yielded a value of 11.2, which, with 4 degrees of freedom, is significant at the .05–.02 level.

nine or ten correctly. Their greatest difficulty came in sorting the dreams of high Barrier subjects. Of nine such dreams, correct identifications ranged from 5 to 6.

The pattern of the results pretty well confirms the fact that the boundary definiteness variable does find expression in dream imagery. It is true that criteria of strict significant difference are not met for the results of most of the individual raters. When one notes, however, that all the results are in the predicted direction and that even with the Yates correction applied, three of the four raters give a chi-square pattern that falls at about the .10 level or better, it would seem that our hypothesis is considerably supported.

MULTIPLE-CHOICE BLOTS

Although it is in a sense anticipating later phases of our work, it would seem logical at this point to report our attempts to measure the Barrier variable by means of a multiple-choice ink-blot technique. Late in our endeavors, after almost all our experimental projects had been completed and the Barrier score seemed to show real promise, we became interested in the possibility of constructing an ink-blot test which would evaluate a subject's degree of boundary definiteness not from his spontaneous responses to blots, but rather from his selection of multiple-choice alternatives presented to him. It was felt that such a multiple-choice procedure would have the advantage of quick administration and quick objective scoring. Although we have not yet been able to develop an instrument which gives results sufficiently correlated with those from the spontaneous Rorschach productions to replace the spontaneous Rorschach method, we have preliminary data which are sufficiently promising to be reported. These data point up the real potentiality for constructing a completely objective psychometric instrument for measuring the Barrier variable.

We were aided immeasurably in our project to construct such an instrument by the work of Wayne Holtzman* who has developed a new ink-blot test series. The Holtzman test consists of a series of forty-five blots (actually two equivalent forms of the test have now been developed) carefully selected by trial and error from among hundreds of experimental blots. The subject is required to give one response per card, thus creating a nearly identical response total for each individual. A series of these ink-blots was selected for use in the development of a multiple-choice Barrier test. Alternate responses for each blot representing a Barrier, Penetration, and neutral response were selected from the large volume of normative data collected by Holtzman. A booklet was prepared listing for each blot the three alternate choices. The order of presentation of the three choices, Barrier, Penetration, and neutral were randomized from card to card in order to prevent the development of any set method of response. The initial experiment with the multiple-choice test involved the use of thirty ink-blots. The Rorschach test, with the total number of responses restricted to twenty-four in the usual manner, was administered to a college group consisting of sixty-five students. The multiple-choice test was also administered. For each blot the subjects were asked to place a plus mark beside the response listed in the booklet which best described the blot, a minus beside the least descriptive choice, and the third choice was to be left blank. The Rorschach test was scored for Barrier responses in the usual manner. Independently and without knowledge of the traditional Barrier score the multiple-choice tests were scored by allowing a weighted score of two for each Barrier response checked with a plus, a score of one for each Barrier response left blank, and a score of zero for Barrier responses marked minus or least preferred. With a total of thirty ink-blots this scoring method offers a possible Barrier score range of 0–60. Actually the range of scores obtained was 26–45, the median score being 35. Ten subjects in the group of sixty-five had to be eliminated either because of failure to follow directions on the multiple-choice test or to record a sufficient number of responses on the spontaneous Rorschach. A total of fifty-five subjects were then available for study.

---

* We wish to express our appreciation to Dr. Wayne Holtzman, Associate Director of the Hogg Foundation for Mental Health and Professor of Psychology, State University of Texas, for his help in the construction of the multiple-choice group test.

Rorschach	Multiple-choice Blots	
	High Barrier	Low Barrier
High Barrier	18	7
Low Barrier	9	21

$\chi^2 = 9.5(.01)$

In Table 3:11 a comparison of the two Barrier score distributions is presented, using chi-square technique. In this analysis the scores of subjects above and below the median on the traditional Barrier scale were compared with their multiple-choice Barrier scores which were also split at the median. As is indicated by the chi-square value of 9.5, significant at the .01 level of confidence, there is a definite tendency for subjects scoring high or low on the one Barrier measure to be similarly high or low on the other Barrier measure. A product-moment correlation of .52 between the two distributions indicates the moderately high degree of relationship between the two tests. An item analysis of the responses to the thirty multiple choice ink blots revealed that actually only eighteen of the blots were distinguishing the high and low Barrier subjects. Twelve blots had little or no discriminatory value.

Rorschach	Multiple-choice Blots	
	High Barrier	Low Barrier
High Barrier	23	7
Low Barrier	4	26

$\chi^2 = 24.4(.001)$

Encouraged by the preliminary findings we proceeded to conduct a second study to test the relationships between the two differently derived Barrier scores. The response alternatives to the twelve blots which failed to differentiate subjects on Barrier score were dropped and new responses selected. Also, ten new blots were added to the series, expanding the test to forty blots and their response alternatives. A second undergraduate class consisting of sixty subjects was tested in a manner identical to the first. The tests were again scored independently. An item analysis of the responses to this second form of the multiple-choice test revealed that the eighteen cards used in the first test and duplicated in the second continued to differentiate high and low Barrier scorers on the traditional Rorschach Barrier index. Also, five of the new cards included in the second test showed promise in this respect. These five cards, when added to the eighteen cards which held up on this repeat administration, formed a test of twenty-three items. A comparison between the distribution of Barrier scores derived from these twenty-three cards and the corresponding Barrier scores from the spontaneous Rorschach yielded a chi-square value of 24.4, significant at the .001 per cent level of confidence (as indicated in Table 3:12). A product-moment correlation of .64 was obtained between the two distributions. Actually this correlation value, as is also true with the value of .52 obtained between the two Barrier score distributions found in the first group studied, is probably attenuated because of the rather restricted range of scores on the traditional Barrier scale.

If the correction formula° for estimating the correlation between two tests in a heterogeneous group, knowing the correlation between the tests in a homogeneous group, is applied, a correlation value of .81 is obtained. This value suggests that there is an appreciable degree of commonality between the two Barrier measures.

It remains to be seen whether a multiple-choice technique can be developed which will be sufficiently equivalent to the spontaneous Rorschach to replace it. But in any case, the data indicate still another level at which the boundary dimension can be tapped. Incidentally, it should also be noted that they support the position taken in Chapter 2 that the Barrier score is relatively independent of a subject's spontaneous verbal facility. That is, the simple choice of a blot alternative does not require more than the simplest of verbal skill; and yet scores based on such choices correlate fairly highly with scores derived from the spontaneous Rorschach productions.

BODY TYPE

Although we had found considerable data in the psychosomatic groups we studied which indicated that the mere experiencing of body symptoms in a given body area did not significantly influence the Barrier score, we were interested in checking on the possibility that general body physique in a normal population might be related to the score. Our position has been that the Barrier score reflects the individual's long-term perception of his body and that this perception is shaped by a wide range of factors, of which the actual body physique is only a very small part. The implications are that the body image, while founded on body experiences, bears little resemblance to the individual's literal

---

° See Garrett (p. 326) for formula for estimating correlation in a wide range from correlation in a restricted range.

body characteristics because the way in which an individual experiences his body from the very beginning is a function of his family experiences and social milieu. The very same body characteristics might call forth one set of responses in a given family group and quite another set of responses in a different family. However, one could argue along the lines that an individual who possesses unusually well-developed body musculature, as compared to the individual with poor musculature, would have body experiences that would make it particularly easy for him to think of his body as having firm, strong boundaries. The very strength of his musculature would stimulate fantasies of boundary toughness and definiteness.

In considering how to check this and similar possibilities, the idea presented itself of relating the Barrier score to Sheldon's somatotypes. It has been established that Sheldon's somatotype procedures are adequately reliable and that they do get at certain dominant features of the individual's body physique. If the Barrier score were to show no relationship to somatotype scores, this would oppose the notion that the Barrier score is significantly a function of an individual's actual body structure.

We were able to investigate this problem operationally in terms of data collected by Margaret J. Cheatham° (60). She obtained Rorschach records, among other measures, from a group of seventy college students. These students had been previously somatotyped according to Sheldon's criteria. The Rorschachs were blindly scored for the Barrier index. However, due to the wide variations in response productivity within the group, it was necessary to limit the number of responses scored in each record. All records over twenty-five responses were reduced to twenty-five. This was done by scoring only the first three responses given to each of the first five cards and only the first two responses given to each of the last five cards. If an individual with more than twenty-five responses did not give the maximum number of responses assigned to any given card, the difference was made up on the next nearest card in the sequence which had more than the maximum allotted to it. It may be noted that Cheatham had previously found that none of the conventional Rorschach scoring categories were significantly related to the somatotype classifications. In our analysis of the data we found that the Barrier scores had a completely chance relationship to the somatotype scores. Therefore, to the degree that Sheldon's somatotypes do represent important dimensions of body structure, one may say that the Barrier score is not determined by actual body characteristics.

° We are very grateful to Dr. Cheatham for the use of these data.

SELF-CONCEPT

It is of importance to clarify the relationship of the body-image variable to the construct of self-concept. To what extent do they overlap and to what degree do they differ? If by the term *self-concept* one means the whole range of complicated attitudes and fantasies an individual has about his identity, his life role, and his appearance, then, the two constructs undoubtedly overlap considerably. While the body-image concept is primarily phrased in the language of body attitudes and body experiences, it is clear that such attitudes and experiences grow out of one's socially determined role and identities. Some previously cited relationships between the Barrier score and TAT attitudes toward the parental figures support this statement. Considerably more data in the same vein will be presented at a later point. We definitely consider the body image to be a condensed formulation or summary in body terms of a great many experiences the individual has had in the course of defining his identity in the world. Illustratively, if an individual perceives his body as ugly and depreciated, it would be assumed that this is a body representation of experiences in some milieu where people reacted to him as if certain aspects of his behavior were ugly and to be depreciated. There is, of course, implicit here the hypothesis that the body image is a sensitive indicator which registers many of the individual's basic social relationships, especially those early involved in his development of a sense of identity.

If one means by *self-concept* the attitudes which an individual expresses about himself verbally, we do not consider the body-image boundary variable to overlap significantly with it. There are now in the literature a great many studies which attempt to measure the individual's self-concept by simply requesting him to rate himself on a variety of traits or to sort a series of statements with self-reference. The assumption is made in most of these studies that the way in which one consciously perceives himself bears a significant resemblance to those aspects of self-organization which influence behavior. This assumption seems doubtful and oversimplified. It appears to us that some of the most important aspects of the individual's concept of himself are either so unpleasant to face or are acquired at such an early preverbal period as to be unavailable for conscious reporting.

Since the Barrier score is derived on the basis of assumptions so contrary to the usual self-concept measure, one would expect the two types of measures to have only a chance relationship to each other. An opportunity for evaluating this point presented itself in some data which had been collected by Robert E. Bills* (35). Bills devised a method for measuring the self-concept which he refers to as the Index of Adjustment and Values. He indicates (34, p. 258) that 124 words with trait value were selected and "were arranged in a vertical list and the words were followed by three blank columns. The subjects were asked to use each of the words to complete the sentence, 'I am a (an) —— person,' and to indicate on a five-point scale how much of the time this statement was like them. This rating was placed in the blank in Column I. Column I sampled, then, the concept of self.

The subjects were also instructed to indicate, in the second blank, a rating which would tell how they felt about themselves as described in the first blank. The ratings are as follows: (1) I very much dislike being as I am in this respect; (2) I dislike being as I am in this respect; (3) I neither dislike being as I am nor like being as I am in this respect; (4) I like being as I am in this respect; (5) I very much like being as I am in this respect. The sum of Column II measured acceptance of self.

The subjects were likewise instructed to use each of the words to complete the sentence "I would like to be a (an) —— person" and to indicate in the third blank how much of the time they would like this trait to be characteristic of them. The same ratings were used as in the first blank. Thus, Column III sampled the concept of the "ideal self."

A discrepancy score may also be derived which represents the difference between Column I and Column III summed without regard for sign. It focuses on the difference between the way the individual currently pictures himself and an idealized version of self.

In the course of one study Bills (35) selected twenty-eight college students whose discrepancy scores were at least one standard deviation above the mean discrepancy score of a standardization group. He also selected twenty-eight students with discrepancy scores at least one standard deviation below the mean. Thus, one group indicated high discrepancy between their stated concept of self and their concept of the ideal self; and the other group showed low discrepancy between these measures. Each subject was individually tested with the Rorschach test. Bills made available to us for analysis the Rorschachs and discrepancy scores of these fifty-six subjects. However, due to difficulties in locating certain records, there were acceptance-of-self scores for only fifty-one subjects; and the simple concept-of-self scores were completely unavailable. But it should be noted that in Bills's various published studies regarding his Index of Adjustment and Values only the acceptance-of-self score and the discrepancy score have shown any degree of significant relationship

---

* We gratefully acknowledge Dr. Bills's cooperation in permitting us to use his data.

to validity criteria. These are the two most functionally meaningful indices derived from the Index.

When the Barrier scores of Bills's subjects were compared with their acceptance-of-self scores by means of chi square, a completely chance relationship was found between the two score distributions. The same chance relationship appeared when the Barrier scores were compared with the discrepancy scores. These results support the view that the Barrier score measures something basically quite different than do self-concept measures which are derived from conscious verbal reports of self-attributes.

REVIEW NOTE

We have attempted in this chapter to trace some of the initial explorations with the body-image boundary measures. In this phase of our work we were interested in determining whether the measures had meaningful relationships to a variety of psychosomatic phenomena, and also to aspects of behavior of normal subjects. These exploratory studies were scattered and diffuse. But the results which emerged were promising and, as will be seen, provided a number of semiverified points of reference which permitted further and more detailed development of hypotheses. Most of the hypotheses to be presented in subsequent chapters grew out of this initial work.

Another task undertaken in this chapter was to show that the Barrier score is a function of the individual's attitudes toward his body. The intent has been to demonstrate that the Barrier score does not reflect either the individual's usual consciously verbalized self-concept or the actual structural characteristics of his body. Rather, data have been presented which link the Barrier score with various measures that presumably tap basic concepts and feelings about one's body.

PART TWO

*Body-Image Boundaries and
Behavior Variations*

··

CHAPTER FOUR

Body-Image Boundaries and Self-steering Behavior

THE SELF-STEERING FORMULATION

UP TO THIS POINT in our series of studies we have tentatively surveyed some of the factors contributing to the Barrier score and have considered its relationships to a number of variables in both psychosomatic and normal groups. This chapter will present more detailed and extensive investigations of the significance of body-image boundary variations in normal subjects.

The results of our preliminary work provided us with some fairly dependable glimpses concerning the kinds of traits and patterns of response one might expect to be associated with differences in boundary definiteness in normal individuals. This preliminary information gave us a basis for making a range of predictions concerning the relationships which should exist between the Barrier score and a number of other variables. Actually we used this information to construct an idealized model of what the high Barrier person is like and then made predictions from the model.

A brief review of some of the salient aspects of the model is in order. Generalizing from our preliminary work, we concluded that definiteness of boundaries is linked with the ability to be an independent person who has definite standards, definite goals, and forceful striving ways of approaching tasks. We visualized the person with definite boundaries as one who sought special success in life and as one who could not easily be diverted by stress or obstacles from goal attainment. We pictured boundary definiteness as carrying with it a facility for expressing tension by attacking and shaping the environment to make it conform to the individual's internalized standards. In another vein, one could consider the individual with definite boundaries as responding to life as if it were a tournament in which each contestant must be somewhat wary of the others yet secure in his own skill and ability to get what he wants. With this model as our guide, we constructed a series of specific

117

hypotheses concerning the relationship of the Barrier score to various modes of behavior. These hypotheses involved the relationships of the Barrier score to the following:

1. Level of goal setting.
2. Need for task completion.
3. Suggestibility.
4. Ability to express anger outwardly when frustrated.
5. Degree of orientation toward self-expressiveness.
6. Ability to tolerate stress.
7. Ability to maintain a realistic orientation in unstructured perceptual situations.

It may be observed that all these variables directly or indirectly concern modes of response that have to do with the individual getting ahead, being effective, expressing his tensions directly, standing up for his own view of things, and being able to establish standards. They are variables which seem to overlap and roughly to constitute a meaningful cluster. We defined what they appear to have in common under the rubric *self-steering behavior*. That is, they all bear on a style of behavior which involves the individual's desire and ability to steer his own special course through the variety of alternatives he encounters in life. It was our prediction that in different contexts high Barrier individuals would show themselves to be significantly more oriented toward self-steering than low Barrier individuals. The remainder of the chapter is taken up with an examination of this proposition.

LEVEL OF GOAL SETTING

Level of goal setting is one of the areas in which we have most thoroughly explored the relationship of body-image boundaries to self-steering. The concern with goals, particularly high-level goals, would seem to be one of the basic characteristics most frequently observed in those who set their own vigorous course in life situations. In Chapter 3 it has already been shown that individuals with Barrier scores above the median are significantly more concerned with high attainment, as defined by our TAT Aspiration Index, than are those with Barrier scores below the median. This was demonstrated in one group and also in a subsequent cross-validation group. However, in order to check thoroughly on these findings and to increase their generality, further studies were undertaken with more groups and also with other measures.

TAT ASPIRATION INDEX

Two further studies, in addition to the two just cited, were made involving the TAT Aspiration Index* which we developed. In one study the subjects consisted of forty-two men and women ranging in age from sixteen to fifty years who were members of families of individuals who had sought psychiatric treatment. They were individually tested with the Rorschach and TAT (1, 2, 5, 6BM, 7BM) as part of a larger project concerned with the characteristics of families of psychiatric patients (103). These subjects were actually selected out of a group of sixty-four, twenty-two of whom were eliminated because their Rorschach records contained less than twenty responses. It was found that the high Barrier subjects produced significantly more aspiration themes on the TAT than the low Barrier subjects. The χ^2 value was 4.8 which is significant at the .05–.02 level.

In a study carried out by Appleby (11) thirty male and thirty female college students were evaluated by means of the group Rorschach (response total controlled) and the group TAT (1, 2, 5, 6BM, 7BM). He found that the high Barrier subjects tended to produce more high aspiration themes than the low Barrier individuals, but the difference was not statistically significant (.10–.20 level).

The results of all the studies in which the Barrier score has been related to the TAT High Aspiration score may be summarized as follows:

(1) In each of the four studies the differences obtained have been in the predicted direction.

(2) In three of the four studies the direction of the differences was statistically significant.

It should be noted that in the Appleby study the selection of some of the subjects was influenced by their willingness to volunteer. This is the only one of the four experimental groups in which volunteering played a part in subject selection. It is possible that this selectivity factor somehow resulted in Appleby's results falling below the level of significance obtained in the other three studies.

MCCLELLAND n ACHIEVEMENT SCORE

The McClelland (212) n Achievement score was the second goal-setting measure against which the Barrier score was compared. McClelland's measure has shown itself to be a sensitive and valid indicator of achieve-

---

* This index has subsequently been used in several studies concerned with the behavior of patients with tuberculosis, and has shown significant power in predicting various phases of behavior (105).

ment motivation in a wide range of studies. In a first study carried out by the writers the data were obtained from material which had been collected by McClelland.* We determined the Barrier scores from the Rorschach records of thirty subjects whom McClelland had studied as part of his over-all exploration of the achievement motive. The subjects were college students. When all records were reduced to a maximum of twenty-five responses, differences in Rorschach response total between those with above median n Achievement scores and those with below median scores was found to be not significant. In relating Barrier scores to n Achievement scores by means of chi square, it was found that the high Barrier subjects obtained significantly higher n Achievement scores than did the low Barrier individuals. The difference was significant at the .05 level.

Appleby (11) too investigated the relationship of the Barrier score to the n Achievement score. His subjects consisted of thirty men and thirty women. He found a phi coefficient of .42 (.05 level) between Barrier and n Achievement in the male group. The relationship in the female group and in the combined male and female groups was in the predicted direction, but not statistically significant.†

A third attempt to relate the Barrier score to the n Achievement score was made by the writers in terms of data collected by Kelly‡ and Fiske (167A) from 123 graduate students in psychology, as part of an over-all investigation of the predictability of success of students training to become clinical psychologists. We determined the Barrier scores from the Rorschach records which had been collected from the graduate students. All records were limited to twenty-five responses by means of the set reduction method. The TAT records of the subjects had been scored for the n Achievement variable. An unusual pattern was found to characterize the relationship of the Barrier scores to the n Achievement scores. The Barrier scores fell on a continuum ranging from 1 through 9, with 1–5 being below the median and 6–9 above the median. When the distribution of above median and below median n Achievement scores was plotted against this continuum, it turned out that those subjects in the 1–2 (low) Barrier category ($n = 25$) had significantly higher (.01 level) Achievement scores than those in the 3, 4, 5 categories ($n = 48$) but not significantly different from those in the above median 6, 7, 8

---

* We gratefully acknowledge Dr. David McClelland's kindness in permitting us to rescore his data.

† It may be parenthetically noted that in this same study Appleby found a phi coefficient of .42 (.05 level) between n Achievement, as measured by the Edwards Personal Preference Schedule, and Barrier score in the male group, but failed to find such a relationship in the female group or in the total group.

‡ We are indebted to Dr. Lowell Kelly for his permission to use these data.

and 9 categories (n = 50). The subjects in the 6, 7, 8, 9 categories were significantly higher (.05–.06 level) than those in the 3, 4, 5 categories. These results indicate that both the very low Barrier subjects and the above median Barrier subjects obtained significantly higher *n* Achievement scores than the moderately low (3, 4, 5) Barrier subjects. Thus, the total above median Barrier group was higher in *n* Achievement than the middle group, which constitutes 65 per cent of the total below median group.

But the question remains as to why the very low Barrier subjects obtained such high *n* Achievement scores. The most logical answer that presents itself has to do with the special motivational factors operating in the situation in which the TAT was administered to the students in Kelly's group. The students had assembled from distant points and were being assessed by a vigorous round of test procedures. They knew that they were being evaluated with regard to their ability to be successful in the occupation they had chosen as a life work. They were under a high degree of stress and exposed to many threatening demands. Since they were students with a degree in psychology, it may be presumed that in general they had had more experience with the TAT than most subjects used in psychological studies and that therefore they had a greater ability to exert controlling influence over the kinds of stories they created. If one assumes, then, that the low Barrier people were the most threatened by the situation and most in need of presenting a good picture of themselves in their responses, it would perhaps follow that they would put out relatively more energy in coloring their stories in a "good" direction (higher achievement orientation) than would the other subjects. This extra effort would result in elevated *n* Achievement scores for the extreme low Barrier group. It is, of course, a well-demonstrated fact that analogous forms of compensatory behavior have occurred in other populations. For example, McClelland (212) reports a study in which low *n* Achievement subjects obtained significantly higher achievement scores on a Sentence Completion Test than did high *n* Achievement subjects.

One must conclude from the three studies described above that the relationship of the Barrier score to the *n* Achievement score is not clear-cut and straightforward. It is true that in all three studies the trend of the results favors the hypothesis concerning the correlation of boundary definiteness with goal-setting level. But one finds the relationship to be attenuated by sex differences in Appleby's study and possibly motivational differences in Kelly's study. Actually these results are not too surprising if one recalls that the behavior of the *n* Achievement score has been shown to be significantly affected by sex differences and situational motivational variables in other studies.

OVERACHIEVERS VERSUS UNDERACHIEVERS

A somewhat equivocal relationship was found between the Barrier score and an index of overachievement versus underachievement in a body of data collected by Rust and Ryan[*] (257). These investigators were interested in the possibility of predicting scholastic overachievement and underachievement from the group Rorschach. Their subjects were undergraduate students at Yale College. They determined for each subject the discrepancy between his actual grades and the level of achievement one would have predicted in terms of an aggregate consisting of his previous secondary school record, his score on the Scholastic Aptitude Test, and his scores on three College Entrance Board Examinations. We were interested in two of their subject groups: the underachievers who obtained grades markedly below their predicted level and overachievers whose grades were considerably higher than the predicted level. Our hypothesis concerning these groups was that the overachievers would tend to obtain significantly higher Barrier scores than the underachievers.

Our analysis of the data involved thirty-five overachievers and twenty-eight underachievers. Chi square was used to determine the significance of the difference in Barrier scores between the two groups. The distribution of Barrier scores was in the direction predicted, but the chi-square value was 3.1 which falls at the .10–.05 level, short of formal significance. Most of the contribution to the chi-square differences were made by the overachievers. Considering the highly select character of the Yale student population, this borderline differentiation of the over-achievers and underachievers may be interpreted as falling in a direction confirmatory of our hypothesis.

CLASSROOM ACHIEVEMENT

Two lines of data will be described, each based on classroom behavior in a university setting. The first line of data was fortuitously secured. In one of our early projects we obtained Barrier scores on a group of thirty-eight women who were taking a summer school workshop course in leadership at the University of Houston. The instructor in this course decided to let the group set its own standards concerning the amount of work that would be minimally necessary in order to earn various levels of grades. The group decided that only those would be eligible for a grade of A who chose to write a rather elaborate term paper. At the completion of the course the instructor found that eleven students had elected to write the paper required to earn a grade of A. What was

---

[*] We are indebted to Dr. Ralph M. Rust and Dr. F. J. Ryan for making these data available to us.

striking was that of the eleven who turned in papers, nine were individuals with Barrier scores above the median of the group; one was at the median; and only one was below the median. Thus, in terms of this real-life behavioral measure, the high Barrier people showed themselves to be definitely more aspiring than the low Barrier people. Our inclination is to place greater weight on this sort of finding than on the formal achievement measure findings, because it represents such direct behavioral data and is so much less a function of second order deductions.

A second line of data concerning achievement behavior in the classroom was obtained in a more formal fashion. An instructor who had had the same students in an undergraduate psychology course which extended over a two-semester period was asked to rank the students relative to two variables:

(1) The degree to which they seemed to have set goals of high achievement for themselves in life.

(2) The degree to which they pursued their goals in class in an independent manner as contrasted to appealing frequently for help.

There were eleven women in this class and only a few men. Since this was so, and since there were likely to be different standards involved in rating men and women for variables like achievement and independence, it was decided to restrict the data analysis to the eleven women. The rho correlation between Barrier score and achievement ranking was .23, which is not significant. The rho between Barrier score and independence ranking was .73, which is significant at the .01 level. It is interesting that McClelland (212) reports a similar pattern of results in some studies having to do with the relationship of the n Achievement score to teacher ratings of such variables as "general independence," "pleasure in success," and "general success motivation." He reports that raters have difficulty in assessing achievement motivation when it is broadly defined (e.g., as general success motivation). But they are able to make more accurate evaluations of the specific behavioral manifestations of the achievement motive (e.g., independence). Quite analogously, the judgments of the rater in our study concerning the general achievement orientation of students did not correlate significantly with the Barrier score. However, the rater's evaluation of the degree of independence shown by the students in the specific classroom situation proved to be significantly linked with the Barrier score.

Over all, a total of ten different studies have been cited which involve the relationship of the Barrier score to various indices of goal setting or degree of achievement orientation. As indicated in Table 4:1, the results have been in the predicted direction in all ten studies. In six of the studies the results were statistically significant; in one the result was at

TABLE 4:1 BARRIER SCORE AND VARIOUS INDICES OF ACHIEVEMENT ORIENTATION

Achievement Index against Which Barrier Score Compared	*Results in Predicted Direction*	*Statistically Significant*
TAT High Aspiration (Fisher-Cleveland)	Yes	Yes
TAT High Aspiration (Fisher-Cleveland)	Yes	Yes
TAT High Aspiration (Fisher-Cleveland)	Yes	Yes
TAT High Aspiration (Appleby)	Yes	No
McClelland *n* Achievement (Fisher-Cleveland)	Yes	Yes
McClelland *n* Achievement (Appleby)	Yes	For male group but not for female or total group
McClelland *n* Achievement (Kelly)	Yes	For a large segment of the group
Yale overachievers vs. underachievers	Yes	Borderline
Classroom behavior	Yes	Yes
Classroom behavior	Yes	Yes

a borderline level of significance. The outcome of one study (Appleby-TAT High Aspiration) was definitely not significant. The two remaining studies gave partial results that were statistically significant; but the significance was subject to special interpretation. It would seem to be a fair statement to say that the main trend of the findings is in support of the proposition that high Barrier individuals set higher goals for themselves than do low Barrier individuals.

NEED FOR TASK COMPLETION

One of the principal connotations of the self-steering concept is the idea of setting goals for oneself and then persisting until such goals are attained. We have already shown that the high Barrier person is concerned with setting big goals, but here we are focusing on the idea of persisting toward any goal which is set, whether it be high or low. It would be anticipated that the individual who is self-steering would find it relatively important to finish up the things he started. If he undertook an ego-involving task, it would become a matter of significance to him to carry it to a point of definite outcome. The person who was not oriented toward self-steering would be more likely to conceive of tasks as things which were imposed from the outside and for which he had little responsibility. For him, a task would be less likely to represent a challenge or a mode of individualistic expression.

It was felt that the Zeigarnik effect would provide an unusually good opportunity for studying the relationships of body-image boundary definiteness to task completion behavior. The Zeigarnik effect refers to a rather complex phenomenon. It would therefore be helpful in clarifying some of the results which were obtained in linking it with boundary definiteness, if the trend of past research in which it has been studied were briefly reviewed.

Since Zeigarnik (361) first observed the tendency for subjects to recall a relatively greater number of incompleted than completed tasks, there has been much energy directed toward observation of this phenomenon. It was noted that individuals show distinct differences in the degree to which they manifest the Zeigarnik effect in their recall. These individual differences in recall have been studied and found to be related to such variables as age (262), ego strength (8, 87, 159), hysterical tendencies (255), type of schizophrenic symptomatology (344), and repression mechanisms (254). It is still far from clear what factors are of paramount importance in the differential recall process. One of the variables that has been most emphasized as an explanatory concept is "ego strength."

Sanford and Risser (262) suggest that the tendency to recall an increasing proportion of incompleted tasks with increase in chronological age is due to the ego maturation correlated with age progression. Alper (8) and Eriksen (87) have both found significant correlations between ego strength and tendency to recall incompleted tasks. But the relationship they find is a complex one which is a function of how ego-involving the tasks are. Jourard (159) has been unable to substantiate directly the relationship of ego strength to task recall, although he did find a significant correlation between task recall and certain Rorschach measures with inferred ego-strength implications. The focus on the ego-strength variable has obscured some of the earlier Lewinian oriented work of Rickers-Ovsiankina (242) and Bennett (28), in which it was shown that the degree to which schizophrenic subjects build up task completion tendencies is a function of firmness of peripheral boundaries.

Winder (344), in the same Lewinian tradition, has more recently confirmed, indirectly, the value of boundary firmness as a concept explanatory of completion-incompletion phenomena. He demonstrated that paranoid schizophrenics, who may be considered to have relatively firm boundaries, recall a greater proportion of incompleted tasks than do nonparanoid schizophrenics whom one may assume to have less integrated and more permeable boundaries. The Lewinians have hypothesized that boundary firmness facilitates the development of segregated tension systems. They indicate that in the absence of firm boundaries tensions are dissipated and do not exert an organized goal-directed influence on the individual. Obviously, the body-image boundary concepts which we have developed in our work are analogous in some ways to the Lewinian boundary-firmness concepts. Indeed, when we noted that boundary firmness had proved to be significantly related to task-completion tendencies in schizophrenic subjects, we were encouraged in our anticipation that the boundary-firmness concept would also apply to task-completion tendencies in the normal range.

We were able to test our basic hypothesis that individuals with definite boundaries would have a greater need to complete tasks than individuals with indefinite boundaries by analyzing some data which had been collected by Jourard[*] (159). Jourard was interested in the relationship of ego strength to recall for completed versus incompleted tasks. One can best describe how the data were gathered by quoting from his paper (p. 52):

> Thirty tasks were devised by the writer so that each could be used as an interrupted or as a completed task by varying the length of the assignment of each task. Thus, for the task "necklace," if it was to serve as an interrupted task, the instructions were as follows: "Make a necklace from these 24 beads such that no two identical beads are touching." If this particular task was to be completed S was given only 12 beads, but with identical instructions.
>
> In order to rule out the effects of serial order on recall, the position of each task in each presentation series was determined from a table of random numbers. The order of interruption-completion was likewise assigned from a random-number table.
>
> The S's were tested singly, one in the morning and one in the afternoon. The general sequence is summarized as follows: (a) introductory comments; (b) administration of the Rorschach test; (c) administration of the I-C test; (d) interview for biographical material for five minutes; (e) S writes out her recall of tasks for three minutes; (f) administration of a series of digit-symbol tasks, lasting 14 minutes; (g) S writes out her recall of tasks again.
>
> In order to induce a set of ego involvement, the I-C test was presented as a college level test of intelligence. The apparatus was drawn from a conspicuously labeled Wechsler box, and a stop watch was displayed and used throughout the record times. Since only 45 seconds were allowed for each task, each S experienced the sensation of being rushed and of failing one half of the tasks. In addition, each S was told that in order to receive IQ credit for a given item, it was necessary that it be completed correctly; partial credit is not allowed. Each item is passed or failed on an all or none basis.

---

[*] We are indebted to Dr. Sidney Jourard for making these data available to us.

The individual Rorschach records collected by Dr. Jourard were administered in the standard manner with the exception that in order to control for total number of responses, each subject was required to give five responses per card. The Barrier scores of the subjects were determined from their total Rorschach records.

There was computed for each subject an index $I/(I + C)$ that denotes the ratio of interrupted tasks recalled to all tasks recalled. This ratio was determined for the first recall and also for the second recall. If our original hypothesis is correct, those with high Barrier scores should have a significantly higher ratio of I to $I + C$ than those with low Barrier scores. That is, the relatively greater concern of the high Barrier subjects about task completion should evidence itself in a relatively greater memory focus on the incompleted tasks.

TABLE 4:2 SIGNIFICANCE LEVELS OF THE CHI-SQUARE TESTS OF THE DIFFERENCES IN RECALL FOR INCOMPLETED TASKS BETWEEN HIGH BARRIER SCORERS AND LOW BARRIER SCORERS

	First Recall	*Second Recall*
Group recalling greater percentage of incompleted tasks	High Barrier	High Barrier
Significance of Differences	Not significant	.01

Table 4:2 indicates that at the time of the first recall memory for incompleted tasks is not significantly different between the high Barrier group and the low Barrier group. However, the difference is in the predicted direction. By the time of the second recall the difference between the group has sharpened, and the high Barrier group recalls a significantly greater proportion of incompleted tasks than the low Barrier group.

In a further analysis of the data, rho correlations were determined between $I/(I + C)$ scores and Barrier scores for the first and second recalls. For the first recall the rho was not significant. A rho of $+.27$, however, which is significant at the 5 per cent level, was obtained between $I/(I + C)$ scores and Barrier scores at the time of the second recall. Over all, then, the data confirm the basic hypothesis concerning the relationship of body-image boundaries to memory for incompleted tasks.

It may be parenthetically noted that our finding that memory for incomplete tasks is linked with degree of definiteness of body-image boundaries is nicely congruent with the previously cited work of Rickers-Ovsiankina (242) and others (28, 344) who showed an analogous sort of relationship in schizophrenic subjects. It would appear that within certain limits the more an individual is characterized by firm (definite) boundaries the more likely he is to build up segregated tension systems that require a specific kind of goal attainment before the tension can be discharged. This boundary approach to the Zeigarnik effect does not necessarily involve disagreement with the viewpoint that ego strength is significantly correlated with differential reaction to task completion-incompletion. It is possible that there is some overlap between the boundary concept and the ego-strength concept. Perhaps ego strength reflects in part the degree to which the individual has evolved boundaries definite enough to give him a clear-cut identity.

SUGGESTIBILITY

One would expect a self-steering person to make his decisions on the basis of his own observations rather than on the basis of arbitrary suggestions offered by others. It would be anticipated, then, that a high Barrier individual would show relatively fewer traits of suggestibility than a low Barrier individual. In attempting to test such a hypothesis, there is, of course, the difficult problem of defining and setting up operational methods of measuring suggestibility. Many different techniques have in the past been utilized in an attempt to measure the suggestibility variable, and unfortunately there is evidence (291, 90) that the intercorrelations among such techniques tend to be low. Even if it be granted that there is no unitary trait of suggestibility, however, the fact remains that subjects do differ markedly in their acceptance of unreasonable propositions and courses of action relative to given individual tasks. We anticipated that the high Barrier person would show less acceptance of unreasonable propositions over a range of tasks than the low Barrier person would.

We were able to test this hypothesis quite directly in terms of a study which had been completed by Ira Steisel * (291). Steisel was interested in the relationship between presumed Rorschach indices of suggestibility and a number of other indices of suggestibility based on behavioral data. We determined the Barrier index for each Rorschach he had collected, and thus each subject's Barrier score could be compared with his several suggestibility scores. In outlining the procedures used by Steisel to measure suggestibility, it is probably best to quote at length from the descriptions which appear in his paper (p. 608):

> Because of the several quite different properties that may be designated by the term, it would seem most wise in studying the relationships between Rorscharch variables and suggestibility to use different measures of that variable. The following tests, the majority of which have been used by previous investigators, were employed in the present study:

---

* We gratefully acknowledge Dr. Steisel's permission to use his data.

1. The Postural-Sway Test. This test was designed by Hull [154] in 1929 and has been used by a number of later investigators [cf. 90, 89, 213]. The apparatus permits the recording of movements of an individual who is initially told to stand still with his eyes closed (or blindfolded) and has repeated to him the suggestion that he is falling forward. The extent of the resultant movement is taken as the index of the subject's suggestibility. Eysenck has indicated that this is the best single measure of what he has termed 'primary suggestibility' (ideomotor).

2. The "Ink-blot Suggestion Test." This test was described by Eysenck and Furneaux [89]. In their study a Rorschach card was shown to each subject and he was presented with two "common responses" and four "inapplicable" responses with the comment that "some people think it looks like that." Each subject was asked if he could see something resembling those percepts in the figures. The authors indicate that the number of such percepts accepted by the subject was his suggestibility score. They further indicate that this is the best index of "secondary suggestibility" (gullibility).

3. Three measures derived from two autokinetic situations were used. The work of Sherif [281], Bray [46], Kelman [168], and Bovard [45] indicates that the apparent movement of a pinpoint of light in an otherwise totally dark room might be utilized to investigate personality processes and social psychological phenomena. They found that, in general, the average extent of movement reported by a subject, when in the situation alone, could be altered to conform to a group average or an average supplied by a planted subject with prestige in a retest situation.

Although Sherif and Bovard do not speak of the obtained measures in terms of suggestibility, they do speak of the individual as accepting social norms. The results of their studies, however, indicate that some measures obtained from the autokinetic situation might be indicative of the degree of suggestibility of an individual.

The subjects used by Steisel were fifty students in an introductory psychology course. Only subjects who gave a minimum of fifteen scorable Rorschach responses and who had no marked physical handicaps were included. Thirty of the subjects were males and twenty were females. It would be well to quote further from Steisel concerning the exact procedures used in the experiment:

> Immediately following the administration of the Rorschach, the "Ink-blot Suggestion Test" was given. Inasmuch as Eysenck and Furneaux [89] did not indicate what specific percepts were used in their study, it was decided to use two popular percepts from Beck's list [18] for the "common" responses. In no case was a percept used in this test that had been given by S during the free association period to the Rorschach cards. On showing each card E said, "Some

people think this looks like a ———. Do you think it resembles that?"

Immediately following this, E and S proceeded to the room in which the autokinetic apparatus was located. —After S was seated in the room and had become dark-adapted the instructions were read. Except for a few minor modifications they were the same as those used by Sherif. Probably the most important change was that S was informed that the light would move anywhere from 1 to 15 inches. Fifty trials were given, the reported amount of movement and the response latencies (time taken to indicate the perception of movement) being recorded for each trial.

After this was completed, S was excused from the room on the pretext that the apparatus needed adjustment. While S was gone E calculated the mean of judgments, determined the *planted* mean (the mean of the estimate that E was to provide in the second situation) and listed all of the scores that he was to give in the retest situation. On the basis of preliminary experimentation, it was decided that the planted mean would deviate 50 percent from the mean estimate made by S in the first situation. For 26 S's (those S's whose initial mean estimates were under 5 inches) this planted mean was higher than the original mean; for 24 S's (those whose mean estimates were greater than fives inches) it was lower. Thus, the attempt was made to influence a lowering of estimates in those S's who gave relatively large responses in the first situation and to raise the scores of those whose estimates were relatively small.

The S was then recalled to the experimental room and was told that the same procedure would be followed as previously, with the exception that E would announce, on each trial, the actual distance traversed by the light. On odd-numbered trials E made his statements first and on even-numbered trials S made his estimates first. The E's estimates were in whole numbers and scattered narrowly around the planted mean. After 50 estimates were obtained from the S, he was again excused from the room. At this point the postural-sway apparatus was set-up.

Upon returning to the experimental room, S was asked to stand with his back to the apparatus while the goggles were fitted. He then was moved until the heated stylus was approximately 2 inches from the back edge of the paper. He was told to stand still, erect, and with his feet together. At the end of the half-minute (baseline) period, E suggested that S was falling forward. Except for minor modifications, the procedure employed was the same as that used by Hull [155, p. 50]. The suggestion was given repeatedly throughout a period of two minutes, during which continuous records were taken of S's bodily position."

Three suggestibility scores derived by Steisel were compared with the Barrier scores.

TABLE 4:3 CHI-SQUARE TESTS OF DIFFERENCES IN SUGGESTIBILITY
SCORES BETWEEN HIGH BARRIER AND LOW BARRIER SUBJECTS

Suggestibility Measures	Group with Lowest Score	χ^2	Level of Significance
Ink-blot Suggestion Test	H.B.[a]	3.9	.05–.02
Postural-sway Test	H.B.	4.1	.05–.02
Autokinetic[b]	L.B.	3.1	.10–.05

[a] H.B.—Above median Barrier scorers. L.B.—Below median Barrier scorers.

[b] This autokinetic index is explained by Steisel (291, p. 611) as indicating: "The degree of correspondence between the S's revised mean estimate of movement (in the second autokinetic session) and the planted mean. In those instances where the planted mean was higher than S's initial mean, this autokinetic ratio was calculated as follows:

$$\frac{M_r - M_o}{M_p - M_o}$$ (where M_o stands for the original mean, M_r stands for the revised mean; and M_p stands for the planted mean)

In those instances where M_p was lower than the initial estimate (M_o), M_r was subtracted from M_o (in the numerator) and M_p was subtracted from M_o (in the denominator) to obtain the ratio. Values ranging from zero (no change in estimates and, therefore, a minimum amount of suggestibility) to values greater than one (indicating a large shift in estimate and a high degree of suggestibility) were theoretically possible."

Table 4:3 indicates that high Barrier subjects were significantly less accepting of inappropriate blot percepts than were low Barrier subjects. The difference is significant at the .05–.02 level. Similarly, the high Barrier subjects showed significantly less sway in response to suggestion than did the low Barrier subjects.* This difference was significant at the .05–.02 level.

Quite different findings were obtained with the autokinetic measure of suggestibility. The low Barrier individuals responded less to the planted suggestion than did the high Barrier individuals. The difference did not attain the .05 level of significance, however. In the process of analyzing this trend which is in the reverse direction from the results given by the other two suggestibility measures, we found that during the first autokinetic session (preceding the session in which a planted mean was introduced) 80 per cent of the high Barrier subjects fell below the median of total reported autokinetic movement. Only 56 per cent of the low Barrier group fell below this median. This indicates that

* Steisel describes the scoring of the Postural-Sway data as follows (291, p. 611): "A baseline was drawn midway between the highest and lowest points in the initial half-minute period, before the suggestion instructions were read. The maximum sway in centimeters, either forward or backward, from this baseline was taken as the sway score for the individual."

there was a tendency (not significant) for high Barrier individuals to perceive less autokinetic movement than low Barrier persons. Therefore, more of the high Barrier than low Barrier subjects must have been subjected to suggestion requiring an *increase* in amount of perceived movement, whereas more low than high Barrier subjects must have been exposed to suggestion to decrease amount of perceived movement. The basic question then arises whether it is easier to produce increase or decrease in perceived autokinetic movement by suggestion. The answer is unknown. But in any case it is clear that the high Barrier and low Barrier subjects were exposed to different types of demands during the autokinetic suggestion period. Consequently, the results obtained for this task cannot be considered to be meaningful.

What is in the forefront of the total results is the fact that the high Barrier subjects are significantly less suggestible in terms of two measures than are the low Barrier subjects. This strongly supports still another aspect of the predictions that have been made concerning the relationship of boundary definiteness to self-steering behavior.

ANGER-OUT VERSUS ANGER-IN

The manner in which the individual deals with angry impulses can tell a great deal about his ability to be self-steering. It is usually in situations of stress and frustration that anger is aroused; and often in such situations there is a conflict between wanting to express the anger in an aggressive self-determined fashion and fear of the consequences of being aggressive. If the individual shows himself able to deal with angry feelings by taking an active aggressive attitude toward the outer world, he is demonstrating the ability to be self-steering under conditions of crisis and strong feeling. The individual who reacts to frustration simply by becoming anxious or blaming himself is adopting an orientation quite the opposite of what one would associate with a life style built around active mastery and structuring of the environment. It would therefore follow that one would expect the person with well-differentiated body-image boundaries to be more oriented toward expression of anger outward against frustrating figures than would persons with less well-defined boundaries.

An opportunity for studying this hypothesis was provided by data previously collected by Funkenstein, King, and Drolette (117A).° They intensively studied a group of sixty-nine Harvard students selected by means of psychological tests, psychiatric interviews, and stress-inducing

---

° We gratefully acknowledge the cooperation of Dr. King and Dr. Funkenstein in making these data available to us.

situations. The individual Rorschach test was among other tests administered to each student. One of the stress-inducing situations to which
the students were subjected was designed to be sharply frustrating and
to elicit strong feelings of anger. This stress situation was incorporated
into a total procedure involving the measurement of various physiological reactions. Consequently each subject was being studied for certain
physiological responses during the course of the period that he was subjected to frustration. The exact procedure involved in the study was as
follows (p. 405):

> The subject was brought into the experimental room, familiar from
> previous nonfrustrating visits, and he was asked to lie on a wooden
> table. He was allowed to rest for at least 20 minutes so that his
> blood pressure might reach a stable level. The experimenter then
> obtained two blood pressure and two ballistocardiograph readings
> at one-minute intervals, after which he gave the following directions:
> "As you know, this machine (the ballistocardiograph) measures
> how much blood your heart pumps and we want to find out if
> your heart pumps more blood when you think. I'm going to give
> you some problems to do in your head so that we can see what
> effect this has on your heart."
> The experimenter then read at a fairly rapid rate a series of 6
> to 10 digits which the subject was required to repeat. (The material
> for this situation, both digit series and problems, was taken from
> Wells and Ruesch). The subject was then asked to repeat each digit
> series backward after the experimenter had finished. Most subjects
> were able to repeat the digits-forward series, so that they began the
> session with successes. Most of them had trouble, however, with
> the longer series of digits-backward and made mistakes. At this
> point the experimenter made remarks such as, "That's not right,"
> or "You missed that one," in an exasperated tone. As the subject
> continued to have difficulty, the experimenter would say, "You
> aren't doing too well on these, let's see what you can do on some
> problems." He then gave a simple problem such as "If 4 pounds of
> beans cost 20 cents, how many pounds can you get for 80 cents?"
> Next came more difficult problems such as, "If 4 men can build a
> house in 6 days, how long would it take 3 men to do it?" On this
> problem most of the subjects gave an answer of less than 6, pro-
> viding an opportunity for the experimenter to retort, "You mean to
> say that 3 men can do it in less time than 4 men? Come on now,
> you know that's not right, you can do better than that!"

About ten minutes after the subject experienced this frustrating situation, he was interviewed and encouraged to describe the feelings and
thoughts he had while being given the problems. This interview was
recorded.

Independent raters then evaluated the recorded material and decided for each subject whether his reaction to the frustration had been marked primarily by anxiety, by anger directed outward against the experimenter, or by anger directed inward in a self-blaming fashion.

Our prediction was focused on the differentiation of subjects showing the anger-in reaction and those characterized by the anger-out response. We anticipated that high Barrier individuals would predominate in the anger-out group and low Barrier individuals in the anger-in group. The Rorschach records of twenty-one anger-out subjects and twenty-one anger-in subjects were available to us. When we scored them for the Barrier variable, we found that the two groups were significantly differentiated in the predicted direction. Thirteen of the twenty-one anger-out group were in the above median Barrier category, whereas only six of the twenty-one in the anger-in group obtained above median Barrier scores. The χ^2 value for this distribution is 5.6 which is significant at the .02–.01 level. Thus, the findings support the hypothesis proposed.

ORIENTATION TOWARD SELF-GRATIFICATION

Another facet of the predictions stemming from the self-steering concept has to do with self-gratification. Our formulations concerning the individual with well-differentiated boundaries suggest that he would be oriented toward self-gratification when adequate opportunities for such gratification presented themselves. The high Barrier person would seek opportunities to supply himself with what he wants. Perhaps another way of phrasing this point would be to say that when the high Barrier person has needs he will take advantage of them. His personality structure will be characterized by relatively few tendencies to deny himself satisfaction when there is reasonable opportunity to attain such satisfaction. The low Barrier person would then be conceptualized as one who, even in the midst of opportunity for self-gratification, is so conflicted that he finds it difficult to permit himself a direct course to such gratification. The low Barrier person would find it hard to perceive himself as an independent being that has a right to do things for himself and by himself. At a later point a detailed examination of the possible personality dynamics which might underlie this type of difference between high and low Barrier individuals will be undertaken (see Chapter 9).

A projective question technique was devised to compare high and low Barrier subjects with regard to their orientation toward self-gratification. Two questions were constructed which posed situations of maximum and unusual opportunity for self-gratification; and subjects were asked to indicate what they would do in these situations. The two questions* were as follows:

(1) If you had one month left to live, how would you spend this time remaining to you?

(2) If you had an unlimited amount of money, what would you do with it?

Both questions place the subject in hypothetical situations in which many of the restraints imposed by reality on self-gratification have been minimized. In the first question, the subject is provided with license for all kinds of special self-gratification by virtue of the common sentiment that if a person has only a limited amount of time left to live he has a right to indulge himself in all sorts of exceptional ways. In the second question, the subject is provided with the extraordinary opportunity of obtaining all those forms of gratification that are usually blocked because of lack of money. Thus the two questions together present the subject with a situation in which he may fantasy extremes of self-gratification. The limitations he imposes on such gratification could then be considered to be a function of his own inhibitions rather than of outside limiting factors.

The projective questions were administered to a group of thirty-seven women and one man who were taking a summer-school graduate course in group leadership techniques. The great majority of the group were schoolteachers. Their median age was thirty-five years. The projective questions were read aloud to them in a group situation and they wrote out their answers. Previous to their response to these questions they were all given the group Rorschach, which had been modified so as to obtain a fixed number of responses.

The replies to the projective questions were all differentiated on a blind basis into two broad categories. One category included those statements which explicitly involved self-gratification and self-satisfaction. The following are examples of statements falling into the category:

"I have always wanted to go to Europe. I would take that trip—going by boat."

"I would buy a new home, furnish it with good furniture, and give my children a good home."

"I would get on a freighter bound for South America and spend the time in as leisurely as possible travel. I would read as many books as I had time."

"I would go to Columbia and get my Ph.D. Then, I would travel in a cream-colored Cadillac convertible and a yacht."

---

* These questions are similar to a number which were used by Frenkel-Brunswik (5) and her group to study the authoritarian personality.

"I would travel over parts of the world until I got tired of traveling. Then I would sit down and relax until I thought of something I wanted to do."

A second category included all those answers which do not explicitly involve self-gratification. Here are some typical statements falling into this category:

"I would do as much as I could for others in making others happy."

"I would set up a foundation which would help people live happier, fuller, more complete, more useful lives."

"If I had one month to live I would like to do things to create happiness for others and forget myself in doing these things."

"If I had an unlimited amount of money, I'd like to spend it in bettering human relations in general—community, state, nation, and over the world."

"I would try to do something that I thought would be pleasing to God, and prepare in some way for the future of my child."

"If I had an unlimited amount of money, I would donate to charities and locate needy families and help them individually."

Actually, most of the answers falling into the second category tended to be self-denying and self-depriving to the point of asceticism.

A nonparametric Median test analysis of the data indicated that the results were significantly in the predicted direction. Table 4:4 shows

TABLE 4:4   CHI-SQUARE TESTS OF DIFFERENCES IN RESPONSE TO THE PROJECTIVE QUESTIONS

Questions	Group with Greater Number of Self-gratifying Answers	χ^2	Level of Significance
1	High Barrier	4.7	.05–.02
2	High Barrier	3.3	.10–.05
1 + 2[a]	High Barrier	6.4	.02–.01

[a] Subjects giving a self-gratifying reply to Questions 1 and 2 were scored as self-gratifying, but subjects giving only one or no self-gratifying answers were placed in the non-self-satisfying category.

that for question 1 the above-median Barrier subjects gave significantly more self-gratifying replies than did the below-median subjects. The same pattern of results was obtained for question 2, except that the difference was only of borderline reliability (.10–.05). As a further part of the analysis of the data, the subjects were categorized into those giving self-gratifying answers to both questions versus those giving self-gratifying answers to only one or none of the questions. Table 4:4 indicates that a significantly greater proportion of above-median Barrier subjects gave self-gratifying answers to both questions than did the below-median Barrier individuals. The difference was significant at the .02–.01 level.

It is interesting to compare qualitatively the answers given by the high and low Barrier subjects. As one reads over the themes of the high Barrier people, one is struck by the zestful and almost excited way in which they anticipate doing self-satisfying things which have previously been out of their reach. There is an air of good humor and release about the way in which they phrase their reactions to the questions. The low Barrier people, however, tend to take a grim, stiffly serious attitude toward the questions. They seem to be made anxious by the opportunity afforded them. Their answers are somewhat defensive and apparently intended to convey a sentiment that might be paraphrased as follows: "I am not selfish. I don't think of myself first. I would think of myself last. I would be public-spirited and do things for others before I allowed myself to have anything." It may be said, then, that both quantitatively and qualitatively the results support the position that firm body-image boundaries are linked with relatively greater ability to gratify oneself in situations where the opportunity is afforded.

MODE OF REACTION TO STRESS SITUATIONS

As indicated earlier, the real test of one's ability to be self-steering occurs in stress situations. It is not difficult for many individuals to maintain an appearance of mastery and forcefulness when they are in easy circumstances; but when problems and complications develop which are threatening, there is a considerable reduction in the number that are able to show mastery behavior. Our model of the high Barrier individuals suggests that he would have particularly good facility for maintaining his equilibrium in the midst of stress. His well-defined boundaries provide him with protection and a base of operations, as it were. The low Barrier person would, on the contrary, be expected to be vulnerable to stress and to find it difficult to maintain his own course through the complications and confusion associated with the stress. It would follow, then, that high Barrier people should show better performance on stress tasks than low Barrier people.

It is not a simple matter to test this hypothesis because there are different concepts of what constitutes a stress and of what methods are best for evaluating reactions to stress (343, 338, 57). Stress has been defined in the pertinent literature as being produced by such varying conditions as a painful electric shock, hostile criticism, failure at assigned tasks, deprivation of sleep, etc. Reactions to stress have also been variously measured: in terms of decline in performance, overt signs of distress, and physiological indices. We have sought to deal with this profusion of definitions by using multiple methods and criteria. That is, we have tested the hypothesis concerning the relationship of body-image boundaries to ability to deal with stress by evaluating it in a number of stress settings. These various settings will now be considered in turn.

S A M   P S E U D O S C O P E

One of the stress techniques we used involved the SAM Pseudoscope which is basically a mirror-drawing task. This stress task was developed in the course of the Air Force research program on selection (153). It requires subjects to trace a pattern under conditions of 180 degrees rotation of the visual field. It is administered with instructions to achieve maximum accuracy and speed. Its stressful aspects are maximized by exposing subjects to flashing red illumination and vibrations of the tracing surface while they are attempting to trace the pattern. Performance is evaluated in terms of two scores. One reflects speed (total time to complete the tracing) and one reflects accuracy (total time spent in making errors). Errors occurred whenever the subject deviated from the pattern he was to trace and made contact with the sides of the pattern. Accumulative times "on target" and "error" are electrically recorded.

Holtzman[*] and Bitterman (153) had collected data by means of the Pseudoscope which we were able to use to test our hypothesis. These data were obtained from ninety cadets in an Air Force ROTC unit at the University of Texas who were also intensively evaluated with a variety of other measures. They were told that they were participating in a study which was part of a larger Air Force research project on the selection of flying personnel. It was pointed out to them that the results would not influence their standing in the service. Among other tests they had taken was the SAM Ink-blot Test, a group-administered form of the Rorschach, which permits subjects to respond to the usual individual Rorschach plates rather than to the blot image projected onto a screen. That is, each subject in the group situation is given his own set of Rorschach cards. The Rorschach responses obtained in this way were scored by us for the Barrier index. All responses over twenty-five were eliminated by the fixed method previously described.

The Pseudoscope behavior of the subjects above and below the Barrier median was compared by use of the nonparametric Median test. This comparison was made in terms of total time and also in terms of error time. The above- and below-median Barrier subjects did not differ at all so far as the total time measure was concerned. The error time score, however, differentiated the two groups in the predicted direction

---

[*] We sincerely thank Dr. Holtzman for the use of these data.

at better than the .01 level ($\chi^2 = 7.4$). The high Barrier subjects were quite obviously superior to the low Barrier subjects in their ability to deal with this stress task. It should be parenthetically noted that the median Rorschach response total of the high Barrier group was not significantly different from the median response total of the low Barrier group; and so one cannot attribute the difference in performance between these two groups to factors related to Rorschach productivity.

There is an important difficulty in interpreting the significance of the difference in stress performance of these two body-image-boundary groups. This difference was one of seven significant differences found in an exploratory comparison of the Barrier score with about forty other scores which had been obtained from the ROTC group by Holtzman and Bitterman. Despite the high level of significance of the individual difference, it might be viewed as a chance result. In order to check this possibility, a cross-validation study was undertaken with a body of mirror-drawing data which had been collected by Sells.[*]

Sells obtained mirror drawings of a star pattern from sixty air cadets. He also obtained the previously described SAM Rorschach protocols from these air cadets. Barrier scores were determined by us from the protocols. We reduced all records over twenty-five responses to twenty-five responses by means of our set reduction procedure. In addition, all records below twenty-five responses were eliminated from the study. This resulted in thirteen subjects being dropped. It was necessary to do this in order to equalize the Rorschach response total in the above-median and below-median Barrier groups. Two indices of performance on the mirror-drawing task were utilized. One was total time to complete the task. The other was the total number of times the subject touched the sides of the pattern in the course of tracing through it. The path taken by each subject in the pattern had been registered by his tracing pencil on the printed pattern which he had been viewing in a mirror. Thus, each pattern could be evaluated in terms of the number of times the pencil line wavered and touched its sides. This score might be considered roughly equivalent to the error score mentioned in the first SAM Pseudoscope study.

The Barrier score proved to have only a chance relationship to the total time score, as defined by the Median test. However, the Median test indicated that subjects with above-median Barrier scores made significantly fewer errors than subjects with below-median Barrier scores. The χ^2 value was 4.4 which is significant at the .05–.02 level. The lack of relationship of the Barrier score to the time score and its significant

---

[*] We gratefully acknowledge the aid of Dr. Saul Sells and Dr. David Trites in making these data available.

relationship to the error score duplicates the results obtained with the SAM Pseudoscope. The results of the first described Pseudoscope study did stand up under cross-validation.

HAND STEADINESS ASPIRATION TASK

A second technique was also used to check the hypothesis concerning the relationship between body-image boundaries and ability to deal with stress. This technique induces stress by permitting subjects to succeed very well at a task and then causing them to fail very badly. Data embodying such success-failure methodology was available from an earlier study carried out by Fisher (97). Among others, twenty normal women participated in the study. Of this number nine were student occupational therapists; five were student nurses; two were student social workers; and four were stenographers employed in a hospital setting. The age range was from twenty to forty-five years, with the majority falling in the twenties. Each subject was individually seen and asked to perform a series of tasks on a hand-steadiness apparatus which is a modification of that described by Dunlap (83).

It consists of a series of eleven equally spaced holes of decreasing diameters drilled near the periphery of a circular brass plate which can be rotated. The brass plate is mounted on a stand and is about chest level for a subject in a sitting position. A stylus about 15 inches long is fixed in front of the plate so that its tip is inserted in the third smallest hole. This stylus is on a pivot which allows it to move freely in any direction. The subject holds the stylus with his favored hand in any way he finds most comfortable. The apparatus appears to be connected to a counter, but actually is not. Consequently scores can be reported to a subject arbitrarily as the experimenter desires.

The instructions to the subjects are: "This is a test to see how steady you can hold your hand and also to find out how well you can estimate your own ability to do things. With your eyes closed try to hold this rod in the middle of the hole as steady as you can. At the end of each trial I will tell you how many times you actually touched the sides of the hole. Then, you will try to estimate in advance the number of times you will touch it on the next trial." The subject is then given a practice trial for thirty seconds with her eyes closed. After the practice trial, ten regular trials are run. Before each trial the subject estimates what she expects to achieve; and at the end of the trial an arbitrary score, and yet one reasonable in terms of the possible achievement score, is reported to her. Following the first trial and for three further successive trials, the subject is permitted to improve her performance progressively in terms of a predetermined pattern. But for the remainder of the trials the subject is told, following each of her performances, that she has done more poorly than she predicted. Arbitrary scores which become progressively poorer are reported to her. The decline is in terms of a predetermined pattern and yet reasonable when considered relative to the previous achievement score.

It was assumed that the subject's degree of disturbance in the face of repeated failure would be reflected in her inability to adjust her achievement estimates to the progressive decline in achievement actually reported to her. One would anticipate that the subject who was most distressed by her failures would seek to deny them by unrealistically maintaining her estimates of performance at the high level they were during the period that she was allowed to succeed. A simple index of such inability to readjust achievement estimates was developed. The index is equal to the difference between the last estimate made under conditions of success and the last estimate made under conditions of failure. A large difference indicates that the subject lowered her estimates as she encountered failure, whereas a small difference indicates that she could not successfully adjust to her failures. When a chi-square test was applied to the difference between above-median and below-median Barrier subjects in this respect, the result was significant in the predicted direction at the .05–.02 level ($\chi^2 = 5.0$). The high Barrier subjects adjusted more realistically to the stressful failure situation than did the low Barrier individuals.

DIGIT SYMBOL DECREMENT

A particularly popular model for studying stress effects involves measuring subjects' Wechsler-Bellevue Digit Symbol performance under non-stress conditions and then obtaining repeat measures of their performance when they are stressed. Degree of decrement or nondecrement in retest scores is used as an index of reaction to the stress. Interest in this method of studying stress effects was stimulated initially by Williams (343) who reported significant correlations between decrement in Digit Symbol performance and several Rorschach indices (e.g., F+ on all cards and F+ on colored cards only). His results suggested that goodness of Digit Symbol performance under stress was correlated with good stable controls such as are presumed to be associated with high F+.

A number of researchers (57, 338) sought to check his results by exposing subjects to stress conditions similar to those he created and noting how the resulting decrements in performance correlated with various Rorschach scores and also other scores (e.g., Taylor Anxiety Scale). By and large, such studies have tended not to confirm Williams' clear-cut findings. Indeed, one of the outgrowths of such studies has been the observation that stress conditions may produce very complex effects on Digit Symbol performance. Thus on one occasion it is observed to decrease the effectiveness of subjects who are considered to be anxious or poorly adjusted in terms of some criterion (338). On another occasion it is observed to facilitate the effectiveness of these subjects and detract from subjects who are judged to be better adjusted (57). In attempting to account for such variations in results, it has been conjectured that within some experimental settings the stress situation is so relatively non-ego-involving that really stable subjects do not respond to it and are not incited to overcome the distracting effect it has on their performance. As a result they do more poorly than they did under nonstress conditions. However, the less stable subject with his low threshold for disturbance is threatened by the relatively non-ego-involving stress and is motivated to do his best to deal with it. He consequently does relatively better under the stress condition than the less threatened stable subject. In still other experimental settings all the subjects apparently experience the stress situation as very ego-involving and threatening. The stable subject copes with the threat effectively and performs well, whereas the less stable subject is so strongly threatened that his performance is disrupted and he does poorly.

Data from two Digit Symbol studies[*] with such contrasting results were available to us and we were able to analyze them in terms of our body-image frame of reference. In one of these studies Westrope (338) had found that a high anxiety group tended to show more decrement under stress than did a low anxiety group. This tendency was not strictly significant but closely approached the five per cent level. In a second study carried out by Carlson and Lazarus (57) it had been found that subjects who were most neurotic in terms of the Winne Neuroticism Scale (345) showed less decrement under stress than those subjects who obtained less neurotic scores. The Rorschach had been administered to subjects in both Westrope's and Carlson and Lazarus' studies; and we scored them in the usual fashion for the Barrier index. Therefore, the relationship of the Barrier score to Digit Symbol decrement under two conditions of stress which had produced rather different patterns of effect in the respective experimental populations could be evaluated.

Westrope Study. Westrope's project involved two groups, each consisting of twenty-four college students (twelve men and twelve women). One group (anxious) was selected from a larger class and included only individuals scoring in the upper 20 per cent of the distribution of Taylor Anxiety scores of a normative group of 2,000 students. The second group (nonanxious) included only individuals in the lower 20 per cent of the distribution.

---

[*] We gratefully acknowledge the kindness of Dr. Martha R. Westrope and Dr. Virgil R. Carlson for permitting us to use the data from their respective studies.

Westrope describes the procedures she used for evaluating reaction to stress in these terms (p. 516–517):

> . . . the experiment was divided into the following parts: (a) Rorschach administration; (b) a training session consisting of practice on the Digit Symbol test, designed to bring Ss to a stable level of performance under non-stress conditions; and (c) a stress period designed to obtain measures of performance on the Digit Symbol test under stress conditions. The above procedures were carried out in two separate sessions separated by a 20–48-hour interval as follows:

Session I

    Rorschach administration
    5-minute rest interval
    7 practice trials, Digit Symbol test

Session II

    5 practice trials, Digit Symbol test
    3-minute rest intervals
    3 trials, Digit Symbol test (control)
    S taken to another room and given stress instructions
    3 trials, Digit Symbol test (stress).

The modified Wechsler-Bellevue Digit Symbol test was administered with the usual 90-second time allowance per trial and a 60-second rest interval between trials. This test represents a modification of the original Wechsler-Bellevue test which consisted of 67 items. Williams modified the latter by repeating the 43 items. Since a preliminary investigation indicated that 110 items were not sufficient for some Ss, 66 additional items selected by using a table of random numbers was added, making a total of 176 items.

Immediately following the last control trial of the training session (Trial 15) each S was taken into another room where three persons introduced as psychologists were seated before a one-way screen. A camera, mounted on a tripod, was in a prominent position against the screen. The remaining apparatus, consisting of a phonograph, an amplifier, a shocking device in series with a variac connected to the 115-volt 60 cycle A.C. supply line, and interval timers for the presentation of light and electric-shock stimuli were placed on a table just to the left of the screen.

The use of the one-way screen was described and S was then taken into an adjoining room on the other side of the one-way screen and seated at a table directly in front of the screen. Mimeographed Digit Symbol test blanks, pencils, electrodes mounted on a leather strap, and a small panel containing a red and a white light rested on the table. This room was in complete darkness with the exception of two #1 Photoflood lamps focused directly on the S. The E attached electrodes to the palm and back of the S's nonpreferred hand and then returned to the observation room.

Instructions for the remainder of the stress period had been previously recorded and were presented by means of the amplifying system. The S was told that: he was being observed by the psychologists who were taking notes and continuous photographs of his behavior; if his performance was not satisfactory, he might receive an electric shock; the flashing of the white light would indicate the shocking apparatus was *on* and the flashing of the red light would indicate his performance was substandard and that he was in danger of being shocked. The lights and shock were then demonstrated.

At the beginning of each trial the white light flashed on. Five seconds later the red light went on and remained on until five seconds after the end of the 90-second trial. At this point a shock of one second's duration was given and both lights went off.

The Digit Symbol test was scored by counting the number of items correctly marked (no half-scores were given). An average decrement score on the Digit Symbol test taken under stress was determined for each individual by subtracting his average score on the three Digit Symbol stress trials from his average score on the last three training trials (control period).

When the Barrier scores and average Digit Symbol decrement scores of the total group were related, it was found that the above-median Barrier individuals tended to show lower decrement scores than the below-median Barrier individuals. As defined by a chi-square test, the difference fell at the .20–.10 level of significance. When the results from the men and women subjects were separately analyzed, the difference in the women's group fell in the same direction but attained only the .50–.30 significance level. The difference in the men's group, however, was very close to strict statistical significance (.10–.05 level). The trend of these results is analogous to Westrope's in that the subjects with high Barrier scores (whom we consider to be particularly self-steering and stable) did better than low Barrier subjects whom we consider to be on the less stable side.

Carlson and Lazarus Study. Twenty-five white male college students constituted the subjects for this study. The experimental procedure whereby their stress reactions were investigated is described as follows (57, pp. 247–248):

> In the first session the subjects were given the Rorschach test.
> . . . After a five-minute rest period, five 90-second trials were given
> on the Wechsler-Bellevue Digit Symbol test with a one-minute break

between trials. Each subject was told that the Digit-Symbol test is part of a standard test of intelligence, and he was encouraged to do as well as possible.

The second session occurred a day or two later. The subject was first given six more practice trials on the Digit-Symbol test. Again one-minute rest periods intervened between successive trials, and a three-minute rest period was interpolated between the third and fourth trials. The last three of these practice trials were designated the "control period" and constituted an estimate of the subject's non-stress performance. Then the subject was taken immediately to another room for three more Digit-Symbol trials under the stress conditions.

The stress conditions to which the subject was exposed were essentially like those described by Westrope. Following the stress period each subject was asked to fill out the Winne Neuroticism Scale. A stress decrement index was calculated for each subject which was equal to the difference between the mean of the control period of performance and the mean of the stress period of performance. A chi-square analysis of the relationship of these stress decrement scores to Barrier scores indicated that above-median Barrier individuals tended to show high decrement and below-median Barrier individuals to show low decrement. The result was significant at the 5 per cent level. This finding is analogous to the Carlson and Lazarus finding that improvement under stress correlated +.54 with scores on the Winne Neuroticism Scale. Subjects showing a greater degree of anxiety or neuroticism on the inventory tended to show more improvement during the stress trials.

The reversal in relationship of the Barrier score to stress decrement in the Carlson-Lazarus data as compared to the Westrope data suggests that the Barrier score is a versatile complex indicator of reaction to stress. Where stress decrement is associated with apparent personality instability, it gives one type of result; and where decrement may be presumed to be a function of not being easily threatened, it gives quite an opposite result. When these results are considered in conjunction with the results from the SAM Pseudoscope and the Hand Steadiness test, there is a pretty good pattern of confirmation of the basic hypothesis concerning the relationship of the Barrier score to ability to deal effectively with stress.

REACTION TO STRESS ASSOCIATED WITH POLIOMYELITIS

The stress situations which have been described up to this point are all a function of artificial laboratory conditions. That is, the subjects were stressed by exposing them to discomfort or embarrassment growing out of an artificial situation created by the experimenter. As long as one relies on such artificial stress techniques, one can never be certain about how ego-involving the situation will become for any particular subject. Some subjects may experience the situation as little more than slightly discomforting. They do not take a laboratory situation seriously. It is probably only in real life settings that one finds crises which can with great certainty be considered stressful to all who experience them.

Every individual who becomes infected with poliomyelitis and who is hospitalized for treatment of this disease is undoubtedly exposed to conditions of tremendous stress. He is faced with possible death, with severe physical incapacitation, with separation from his family and friends, and with inability to care for himself. Can the individual's reaction to this sort of stress be predicted from the Barrier score? Kenneth Ware (324) in collaboration with the writers attempted to answer this question. The Barrier score of each of fifty-nine patients was determined from protocols which had been obtained by individual examination. Only those patients were studied who gave at least fifteen Rorschach responses. Furthermore, all records over twenty-five responses were cut down to twenty-five by the set reduction method. In this way the influence of response total upon the Barrier scores could be considerably controlled.

The criterion used for evaluating how the patient adjusted to the hospital stress situation were ratings by various hospital personnel. Thirty-two of the patients were rated by three staff physicians and a psychologist who divided them into a "poorly adjusting" group and a "well adjusting" group. These raters knew each patient intimately as the result of months of observation. Three of the four raters agreed in their evaluations of twenty-eight patients. In only four cases did the raters split evenly in their disagreement. These four cases were dropped from the study. Generally the raters showed high agreement in their judgments concerning the adjustment level of the patients.

The adjustment level of the remaining group of twenty-eight patients was rated by a social worker. Her ratings were originally made on a nine-point continuum, but for purposes of the present study were dichotomized into "good" and "poor" adjustment. Her ratings actually represented a summary indication of what she felt to be the consensus of the hospital staff members about each given patient. She was familiar with their opinions as the result of participation in many staff meetings in which the progress of all patients was discussed.

Before determining the relationship of the patients' Barrier scores to their hospital adjustment scores, an analysis was made of several variables which might have had a complicating influence in interpreting any results obtained. First of all, the relationship of Rorschach response total to Barrier score was checked by means of a chi-square test and found to be of a chance order. Secondly, the Barrier score was related to length of period intervening between time of development of acute symptoms and time at which Rorschach was administered. This relationship also proved to be of a chance order. Finally, the Barrier scores of the fifteen patients in the group considered to have the most serious physical disabilities were compared with the fifteen considered to have the minimum of physical disability. Chi square indicated a chance relationship between the variables. Apparently, then, the Barrier scores of these polio patients were not a function of response total, or of point in the illness sequence that the Rorschach was administered, or of the actual degree of physical disablement present.

In the patient group whose hospital adjustment level had been rated by three physicians and a psychologist, the Barrier score tended to differentiate significantly in the predicted direction those who adjusted well to their illness and those who adjusted poorly. The χ^2 was 4.0 which is significant at the .05–.01 level. In the patient group rated by the social worker the findings were likewise significantly in the predicted direction. The χ^2 was 5.3 which is significant at the .05–.01 level. When the two subject groups were combined into a total group of fifty-six patients, the chi-square test indicated that the Barrier score differentiated the well-adjusted from the poorly adjusted at the .01 level ($\chi^2 = 9.2$). These results are clear-cut in their indication that the individual with definite boundaries adjusts better to the stress of a serious illness than does the individual with relatively indefinite boundaries.

PERCEPTUAL STABILITY

One of the more speculative hypotheses we ventured on the basis of the self-steering model was that ability to maintain a realistic orientation in unstructured perceptual situations would be linked with degree of boundary definiteness. It is obvious that in an unstructured perceptual situation the individual loses the guidance of many of the cues upon which he ordinarily depends. He has few "outside" clues upon which to found his judgments, and is therefore maximally thrown back upon his own internalized standards. Thus, an individual who is placed in a room so dark that all visual cues are obscured and who is asked to adjust a luminous rod to the vertical is forced to make the adjustment on the basis of his own individualized frame of reference. We presumed that in this sort of situation the high Barrier person would probably have an advantage over the low Barrier person. If the high Barrier person does indeed have a special ability for independent action and for following a course based on his own specifications, would this ability not facilitate his adjustment in a poorly defined perceptual situation? Would he not be better able to muster a frame of reference to substitute for the more usual reference points which had been obliterated in the experimental situation?

The opportunity for evaluating these speculations was presented in terms of a line of study pursued by H. A. Witkin* (348). Witkin demonstrated in an elaborate series of investigations that individuals differ markedly in their ability to evaluate spatial relationships when the usual visual cues are removed. Illustratively, he found that one individual who is placed in a dark room becomes completely confused concerning the true vertical and yet another may retain his bearings remarkably well. He developed a whole battery of perceptual tasks for evaluating the degree of dependence the individual has upon immediate visual field cues in this respect. In the course of a major study (348) of the personality correlates of individual differences in dependence upon visual field cues, he obtained individual Rorschach records, among various other tests administered to the subjects. He made some of these Rorschach records available to us so that we could determine if the Barrier score was related in the predicted direction to the perceptual task measures. If our hypothesis was correct, the high Barrier subjects should show significantly less dependence on the visual field cues than the low Barrier subjects. The hypothesis was checked in the following manner. Witkin sent to us the Rorschach records for ten male subjects at the extreme of the field-dependent end of the perceptual continuum and ten from the field-independent end. Each subject's position in the perceptual distribution was based on a composite score for the rod-and-frame test and the tilting-room-tilting-chair test. All the subjects were Brooklyn College students. We were not given any information concerning the positions of these subjects in the perceptual distribution and scored the Rorschachs blindly.

It would be well at this point to describe the two spatial orientation tests from which the composite field-dependence-field-independence scores were derived. Witkin says of the rod-and-frame test (p. 25):

> This test evaluates the individual's perception of the position, in relation to the upright, of an item within a limited visual field. The subject is placed in a completely darkened room, facing a luminous frame which surrounds a movable luminous rod. With the frame tilted, the subject is required to bring the rod to a position that he perceives as upright. For successful performance of this task the subject must "extract" the rod from the tilted frame through reference to body position. The subject is tested on some trials while

---

* We are indeed grateful to Dr. Witkin for his cooperation.

sitting erect, so that it is relatively easy to refer to the body in establishing rod position, and on other trials while tilted, so that it is more difficult to use the body. On all trials a large tilt of the rod when it is reported to be straight indicates adherence to the visual field; a small tilt indicates independence of the field and reliance on the body.

Witkin describes the tilting-room–tilting-chair test as follows (p. 27):

> Whereas the rod-and-frame test evaluates the subject's perception of the position of an item within a field, this test evaluates his perception of the position of his body and of the whole surrounding field in relation to the upright. The way in which the subject establishes the position of his body is determined by seating him in a tilted field, and requiring him to bring his body to a position that he perceives as upright. If he tilts his body far in the direction of the tilted field in order to make himself straight, he is judging his position in terms of his apparent relation to the field. If, on the other hand, he brings himself close to the true upright, he is resisting the influence of the field and showing marked awareness of pressure sensations. To determine the manner in which the subject establishes the position of the whole surrounding field, the room in which he is seated is tilted, and he is asked to bring it to an upright position. If he reports the room straight at its initial tilt, he is accepting its vertical axis as the true upright. If, on the other hand, he succeeds in making the room truly straight, he is perceiving its position in relation to the felt position of his body.

The Barrier scores of the twenty subjects were found to be related to their composite spatial orientation scores in a completely chance fashion. This negative finding was later confirmed from a body of data collected by Holtzman and Bitterman (153). In the course of this study rod-and-frame measures and Rorschach records (as part of a larger battery) were obtained from ninety-six ROTC students at the University of Texas. The Barrier scores derived from the Rorschachs showed only a chance relationship to the rod-and-frame scores. The findings suggest tentatively that body-image boundary definiteness is not related to ability to be independent of the visual field in dealing with spatial orientation tasks. This is the one hypothesis out of the seven proposed concerning body boundaries and self-steering behavior which seems not to be supported. A tentative explanation of this negative result will be offered in the summary comment section which concludes this chapter.

SUMMARY COMMENT

Seven areas of behavior have been studied in the process of determining whether individuals with definite body-image boundaries take a more self-steering orientation toward life than do individuals with poorly defined boundaries. By and large, the results obtained do indicate that degree of boundary definiteness is linked with the ability to be self-steering. It is true that in some instances the results have been a bit vague and even directly contradictory. But the over-all trend of the findings has conformed well to the predictions that were made. It is perhaps of particular significance that the one area in which predictions proved not to be clearly successful had to do with a rather pure perceptual type of situation.

The high and low Barrier individuals did not differ in their ability to maintain an accurate orientation toward spatial relationships in a situation in which most of the usual spatial defining cues had been removed. One may speculate that the lack of differentiation in this instance is a function of the relatively impersonal nature of the spatial localization tasks. With the exception of the Witkin type of task, all the others described in this chapter have obvious social and ego-involving connotations. Most of the other tasks were either deliberately made ego-involving or were phrased in terms that have social and interpersonal meaning. The Witkin type of task has no apparent interpersonal implications and would probably have no consistent ego-involving significance to a great many subjects. Does this not raise the possibility that the Barrier score is related to self-steering behavior only in so far as that behavior occurs in a socialized ego-involving context that has to do with relating to people? Or to put it in another way, may it not be that the individual with definite boundaries does not exceed the individual with indefinite boundaries in ability to structure effectively those situations which are abstracted and removed from the level of social interaction? This raises the possibility that, while the Barrier score is not linked with spatial localization ability in the abstract Witkin situation, it might prove to be linked with such ability, in a situation where one had been motivated to define the ambiguous spatial positions of people who were of personal significance to the subject. What had been an abstract perceptual task might become an undertaking with social interaction import that would tap a different level of response. The tone of this line of speculation is at least partially supported by findings to be presented in a later chapter which indicate that body-image boundaries are developed primarily as part of a process of structuring and stabilizing relationships with people and relatively less so with things.

The self-steering orientation of the high Barrier person is an advantage in many situations; however, there are indications that such an orientation may be disadvantageous in some settings. For example, we found in a sample of ninety-eight ROTC students[*] at the University of Texas

---

[*] These were subjects who had participated in the earlier referred to study conducted by Holtzman and Bitterman (153).

that those with high Barrier scores were rated by their officers as having significantly lower officer potential than those with low Barrier scores. The chi square was significant at the .05–.02 level. It is true that this was only one of a limited number of significant findings in a long array of statistical tests, but still it is suggestive. Our interpretation of the finding is not that high Barrier people have less leadership potential than low Barrier people, but rather that they make a poor impression upon officers because of their tendencies to be independent and to resist subordination. This interpretation raises the general possibility that in a setting where obedience and conformance to the wishes of a leader are of prime importance, the self-steering attitude of the high Barrier person may very well get him in trouble with the leader. He is perhaps not able to give up his own standards sufficiently and so evokes disapproval. It would appear that a high Barrier person is less able than the low Barrier person to adapt to situations which require a high degree of subordination of one's identity.

Some special comment should be made concerning the relationship of our body-image boundary typology to the achievement typology implicit in McClelland's comparisons of those with high achievement motivation versus those with low achievement motivation. The fact that the Barrier score tends to be significantly linked with the n Achievement score indicates that there probably is some overlap between the two typologies. The possibility of such overlap is further underscored when one notes that some of the behavioral characteristics reported by McClelland to go along with a high achievement level are analogous to those referred to in the self-steering cluster. For example, McClelland states that Atkinson (13) found that the n Achievement score is positively correlated with the tendency to recall relatively more ego-involving incompleted tasks than completed tasks. We found this same tendency to characterize high Barrier as contrasted to low Barrier subjects. Despite such overlap, however, we consider the Boundary score to be getting at a basically different dimension than the n Achievement score. This is, of course, indicated by the fact that in some populations we have found the two measures to be only tenuously related. We picture the n Achievement score as a measure of the intensity of a certain type of motivation. We conceive of the Barrier score as an indicator of the degree to which the individual has been able to establish a separate stabilized identity. It does seem to be true, other things being equal, that the individual with definite boundaries feels safer and more capable about setting high goals for himself than the individual with indefinite boundaries. There are many situations in which other things are not equal, however, and in which the relationship between the Barrier score and the n Achievement score could be altered. Thus, an individual with indefinite boundaries may feel insecure about setting high goals and may wish to avoid doing so; but at the same time his very insecurity may drive him to compensatory high reaching achievement that has face-saving value. Or, one can picture an individual with definite boundaries who has achieved a great deal and is so sufficiently saturated that his achievement fantasies are moderate and muted. It is at this point our "educated" guess that the Barrier score and the n Achievement score tap two different aspects of the individual's personality system.

CHAPTER FIVE

....

Boundary Variations and Values

THIS CHAPTER is concerned with an analysis of the differences in values and interests of individuals with varying body-image boundary characteristics. We were stimulated to explore the relationship of value orientation to boundary characteristics by the fact that persons with different Barrier scores differ systematically in so many other aspects of their behavior. That is, there seem to be variations in broad style of behavior associated with variations in Barrier scores. The question arises as to whether the differences in style of behavior are sufficiently broad to be reflected at the level of verbally expressed interests and values. Do the individual's boundary characteristics influence or shape the superstructure of values which he builds up? If such an influence could be demonstrated, it would point up the pervasive determining effect of degree of boundary definiteness upon almost all phases of the individual's personality.

The problem of measuring values and interests is fairly complicated because there is a diversity of measuring instruments and only partial agreement as to what variables these instruments tap. A good example of the complications involved is provided by the Allport-Vernon Study of Values which is one of the more widely employed value measures. Thus, Brogden (50) points out that although the test is supposed to measure six different value areas, the manual accompanying the first edition of the test reported high correlations between several of the values. Brogden further notes that various factor analysis studies of the test, including his own, have found that it measures values not embraced by its six stated categories. The situation is further confused by the fact that some, e.g., Lurie (202A), consider the test to measure fewer than six values; whereas others, e.g., Brogden (50), indicate that the test actually measures more than six values. Similar disagreements may be found concerning the Strong Vocational Interest measures and other standard interest measures.

We therefore decided to sweep widely with a variety of tests rather than to depend on any one or two measures. It was hoped that the relationships obtaining between the Barrier score and a wide range of

153

value and interest measures would make it easier to detect broad patterns which might be overlooked in a study involving just one or two techniques. Furthermore, if similar relationships appeared between the Barrier score and several equivalent or similar-sounding value scores from different tests, more faith could be placed in such results than in a relationship involving just one measure of any given value area. We were also particularly fortunate in being able to check some of the results secured from the usual "paper-and-pencil" interest and value tests by comparing them to findings obtained by scoring the Barrier aspect of the Rorschach protocols of many of Anne Roe's (250) original scientist groups. This added considerable generality to some of the results from the paper-and-pencil tests.

There follows now a presentation of the data from three separate studies involving interest and value measures. These studies were either carried out by the writers or instituted at our suggestion. The findings of the three studies will be integrated and discussed. They will then be compared with the results obtained in analyzing Anne Roe's scientist groups.

STUDIES INVOLVING MEASURES OF INTEREST AND VALUES

(1) The first study to be described was done by Appleby (11). As part of a larger project having to do with body-image boundaries, he investigated the relationship of the Barrier score to the Allport-Vernon Study of Values and the Thurstone Interest Schedule. There are six value areas presumably measured by the Allport-Vernon Study of Values: theoretical, economic, aesthetic, social, political, religious.

There are ten areas of occupational interests which are assumed to be tapped by the Thurstone Interest Schedule: physical science, biological science, computational, business, executive, persuasive, linguistic, humanitarian, artistic, musical.

Appleby secured these tests on a group basis from thirty men and thirty women who were undergraduate students at the University of Houston. He also obtained group Rorschachs limited to twenty-four responses. These Rorschach records were scored by the writers for the Barrier variable.

In analyzing the results of the total group of subjects, Appleby found that there was a phi coefficient of $-.27$ between the Barrier score and the Theoretical score of the Allport-Vernon Study of Values. That is, subjects with high Barrier scores tend to score low in the theoretical category and those with low Barrier scores tend to score high in this category. Allport and Vernon define the theoretical category as follows:

The dominant interest of the theoretical man is the discovery of truth. In the pursuit of this goal he characteristically takes a "cognitive" attitude, one that looks for identities and differences, one that divests itself of judgments regarding the beauty or utility of objects, and seeks only to observe and reason. Since the interests of the theoretical man are empirical, critical, and rational, he is necessarily an intellectualist, frequently a scientist or philospher.

Appleby found with reference to the Thurstone Interest Schedule that there was a phi coefficient of −.36 (.01 level) between Barrier score and physical science interests; a phi coefficient of +.27 (.05 level) between Barrier score and linguistic interests. None of the other seven Thurstone occupational interest categories were significantly related to the Barrier score.

It would be well at this point to define clearly the three occupational categories that were significantly related to the Barrier score.

The *physical sciences* category refers to preferences for such occupations as physicist, mechanical engineer, chemist, mathematician, and astronomer. Thurstone (316) says apropos of this category, "The theoretical category in Spranger's classification spreads over several of our categories but it is perhaps best represented in physical science."

The *humanitarian* category refers to preferences for such occupations as YMCA secretary, recreation director, child welfare work, social service work, and missionary. Its highest negative correlation with the other occupational categories (−.37) is with the physical sciences.

The *linguistic* category is represented in preference for such occupations as journalist, magazine writer, lawyer, diplomat, and radio commentator. Thurstone (316) says it "represents interest in language as communication rather than as art." Of its two highest negative correlations (−.25) with the other nine occupational categories, one is with the physical sciences.

The results from the Thurstone Interest Schedule tend to fall in the same direction as those obtained from the Allport-Vernon test. If one considers that a preference for theoretical alternatives in the Allport-Vernon test represents a choice of scientific activities and of an orientation heavily weighted with the outlook of the physical scientist, then the negative correlation of the Barrier score with this category is congruent with its negative correlation with the Thurstone physical sciences category.

It is noteworthy that the two Thurstone categories (humanitarian and linguistic) with which the Barrier score is significantly *positively* correlated are among the Thurstone scores showing the highest negative correlations with the physical sciences. It may also be noted in studying the matrix of intercorrelations of the ten interest scores that the humanitarian score shows one of its two highest positive correlations (.37) with the linguistic score. Similarly, this represents one of the three of the highest positive correlations of the linguistic score with the other nine scores. This is an important point because it indicates that there is a relatively high degree of commonality between the only two interest scores with which the Barrier score showed a significant positive correlation. In speculating about what the humanitarian score and the linguistic score might have in common, one is struck by the fact that they both involve occupations in which there is an emphasis on contacting people and communicating with them at a rather emotionally involved level. The missionary, the person in social service work, and the vocational counselor (who typify the humanitarian occupations) might be characterized as people seeking to communicate certain standards and feelings to others and to influence their outlook. The writer, the lawyer, and the person in the diplomatic service (who typify the linguistic occupations) appear to be people who are also primarily concerned with communicating emotion-laden ideas to others and with stimulating them to accept a particular outlook.

It is surprising that the persuasive score did not also correlate with the Barrier score, since it too is heavily weighted with occupations involving communication with others with the intent of influencing them. One possible explanation may be that there are many occupations in this category having to do with mass political or propaganda communication (e.g., politician, political speaker, publicity writer). Such mass political or propaganda-communication occupations are generally absent from the humanitarian and linguistic categories.

How may the results of the Appleby study be summarized? First of all, the indications are that the more definite an individual's body-image boundaries, the less likely he is to be interested in the physical sciences or to have a value orientation emphasizing the importance of things and abstractions. Secondly, it would appear that the more definite an individual's boundaries the more likely he is to be interested in activities which focus upon communicating with other people about matters that are of emotional significance and are ego involving.*

(2) The second study concerns an analysis of data which was originally collected by Kelly,† Fiske, and others (167A) as part of their investigation of the factors involved in success in clinical psychology. The VA clinical psychology trainees who served as subjects in this study

---

* It should be reported that Appleby also used the F-scale as part of his battery of measures. He found the Barrier score to be unrelated to the F-scale. This supports the nonsignificant relationship between Barrier score and F-scale found by the writers in a study of 86 college students, which is described in Chapter 3.

† We wish to thank Dr. E. Lowell Kelly for making these data available to us.

took a large number of tests, among which were included the individual Rorschach, the Allport-Vernon Study of Values, and the Strong Vocational Interest Blank. The Rorschach records of 123 subjects were scored for the Barrier variable. Records exceeding twenty-five responses were

TABLE 5:1   CHI-SQUARE TESTS OF RELATIONSHIP OF BARRIER SCORE
TO INTEREST-VALUE SCORES OF KELLY'S VA TRAINEE GROUP

Interest-Value Scores	Group with Higher Score	Level of Significance
Allport-Vernon		
Theoretical	L.B.[a]	N.S.
Economic	H.B.	N.S.
Aesthetic	N.D.	
Social	L.B.	.06–.05
Political	H.B.	.07–.05
Religious	N.D.[b]	
Strong		
Group I........Professional	L.B.	.01
Group II.......Quantitative science	L.B.	.01
Group V........Social service	N.D.	
Group VIII......Accuracy-efficiency	N.D.	
Group IX.......Sales	H.B.	.02–.01
Group X........Persuasive	N.D.	
Sales manager	H.B.	.05–.01
Real estate salesman	H.B.	N.S.

[a] L.B.—Subjects below Barrier median. H.B.—Subjects above Barrier median.
[b] N.D.—No difference. N.S.—Not significant.

reduced to twenty-five by the set reduction method. All the Allport-Vernon scores were available for analysis, but only the following Strong scores:

STRONG GROUP SCALES

Group I
Group II
Group V
Group VIII
Group IX
Group X

STRONG INDIVIDUAL SCALES

Sales manager
Real estate salesman

Table 5:1 indicates the pattern of relationship that was found between the Barrier score and the Allport-Vernon and Strong scores. The above-median and below-median Barrier subjects are differentiated by two Allport-Vernon scores at a borderline level of significance. The low Barrier group is higher in social values and lower in political values than the high Barrier group. These differences fall at about the .07–.05 level. It is incidentally worth noting that the high Barrier subjects tend to score lower in the theoretical category than the low Barrier subjects. This difference is not at all significant but is in the same direction as the result cited in the Appleby study.

A clearer conception of the two borderline differences found which involve the social and political categories would probably be provided if the definitions of the two categories were reviewed. Allport and Vernon define the social category as follows:

> The highest value for this type is *love* of people. . . . The social person prizes other persons as ends, and is therefore himself kind, sympathetic, and unselfish. . . . Spranger adds that in its purest form the social attitude is selfless and tends to approach very closely generally have high power value.

They describe the political category as follows:

> The political man is interested primarily in *power*. His activities are not necessarily within the narrow field of politics; but whatever his vocation, he betrays himself as a Machtmensch. Leaders in any field generally have high power value.

The differences between the high and low Barrier groups with regard to the social category suggests that the above-median Barrier subjects are less willing than the below-median subjects to endorse an extreme number of alternatives which favor a self-sacrificing, charitable attitude toward others. Emphasis should be placed upon the fact that the difference represents a differentiation at an extreme point in the social range rather than in the more usual ranges. The subjects involved in the Kelly-Fiske study were a highly select group and their median social score was in the 80–90 percentile of the Allport-Vernon norms. The high Barrier subjects were distinguished by the fact that they obtained fewer social scores in the 82–95 percentile range than did the low Barrier individuals. Their social scores tended to fall more toward the norm response of a college population.

The difference obtained with regard to the political scores indicated that the high Barrier group was more accepting of political values than the low Barrier group. However, here too the differentiation involved extremes. The median political score of the total group was at about the thirty-eighth percentile, as defined by Allport-Vernon norms. The high

Barrier subjects differed from the low Barrier subjects in that they more nearly approached the average (fiftieth percentile) degree of preference for political values. The low Barrier subjects were not accepting of the average degree of political orientation usually found in a college population.

It is difficult to interpret the two differences in Allport-Vernon values between the Barrier groups because the differences involve extremes of the two-value continua. One notes that in both instances the high Barrier group falls away from the extremes and in the direction of norm values. It is possible to interpret the results as indicating that the high Barrier individuals endorse a more direct and forceful system of values regarding interaction with others than do the low Barrier people. Thus they endorse fewer alternatives which involve being soft-hearted and self-sacrificing in dealing with others. But at the same time they favor more alternatives which involve influencing and directing people in order to attain certain power goals. Over all, the high Barrier people seem more identified than the low Barrier people with an approach that implies a "normal" amount of pressuring and manipulation of others.

Table 5:1 indicates that there were a number of the Strong interest categories that significantly discriminated between the two Barrier groups. The low Barrier subjects scored significantly higher than the high Barrier subjects in both Group I (.01 level) and Group II (.01 level) interests. But the high Barrier subjects scored significantly higher on the Group IX (.02–.01 level) interests and the sales-manager category (.05–.01 level). Before proceeding to an analysis of these differences, let us review the definitions of the particular interest categories involved.

Group I embraces a pattern of interests found to be typical of such occupations as physician, dentist, architect, artist, and psychologist. This category apparently refers to the degree to which individuals have interests typical of professional people in general.

Group II includes interest patterns represented in such occupations as mathematician, physicist, engineer, and chemist. It may be considered to refer to the degree to which persons have interests similar to those of quantitatively minded scientists.

Group IX involves three occupations: sales manager, realtor, and life insurance salesman. It does not include all sales occupations. Indeed, Strong (301) specifies three types of salesmen who do not fit this category: salesmen of a public utility company, salesmen of engineering goods, and house-to-house canvassers.

Sales manager is part of Group IX. It indicates the similarity of the individual's interest pattern to that of a sample of sales managers. Strong (301) cites the following correlations of the sales-manager score with other scores he considers pertinent:

CORRELATION OF SCORES OF SALES MANAGER WITH—

Production manager	.01
Personnel manager	.36
Accountant	.23
President of company	.52
Advertising manager	.41

It is interesting that the highest correlation is with the pattern obtained from presidents of companies. When one further considers that the sales manager is an individual who directs or manages the work of a group of employees, it would appear that the sales-manager pattern is related to an interest in dealing with people in a managing or directive capacity.

The fact that the high Barrier group obtained significantly lower Strong Group II* (quantitative science) scores than the low Barrier group is nicely congruent with the results found in the Appleby study. Appleby reported a phi coefficient of −.36 between Barrier score and the physical science category of the Thurstone Interest Schedule. In a related vein, he found a phi coefficient of −.27 between Barrier score and the theoretical category in the Allport-Vernon test. This theoretical category has been considered by some (e.g., Thurstone) to overlap considerably with an interest in the physical sciences.

Apropos of this point, it may be noted that in a study carried out by Sarbin and Berdie (263), two of the Strong group scores were found to be positively correlated with the Allport-Vernon theoretical score and one score negatively. The two positively correlated categories were Groups I and II; the negatively correlated category was Group IX. In the results from Kelly's data which were obtained, Groups I and II show an inverse sort of relationship with the Barrier score and Group IX shows a positive linkage with the Barrier score. Thus the two Strong scores found by Sarbin and Berdie to be positively correlated with the theoretical category are inversely related to the Barrier score; and the relationship is reversed for the Strong score we found to be negatively correlated with the theoretical category. This pattern of results strongly supports the conclusion that high Barrier people are less interested than low Barrier people in the physical sciences and in a way of thought that would be associated with a theoretical orientation.

The meaning of the significantly higher Group I scores that we found to characterize the low Barrier subjects is not immediately apparent. Why should the high Barrier people be low and the low Barrier people be high

---

* It should be noted that clinical psychology trainees as a group score well above the middle of the Strong continuum as far as Group I is concerned. The median value for the group falls at about the middle of the B+ rating, on a total continuum extending over six units (C, C+, B−, B, B+, A).

in terms of an interest category involving various professional groups (e.g., dentist, physician, architect)? The only explanation that could be formulated was in terms of results obtained by Strong when he factor-analyzed his various interest scores. One of the five factors that emerged was a science factor. Its composition is suggested by the following listing of the interest categories with related positive and negative loadings:

POSITIVE LOADING	NEGATIVE LOADING
Physician	Personnel
Artist	Y Secretary
Dentist	Life insurance
Chemist	Real estate
Engineer	Sales manager
Physicist	Banker

One can see that most of the interest categories of Group I have positive loadings in this science factor. Furthermore, the physicist and engineer scores fall into this same factor area, as do the physician and dentist scores. This suggests that Group I (despite the fact that it includes artist) is heavily saturated with interests typical of a science orientation, particularly the physical sciences. If this is so, one would conclude that the significantly higher Group I scores of the low Barrier group are a function of the fact that this group is more interested in the physical science type of activities than the high Barrier group.

The significantly higher Group IX scores and also sales-manager scores (subgroup of Group IX) of the high Barrier subjects suggests that a degree of body-image boundary definiteness is linked with interests in influencing, persuading, and guiding people. It would appear that above-median Barrier individuals have a greater interest than below-median Barrier persons in interacting with others in such a way as to have a directive and steering impact upon them. It is parenthetically of interest that the sales-manager category was found by Strong to have a significant negative loading in the science factor, which is heavily loaded on the positive side with occupations from Group II. It is rather impressive how analogous to some of Appleby's results are the findings involving the Strong Group IX and sales-manager scores. In Appleby's data, a degree of boundary definiteness seemed to go along with some degree of preference for the linguistic and humanitarian occupations in the Thurstone Interest Schedule. Appleby's results were interpreted by us as indicating that high Barrier persons are more interested in contacting and communicating with people than are low Barrier individuals. One may similarly interpret the results related to Strong's Group IX scores. Here too the high Barrier person indicates a preference for a pattern associated with making a strong communicative contact with others.

(3) The third study to be described is a rather small-scale project carried out by the writers. It involved thirty-eight students who were taking an introductory psychology course at the University of Houston. There were twenty-one men and seventeen women in the group. Barrier scores were secured in the usual manner from Rorschach records obtained on a group basis and with instructions that fixed numbers of responses be given to various cards. In addition, the following value and interest measures were administered on a group basis: The Morris-Jones (222) Ways to Live Measure, The Allport-Vernon Study of Values, and The Thurstone Interest Schedule.

The Allport-Vernon test and the Thurstone form have already been described in detail. The Morris-Jones Ways of Life form needs to be described, however. This measure of values consists of thirteen separate paragraphs, each describing a possible way of life. The subject is asked to indicate his liking for each way of life by rating it on a seven-point scale ranging from "I dislike it very much" (rating of 1) to "I like it very much (rating of 7).

There follows now an example of one of the ways of life enumerated:

> Way 7. We should at various times and in various ways accept something from all other paths of life, but give no one our exclusive allegiance. At one moment one of them is the more appropriate; at another moment another is the most appropriate. Life should contain enjoyment and action and contemplation in about equal amounts. When either is carried to extremes we lose something important for our life. So we must cultivate flexibility, admit diversity in ourselves, accept the tension which this diversity produces, find a place for detachment in the midst of enjoyment and activity. The goal of life is found in the dynamic integration of enjoyment, action, and contemplation, and so in the dynamic interaction of the various paths of life. One should use all of them in building a life, and no one alone.

Some of the other ways of life advocate such diverse propositions as, "A person should let himself be used"; "Enjoyment should be the keynote of life"; "The use of the body's energy is the secret of a rewarding life."

The thirteen Way of Life paragraphs were read aloud to the subjects, and they indicated their ratings of each on a sheet which contained printed reproductions of the paragraphs.

When the subjects' Barrier scores were related to their Way of Life scores, the results were, by and large, not significant. Chi-square tests were made of the relationship of Barrier scores to the ratings for each way of life. The median of the the thirty-eight ratings for each way of life was used as the cutting point for splitting the group relative to the

given way of life. Twelve of the thirteen ways of life were not significantly related to the Barrier score.

Way of life 7 was found to be more preferred by high Barrier subjects
than low Barrier subjects. The differentiation ($\chi^2 = 2.6$) fell just short
of the 10 per cent level of significance. However, when there was tabulated for each subject the number of times that Way of Life 7 was rated
either highest or tied for highest rating in his array of thirteen evaluations,
it was found that such highest ratings occurred significantly more often
in the high Barrier group than in the low Barrier group. This difference
was significant at the .05–.02 level. Ordinarily, one such significant result
out of thirteen tests of significance should be dismissed as probably a
chance finding. Perhaps it *is* a chance finding. The fact, however, that it
was Way of Life 7 which proved to be differentiating has special implications. The exact content of this way of life was quoted in the example of Way of Life paragraphs which was just offered. It is
the only one of the thirteen which advocates accepting "something
from all other paths of life" and which does not emphasize just one style
of living. Morris and Jones state (222, p. 533), "Way 7 stresses flexibility
and many-sidedness, and explicitly provides a place for contemplation
and enjoyment as well as for action."

"Furthermore, in the course of comparing ratings of the Way of Life
given by students in various countries (the United States, India, Japan,
China, Norway), Morris and Jones discovered that it was Way of Life
7 which more than any other distinguished the United States students
from the others. The United States students showed a much higher preference for this Way of Life than any of the other student groups. The
United States students obtained a scale value of 1.24 for Way 7, with
the next highest value in the United States group being .80 (for Way 1).
The students from Norway showed a scale value of .66 for Way 7; Chinese
students were represented by a value of .51; and they in turn were followed by students from India with a value of .46, and finally Japanese
students with a value of .21. Thus, the United States scale value for Way
7 was not only the highest in the United States group, but also just about
twice as great as the corresponding value for any of the other student
groups. This suggests that Way 7 taps something of relatively unique
import to the students of the United States group.

One might interpret the over-all Way of Life results as indicating that
the high Barrier subjects are differentiated from the low Barrier subjects
not so much by their preference for any one specific way of life, as by
their choice of a middle position which accepts aspects of a number of
ways of life as good. This interpretation of the results would fit fairly
well with most of the findings from the Appleby and Kelly-Fiske data

which indicated the relatively greater preference of high Barrier people for communicating and interacting widely with people. That is, one might expect individuals who express a preference for activities which emphasize personal interaction with others to be more accepting of a range of life styles than individuals who are relatively less interested in communication with others. To put it another way, since low Barrier subjects evidence a greater inclination than high Barrier subjects to be interested in things rather than people, might one not expect them to be less motivated to take a positive orientation toward the diversity in people?

In the subject group being described the Allport-Vernon scores proved to be minimally related to the Barrier scores. There is a slight tendency for the high Barrier subjects to obtain lower theoretical scores than the low Barrier subjects. But the trend is far from significant. When the score distributions of each value category were split at the median and compared to the Barrier scores by means of chi square, all the results were of a chance order. The same chance results occurred when the middle score defined by the Allport-Vernon norms for each value category was used as the splitting point. One significant difference did emerge when a tabulation was made of the number of times each value category was the highest score (or tied for highest score) in the above-median Barrier group and the below-median Barrier group. It was found that the aesthetic value appeared in first position more often in the high Barrier group. .Yates's correction was applied to the chi square because of the small expected frequency in one cell. This corrected value was 3.8, which is significant at the .05 level. One cannot attach too much importance to the finding, because it failed to appear in the Appleby study and in the Kelly-Fiske data. It is interesting, however, that the high Barrier group should show a greater leaning toward the aesthetic outlook, since the aesthetic orientaton is one that stands in considerable contrast to a theoretical or physical science pattern of preference.

The results obtained from this group for the Thurstone Interest Schedule were of a chance order. Each Thurstone vocational category was split at the median value of the thirty-eight scores made by the subjects for that category. The scores for the various categories were compared with the Barrier score by means of chi square. There were no significant findings and even a lack of clear-cut trends. It is not apparent why the Thurstone Interest Schedule should give such chance results in this group in contrast to the positive results in Appleby's data. Possibly it is due to the smaller number of subjects in the study being presently described. There were sixty subjects in Appleby's group and only thirty-eight subjects in this group. However, the fact that there are no visible trends in the results which could be considered parallel to Appleby's findings implies that the relationship between the Barrier score and the Thurstone scores are rather unstable. One might take the same view concerning the fact that the relationship found by Appleby between the theoretical category of the Allport-Vernon test and the Barrier score was not significantly duplicated in the present results.

The total pattern of results from the three studies which have been described are moderately supportive of two generalizations:

(1) Low Barrier individuals manifest a relatively greater preference for the exact quantitative sciences than do high Barrier individuals.

(2) High Barrier persons indicate a greater preference for personal, influential communication with others than do low Barrier persons.

One cannot escape the fact that these conclusions are mainly based upon what subjects report about themselves. The conclusions are derived from relationships between Barrier scores and various self-descriptive statements made by subjects in reply to inventories which pose questions and choices. One should probably not generalize very far from such data about the degree to which boundary definiteness would bear a relationship to real-life behavioral manifestations of interest-value preferences. Fortunately, however, we were able to secure behavioral data relating to the occupations individuals had actually chosen; and this made it possible to check the meaningfulness of the results obtained with various inventories. Such behavioral data were made available to us by Dr. Anne Roe* who had in the course of her work collected Rorschach protocols from a number of occupational groups. The results we obtained from studying her data are described in the section that follows.

BARRIER SCORE DIFFERENCES AMONG VARIOUS OCCUPATIONAL GROUPS

As she has described in detail elsewhere (248, 249, 250), Anne Roe studied a series of eminently successful and creative persons in various fields. She evaluated by means of interview, Rorschach, and other procedures many outstanding research figures in physics, biology, psychology, and anthropology. In addition, she evaluated a group of eminent artists. She sought to establish control groups against which to compare the eminent individuals by securing group Rorschachs from members of university faculties in corresponding areas of specialization. The Rorschachs secured from the various categories of subjects were scored by the writers for the Barrier variable. All the individual records exceeding twenty-five responses which were obtained from the eminent subjects were reduced to twenty-five by the set reduction method. This was also done with the protocols obtained from the control groups. Indeed, there

---

* We are very grateful to Dr. Anne Roe for permitting us to study her data.

was such an abundance of control subjects that it was possible to use only records which had at least twenty-five responses. This means that the Barrier scores of all the control group individuals are based on a response total of twenty-five responses.

In addition to the groups made available by Anne Roe, a mixed group of eminent mathematicians and chemists was provided by data collected by Donald Walker° as part of a study of creativity. The individuals in his group consisted of six mathematicians and twelve chemists, all of whom were as outstanding in their field as the eminent scientists whom Anne Roe studied. Individual Rorschachs had been obtained from these subjects. In scoring the protocols for the Barrier variable, all responses over twenty-five were reduced to twenty-five by the set reduction method. The median Rorschach response total of this group was twenty-five. All the eminent groups, except one, which were studied by Roe likewise had median response totals of twenty-five. The one exception were the biologists who had a median of twenty-two. In general, one may consider the various eminent groups as roughly comparable as far as Rorschach response total is concerned.

TABLE 5:2   MEDIAN BARRIER SCORES OF EMINENT AND OF NONEMINENT
PERSONS IN CORRESPONDING AREAS

Occupational Group	Eminent	Noneminent	Combined
Psychology	6 (N = 9)	5 (N = 40)	5 (N = 49)
Anthropology	5 (N = 9)	5 (N = 16)	5 (N = 25)
Art	4 (N = 20)	a	a
Physics	3 (N = 15)	4 (N = 34)	4 (N = 49)
Biology	3 (N = 12)	4 (N = 40)	4 (N = 52)
Mathematics-Chemistry	3 (N = 17)	a	a

ª There were no controls for the artists, mathematicians, and chemists.

Table 5:2 shows that there is a hierarchy of median Barrier values for the eminent groups. Psychologists, anthropologists, and artists are highest, with respective median scores of 6, 5, and 4. The physicists, the biologists, the mathematicians, and chemists all fall at the lower end of the Barrier continuum, with median scores of 3. The small number of eminent subjects in each of the occupational areas prevented a statistical test of the differences in scores between specific groups. It is interesting, however, that the lowest Barrier scores are obtained by individuals in the exact quantitative sciences. In contrast, the psychologists, anthropologists, and artists may be described as doing a type of work which focuses on peo-

° We are indebted to Dr. Donald Walker for permitting us to study his data.

ple and human emotions. One notes in Table 5:2 that the combined psychologist, anthropologist, artist group obtains significantly higher Barrier scores than the combined physics, biology, mathematician, chemist group. The difference is significant at the .05–.02 level. Such results are certainly confirmatory of the findings which emerged from the previously cited studies in which various value and interest measures were related to the Barrier score. It will be recalled that these studies indicated that degree of boundary definiteness was negatively linked with degree of interest in the exact quantitative sciences and positively linked with interest in personal, communicative interaction with others.*

A review of the findings of the noneminent control groups also proves to be confirmatory of this trend. Table 5:2 indicates that both the psychologists and anthropologists have higher median Barrier scores than the physicists and biologists. Table 5:3 points up the fact that the psychologists have significantly higher (.05–.02) Barrier scores than both the physicists and biologists. The small number of subjects in the anthropology control group prevented tests of significance of its relationship to these two groups.

It should be observed that the biology and physics groups do not differ from each other in Barrier score. A comparison was made of the Barrier scores of the combined psychologist and anthropologist group with the combined physicist and biologist group. Table 5:3 establishes that the psychologist + anthropologist group has significantly higher (.05–.02) scores.

Table 5:3 also presents a comparison of Barrier scores of the occupational groups when each group represents a combination of both the eminent and noneminent scientists. The psychologists very significantly

---

* It may be parenthetically noted in Table 5:2 that most of the eminent creative groups do not have Barrier medians higher or even as high as medians characteristic of average undergraduate college students. Apparently, boundary definiteness is not related to the special kind of creativity which is typical of these eminent individuals. Indeed, the fact that scientists in the physical sciences are inclined to fall at the low end of the Barrier continuum is a somewhat refreshing contrast to the bulk of the findings earlier presented which imply that the high Barrier person is generally superior to the low Barrier person in the way he deals with situations. It would appear from the present data that the indefinite-boundary person is likely to excel the definite-boundary person in an area of activity that has unusual status and importance in our culture.

It is intriguing, apropos of the relatively low Barrier scores of the physicists, that Anne Roe (250) raised the question as to whether or not the theoretical physicist's superior ability to manipulate size concepts so abstractly is a function of the fact that he can freely separate them from his body image, which she conjectures is relatively poorly developed. She observed a very high incidence of severe childhood illnesses among the theoretical physicists and wondered if this might lead to an impairment of body image. She suggests that it would be easier to discard an unsatisfactory body image because of its unsatisfactoriness and thus be free to manipulate size concepts loosely and without reference to body standards.

TABLE 5:3   CHI-SQUARE ANALYSIS OF DIFFERENCES IN BARRIER SCORES
BETWEEN PERSON-ORIENTED AND THING-ORIENTED DISCIPLINES

Comparisons	Eminent		Noneminent		Combined	
	Group with Higher Score	Significance Level	Group with Higher Score	Significance Level	Group with Higher Score	Significance Level
Psychology vs.						
Physics	Psy.	a	Psy.	.05–.02	Psy.	.001
Biology	Psy.	a	Psy.	.05–.02	Psy.	.001
Anthropology vs.						
Physics	Anthro.	a	Anthro.	N.S.[b]	Anthro.	N.S.[b]
Biology	Anthro.	a	Anthro.	N.S.	Anthro.	N.S.
Art vs.						
Physics	Art	a		c		c
Biology	Art	a		c		c
Psychology + Anthropology vs.						
Physics + Biology	Psy. + Anthro.	a	Psy. + Anthro.	.05–.02	Psy. + Anthro.	.001
Psychology + Anthropology + Art vs.						
Physics + Biology + Mathematics + Chemistry	Psy. + Anthro. + Art	.05–.02		c		c

[a] The N in these groups is too small to permit meaningful statistical tests.
[b] N.S.—Not significant.
[c] Scores of noneminent artists or noneminent mathematicians and chemists were not available.

(.001) exceed the physicists and biologists in Barrier scores. The anthropologists exceed these two groups also, but the differences are not significant. The combined psychologist + anthropologist group obtains significantly higher (.001) Barrier scores than the physicist + biologist group. There is no difference between the physicists and the biologists.

It is clear throughout the comparisons involving eminent, noneminent, and combined groups that it is the psychologists who most consistently and significantly exceed the physicists and biologists in boundary definiteness. The anthropologists do evidence consistent (but not significant) tendencies toward higher Barrier scores than the physicists, biologists, chemists, and mathematicians in the eminent group; and they do show the same tendencies (but not significant) in the noneminent group comparisons. What is most important about the over-all results, however, is that combined groups consisting of those occupations which involve communicating with and about people are consistently significantly higher in their Barrier scores than combined groups consisting of occupations that focus on things and abstract concepts. These results, when considered in conjunction with the analogous findings from the value and interest studies, firmly indicate that differences in value orientation do go along with differences in body-image boundary definiteness.* It would appear that an individual's boundary characteristics may exert an influence on the degree to which he directs his interests and activities toward people as contrasted to things and abstractions. All sorts of questions come to mind concerning the reason for this phenomenon. Does the individual with indefinite boundaries show a greater inclination to deal with things rather than people because he feels uncomfortably open and vulnerable to how people respond to him, but does not have to concern himself about such response when he is responding to things? Is the individual with indefinite boundaries more inclined to deal with things because he feels less decisively demarcated off from the "thing" aspects of his world? That is, perhaps the low Barrier person can identify himself more with things because he does not experience his body so clearly as possessing a personal or humanized identity as does the high Boundary person.

This idea leads into still another concerning the possibility that the high Boundary individual is one who has developed definite boundary concepts (which emphasize his unique human identity) because he has had relatively satisfying experiences with people in the process of growing up. Might one say that the individual with definite boundaries is more interested in influencing and communicating with people than the indefinite-boundary individual because the definite-boundary individual's past experiences with others have been more rewarding and thus have led him to expect greater rewards from personal interaction?

---

* The fact that there are differences in personality between physical scientists and individuals interested more in the study of people and human events has been previously demonstrated by Roe (250) and also by Teevan (309).

....

CHAPTER SIX

Case Studies of Normal Individuals Who Differ in Body-Image Boundary Characteristics

PRELIMINARY COMMENTS

OUT OF THE numerous studies which have been described some fairly definite information has emerged about the personality traits and tendencies associated with body-image boundaries of varying definiteness. However, this information suffers from the deficiencies inherent in the fact that it is derived from generalizations about statistically significant differences between modal frequencies. It is information abstracted from relationships observed to hold true in terms of groups of individuals. It is therefore information which lacks flesh-and-blood quality. Despite the fact that we had accumulated large stores of data concerning body-image boundary phenomena, we found it difficult to visualize the differences between high and low Barrier persons in terms of real life, everyday behavior. We could not associate a meaningful personalized identity with high and low Barrier persons. It was as if one knew the names of several persons and had available their scores on various psychological tests, but knew little about their actual life histories. Such persons would remain abstractions, and probably be unrecognizable if one were to meet them personally.

We consequently felt that it would have great clarifying value to study in detail the life patterns of a number of individuals who differed in boundary characteristics. If one compared the biography of a high Barrier individual with that of a low Barrier individual, would there be clear-cut differences in the way they had lived? Would they have grown up differently? Would they have related to people differently? Would they have evolved contrasting ways of dealing with basic life problems? It was our intent to explore such questions by means of a rambling impressionistic analysis of detailed biographical information. In this chapter we shall forget about statistical significance and undertake an intuitive common-sense appraisement.

The sort of concrete, intimate life data about normal persons in which we were interested is not easily obtained. It requires a special situation with unusual incentives to motivate a normal individual to tell a great deal about himself. He does not have the press of anxiety or the desire for relief which stimulates the patient in psychotherapy to reveal himself to the therapist. We were fortunately able to side-step much of the tremendous labor involved in compiling this kind of information from normal subjects by making use primarily of data which had already been collected by Smith,* Bruner, and White (286). As part of a project concerned with the relationship of personality characteristics to opinion about Russia, Smith, Bruner, and White studied the life patterns of ten adult men, all married and all, with one exception, pursuing their livelihood in the Greater Boston community.

These men were not chosen as a representative sample from the population, but were obtained through personal contacts. One of the aims of the selection was to secure men sufficiently intelligent to be verbally productive. The ten men did represent a wide range of social backgrounds and walks of life. The range of their occupations was as follows: law clerk, salesman, journalist, factory operative, factory worker, accountant, shopkeeper, contractor, civil-service administrator, real estate agent. They were paid to serve as subjects, and were studied for some fifteen weekly two-hour sessions. They were interviewed in great detail about all phases of their life, interests, activities, and fantasies, and were evaluated with the Rorschach and other projective and also intellectual tests. Thus was accumulated a rich fund of data concerning each of them. When their Rorschach records were made available to us, we scored them for the Barrier variable. We found that only two of the men were clearly in the low Barrier group and most of the others were definitely in the high Barrier category. Since it was our arbitrary intention to compare the life styles of at least three high Barrier men with three low Barrier men, it was necessary to look elsewhere for a third low Barrier person. In order not to introduce any special bias into this selection, it was decided to study a series of normal persons and to take the first in the series that happened to be low Barrier.

As it turned out, the first person we studied was low Barrier. This man was referred to us by a vocational counselor who worked in the tuberculosis section of a Veterans Administration hospital. We had asked the counselor to keep his eyes open for a man in his thirties or forties who looked reasonably normal and who would have the verbal facility and motivation to participate in a study requiring him to reveal a good deal about himself. The man proved to be very willing to participate in the study. He was evaluated by means of ten hours of inter-

* We acknowledge with gratitude Dr. M. Brewster Smith's cooperation in making these data available to us.

viewing and also the Rorschach and Thematic Apperception tests. His Barrier score was not determined until the very last phases of the evaluation in order to avoid biases that might be introduced by knowing whether he was a high or low Barrier person. The choice of which of the high Barrier men to compare to the low Barrier men was made by selecting three from the high Barrier group who best matched the low Barrier men in terms of occupational level, religion, and general socioeconomic level. The three high Barrier and three low Barrier subjects singled out are listed below, along with certain descriptive data about them.

HIGH BARRIER

Name	Age	Occupation	Education	Barrier Score
Charles Lanlin	41	Salesman	High school Business school	10
Ernest Daniel	37	Factory operative	3 years high school	9
Clarence Clark	43	Accountant	High school Business school	7

LOW BARRIER

Name	Age	Occupation	Education	Barrier Score
Hillary Sullivan	46	Journalist	2 years high school	3
Sam Hodder	48	Factory worker	6 years grade school	3
Jim Gibson	44	Schoolteacher	College graduate Working on Master's degree	3

It is, of course, true that many biasing factors entered into the choice of the eleven subjects who constituted the original pool from which the present six were selected. They were very far from being a random sample. Since they were all chosen, however, without our having any knowledge of their Barrier scores, it is clear that selection was not contaminated by the body-image variable itself. Furthermore, since there were only three subjects with Barrier scores below the usual median, the choice of low Barrier subjects from the pool of eleven cases could not in any way be arbitrary. There might possibly have been some room for arbitrary decisions in selecting three high Barrier cases from the five cases that did have Barrier scores well above the usual median. This possibility was minimized, however, by the fact that of the two high Barrier individuals eliminated one was discarded on the basis of his special religious affiliation and the other because of his unusually high socioeconomic background.

The analysis of the data from the six men will proceed as follows. First, detailed accounts concerning the high Barrier men will be presented. Then, detailed accounts of the material from the low Barrier men will be described. Finally, impressionistic cross comparisons of similarities and differences within Barrier categories and across Barrier categories will be made. In order to avoid prejudice in the selection of what material to present about the subjects who are described in the book *Opinions and Personality* by Smith, Bruner, and White, all pertinent statements in the book will be paraphrased which specifically concern background and behavior and which are not repetitious.

HIGH BARRIER MEN

CHARLES LANLIN

Charles Lanlin, a forty-two-year-old man, was a salesman of household appliances. He had been a clerical worker with the same appliance company for nineteen years and had only recently become a salesman. He had been chronically dissatisfied with his clerical work and had sought during the last eight years that he was on that job to express himself in union activities. Previous to his work with the appliance company, he had briefly held a position in a bank, but he had quit because the work was "too gloomy." Before that he briefly worked in the time-study department of a manufacturing company, but had left because of the low popularity of the time-study department among the rank and file of workers in the company.

He had completed high school and business trade school. He was a Catholic, who, although not deeply religious, maintained a close orthodox relationship with the church. There was an income of $5,000 a year available to him, partially from his salary and partially from income from property left by his father. He lived in a middle-class suburb of Boston. His health had been consistently good, except for symptoms of a suspected ulcer which had occurred eight years previous to the time he was studied. He still adhered to a diet which had been suggested by his physician at that time.

Terms like *well-fed* and *well-cared-for* are used to describe his appearance. He was heavy in physique and of medium height. He smiled often and easily enjoyed a joke. He seemed to want to be pleasant and amiable to people. It seemed important to him that he dress well. Indeed, he emulated the example of a successful junior executive. One was struck with the care he took with his appearance. He never seemed to be in need of a shave, a pressing, or a shine. Yet, he did not overdress. Most of the time he was quite talkative and tended to ramble in a tangential manner. His speech was full of images of warmth and humor.

Charley's father had come to Boston in his teens from New Haven, Connecticut, where he was born of parents of German origin. Lanlin, senior, completed grammar school, but did not go further because of the poor financial condition of his family. He was an economical man who worked with great energy. Over a period of time he became the manager of a food store in a Boston suburb. By hard work and economy he saved enough money to purchase some heavily mortgaged property on which were some neighborhood stores. This property became a dominant interest in his life and he lavished a great deal of his time and energy in keeping it in good repair. Charley indicated that the family could rarely leave town for more than a day at a time because of his father's anxiety about how the property would fare in their absence. After a number of years Lanlin, senior, paid off the mortgage and finally owned mortgage-free property.

He was thirty-four and his wife was thirty-one when Charley, an only child, was born. He was a tightly bound up, purposeful person who was the head of the family. He was described by Charley as "calm, deliberate, and very much of a planner." As a child, Charley accompanied his father on his frequent missions to tend to his property, but during this time they were not emotionally close to each other. In his descriptions of his mother Charley indicated that she was impatient and quick-tempered; but he seems to have felt closer to her than to the father. She tended toward a sad outlook, and apparently became increasingly moody with the years. Often she would complain to Charley about his father; and particularly she registered dissatisfaction with his father's stinginess. Charley felt that his parents were not specific in their vocational wishes for him, but that they did have in mind some vague clerical or administrative career in business. He had no clear-cut vocational aims of his own. After completing high school he took a year's course at a commercial school because his father recommended that he do so. It was his complaint that his parents had not pushed him enough. He said (286, p. 127), "I wish my father had made a point of seeing to it that I went on in my education. Oh, he didn't stop me, of course, but he might have pushed me on further. What I had seemed a lot and was a lot in comparison to his own education, and I suppose the transfer to college wasn't very widespread then. But I do wish he'd pushed me a little further."

Generally, he played a good-boy role in relation to his parents. He accepted his father's authority rather completely and it rarely required more than a request to get him to do things. Smith, Bruner, and White note (268, p. 128):

In his Autobiography, Charley stated:

I soon learned that when my father said, "NO," he meant "NO" and any further discussion or attempts to persuade was a waste of time, but in my mother's case, I could generally prevail, not through tantrums, which neither would stand for, but by kidding her along, a little soft soaping, and she would laugh and give her O.K.

My father never punished me, perhaps because, when he told me something he did not want me to do, he would leave a definite impression that it would be wise to follow his suggestions. If he saw me doing something which he did not approve, all he had to do was say my first name, and from the way he said it, and tone of voice was enough for me, because that tone was not used often, but when it was "Stop!!" would bounce from one side of your head to the other. In my mother's case, she would take a good righthand swing, only one, and none ever landed, as I could see it was coming, and I would leave that spot pronto, and from there on, it would be a bawling out.

After Charley's father paid up the mortgage on his property he retired from the food store and became a full-time landlord. Economic conditions at that time eased considerably for the family, and such things as a car and a radio were purchased. Lanlin, Senior used some of his newly available free time to take the lead in his neighborhood Chamber of Commerce and eventually became Treasurer and President. He died when Charley was twenty-nine.

Charley started to work part time in a grocery store when he was still a young adolescent. He gave his father all the money he earned. Following the completion of his one-year business-school course he undertook several jobs for brief periods which did not satisfy him. Finally he obtained a position with a household appliance company, and he was still with this company at the time of the study twenty-one years later. He spent nineteen years in the pay-roll department of this company. A good part of the time he found the work repetitious and not able to provide outlets for his creative urges. He did, however, like the security of working in a well-established company that guaranteed seniority and retirement pay. But finally after nineteen years, his dissatisfaction with the routine of his job mounted to a point where he arranged to be transferred to the sales division of the company. His work in this division involved selling appliances in a store which he managed for the company. He derived much satisfaction from his new assignment. It pleased him to be in a position where he was actively communicating with people and had to devise ways of getting through to the various kinds of personalities he encountered in his customers. Also he felt that in selling he was doing something more constructive for his company than he had done in his clerical job. He felt that all the work that went into the company's product would be to no avail unless the final step of sales to a consumer had been achieved. Thus he could see himself as having special status in the company's scheme of things.

His patterns of leisure-time activity were rather simple and conforming. In childhood he had often played alone, especially because he was an only child. Apparently his mother was surprised at how self-sufficient he could be for long periods and she remarked that he was rarely any trouble. As he got older he read moderately and engaged in a lot of competitive sports. He was above average in athletic proficiency. He did not recall any teachers as having had an outstanding influence on his life. In high school he was active and well liked. He had a lot of friends whom he continued to see in later life. At a recent reunion he was elected officer of his class. Fights were fairly common during his period in school; he learned not to look for fights, however, but rather to accept challenges that were delivered. He found that he fought more successfully when he was the challenged one rather than the aggressor.

Charley revealed little about his sexual history. He is quoted as saying (286, p. 31): "Sex did not worry me . . . neither did it tease or annoy me. It just drifted along in a gradual sort of way." Although he went to dances quite often, he usually did not take the same girl consistently. His marriage occurred when he was twenty-five. His wife was an active friendly person. During their sixteen years of marriage they had four children.

When Lanlin was asked in the course of an interview "What things really matter to you?" he emphasized the importance of his marriage, his children, and his home. He also emphasized work and the ability to get along with people. He said (286, p. 131), "I can't think of much of anything else that goes on in this world besides your home and your work." Most of his time away from work was shared with his family. He took the role of father and guide to his children very seriously. It was a prime idea for him that his children should be healthy and well adjusted. He felt that a father should know all about his children and participate in their activities. He tried to give them individual attention. Each day he sounded the children out and obtained a detailed account of their experiences. At times he reacted to this role of the good interested father as demanding and trying. He felt that it involved carrying a heavy load, and it would periodically leave him feeling drained to the point that it interfered with the efficiency of his work.

His interactions with his wife were rather standardized and fixed. They did pretty much the same things from day to day. Lanlin described his wife as an industrious person who would often do household chores right up to bedtime. It was customarily at bedtime that they talked about the important events of the day and she usually agreed with the decisions he had made. He described her as being on the cheerful side and having a good sense of humor.

One of her main influences upon him had been to make him feel that it would be foolish to attempt a radical change in jobs, when he had on occasion toyed with the idea. He reported that sexual relations were no longer of much importance in their marriage.

Participation in union affairs played a major role in his life, particularly during the time that he was so fed up with his clerical job. It became a major outlet through which he could gratify his wishes for status and recognition. He noted in his autobiography (286, p. 135):

> In the course of events our company became unionized and I was elected by ballot at the Union Hall as a member of the Labor Relations Committee of our Local. I was elected and reelected and served eight years on this Committee. . . .
>
> Soon I was elected to perform other duties for my Local, such as delegate to State conventions, delegate to the National Convention in Omaha, member of the New England Board of the Union, etc., as well as keeping up my own labor relations work in my Local. I would assist in wage negotiations for other locals in my field in New England, was a member of the joint Wartime Labor-Management Committee, appeared at the State House on bills, was Company Chairman of the United War Fund Drive, and Company Chairman of the Red Cross Drive.

In his union work Charley was consistently conciliatory in his attitude. He felt that there was no basic conflict between labor and management. From his viewpoint the more business prospered the more the union had to gain in terms of being in a better position to ask for wage increases. He felt that most strikes were not necessary. In general he performed his union duties with considerable skill.

The role of property owner was also important in his life. He had inherited property from his father and conscientiously cared for it. The income from the property made a big difference in the way of living he could afford for his family. His careful supervision of the property was modeled after the example set by his father. He indicated that he had always admired his father's hard-working attitude in this respect. In his management of the property he pressed to obtain as high rents as possible; and he had been told by some of his tenants that he drove a hard bargain. It is clear, though, that the property was a source of anxiety, too. For example, he worried considerably when vacancies occurred in his stores. The fact that he owned property seemed to strengthen his middle-class identification. Perhaps this is best symbolized by his active participation in the neighborhood Chamber of Commerce. It should be noted that his participation in community activities was one of his chief ways of making interpersonal contacts outside of his job and family. He had few, if any, extremely close friends.

His manner of getting along with others was based on being reasonable and controlled. It was difficult to stir him to anger and he tended to adopt a placating attitude toward the anger of others. Ordinarily it required a long series of frustrating events to get him to boil over and this usually occurred only in the privacy of his family. His emotional responses in other areas, too, were on the restrained side. Control seemed to be markedly important to him. Through control he hoped to win respect and to fulfill the role of the "good guy." He seemed to have little conflict in deciding what was expected of him in terms of his role. At times the restraint he imposed upon himself was a bit stifling, and he enjoyed getting into permissive situations where he could relax. For instance, he liked to sit quietly in church, especially when there was no service. Although he described himself as a worrier, most of his anxieties seemed to be focused on and confined to family and business matters. He seemed not to have any widespread, diffuse anxieties that might be seriously disruptive.

ERNEST DANIEL

Ernest Daniel was married and had four children. He was thirty-eight years of age, of Irish descent, and a Protestant. At the time studied he was working as a factory operative and made a wage of $2,500 a year. He was a short, strongly built man who conducted himself in a calm and confident fashion. He apparently enjoyed participating in the study and the opportunity it gave him to express his opinions. It pleased him to be able to "shoot off his mouth" and have an attentive audience.

He was the second of two children. He had an older sister. His father was a railroad engineer who despite a fairly low income was able to establish a home in a middle-class area. Ernest and his sister were brought up in a middle-class tradition that involved emphasis on morality and religion. He reported that his mother and father were usually in rather good agreement about how one should conduct oneself and about educational goals, but they often disagreed about financial matters. His mother seemed chronically dissatisfied with their financial condition. He was critical of his mother's attitude in this respect. He felt that she was obsessed about money and was too ambitious. At times she threatened to leave the children when they irritated her, and they would become frightened at the possibility. Ernest recalled that his sister pushed him around and would not reciprocate his offers of friendship. He seemed to be jealous of his sister, who more openly opposed their parents than he did and who had gone on to obtain training as an accountant, a position which gave her relatively high status and a good income. It is interesting that she was a good mathematician and he thought of himself as a poor one.

His best relationship in the family was with his father who was a rather intelligent, shy individual. Father seemed remote and this was enhanced by the fact that he was often away from home because of his work. Despite this remoteness, however, Ernest admired him and had much affection for him. Smith, Bruner, and White note (286, p. 190), "The father served, nevertheless, as a model and object of admiration; Ernest considered himself a 'carbon copy' of his father, whom he rated by all odds the most important influence in his life."

In school Ernest did well. He completed grammar school and three years of high school with ease. Apparently learning was easy for him and he was well liked by his teachers and schoolmates. He participated very actively in rough sports and did unusually well. This was true despite his short stature. While in school his vocational plans were vague and he indicated that his parents gave him little guidance in this area. However, he had had clarinet lessons and two of his friends who were musically inclined persuaded him to leave high school and enter a local music school in order to obtain training for playing in an orchestra. For two years he attended this school and then decided that he was not good enough to earn a living playing music. He tried various jobs and finally obtained a position in a factory with the help of his minister. At this time he was thirty-two years old and he had just had a third child. The factory job was highly routinized and monotonous and had little intrinsic interest for him. The level of ability required to do the job was below his actual intellectual potential (Wechsler-Bellevue IQ 128).

But he did find in this job situation an opportunity to participate in union activities which became an outstanding source of gratification to him. Union work became one of the dominant interests of his life. He worked his way up from being a steward of his department to being vice president of the state organization. His opinion became important in union affairs and he exerted a good deal of influence. As part of his role as a union leader, he read the newspapers intensively and tried to keep himself informed. He liked to debate union policies and wrote letters to congressmen about labor issues. It was his feeling that participation in union affairs had made him a better, stronger man and had taught him a great deal about how to get along with people. To be a part of the union group with its common purpose added to his sense of security. His interest in union work represented a direct following in his father's footsteps, for his father had eventually become a paid union official. It was one of his disappointments that he was not able to rise high enough in the union to occupy a paid union position in similar fashion. One of the paradoxes of Daniel's life was the contrast between the energy and ambition he put into his union work and his passivity about trying to improve his personal economic position. He had shown little interest in finding a job that measured up to his potential ability. It seemed as if there were underlying feelings of inadequacy that kept him from seeking higher goals economically.

Apparently he devoted a lot of time and energy to his children. He wanted to give them the friendly closeness which he felt he had had little of in his own family group. But he was pessimistic about ever having the money to give them a specialized education. This pessimism was part of a tendency to see life as a dog-eat-dog situation with rather gloomy prospects. But at the same time he seemed to believe that life could be good and that people could be happy if they were rational and cooperative. Religion and morality were in this sense important to him; and he felt that it was his duty to implant adequately moral standards in his children. He was inclined to identify future social progress with the achievements of trade unionism. He endorsed the policies of the CIO which he saw as embodying an extensive program of social security.

CLARENCE CLARK

This man was a forty-one-year-old accountant who had been with the same company for eighteen years. His life pattern was characterized by few swings or variations. He avoided the unusual and the unplanned. He early adopted a fixed way of life to which he consistently adhered. The style of life he had adopted was such as to maximize security. His height was average; he was rather slender, and it was his custom to dress inconspicuously. He spoke in a carefully enunciated fashion, but said relatively little unless questioned. During the initial interviews he was highly suspicious as to what would be done with the material that was obtained. But he gradually became more comfortable and later asked the interviewers for their opinions about various problems.

Social class ideals were prominent in his background. Although his parents had only a lower-class income they sought to live by middle-class standards. His father, who had had only a grammar-school education, was a night janitor of a school building and had to work intensely hard. His duties required eighty-four hours of work a week; and the pay was so poor that he sought supplementary income from extra part-time jobs during the day. Clarence's father was a paragon of virtue in that he worked hard, never drank or smoked, and professed high moral standards. His energy was such that despite his low-status job he was able to maintain his family in a "better neighborhood." Clarence's mother had had a high-school education and came from a middle-class background.

Clarence began to work in his spare time at the age of thirteen, and continued to work in this fashion until he completed a two-year business-college course. From then on he worked as an accountant. At the time of the study he had a job paying $3,500 a year with a stable concern. He was the head of his department and had three men working for him. This job was the highest he could probably obtain in his company and he had ideas of looking around for something better; but inertia linked with the security of the immediate situation prevented him from doing so. The mechanics of his work interested him. He liked to work with numbers and he liked the perspective he obtained on the company's operations from his statistical computations. Furthermore, the interactions he had with fellow employees were harmonious and friendly. But he stated that he had to work too hard and that he did not receive enough recognition for what he did.

Clarence's early background was saturated with ideas about attaining high social and economic goals. His parents highlighted the importance of getting an education. He said (286, p. 204), that his father's "one ambition was that I should get an education, and he'd go without a shirt in order to pay my way in school." He described his mother as urging him to be open and friendly with people and also tidy and punctual. But at the same time she seemed to be overconcerned about his safety and did not like him to play rough games. Clarence indicated that his older sister and only sibling was his mother's favorite. As a child he apparently played considerably by himself. He experienced his father as distant and reserved. He said that for this reason he was determined that his own son should not have a similar experience, and so wanted to be a close companion to him. As he was growing up, Clarence was strongly impressed with the sacrifices his parents were making to give him things. He felt very obligated to them and quickly built up a sense of guilt if he hurt them in any way. There was an atmosphere about the house which made for a well-controlled, compulsive, orderly way of behaving. Clarence considered himself to be more like his father than his mother.

He married when he was twenty-nine years of age. His wife was a sociable person who easily established contacts with people and who in that sense filled in an area in which he was only moderately adequate. There were two children born of the marriage. At the time of the study Clarence had a seven-year-old son and a ten-year-old daughter. He left the care of his daughter entirely to his wife, but devoted much time and energy to his son. The problem of bringing up his son was a very serious matter to him; he felt that it was his duty to mold his character in certain directions, even if it meant inflicting punishment. When his son got into difficulties of any sort, such difficulties concerned him not only in their own right but also in so far as they implied that he had not done a good job as a father.

His life was lived in a rather narrow fashion. He had few, if any, friends outside of his job and his family. He engaged in few social activities and even avoided the movies and radio programs. Attendance at church was a regular part of his routine. Every Sunday he and his family went to a Roman Catholic church. When he was at home he worked around the house and apparently gave a lot of thought to financial matters. One of his big ambitions was to reach the stage where all his bills would be finally paid. On the whole he lived an orderly life that seemed quite stable. He showed signs of struggling with feelings of inferiority and dissatisfaction, but his anxieties were maintained within manageable bounds.

He was not much interested in political or world affairs. His opinions about current issues tended to be conventional and were phrased in a way least likely to stir up opposition. Money and morality were the things about which he had the strongest opinions. He was in favor of decency, respectability, and diligence. Religion appeared to him as fundamental to being a moral person. But religion as he conceived it was in the nature of a contract with God who rewards us if we obey certain rules.

LOW BARRIER MEN

HILLARY SULLIVAN

This forty-eight-year-old man was pretty much self-educated. At the time of this study he worked irregularly as a newspaperman. He had been a Catholic but had left the Church and become a Communist. His physical health was generally good. The appearance he presented was that of a large, heavy person who dressed neatly. There was awkwardness in the way he carried himself. He enjoyed talking and was often warm and witty.

He was born in 1898 in Whitney, Connecticut, as the oldest son and second child. Six other children were to follow in the next twelve years, of whom three survived to maturity. Hillary's father was Catholic, native-born, a knitter in a textile plant, and had had a grammar-school education. He had broad interests for a person of his background. Hillary felt very positively toward his father, and when he died of tuberculosis at the time that Hillary was only fifteen it was experienced as a great loss.

Hillary could not recall that his father had any faults. He described him as (286, p. 172) "the finest looking man I ever saw . . . just handsome. A gentle person. . . ." Further, he had this to say about him (p. 172): "I'd say his strongest point seemed to me to be that he had a kind of kindly, calm philosophy. For example, when my mother was blowing off her top and sprinkling holy water on everybody from top to bottom in the house, raising hell, my father would sit calmly and look out of the window. And he'd sort of try to calm things." Hillary also described his father as talented and imaginative and a "minstrel type of Irishman." He indicated that his father had enjoyed entertaining people by doing imitations and reciting Shakespeare and that he had participated in amateur plays and also in semipro baseball. He referred to his father as having been quite a radical for his day, who strongly supported unionism and once tried unsuccessfully to organize the plant at which he worked. Father was Hillary's hero and his main identifications were with him.

Despite the positive way in which he felt about his father, he did not find home life pleasant, because of his poor relationship with his mother. He described her as the villain of the family, a matriarch and disciplinarian. He felt constantly under attack from her. She acted as if the children were always doing something wrong and about to bring disgrace on the family. She tried to control the family by playing off the children against each other and against their father. Hillary said of her (286, p. 173):

> She didn't force you to do anything. She was a person who got you to do things by guile . . . never gave me or anyone else any affection that I know of. I've asked and they say no. . . . Impressing on me how important . . . not "how important" but how imperative it was to bring home what I made . . . and that they'd starve and all that sort of thing. And she always impressed on us how hard she worked . . . always telling us that our father was no good . . . which was all a lie.

As a boy he had felt humiliated by her because she had made him wear hand-me-downs, including girl's clothes. His attitude toward her was one of deep resentment. In later years she was hospitalized with paranoid symptoms.

When his father died, Hillary interrupted his formal education at the point where he had completed two years of high school. He had not found school particularly enjoyable but had become intensely interested in reading books. His first full-time job was as baggagemaster at the Whitney station. He quit this job to join the Navy, served briefly, returned to his railroad job, and then went back into the Navy again for a short period. During this second enlistment he traveled widely and enjoyed what he saw. He returned again to civilian life, and after trying a number of local jobs, embarked on a four-year period of bumming around the country. He was accompanied by a friend, and when this friend accidentally died, Hillary returned to Whitney where he worked irregularly in the mills. During this time he also sold "booze" in New York. In 1925 he started to do newspaper work and continued to do so until about 1933. It was during this period that he developed symptoms of claustrophobia in subways and theaters. He also began to drink heavily and in his early thirties he suffered from delirium tremens.

At the age of thirty he married a woman whose social background was much like his. She had worked in a factory since she was twelve. They were married for eight years and had one child, a boy. Then they were divorced. The divorce was apparently precipitated by his drinking, and the wife obtained custody of the child. Hillary described his wife as having the characteristics of a compulsion neurotic. He said they got along "pretty well" in the early phase of their marriage, but that their relationship was never close. The divorce was disturbing to him mainly because it meant losing his son. He had only periodic and "deliberately casual" contact with his son after the divorce.

Following his separation from his wife and son he obtained work on a WPA Writers' Project. At this time he gave up drinking. It was while he was on the Writers' Project that his Communist allegiance began to take shape. Several of his coworkers were Communists and he was impressed with what they had to say. Their views offered him a guiding philosophy of life—and he was very much in need of one. Communism became the center of his life; and most of his reading and discussion became directed to issues pertinent to his Communist values. He did not join the Communist Party because he was afraid that if it became known he would have difficulty in obtaining jobs. Russia became a symbol of perfection to him and Communist ideology provided him with an area in which his thinking could be sure and definite.

With the outbreak of World War II he went through a whole series of jobs. He did manual labor in the textile mills, and was successively a guard, clerk, and investigator. In 1945 he returned to newspaper work in Boston. This work was not steady but provided him with a sufficient income. At the age of forty-four he married a second time. His wife was a semiprofessional woman. Here is his description of how their marriage occurred (286, p. 175):

> This girl has always lived away from home, never had a home and she's a marvelous companion. And the group we knew went away to war . . . broke up, so we were the only ones left. She was working in one place and she said . . . I said, "you've got a problem and I've got a problem; let's get married." And she said, "we will some day." And we'd meet and talk about it, and then we got an apartment . . . and so (laughs) we got married.

Their relationship in the marriage was founded mainly on intellectual companionship. His wife kept her own job and her own friends and was not dependent on him financially.

In his general contacts with people Hillary sought to establish informal friendships. He was most comfortable when things were pleasant. If he had to relate to people who disagreed with him, he was likely to cover his hostile feelings by clowning a bit. However, he was inclined toward strong impulsive emotionality. At times he would have sharp fits of temper. The most characteristic thing about his emotional life was his high level of anxiety. As a child he was disturbed by dreams about being buried alive and later he had claustrophobia and fears of falling from high places. After his divorce he felt disoriented and feared he was going insane. At times he would become extremely depressed and get the feeling that he was the only person in the world. This would be accompanied by a shaking of his body all over. Hillary had become somewhat resigned to his chronically disturbed state of mind and did what he could in small ways to comfort himself. Although anxiety dominated the picture, he could at times be quite aggressive. He had a paradoxical sense of humor that made a hostile and disconcerting impact. His relations with the average person he did not like fluctuated between a satirical condescending niceness and trying to shock.

SAM HODDER

Sam Hodder, a forty-eight-year-old man, was a factory operative who earned $2,700 a year and who had completed six years of grade school. His life pattern had been so diverse and helter-skelter that it was difficult to determine the order in which things had happened to him. He spoke in an ungrammatical way and used a lot of slang and profanity. He read little and was unconcerned about most abstract matters. It was difficult for him to conceptualize at an abstract level, despite a Wechsler-Bellevue IQ of 113. His sources of information about things were mainly friends with whom he had conversations. He seldom listened to the radio and would only briefly survey any newspapers or magazines with which he came in contact. His bearing was cheerful and he usually appeared to be at ease. His approach to the interviewers was frank and open, and he did not seem interested in impressing them.

At the age of three months he was turned over by his mother to her parents for rearing. He never knew his father. The relationship between his mother and father must have been just a passing one. His mother lived near her parents after she gave him to them, but she had little to do with him as he was growing up. He recalled his grandmother as a warm friendly person who gave him considerable attention and who sought to make a devout Catholic of him. In the early years of his upbringing she did a satisfactory job, but when he became older and more active she lost control over him. He did incidentally recall that she dressed him in clothes which other people made fun of. Her ability to influence him declined precipitously when he was still a boy, and he missed school and church whenever he pleased. Most of the time he stayed away from home and participated in gang activities. His grandfather was a shoemaker. Often he was drunk and generally he was not a very impressive figure. His influence over Sam was minimal from the time he was six or seven years old.

Gang life was of outstanding importance to Sam. He was tall and strong and able to establish himself as a fighter with leadership ability. To be a member of the gang gave him a sense of solidarity and security that he missed in his other relationships. The tradition of the gang to which he belonged was defiance of authority. An endless battle was fought against the school, truant officers, and police. Trickery and cheating were dominant in the gang's tactics. As the members of the gang grew older, the seriousness of their delinquencies increased and some of them became habitual criminals. Sam rejected the criminal role, however, and went to sea as a sailor. He stayed at sea for a few years and had adventures in many parts of the world. Then he came back and tried his hand at various jobs. He had his own business delivering coal and ice for about two years. But when he was thirty-two he took a job with a large company for which he was still working at the time he was interviewed. He enjoyed the security of this job and liked the people who were his coworkers. Also he felt that his work was important and responsible because carelessness could result in the destruction of expensive materials. When his plant was unionized he played a part in the process.

He married at the age of twenty-five "for love," and felt that in general his relationship with his wife had been satisfactory. They had had one daughter. He pictured his wife as a quiet person who had held the marriage together despite his heavy drinking. His wife's mother lived in the same building and gave her daughter considerable support during stress periods. When he drank he was not violent toward his wife nor did he spend the housekeeping money. The attitude which he expressed to the interviewers about his wife and daughter were affectionate and kind; but they got the impression that his family life was of secondary importance to his outside life with men friends. He spent the greater part of his free time away from home and in the company of male companions. His contacts with these friends occurred in such varied settings as Alcoholics Anonymous, groups formed to carry out community projects, and bars where he imbibed only soft drinks in order not to risk the temptation of getting drunk. The great importance of membership in male groups for him during adulthood mirrored the importance that participation in the gang had played in his childhood development. The sociability of such groups helped him to defend against feelings of anxiety and inferiority. Smith, Bruner, and White conjecture that the great amount of drinking he did for a good part of his life was not to allay anxiety in a direct sense but was to reinstate (p. 200) "the happy-go-lucky, irresponsible atmosphere of the boyhood gangs, thus easing the strain of settling down to respectable middle-class adulthood." He actually began to drink at the age of ten or eleven years when helping out on a beer delivery truck. His drinking continued to increase with a wide variety of companions and eventually he was hospitalized twice. Once he had an attack of delirium tremens. After he married he stopped drinking for eight months, but then resumed it. While drinking he never attacked his family and continued to hold his job. At the age of forty-five he gave up drinking following his contact with representatives of Alcoholics Anonymous.

Religion was important in Sam's life. His knowledge of the specific teachings of the Roman Catholic Church was vague but he did seem to believe in a Higher Being who had placed man in the world and decided what was right and what was wrong. He identified religion with order and meaning in the world. He believed that people should control their impulses and give the other fellow a fair chance. If one were unfair, it justified others being in turn unfair to him. Sam indicated that he felt most people were fundamentally decent. There were few issues about which he had any bitterness to express. He felt that the American economic system was a good one. But he did favor all possible social security measures.

JIM GIBSON

Jim Gibson was the only subject who was personally studied by either of the writers.* He was a forty-four-year-old man who was recuperating from tuberculosis in a VA hospital in Texas. He was a schoolteacher by profession, but had been unable to work for over a year because of his illness. When asked to volunteer for the study, he was very obliging and agreeable, and showed not the least hesitation. During most of the interviews he presented a calm mien and spoke in a soft voice that varied little. It was difficult to detect strong emotion in his responses because he kept such level control over himself. At times when he was talking about things with deep emotional significance, his inner disturbance was revealed in a visible hand tremor. He was a man of medium height and build with a soft clear skin that had a baby-pink hue. He bore himself in a manner intended to emphasize dignity and the idea that he expected fairness and respect. Indeed, one of the important themes that ran through the descriptions of his life was his concern that people be sincere with him and not try to deceive him. When he was discussing people who had tried to fool him in some way, he most definitely evidenced signs of deep anger. As more data about him accumulated, it became clear that he found it hard to trust people and that he had been highly suspicious of most of the past significant figures in his life. When he was asked at one point what sort of thing would be most likely to make him angry, he replied, "Lying to me will upset me quicker than anything else." In his discussion of various political figures, his primary criterion for liking or disliking them seemed to be whether they were "two-faced" or not.

Jim Gibson was born near a small town in Texas on a farm which his

---

* Fisher

father owned. Of five sibs he was the second oldest. He was preceded by an older brother and followed in sequence by two sisters, a brother, and then another sister. At the time of his birth his father was a prosperous farmer who owned considerable land and who worked part-time teaching in a nearby school. His father had studied law at the University of Texas but had not completed his law work. He did earn enough credits to get a teaching certificate. Apparently he was an unusually adventurous person who worked hard and tried his hand at many enterprises. He put much energy into buying up land and staking families to farm this land for a share of their harvest. Gibson in reminiscing about his father said, "I've never seen a man work harder than him. He taught school. He considered it a public service. He was in the state legislature for one term. He was a Mason. He took an active interest in the rise of labor unions. He made a series of speeches over the county about it. The labor unions hired him to do it. He was always active in church affairs, handling the business end of problems. He liked sports very much. He was very strict in discipline with us. He believed that what he decided was it and it better be."

He reminisced further about his father's interests: "He raised us up to play baseball from an early age. One of us should have been a baseball player. He liked to swim. Lots of times on the way to town he would stop the car and take his clothes off and go swimming in a swimming hole and the whole family sitting in the car waiting for him. People probably thought Papa was. . . . You could never tell exactly what Papa was going to do next. If everybody thought it was too cold to go hunting, that's exactly what he would do. . . . His extravagance was his main weakness. He never figured the economic way. He was like a bull in a china shop when he went to do something."

Jim went on to indicate that his father lent money freely to almost anyone who asked and that he lost a great deal because many never repaid him. He noted, "Father wasn't a good businessman. He was too good-hearted." In several contexts he indicated that his father was the boss of the household and the final authority on matters of discipline. What stands out in Jim's descriptions of his father is the fact that he was a unique sort of fellow who had originality and drive and who could rarely channel his energies into just one enterprise. He was interested in many things and tried to play numerous roles (e.g., farmer, schoolteacher, legislator). There were a number of striking contradictions in his style of behavior. He was devoted to making a lot of money and yet spent part of his time teaching school. His devotion to making money stands in contrast also to the easy way in which he lent money to others, even if they were bad risks. His unusual style of behavior is illustrated further by the fact that he played an important conventional part in community affairs and yet was willing to lecture in favor of labor unions at a time when union sentiment was highly unpopular, simply because he felt that it was right to do so. He was a serious, strict man and yet would impulsively keep the family waiting in the car while he took a swim in the old swimming hole.

Gibson did not feel close to his father. In many ways his closest contacts came with him when he was issuing instructions about the work that had to be done that day on the farm. He felt that his father's favorites in the family were the oldest sister and the youngest brother. Most of the time he apparently felt cowed by his father and could not escape the sensation that he had to subordinate himself to his many purposes and goals. When Gibson was about eleven, his father developed tuberculosis. In the three following years before he died, the father was a semi-invalid who periodically went off to a sanatorium for treatment. Just prior to his becoming ill he lost a good part of his money as the result of a decline in farm prices. Consequently his illness found the family in poor financial condition, and he would never stay at a sanatorium long enough for a complete cure because he felt obligated to return home and lighten the burden which was being carried by the boys who were running the farm.

Gibson was fourteen when his "Papa" died. It was in the midst of the depression and things had become so bad that there was a scarcity of food. His mother used some insurance money to move the family to a small Texas town and to go to business school long enough to become qualified as a secretary. She also began to review teaching subjects and obtained a teaching certificate at the age of thirty-nine. About this time also she set up a boardinghouse which her children helped her to run. Gibson emphasized how courageous his mother was in raising six children under such circumstances. He described her as taking on the responsibility of the family with great determination and subordinating everything else to insuring their economic survival. He said of her, "Mama was the big boss—Mama was a great psychologist. She never used brute force. She encouraged us to want to be something. She got me to work according to her plans." He focused on the fact that she maneuvered him into doing things. He could always sense what she expected of him and felt that for the good of the family he ought to accede. In his accounts of this period he elaborated greatly on how deprived he was. He had only a few old clothes to wear and was ashamed to go out socially for this reason. He recalled that he rarely had any money of his own and that his mother never trusted him with money. "I am inferior at handling money because I never had any. I never got the knack of holding money. I spend it as soon as I get it." He complained that his mother decided too many things for him. "If I'd let her, I could go home today and she'd tell me what to do." There was considerable resentment in his voice as he recalled this material. He contrasted her philosophy of life with Papa's as follows: "Mama in her efforts gained something back in a material way for herself.

By sixty she owned her own home. But Papa was free in giving help to anyone who asked. Mama believed more in taking the beam out of her own life before she took the splinter out of her neighbor's."

It is interesting that in the interview following this expression of negative feeling toward his mother, he was apologetic and guilty. "Maybe I exaggerated my feelings toward my mother. I overemphasized my feelings toward her and her inclinations to determine my plans. It was her interest in us rather than in herself that determined that." It is clear that he felt extremely controlled by mother and pretty much subordinated to her goals. He felt that he had no right to individual expression which might conflict with her aims. In this respect it is worth noting that his older sister did not marry until she was in her late forties because she felt obligated to live with her aging mother. She too apparently felt that she must subordinate her own life goals to those of the mother.

In a related vein, Gibson produced one Thematic Apperception Test story involving a mother and son in which the son was depicted as being in serious trouble and danger. Despite the fact that it was the son who was in danger, however, Gibson felt obligated to focus the major part of the story in a pitying way on the indirect suffering the son's danger would cause the mother figure. The implication was that the son's anxieties must be considered unimportant relative to those experienced by mother.

After graduating from high school, Gibson decided to go to a small teachers college in the vicinity and to obtain a degree in education which would permit him to get a teaching certificate. He had limited funds and worked at a variety of jobs to make enough money to attend school. It took him several years longer than usual to obtain his degree because of economic difficulties. At the age of twenty-one he developed some signs of tuberculosis and spent four months in a sanatorium, where he was completely cured. While still completing school, he married a seventeen-year-old girl. He was twenty-five at the time. He had known the girl for a year and she had just graduated from high school. Her father was a prison guard and former Texas Ranger, and was quite hostile to anyone courting his daughter. On several occasions he threatened to shoot Gibson if he came around the house. Gibson won the girl's mother over to his side, however, by writing a long love poem. When her daughter showed her the poem, she was so impressed with the feeling in it that she told her daughter she ought to hold onto a man who cared so much about her. Generally, though, one gets the impression that when the marriage finally occurred Jim Gibson's mother and his wife's father were opposed to it. In commenting on his mother's resistance to the marriage he said, "Mama was always proud. They weren't in *Who's Who* and she took the father for a common prison guard. . . . Mama wasn't ready for me to get married. She hadn't picked a person for me to marry yet."

He described his wife in the following terms: "She was shy. Pretty girl. Very attractive. . . . She had a good mind. Quick. Smart woman. She won first place in dramatic acting in the state. I think she would have made a wonderful actress. She was very cool. Not a spitfire type. You could stick a .45 in her back and mean it and she wouldn't show it in her face. I think she was part Indian. Her mother looked like a part Indian. She developed a rather sexy appearance in later years. By twenty-five she was very beautiful—I was very jealous of the attentions she showed to other men."

One year after the marriage she had a stillborn child. About a year later a boy was born and three years later a girl was born. None of the pregnancies were wanted and she became so depressed after the birth of the boy that she attempted suicide by cutting her wrists. There was constant tension and disagreement between Gibson and his wife and during the eleven years of their marriage they fought a great deal. He was very jealous of her relationships with other men.

About two years after their marriage he finally graduated and got a low-paying job teaching the elementary grades in a country school. His wife was very critical of his earning capacity and demanded that she be permitted to take a job and hire someone to take care of the children. At the time of World War II the tension between them had become so great that he impulsively joined the Air Force. He told her that he was doing it because his wages as a private plus his allotment benefits would be greater than the amount he could make as a teacher. He told her he hoped this would satisfy her. During his period in the Air Force they drifted further apart. They did live together for three more years after the war, but things went from bad to worse. Finally they were divorced. He subsequently went through a period of deep depression and drinking and returned to live with his mother for a while in order to pull himself together.

During the period of his life preceding the divorce he had engaged in a great variety of occupations. Shortly after his marriage he worked part time as a reporter. He particularly covered stories concerned with executions of prisoners in a nearby prison. After witnessing eleven executions he quit the job in disgust. Then he started an ice-delivering business of his own to make enough money to finish his college work. When he graduated, he worked for almost four years as a teacher. It was at this time that he enlisted in the Air Force and was in the service for three years. He found the whole experience unpleasant and was unable to advance beyond the rank of private, first class.

When Gibson came out of the service he decided not to go back into teaching. He worked as a truck driver for a short period. Then he got a job as a pay-roll clerk, but was fired after a number of months. He got another job as a clerk for a short period. Finally he returned to teaching in country schools and continued to do so until the time of his divorce. Following his divorce he sold insurance briefly; then he was a credit manager for a dairy for about a year, and once again returned to teaching. He proceeded to teach in various schools for about five years until he developed tuberculosis and had to be hospitalized. It was during this hospitalization that he participated in the present study.

At a period subsequent to his divorce it was agreed that his son should live with him and his daughter with her mother. About this time, too, he decided to remarry. His second wife was a widow a year older than himself. Apparently tension very quickly developed between them. He came to feel that she had married him to exploit him in some way. One of the issues about which they particularly differed was how his son, who was living with them, should be treated. He said, "She was busy all the time trying to run my boy off. I felt she tried to frame the boy. She made the boy rebellious. . . . When she picked on the boy, she might just as well have hit me on the head. I had to step in." She would accuse the boy of wrongdoing and he would defend him.

They argued and fought for two years in this fashion until Gibson became ill with tuberculosis and left for the hospital. His son remained with his wife but their relations soon became so strained that she insisted he could not stay with her any more. Gibson reacted to her refusal to care for his son as a sign that he could no longer live with her and instituted divorce proceedings which shortly afterwards became final. His son went to live again with his mother. But when Gibson heard that he was running around with a "wild crowd," he felt obligated to leave the hospital before completely cured in order to set up a home for him where he could exert some controls over him. He leased a small farm and set out to run it with the help of his son. But once again his tuberculous symptoms became acute and he had to return to the hospital. He wanted his son to go live with his mother. But after some discussion it was decided that the boy (then about age sixteen) would remain by himself on the farm and live there while attending school. Later, however, while on leave from the hospital, Gibson paid a surprise visit to the farm and found his son depressed and living in filth, and he decided that the only way out of the whole dilemma was for the boy to join the Army. He felt that in the Army the boy would get supervision and further education. The boy took his father's advice and joined the Marines.

In describing his son, Gibson tended to focus on his shady side. He kept referring to the idea that there might be more bad qualities about his son than he fully realized: "He probably tells stories freely. He makes things look right. I don't worry too much about him because I know he won't do things unfair to others. My son is not inhibited mentally. I worry about it sometimes. I worry it may cause him to have a brush with the law. Sometimes his behavior doesn't fit social approval." He went on at great length about one incident in which the school coach had caught his boy doing something "very bad," but refused to tell him what it was and simply said that they had settled it between them. He indicated that he frequently detected an attitude of resentment on his son's part toward him, as if he felt "he hasn't been treated quite right. He never could forgive us for the divorce." It was apparent, in general, that he felt quite guilty about the times he had left his son on his own. He was also uneasy about whether he had done right in encouraging him to join the Army at such an early age. One could see that his behavior toward his son had erratically fluctuated between uneasy overconcern, rather authoritarian overcontrol, and guilty indifference.

In planning for his future after leaving the hospital, Gibson had considered three possible lines of work. One possibility was to return to the same sort of teaching he had been doing at the time he became sick. An alternative revolved about the possibility of establishing a company which would contract to clean public buildings. The labor force of this company would consist mainly of men who wanted to earn some extra money working at a part-time evening job apart from their regular line of work. The third possibility Gibson considered was to buy some prospecting equipment and go out searching for uranium. This was more on the order of a fantasy than a seriously considered possibility.

OVER-ALL IMPRESSIONISTIC ANALYSIS

A review of the information which has been presented concerning the high Barrier and low Barrier individuals suggests that there are numerous fairly obvious differences between them. These differences have been roughly grouped into categories which will be described below.

EARLY LIFE

The high Barrier individuals seem to have grown up in family groups in which there was at least a moderate degree of structuring of values and setting of positive goals. That is, one or both of the parents had pretty definite ideas of how things should be done and devoted energy to inculcating such ideas. Just the opposite seems to be true of the low Barrier persons. One is impressed with the relative disorganization and the lack of definite, explicitly phrased standards in their early family life. Their upbringing was guided by fewer positive standards and fewer broad concepts. It would be well to illustrate and expand upon what has been said by reviewing some of the main facts about the early life of each subject.

Let us begin with the high Barrier individuals.

Lanlin was an only child whose father and mother were struggling to establish themselves as members of the middle class. His father was a frugal and hard-working man who was focused on maximizing the value of his property. He described him as "calm, deliberate, and very much of a planner," the family disciplinarian, a man who meant "no" when he said "no." Father represented a business ideology and was a person of definite opinions. Lanlin described his mother as one with whom he had a close emotional relationship. He was her confidant and learned how to get on the best side of her. He did, however, see her as moody, impatient, and quick-tempered.

Daniel grew up in a family which maintained its home in a respectable middle-class neighborhood. He was one of two children who were given a middle-class upbringing with an emphasis on morality and religion. His strongest positive relation was with his father, a railroad engineer, who was shy and remote and yet a source of considerable affection. Daniel considered himself to be a "carbon copy" of his father. He described his mother as impulsive, dissatisfied with their financial status, and quite punitive. She would at times threaten to leave the children if they displeased her.

Clark was raised in a family in which the parents were attempting to maintain middle-class standards on a lower-class income. His father was a janitor of a school building and worked extremely hard. He was industrious, never smoked or drank, and observed the highest moral standards. Clark's upbringing emphasized bettering one's position in life. He indicated that his father's "one ambition was that I should get an education, and he'd go without a shirt in order to pay my way in school." His mother was of middle-class origin. She agreed with the father's educational aspirations for him. She taught him to be tidy and punctual and found it difficult to let him go out and play rough games with other children.

Now, let us review some of the facts about the low Barrier individuals:

Sullivan was one of seven children born to poor parents. His home life was not pleasant. His mother sought to control the family by playing off the children against each other and against their father. She later had to be hospitalized for paranoid symptoms. Sullivan saw his mother as all villain. "She doesn't force you to do anything. She was a person who got you to do things by guile." Sullivan pictured his father as a talented person of broad interests, "the minstrel type of Irishman," who could do imitations, recite Shakespeare, and play semipro baseball. He was somewhat of a radical for his day. He died of tuberculosis when his son was fifteen. His wife rather than he was the disciplinarian of the household.

Hodder was, at the age of three months, turned over by his mother to her parents for upbringing. He never knew his father. His mother had little contact with him after he went to live with his grandparents. He described his grandmother as a friendly and kindly person who was probably an adequate mother during his infancy, but who lost her influence over him when he became an active boy. He learned to do as he pleased and would skip school and church attendance. His grandfather was a shoemaker who was often drunk. The grandfather apparently failed to supply any sort of meaningful model with which Hodder could identify. Hodder spent most of the time with a neighborhood gang and was continually involved in various delinquencies.

Gibson, one of six children, spent his early years in a rather well-to-do Texas farming family. His father was the disciplinarian and boss of the household. He was an unusual fellow who was constantly engaged in many ventures. He did things on impulse and would often get involved in activities that seemed strange or radical to others. He made a lot of money from his economic ventures, and lent it freely, and eventually lost most of it because of investment risks he took. He died of tuberculosis when young Gibson was fourteen, but had been an invalid for several preceding years. Gibson's mother took charge of the family after the father's death. She became the big boss. She exercised extreme control over everyone in the family, but her control techniques were indirect. "Mama was a great psychologist. She never used brute force. She encouraged us to want to be something. She got me to work according to her plans." Gibson recalls that during his mother's reign they were extremely poor and deprived and that he was ashamed to go out socially because he had only a few old clothes to wear. He recalls also that his mother never trusted him with money. He emphasized that her values were very different from his father's, in that she wanted to profit from people whereas his father liked to help others.

One is immediately impressed with the differences in the amount of parental support and guidance that was available to the high Barrier versus the low Barrier individuals. All three of the high Barrier men were brought up by their own parents, had few sibs, and did not lose either of their parents by death while they were still children. One of the low Barrier men (Hodder) was deserted by his mother when he was a baby and never knew his father. The other two low Barrier individuals both lost their fathers while they were still young adolescents, and their fathers were semi-invalids for some time before dying. Furthermore, these two men were both members of families in which there were large numbers of sibs (five or more) competing for the available resources. Such data suggest that the development of definite body-image boundaries may be partially a function of how much help and support is available from the parents. In the absence of certain minimum parental contributions, the individual may be permanently handicapped in developing firm boundaries.

There seems also to be quite a difference between the high and low Barrier men with respect to the definiteness of the goals which were set for them and the directness or openness with which such goals were enforced. The three high Barrier individuals were members of families in which there was an explicit emphasis on achievement, particularly in terms of economic success, and attaining the material things associated with middle-class status. One of the guiding values in these families was to climb the ladder of social and economic success. For example, Clark's father frequently emphasized the value of bettering oneself and of getting an education so as to be qualified to rise in the world. Lanlin's father was forever pointing out the importance of accumulating property. Daniel's mother was obsessed with money and bettering the family's financial condition. One finds little of this type of goal setting in the case of two of the low Barrier men (Hodder and Sullivan). They both grew up in family settings in which the goal was not to rise in the world, but simply to survive. Just to get along from day to day was an accomplishment. In the instance of Gibson, the third low Barrier individual, one finds that his father was interested in economic achievement; but it was an interest much diluted by other goals, some of which were antagonistic to economic attainment. For example, his humanitarian interests led him to lend considerable money to people who were bad risks and he lost a good deal financially for this reason. His concern with economic attainment was not as singleminded and intense as it was in the high Barrier families. These observations derived from the biographical data are certainly congruent with the earlier described findings that high Barrier subjects tend to obtain significantly higher achievement and aspiration scores on various measures than do low Barrier subjects.

Another phase of the differences in the goal-setting behavior of the parents of the high Barrier versus the low Barrier men has to do with directness and openness. It would appear that at least one of each set of parents of the high Barrier men tended to impose their controls in a sharp unconcealed fashion. They openly assumed their right to expect certain kinds of obedience. Thus, Lanlin indicated that when his father said "no," he knew that was final. Clark was never in doubt about what his father expected of him. His father would sit down with him and spell out what he was doing wrong and how he was falling short of expectations. Daniel's mother was very open with her criticisms and would threaten to leave him if he continued to displease her. Quite in contrast, a number of the parents of the low Barrier men were described as relying more on indirection and concealed intrigue to maintain control over their children. Sullivan referred to the fact that his mother tried to control the family by playing off the children against each other and against father. He said of her, "She was a person who got you to do things by guile." Gibson likewise described his mother as never forcing him to do anything directly, but somehow maneuvering him into fulfilling her expectations. In Hodder's case the substitute parental figures simply did not have enough energy and interest to influence him much either directly or indirectly.

It is of interest to note that the two fathers who were actually present in the lives of the low Barrier men (Hodder did not know his father) differ from the fathers of the high Barrier men in that they were apparently less conventional and more likely to do unusual, unpredictable things. The fathers of the low Barrier men are described as having atypical, plastic, dramatic, and intense feeling qualities about them which are not attributed to the fathers of the high Barrier individuals. The low Barrier men would seem to have had greater difficulty in picturing their father's in straightforward simply defined terms. They could not easily classify and unify their knowledge about the father and put it in a clear-cut mold. Their fathers deviate more from expected paths than do the fathers of the high Barrier men.

Sullivan described his father as having multiple major interests, as a "minstrel type of Irishman," someone who was an entertainer and a skilled baseball player, a radical for his time. Gibson similarly referred to his father as a man of many interests and enterprises: farmer, schoolteacher, member of the state legislature, and a pioneering supporter of union activities. He was also the man who, when he got the urge to take a swim while driving his family to town, would seek out the nearest swimming hole and dive in—with the whole family meanwhile waiting for him in the car.

The fathers of the high Barrier men are depicted as being of quite a different species. Lanlin characterized his father as having one primary interest in life: to look after his property. He also recalled that during the greatest part of his childhood his father had little time for anything else and could hardly drag himself away even for a few days of vacation. Clark described his father as a person who worked most of his life as a janitor. He was on duty eighty-four hours a week and in addition took other odd jobs. His whole life outside his family seems to have been built around the activities involved in being a janitor. Daniel said little about his father which would suggest that he had many of the multirole qualities assigned by Sullivan and Gibson to their fathers. Daniel's father seems to have put most of his energy into matters either directly or indirectly related to his work as a railroad engineer.

On the whole, then, it would appear that the high Barrier men were not only exposed to more explicit information about parental expectations than the low Barrier men, but also had less fluid and less complex images of the father after which to model themselves. The high Barrier men found their parents more straightforward in the way they exerted control. On the basis of such data one might hypothesize that the individual finds maximum opportunity for building up definite boundaries in a family setting in which expectations are firm and clear, in which modes of control are open and well defined, and in which parental models are representative of devotion to a limited number of primary values and lines of living. Apropos of this point, it is noteworthy that in several studies described earlier in this book the high Barrier subjects were found to have a more definite image of the parental figures than the low Barrier subjects.

WORK HISTORY

There is quite a difference in the work pattern and work habits of the high Barrier versus low Barrier men. Generally, the high Barrier individuals have shown more interest in work, have been able to choose a definite line of work with less preliminary trial and error, have more consistently remained in one line of work, and have given work activities a greater part in their total life.

Let us consider the work backgrounds of the high Barrier men:

Early in adolescence Lanlin began to work at a grocery store after school and on Saturdays. During high school he worked Saturdays for a department store. After completing a year's business course at a commercial school, he took a job in a bank where he remained only briefly because he decided it was "too gloomy" and therefore quit. He then worked for a very short time in the time-study department of a large manufacturing company. He quit because he found the antagonism of the factory workers toward time-study men very unpleasant. He next obtained a position as a clerk in a household appliance company. He held this job continuously for nineteen years; and the only other job change he made was to transfer, after nineteen years, from the department in which he was working to another division of the same company. During his time with this company he put a great deal of energy into serving as a representative for the union in negotiations with the company. He became very prominent in union affairs and was assigned labor relations tasks in various parts of New England. Apparently he got great satisfaction out of his union work.

Clark was thirteen when he began to work at a spare-time job in a store. He held a variety of such jobs until he finished a two-year business-college course. Upon completing the course, he took a position with a company as an accountant and had remained with that company ever since, for a total period of eighteen years. He rose to be head of his department, with three men under him. He enjoyed most aspects of his work and strongly identified with many activities which occurred within the company framework. He had little social life outside of company activities.

Daniel considered for a while, after finishing three years of high school, that he might go into musical work. He studied music for two years and then decided he was not good enough to make a living that way. He held a succession of miscellaneous jobs and finally secured work in a factory, where he has remained ever since. He performed monotonous work whose difficulty was below his potential ability. He got involved in the activities of the local union, however, and this became his real prime interest on the job. He started as the steward of his department and worked his way up to become vice president of the state union organization. His hope was that eventually he would become a paid union official. Both at work and outside of work his mind was constantly occupied with union affairs.

A review of the work histories of the low Barrier men presents some contrasting patterns:

Sullivan completed about two years of high school. He left his first full-time job as baggagemaster at a station to join the Navy. After brief service he returned to his railroad job, but rejoined the Navy for a short period. Upon returning to civilian life a second time, he and a friend spent four years bumming around the country. Following this period he worked in several mills and sold "booze" on the side. After about a year he obtained a minor newspaper job and remained with this work for seven or eight years. During the depression he lost this job and tried to make a living in such ways as selling beer, selling Christmas cards, and working for the WPA. He was affiliated for a while with a WPA Writers' Project. At the time of World War II he had another whole series of jobs ranging from guard and clerk to investigator. Finally, about the end of the war, he returned to newspaper work of an irregular sort. He was still doing this work at the time he became a subject for this study.

Hodder's work background was rather scattered. He had lived in such diverse ways that it was hard to reconstruct the sequence of his past. He completed six years of grade school. He went to sea and after various adventures returned ashore and tried a variety of jobs. For two years he had his own business delivering coal and ice. At the age of thirty-two he obtained a factory job which he was holding up to the time of the study.

Gibson began his work career in early adolescence by helping his father run their farm. Later, in order to finance his way through teachers college, he did a great number of different kinds of work, varying from part-time reporter to being owner of an ice-delivery service. Upon graduation from college he took a position teaching in a rural school where he remained for about three years. He resigned this position and volunteered to join the Air Force where he was trained as a mechanic. When he left the service about three years later, he decided to look for something more remunerative than teaching. He tried his hand unsuccessfully at truck driving and some miscellaneous clerical jobs. He returned to teaching in various rural schools and continued to teach for several years. Then once again he tried his hand at a variety of jobs ranging from selling insurance to being credit manager for a dairy. He returned to teaching and remained in this field for five years until he developed tuberculosis. During a brief absence from the hospital he tried to set up his own farm, but failed and had to return to the hospital. In anticipation of leaving the hospital when he attained full recovery, he was debating between going back to teaching or starting a company which would contract to clean public buildings.

If we review the data cited above we find that the three high Barrier men have all spent a good part of their adult lives working for one company. Lanlin and Clark experimented very little before finding what appear to be permanent job niches. Daniel had more difficulty in hitting upon a stable job situation, but still relatively less than the low Barrier men. Two of the low Barrier men (Sullivan and Hodder) wandered about (bumming and going to sea) rather aimlessly in distant places for a number of years before they could establish an even moderately stable work pattern. They showed a restlessness that was incompatible with an ordinary, routine job. It is also true of Gibson that he was delayed to an unusual degree in settling down to a particular occupation. He attended teachers college on and off for many years before he finally got his degree. During those years he held many different kinds of jobs for varying periods of time. Even after he got into teaching he kept changing his mind and trying his hand first at one thing and then at another.

The two body-image groups may be compared further with regard to the effort and enthusiasm they have invested in their total job situations. Lanlin and Daniel have not only worked consistently at one job for a long time, but also have put great effort and enthusiasm into the union activities growing out of their job situation. Lanlin was a leading figure in his union, as was Daniel. Clark has apparently put enough effort into his work to become the head of his department. At the other extreme, one notes that Sullivan has only a part-time job and that his work plays a minor part in his life. Hodder sees as one of the chief assets of his job the companionship of his fellow workers. He has plodded along at his routine work and has not invested much energy in other aspects of the job situation (e.g., the union organization) in the way that Daniel (high Barrier) has, who also holds a routine factory job. Gibson has for periods exhibited enthusiasm for some of his jobs, but he waxes and wanes. Few, if any, of his jobs have been sufficiently rewarding to him to remain a major interest in his life. He keeps looking for a job that will be satisfying enough to hold his interest.

In summary, one might say that the high Barrier men show a job pattern that more closely fits what is expected of a man in terms of middle-class standards than does the pattern typical of the low Barrier individuals. The low Barrier men have tended to show a more restless, more wandering, less consistent, and less channeled style of dealing with the whole issue of earning a living.

MARRIAGE AND CHILDREN

The high Barrier men tend to be different from the low Barrier men both with regard to their marriage histories and their behavior toward their children. Those in the high Barrier group seem to have set up more stable marriages, to have committed themselves to more definite and fixed contributions to their spouses, and to have been more motivated to develop close relationships with their children.

A brief review of the pertinent data concerning the high Barrier men follows:

Lanlin married at the age of twenty-five and at the time of the study was still married to the same woman. He said that his wife was a good mother and a fine person. During their sixteen years of marriage they had four children. He spent almost all of his time away from work with his family. His relationships with his wife were very routinized, and each made his contribution to the family without much fuss or friction. He expressed great interest in understanding his children and felt he ought to spend a lot of time with them.

Clark married at the age of twenty-nine and he and his wife had two children. His family was one of his main areas of interest. He spent most of his time outside work at home. Frequently he affirmed that he wanted his children to have a good upbringing. He indicated that he wanted to give his son the companionship which had been lacking in his own childhood. He wanted to mold his character. But he gave much less attention to his daughter whom he pretty much left to his wife to rear.

Daniel was married in his twenties and had three children. There are little data concerning his relationships with his wife and children. It is indicated that he tried to give his children the friendly support which he felt he had not gotten as a child.

Now to consider the low Barrier men:

Sullivan married at thirty. He and his wife were married eight years and then were divorced. His wife secured custody of their one child, a boy. He said that during the earlier years of their marriage they got along pretty well, but that the intensity of their relationship was low. He felt very hurt by the loss of custody of his son, with whom he maintained only distant contact. A number of years later he remarried. His relationship with his second wife was based on intellectual companionship. She kept her job and was not dependent on Sullivan financially. Clearly he did not assume in this second marriage many of the usual obligations of a husband.

Hodder was twenty-five when he married. He said he married for love and felt the marriage had been satisfactory. He felt that his wife had held their marriage together in spite of his heavy drinking. He spoke of her and his daughter affectionately, but the interviewers got the impression that his family life was secondary in importance to the companionship of his men friends. He spent almost all his free time away from home.

Gibson married at twenty-five. There were two children by the marriage, a boy and a girl. Gibson and his wife had a stormy relationship from the very beginning and were divorced about ten years later. Several years following his divorce he remarried a widow, but after two or three years this marriage ended in divorce also. Gibson has periodically shown great interest in his son, but somehow he has never been able to sustain a continuous relationship with him. Their last parting occurred when he urged the boy to join the Army.

In reviewing the data concerning marriage and family relationships, one finds that none of the high Barrier men have been divorced; whereas two of the low Barrier men have been involved in one or more divorces. Furthermore, the one low Barrier individual who has not been divorced (Hodder) indicates that it is only because of his wife's efforts that the marriage held together. Two (Lanlin and Clark) of the three high Barrier men are described as spending a great deal of time at home with their wives; and all are depicted as voicing unusual determination to contribute interest and companionship to their children. The situation is different in the low Barrier group. Sullivan has a rather casual relationship with his second wife and rarely sees his child by his first marriage. Hodder spends almost all his spare time away from home. Gibson is now divorced for a second time and has only rare contacts with his children. Once again it may be said that the behavior of the high Barrier individuals conforms more to conventional middle-class standards of propriety, obligation, and regularity.

MISCELLANEOUS FACTORS

The low Barrier men evidence in still other ways their tendency to take less normalized paths through life than do the high Barrier men. One notes that all the low Barrier individuals have had significant difficulties with drinking too much. Two (Sullivan and Hodder) of the three have had in the past to be hospitalized for delirium tremens. Hodder showed clearly delinquent behavior during early adolescence. Sullivan was troubled by claustrophobia in his late twenties; and at the time of the study he had periodic spells of extreme depression and disorientation when he would get the feeling that he was the only person in the world and shake all over. None of the high Barrier men are reported to have had trouble with drinking and there are no references to their showing deviant delinquent or neurotic behavior. There was some suspicion of a gastric ulcer in Lanlin's case, but it apparently never materialized as a definite symptom.

INTERPRETATIVE COMMENTS

Most of the biographical data have been congruent with the results of the various previously cited objective studies which suggested that the high Barrier person exceeds the low Barrier person in stability, degree of concern with high achievement, need for persistence at tasks, and definiteness of relationships with parental figures. In general, the high Barrier person seems to be a more solid citizen and more likely to keep his nose to the grindstone in pursuit of the goals that society considers important. The high Barrier person seems to be more effective in obtaining conventional rewards and satisfactions from life. He is also more likely to take up and continue to bear the responsibilities expected of an adult in our culture.

It is easy to slip into the viewpoint that there is something inferior about the low Barrier individual. One can succumb to the fallacy of focusing on the "goodness" of the high Barrier person's adjustment and the "poorness" of the low Barrier person's mode of adjustment. In the first place, of course, it should be borne in mind that such a contrast involves comparing people at the extremes of the Barrier continuum. Most people are, after all, not to be clearly classified as low or high Barrier, but rather as falling in the middle regions of the continuum.

As far as those who do clearly represent the high Barrier versus low Barrier orientation are concerned, it is a matter of viewpoint and of values as to how one rates their style of life. If one focuses on conventional achievement and being effective in terms of usual societal norms, then the high Barrier person may stand out as superior. However, one may look at the low Barrier people and see them as less confined to main channels and less willing to submit to broad societal expectancies. In that sense, they are freer than the high Barrier persons. It is as if the low Barrier people, having less definite boundaries, were by that fact more likely to wander into deviant channels and to develop atypical behavior patterns. They apparently have a greater probability of doing things like bumming around the country or joining the Navy to see the world. They go off on tangents disapproved of by society, even at the cost of great anxiety and severe neurotic symptoms. They are apparently more disordered persons than the high Barrier people. But by the same token, their greater disorder may increase their chances for experiencing life outside of its usual mold. They seem to experiment to a greater degree with the basic aspects of life (e.g., work and marriage) and to act more like children who have not yet made up their minds about how life should be lived.

There are two trends in the biographical material which are difficult to reconcile with some of the formulations from the more objective data that have been described. The biographical material indicates that the low Barrier men are in general very friendly and enjoy social interaction. They enjoy their "buddies" and like kidding and horseplay. But various findings from the objective data suggest that low Barrier people are more oriented toward things than people and that they are relatively poor in their ability to empathize with others. At one level, the biographical and objective data are certainly in conflict concerning this point. Perhaps they are not fundamentally contradictory, however, if one considers that although the low Barrier men whose biographies were evaluated can be very engaging and do enjoy social exchange, they have had great difficulty in establishing lasting intimate relationships with others. They show a pattern of conflict with their spouses, divorce, and relative superficialness in their contacts with their children. They may seek fairly superficial relationships with others, but be repelled from more intimate commitments. Thus, one might conjecture that if the high Barrier individual does have relatively more interest in interacting with people than the low Barrier individual, the distinction applies to intimate interaction rather than to less ego-involving modes of relationship.

A second area of apparent conflict between the biographical data and the objective data has to do with the issue of expressiveness and impulse release. The objective data suggested that high Barrier people were more likely than low Barrier people to release impulses freely. For example, they were more likely to gratify themselves when the opportunity presented itself and more likely to express anger outwardly than inwardly when frustrated. But the biographical data give one the impression that it is the low Barrier men who have most often done things on impulse and that it is the high Barrier men who have most consistently held to a straight and narrow life channel even when this channel was frustrating. A key question in probing this inconsistency is whether the more impulsive behavior of the low Barrier men represents real impulse gratification or whether it is the erratic bursting out of impulses too long held in check. One wonders whether the aimless bumming around of some of the low Barrier men was gratifying or whether it was flight from a situation that had become intolerable. Was the bumming around a retreat that actually further prevented the individual from getting some of the things he wanted out of his life? One notes in the biographical material also that, even though the high Barrier men do make themselves stick in frustrating channels, they are more likely than the low Barrier men to seek compensatory release in a kind of activity that will balance out the frustration. For example, two of the high Barrier men worked for years at jobs which they found unrewarding. However, they both turned to union activities in the job situation, and got immense gratification out of the status and success resulting from their activities in this area. This would seem to be a more effective long-term mode of self-gratification than simply retreating to doing nothing or aimlessly running off to distant places.

....

CHAPTER SEVEN

Body Image and Patterns of Group Behavior*

NORMAL GROUPS

UP TO THIS point the concept of body image has been described only in terms of its relevance for individual personality characteristics. A considerable area of personality correlates has been mapped out as bearing some relation to body image. Although such characterization has thus far been restricted to a description of individual behavior, it seemed logical to assume that the striking individual trends uncovered should have application to group behavior. A body-image index, such as the one being presently pursued, may be conceptualized as indicating the way in which the individual sets himself off from others. The whole concept of body-image boundaries has implicit in it the ideas of the structuring of one's relations with others. It would seem to follow that if the body-image concept has something to do with the kind of defensive barriers an individual establishes about himself, an understanding of these barriers or peripheral boundaries should tell us something about the nature of that person's interactions with others.

Accordingly we set out to explore the behaviors in small group settings of individuals with high versus low Barrier scores. Aside from two specific predictions, described at a later point in this chapter, we were mainly interested in exploratory observation of high and low Barrier persons in the course of group interaction. This kind of setting seemed to represent an ideal opportunity to observe the actual extension in a real life situation of the many hypotheses concerning these individuals drawn largely, up to this time, from fantasy and test data. We wondered whether the achievement-success orientation so frequently encountered in studying individuals would appear in a group setting. Would high Barrier members tend to be group leaders, to organize and conduct groups in which they were members? And low Barrier individuals, what could we expect of them in a group setting? Would they attempt to compensate for their lack of personal aggressiveness by a show of bravado in groups? Or

---

* A portion of this chapter appeared in *Human Relations*, Vol. 10, No. 3, 1957.

would they prove to be more quiet and retiring? These were some of the questions we had in mind in applying the body-image index to group behavior. Not only were we interested in the degree of overlap with previous findings, but also in the form and nature such behavior would take in a group process.

Questions and speculations such as these led us to apply the body-image concept to the study of small-group behavior. Examination of the available literature revealed that, although extensive work has been done in investigating the characteristics of group behavior, little experimental work is available relating individual personality traits to group functioning. This point was recently highlighted by Haythorn (144), among others. In his attempt to alleviate this situation he was successful in establishing some individual personality correlates with group activity. For example, he found that such individual traits as insight, cooperativ ness, and efficiency, as measured by Cattell's Personality Factor Questionnaire, promoted group functioning. On the other hand, "striving for individual prominence" (ascendance versus submission) reduced group cohesiveness and friendliness.

Bell and French (20) concluded that individual characteristics measured by the Cattell scale accounted "for over half of the variance in leadership status within the average small group." Using more common clinical measures, such as the Rorschach test, Bass, et al. (17) were able to find Rorschach predictors of Leaderless Group Discussion (LGD) behavior. A large number of responses on the Rorschach or a record rated as "highly energetic" or as having "strong imagination" were all identified with active LGD behavior. On the other hand, ratings on the basis of clinical data have not always been found significantly related to group-behavior ratings. In a study reported by Fouriezos, Hutt, and Guetzkow (108), ratings of individual personality needs on the basis of clinical data were found to be unrelated to the same ratings on the basis of group behavior. A large and extensive literature on small-group behavior will not be reviewed here. Several excellent summaries exist; for example, Hare, Borgatta, and Bales (142), Borgatta (43), Deutsch (80), and Roseborough (253) offer such reviews. Regardless of which position is taken as to the importance of individual and situational factors in influencing and determining small-group behavior, there is a strong continuing need for more understanding of the relative contribution from both sources.

HYPOTHESES

The question posed concerns the ways in which individuals with highly contrasting body images would differ in their behaviors in small-group interaction. Specifically, an experiment was designed to explore the behavior of small groups composed entirely of individuals selected for their commonality of body-image schema. As suggested by the brief survey of the literature cited above, there seems to have been little or no work done in this direction, namely, the formation of "pure" groups on the basis of some personality variable and the subsequent evaluation of the differential character and behavior of such groups. Accordingly we attempted to test the question as to whether a small group composed of individuals with high Barrier scores would differ significantly in behavior while carrying out assigned group tasks from a group with members having low Barrier scores.

In the present experiment two predictions were made about the behavior of the groups under study. The first prediction has to do with the degree of high aspiration and achievement orientation displayed by the groups. This aspect of group behavior was selected for study because it is a highly important factor in nearly all types of group functioning. The ability to predict the kind of group that will "get things done" is especially valuable. Many studies (17, 20, 253) have been devoted to this aspect of group behavior, reflecting the widespread interest in group achievement. As has been mentioned, previous experience with our body-image schema established that high Barrier individuals show the greater concern with achievement and high aspiration in comparison with those scoring low on the Barrier index. Accordingly, in the present study it was predicted that groups composed of high Barrier members would show a relatively higher degree of concern about achievement and success in the course of carrying out a variety of group tasks than would groups with low Barrier members.

A second prediction involves the degree of interest and concern shown by the high versus low Barrier groups in respect to the value of the individual and his importance in human relations. In this case a comparison was made between a philosophy of humanitarianism, on the one hand, versus the alternate view that human relations are relatively unimportant and that human behavior is regulated by external and impersonal forces. Interest in this subject arose from suggestions in our earlier work that individuals differing in their body-image schema probably also differ in their broad philosophy toward life. There were indications that high Barrier persons were more dedicated than low Barrier persons to the feeling that it is the individual and his own efforts that determine his fate. This kind of philosophy also involves the idea that it is not external or impersonal forces that dominate human behavior, but rather the nature and degree of interpersonal relations involved. Such a distinction in orientation toward life would seem to be important for any group activity having to do with how human beings get along and relate to one another. For the purposes of this study, the prediction was made that in comparison with the low Barrier groups, those groups with high Barrier members would show a more humanitarian orientation in their behavior.

METHODOLOGY AND SUBJECTS

Three separate studies were conducted. The first two populations investigated consisted of university students. A third population consisted of student dietitians at the Houston VA hospital. Group Rorschachs were administered to each population. These were then scored in terms of the Barrier index. All Rorschach records were held equivalent as to the total number of responses by limiting total production of each subject to twenty-four responses. Subjects who varied widely on the body-image index were then selected to participate in the small-group experiments. Two basic small groups were set up in each of the subject populations. That is, for each population studied there was one small group consisting of individuals with uniformly high Barrier scores. A second group was established composed of members scoring uniformly low on the Barrier index. The groups ranged in size from five to eight persons. Within any given subject population the groups contained the same number and sex distribution. All the subjects were women with the exception of one of the university populations where each small group contained one man.

Each group was brought together and assigned tasks designed to elicit a range of behavior. All the individual groups were asked to perform the following tasks: (1) To make up as a group two spontaneous stories. That is, all members of the group were to work together and construct stories they could agree on. (2) To discuss as a group the question of what makes for success in our culture. They were to decide together the five most important traits needed for success. Each group was observed by one or the other of the authors. Detailed notes were made of how each group proceeded to carry out its tasks. The stories and discussion material were recorded as verbatim as possible. In addition to the two tasks previously described, the student dietitian groups were asked to discuss two other problems. One of these additional discussion topics had to do with working relations with kitchen employees. The students were asked to discuss ways of improving relationships with kitchen personnel. They were to agree on and list five means of bettering such working relationships. A final discussion topic concerned means of establishing good relationships with ward patients. Again the students were asked to agree on and list five methods of improving such relations. These additional tasks were required of the dietitian population in order to obtain more complete and varied data on their philosophy about how people should get along together.

Each population investigated constituted a separate study and several weeks intervened between each experiment. Thus one may view the entire project as consisting of one original exploratory study followed by two efforts at cross validation and confirmation.

Four experienced clinical psychologists were asked to evaluate the spontaneous stories and discussion material. Each rater worked independently and without knowledge as to which of the small groups produced the data. The procedure was for one of the authors to read randomly to a rater the various stories and discussion formulations of the groups. Following the reading of any pair of stories or discussion material summaries, each judge made two ratings having to do with the previously described original hypotheses of this study. First he indicated which of the two stories or discussion records revealed the more interest and concern with themes of high aspiration and achievement. Secondly, he rated the same data as to the degree of concern with the philosophy of humanitarianism, i.e., the idea that personal relationships and human dignity are of paramount importance in human behavior.

In addition to the four individual judges used, two *groups* of judges also made the same evaluations. Raters working as a group were originally employed because it was felt that the material produced by the small groups was too complex for individual analysis. Experience soon proved, however, that independent raters could analyze this material without difficulty. One group of raters consisted of three clinical psychologists other than those who had acted as individual judges. This group rated the assigned material from one of the university populations. A second group of judges was made up from student dietitians not involved in the group study. These judges evaluated the group material from the student dietitian population. All the judges were informed at the outset only as to the number and sex of the individuals comprising each group. In the process of differentiating the productions of the high Barrier groups from the low Barrier groups, the four individual judges made a total of twenty judgments. The group of judges who rated only the material from one student population made a total of six separate judgments. The dietitian judges who rated only the group material from the student dietitian population made a total of eight ratings.

RESULTS OF THE THREE EXPERIMENTS

The most obvious finding that emerged from this series of studies has to do with the pattern of participation in each of the small groups. Qualitative observation indicated that groups composed of individuals with the more definite body boundaries showed a consistent pattern of equal participation. Each person sought to express his views and no one individual emerged as a definite leader. There was much cross discussion and a large volume of talk. Furthermore, the atmosphere was more free and there was a great deal of kidding and joking. Themes of hostility or sex, which usually stir up anxiety in groups, were discussed in an open and relaxed manner. On the other hand, the groups comprising individuals with less definite body boundaries behaved differently. In these groups the members tended to sit passively and wait for one individual to take the lead and tell the group what to do. The volume of talk was limited and little spontaneity was evident. Joking about sexual topics or discussion of hostile behavior was absent. The atmosphere was somewhat like that of a classroom in which the pupils wait for instructions from the teacher. Consequently, the spontaneous stories of the low Barrier groups tended to consist of a series of discrete episodes offered by separate individuals. In the case of the high Barrier groups the stories were much better integrated and more obviously a cooperative venture. The atmosphere in the latter groups may be characterized as being more democratic, spontaneous, and lively than in the low Barrier groups.

In Tables 7:1 and 7:2 the results of the ratings of the group stories and discussion material are presented. It will be noted that the four individual judges and the two groups of judges demonstrated a high degree of uniformity in their ratings. It will be recalled that each rating involved a simple decision as to which of two behavior samples indicated higher achievement orientation or the more humanitarian outlook. By chance alone each judge or group of judges would have placed only one-half of their total number of ratings in agreement with the experimenters' hypotheses. Tables 7:1 and 7:2 reveal that two judges made their ratings in complete agreement with the hypotheses. One judge disagreed on two decisions, one on six, and the two groups of judges agreed with the hypotheses perfectly on a smaller number of ratings. Examination of these two distributions of ratings by chi-square analyses yields chi-square values of 16.0 in the case of the achievement variable and a chi-square value of 16.5 in the case of the humanitarian variable. Chi-square values of this magnitude are significant beyond the .001 level of confidence, assuming one degree of freedom. In both these analyses the total distributions of judges' ratings on each variable were placed in a fourfold table. The actual ratings of the judges were compared with a chance distribution of the ratings, assuming that by chance only one-half the ratings would have been in one direction.

The results of these analyses demonstrate that judges working on a blind basis were in agreement far beyond chance expectancy in recognizing the stories and discussion material as having definitely contrasting features. In line with the experimenters' original hypotheses, these raters named the productions of the high Barrier groups as having the greater concern with themes of high aspiration and achievement. They were in agreement with the authors in recognizing the stories and discussion material of the high Barrier group as being more focused on a humanitarian

TABLE 7:1   JUDGES' RATINGS OF GROUP STORIES AND DISCUSSION
MATERIAL ON ACHIEVEMENT-ASPIRATION

Rater	Total No. of Judgments	Judgments in Agreement with Original Hypothesis
Judge 1	10	10
Judge 2	10	10
Judge 3	10	9
Judge 4	10	7
Psych. group	3	3
Diet. group	4	4

TABLE 7:2   JUDGES' RATINGS OF GROUP STORIES AND DISCUSSION MA-
TERIAL ON HUMANITARIANISM

Rater	Total No. of Judgments	Judgments in Agreement with Original Hypothesis
Judge 1	10	10
Judge 2	10	10
Judge 3	10	9
Judge 4	10	6
Psych. group	3	3
Diet. group	4	4

philosophy than is the case of groups with members characterized by less
definite body-image boundaries.

The individual raters who evaluated the group productions made some
interesting comments in a consistent manner concerning the groups.
Three of the four individual judges, on the basis of the story material,
made the spontaneous remark that they would rather have as personal
friends the members of the high Barrier groups. This choice seemed to
be a result of the observation that these subjects expressed themselves
more freely and with greater emotional latitude than did the low Barrier
individuals. The judges' attitude in this respect is important, since it
tends to support the prediction that the high Barrier groups manifest
relatively greater positive interest in human relations and the importance
of the individual. Apparently some of this same feeling was communicated to the judges and influenced them in their preference for members
of these groups as personal friends.

It is incidentally worth mentioning that one of the university classes
studied demanded and was given a class hour following the experiment
in which the members asked questions of the experimenters concerning
the nature of the study. Quite strikingly, members of the high Barrier
group took over and dominated this meeting almost completely. They
were persistent and intense in their questioning of the authors. This kind

of behavior within a larger type of group setting is further evidence of the assertive orientation of the high Barrier group members.

CONTENT OF THE GROUP PRODUCTIONS

The ratings and observational data yielded some clear differences in group behavior and attitudes between the high and low Barrier groups. An even more graphic illustration of the differing philosophies held by these groups can be found in the actual content of the group productions. First of all, the spontaneous stories told by these groups provide an interesting contrast in content and theme. For example, in one of the university populations the high Barrier group told the following story:

"Individual has grown up and finds he was an orphan. He's a politician, just starting his political career. They begin to smear him. He traces back and finds he's the illegitimate son of King George. He's going to show that heredity doesn't make a man bad. Even though he's from a stupid family, he does well. Horatio Alger story."

But the following story was told by the group with low Barrier members:

"An old squeaky house, no one lived there, all hidden by brush, haunted; mysterious people used to live there. They had a candle burning in the window and it still did after they left. It would burn every night. One day two kids decided to go up there. They found the candle and got scared and ran away. A man came along and wondered why they were running. He was the son of the people who burned the candle and came home the night they died in an auto accident. He never saw his parents and he put a candle in the window for them. It burns all the time for them."

These stories point up a number of interesting and differentiating aspects between the two groups. In the first story, given by the high Barrier group, the theme of struggle against odds, even against heredity, is apparent. A theme of achievement and success highlights the story. A certain degree of humor and saucy impertinence toward authority is also apparent. Most important of all is the idea that the individual gets something done and changes his status only through his own efforts. In contrast, the second story, produced by the low Barrier group, contains no theme of achievement or success. This is a far more disorganized and aimless story. People behave in a certain way not from any inner conviction of good orientation; rather, they do what tradition and custom has established. Thus, the man burns the candle in a window in some kind of fixed ritual.

Even more striking in differentiating the high and low Barrier groups were the special discussion tasks added to the total assignment of the student dietitian groups. In this case the two small groups were given special discussion topics pertinent to their own activities. They were asked to discuss ways of getting along better with kitchen employees and with ward patients. These discussion topics were assigned to elicit in greater detail the respective viewpoints of the two groups in regard to inter-personal relations. The group with high Barrier members listed the following five suggestions for better working relations with kitchen employees: (1) Be friendly. (2) Be interested in them. (3) Know theory of dietetics. (4) Compliment employees when they make a correct decision. (5) Pitch in and help.

In contrast to these suggestions, the group with low Barrier members offered the following five methods of improving working relations with kitchen employees: (1) Kitchen employees should have more training. (2) Better schedules for them. Expect them to be at work and not leave early. (3) More supervision of them. (4) Better understanding of where employee's job leaves off and dietitian's begins. (5) Development of better attitude on their part.

The attitudes expressed in these two separate group discussions are in nearly complete opposition. In the case of the five suggestions made by the high Barrier group, the entire emphasis is placed on consideration of the employee as an individual. Respect is expressed for his importance, and his feelings and reactions are recognized. Compare this philosophy with that contained in the five suggestions made by the low Barrier group. Here the emphasis is on greater structuring of hierarchical relationships. The individual and his feelings invite no interest. Rather the position is taken that personal feelings are unimportant. People get along best when strict codes of conduct are established. The distinction in these two opposing frames of reference is sharp.

IMPLICATIONS OF THESE GROUP STUDIES FOR INTERPER-
SONAL RELATIONS

It is clear from the results described that the extreme groups do differ in their conception of how people make their way in the world. Two distinct patterns of group interest and interaction emerge from this study. These patterns are sufficiently broad to justify referring to them as representing two different philosophies about human behavior and personal interrelations. One type of philosophy emerges from the behavior and attitudes expressed by the groups composed of members with a body-image schema of firmness and definiteness. Assertiveness, self-initiative, and achievement orientation characterize their approach to their environment. Not only do they talk more in their group discussions about getting things done, these same groups were also observed to indulge in greater amount of interaction, free expression, and initiative, in contrast to the groups with low Barrier members. This proved to be true not only for the planned group meetings but also for informally observed activity outside the experiment proper. This display of assertion and initiative took place without the guidance or prodding of a leader. In contrast to this pattern of group interaction is the type of interchange observed in the groups with members having less clearly defined body-image boundaries. In these groups a far more passive and inert kind of group interplay occurred. Members tended to sit back and await the emergence of a leader who then structured their mode of conduct for them.

It should not be assumed that high Barrier groups are aggressive in the sense of being inconsiderate of others. Rather their life style also includes a high regard for the importance of the individual. Interpersonal relations are seen as ordered along a feeling basis rather than controlled by hierarchical rules and regulations. At first glance the tendency of the high Barrier groups to show so much interest in the welfare of the individual may seem paradoxical. Why should aggressive and striving groups pause to consider the interests of others? One explanation may be found in the nature of the body-image schema shared by the members of these groups. Since definite body-image boundaries imply definiteness of purpose and confident self-steering, such individuals probably experience relatively little threat in their interactions with others. This explanation becomes even clearer when the pervading philosophy of the low Barrier groups is examined. Their philosophy emphasized the strict hierarchical structuring of human relations. People were seen as behaving in a certain way not because of individual assertion, but rather according to tradition or because it was "the thing to do." Subordinates, such as kitchen help, were to be encouraged in their work not by the dietitians becoming more interested in them and liking them as people, but by establishing stiffer rules and regulations. The emphasis is placed on establishing some kind of external firmness and structure in the guise of rules and codes of conduct with which to order interpersonal relations. Such ordering of people reduces the possibility that unexpected things can occur against which there seems to be no defense by the individual in terms of his own strength.

A general pattern of personality characteristics emerging from previously described studies of body image and individual behavior as well as the group behavior described in this chapter can be seen. It will be recalled that the high Barrier person was found to have a constellation of interests centering about such areas as humanitarianism, contacting, and in general, communicating with people. At the same time the high Barrier individual expresses little interest in things, in theoretical rumination, or in general, in quantitative aspects of life. Low Barrier individuals, however, indicate a preference for theoretical matters, for a quantitative approach to life. Theirs seems to be a life of things rather than people. This same pattern of interests and attitudes was also reflected in the results of the application of the body-image index to Roe's data, as described in Chapter 5. Physical scientists were found to be significantly low on the Barrier score, while in contrast, trained and experienced personnel in the social sciences, anthropologists, and psychologists made unusually high Barrier scores. Again the distinction appears to involve a tendency on the part of high Barrier individuals to seek a way of life in close contact to others, sensitive to the needs of others. Those in the physical sciences, on the other hand, score low on the Barrier index and devote themselves largely to a world of things.

The findings concerning the relationship of body image and group behavior seem to be closely related to this same pattern of life orientation. Groups with high Barrier members demonstrate an interest in people and individual feeling. They press forward and stimulate one another in their search for human contact. Low Barrier groups were noted to be more impersonal. They remained relatively inactive in group participation and sought guidance for their conduct in objective rules and regulations.

Other theoreticians have described behavioral types which closely approximate some aspects of the Barrier concept highlighted by the results of the group studies. Perhaps most striking is the analogy to Riesman's (245) inner-, other-, and tradition-directed types. Considering the completely disparate data from which Riesman evolved his typologies as compared with the body-image index, one is all the more impressed by the similarities evident. For example, the inner-directed person is considered by Riesman to have acquired early in life a kind of internalized 'gyroscope" enabling him to chart a relatively independent and stable course in life. This type of person is thought to rely but little on external codes and traditions for guidance but rather to guide himself by a strong, inner goal-directed sense. He is even "at home abroad" because of his strong, inner psychological gyroscope. The inner-directed person is also felt to be ambitious, success-oriented, forceful, and to have a high level of self-awareness.

In many respects this description approaches that advanced concerning the high Barrier person. This is especially so in respect to Riesman's use of the gyroscope analogy of inner direction. *Self-steering* is the term applied by the authors to the high Barrier individuals. Both concepts make use of the idea of some kind of self-centered sense of purpose and being in life. Riesman's two other types, tradition-directed and other-directed, are credited with behavior remarkably similar to that described in the present low Barrier groups. Riesman feels that these two types are lacking any strong, inner sense of direction. They conduct themselves by relying on tradition, social codes, ethics, or on the opinions and influence of friends and associates. Here the similarities of Riesman's types to the body-image types end, for in other important aspects they are quite different.

Of course the groups described in this chapter represent a special situation. Members were carefully selected in order to maximize group differences in behavior. Only further research with this body-image variable can determine the extent to which these findings can be generalized for less saturated groups. Unanswered, also, is the question as to the effect on group behavior of intermixing various kinds of body-image types. In any event, the present studies have shown that an individual personality variable has relevance for predicting some aspects of small-group behavior. One would conjecture that the Barrier variable is relevant to group behavior since it gets at the degree to which individuals establish boundaries about themselves. In a sense, the body-image index furnishes an understanding of the way in which the individual sets himself off from others. Even though this body-image variable is an individual personality measure, implied in the concept is the notion of how the individual structures his relations with others. Does he set himself clearly apart from others and thus, with his own boundaries clearly defined, feel free to interact with others? Or, on the other hand, does he have difficulty in setting himself off from others and therefore seek some kind of external structuring of personal interactions which will artificially supply this separation?

FURTHER VALIDATION OF THE RELATIONSHIPS BETWEEN BODY-IMAGE BOUNDARIES AND SMALL-GROUP BEHAVIOR

Following the various studies described above involving small-group behavior, an opportunity arose permitting still another cross-validation study of our findings. In August, 1956, the second annual session of the Human Relations Training Laboratory convened for a two-week period at a ranch near Las Vegas, New Mexico.* Delegates attended this laboratory in order to receive training and experience in the functioning of small groups. As a by-product of the conference a great many varied measures of group interaction were obtained. In addition a group Ror-

---

* The research material presented in this section was collected at the Human Research Training Laboratory jointly conducted by Kansas State College, Southern Methodist University, the University of Texas, and the University of Colorado. The research data was collected under the direction of Dr. Robert R. Blake and Mrs. Jane S. Mouton of the Department of Psychology, University of Texas. The research program itself and a detailed description of the conference are reported in a monograph, "Personality Factors Associated with Individual Conduct in a Training Group Situation." See Bibliography, #37.

schach was elicited from each delegate permitting a comparison of the Barrier index with a host of other social and group interaction measures.

In order to place in proper context the application of the Barrier index to the Training Laboratory research data, a brief description of the conference is necessary. A more detailed account of both the conference and the research program conducted by Dr. Robert R. Blake is available in the monograph referred to in the footnote of the previous paragraph. Based in part on the original studies in group dynamics held annually at Bethel, Maine, the Training Laboratory provides an opportunity for the training of individuals in the functioning of small groups. These individuals are formed into groups which operate in a unique setting and without any of the traditional formality of group structure such as a formal agenda, a secretary, a president, or even a formal group leader. Delegates attending the Laboratory come from a variety of fields such as industry, education, public health, and community services. Among them are numerous people with managerial or supervisory responsibility and with high levels of professional training.

Blake and Mouton (37) describe the Laboratory in the following manner:

> The training group has no "work" problem in the ordinary sense. It has only members who are free to discuss whatever they are able to discuss. Its members do not interact through a formal agenda, role structure, under pressures to produce "specific" results, nor in terms of ordinary time pressures. Personality characteristics, therefore, may be expressed more freely. It has eight or nine people composing the group; it has a trainer; yet as soon as group action starts the trainer is seen to act differently than an ordinary leader in a typical problem-solving group. There is no differentiated role structure; that is, there are no differences in roles that people are assigned either in composing the group or in its beginning phases. The training group has none of the ordinary parliamentary rules or work procedures imposed that have been crystallized and formalized in the long tradition of western culture. Without output and time pressures and with the possibility of trying and analyzing consequences of various procedures and actions, it is possible to investigate more easily relationships between personality and individual conduct within the group since basic personality factors are not restricted from expression by the same degree of conscious control that appropriately is exercised in a work group type of situation.

Twenty-four delegates, twelve males and twelve females, attended this session of the Laboratory. Three groups of eight members each were formed with equal division in each group in respect to sex. Personal acquaintance within groups was also avoided by placing personal friends in different groups. The three small training groups met one and three-quarter hours per day each of the ten work days of the conference. Membership within the groups was held stable throughout the entire Laboratory session. One staff member served as observer or trainer for each group meeting. Blake and Mouton (37) describe the function of the trainer as follows: "The trainer is concerned with the psychological processes that arise as interactions occur among members of the group. He does not act as a chairman, giving the group a topic to analyze or an agenda on which to work. His primary role is that of calling attention of members to certain critical events that have significance for understanding the psychological properties of problem-solving groups."

In studying and predicting the behavior of the Laboratory delegates in the small training groups, Blake and Mouton measured two personality dimensions. One was language skill and the second was the ascendancy-submissiveness dimension. A forty-item, four-alternative, language-facility test was devised from past issues of the *Reader's Digest*. The Allport *A-S Reaction Study*, forms A and B, were used to grade the degree of ascendancy-submissiveness of the group members. These two tests were administered on the first and second days of the Laboratory session. The test results in no way influenced the formation of the small training groups, as these had already been established. The two tests served as measures for predicting a great many different aspects of individual behavior in the group training sessions. A detailed report of the results pertaining to the measures is available in the previously mentioned monograph (37).

For the purposes of the present study it is important to note that the Barrier index was found to be completely unrelated either to the language facility or to the ascendancy-submissiveness dimensions as utilized by Blake and Mouton. The relationship of Barrier score to these two measures was studied in the following manner. On the twelfth day of the Laboratory meeting the group Rorschach was administered to the twenty-four delegates.* The total number of responses given was controlled in the usual manner, and the records were scored for Barrier responses. The range in Barrier score for this group was found to be 2–9, and the median Barrier score 4. Rank order correlations of .15 and .25 respectively were obtained between Blake's language-facility and A-S measures and the Barrier scale. Correlations of this magnitude are not statistically significant. This point is important since Blake and Mouton had found various significant relationships between the language-facility and A-S measures and group behavior. We may conclude that any relationships found between Barrier score and group behavior are not a function of variables sampled by these two particular measures employed by Blake.

---

* We are indebted to Dr. Robert B. Morton, Chief Psychologist, VA Hospital, Houston, Texas, a delegate to the Laboratory, who collected the Rorschach data.

Although Blake and Mouton employed many different measures of group behavior, only one measure offered an opportunity to check some of our previous findings relating body image to small-group behavior. This measure is a twenty-two item sociometric type of questionnaire. Blake and Mouton report that the "questionnaire is one employed previously in therapy and training groups and known to contain items of a kind that group members feel able to answer with a significant degree of reliability and accuracy." The questionnaire was administered on the

TABLE 7:3   GROUP BEHAVIOR QUESTIONNAIRE *

1. Which two members of the group can most easily influence others to change their opinion? _____

2. Which two are least able to influence others to change their opinions? _____

3. Which two have clashed most sharply in the course of the meetings? _____

4. Which two are most highly accepted by the group at large? _____

5. Which two are most ready to protect and support members who are under attack? _____

6. Which two have been most able to operate effectively without direction and support from a process analyst? _____

7. Which two have shown the strongest need for direction and support from the process analyst? _____

9. Which two are most likely to put group goals above personal goals? _____

10. Which two are most likely to put personal goals above group goals? _____

11. Which two have shown the greatest desire to accomplish something? _____

13. Which two have wanted to avoid conflict in the group discussion? _____

15. Which two tend to withdraw from active discussion when strong differences begin to appear? _____

16. Which two have sought to help in the resolution of differences when they have arisen between others? _____

18. Which two have wanted the group to be warm, friendly, and comfortable? _____

20. Which two have tried to do the most to keep the group "on the ball"? _____

21. To which two do you usually talk the most? _____

22. To which two do you usually talk the least? _____

---

* Devised by Blake and Mouton (37). Question numbers refer to the original item numbers. Five items not considered appropriate to the present study were eliminated.

fifth and again on the tenth day of training. Actually only seventeen of the twenty-two items of the sociometric questionnaire appeared appropriate to the present study. That is, the present investigation was designed to provide an approximate replication of the three previous studies relating Barrier score to small-group behavior. The seventeen sociometric items selected in advance for analysis appeared to approximate the hypotheses previously investigated; but the five items omitted had nothing to do with these hypotheses.

In Table 7:3 the items selected for analysis are listed. For every item, each member nominated two persons from his own training group. Scores on this questionnaire consist of the number of nominations received by each delegate. The possible range of nominations is 0–7, delegates not being permitted to nominate themselves.

It will be recalled that the previous studies relating Barrier score to small-group behavior established consistent behavioral patterns for high versus low Barrier group members. Thus, in comparison to low Barrier groups, high Barrier groups operated with a minimum of group structure, no formal leader, and group discussion was free, relaxed, and more spontaneous. High Barrier personnel were more friendly, more anxious to get something done, and more willing to express personal feelings, including such emotionally charged feelings as hostility and aggression. On the other hand, low Barrier members avoided open conflict in a group, leaned heavily on an authority figure, and relied on traditional rules and regulations of social conduct.

Proceeding on the basis of these findings, we made the following predictions in respect to number of nominations on the sociometric questionnaire:

(1) That high Barrier members would receive significantly more nominations than low Barrier members on items 1, 4, 5, 6, 9, 11, 16, 18, 20, and 21.

(2) That low Barrier members would significantly exceed high Barrier members in number of nominations for items 2, 3, 7, 10, 13, 15, and 22.

The distribution of Barrier scores was divided at the median, those scoring at or below the median Barrier score of 4 being classed as "low Barrier." Those scoring 5 or more on the Barrier index were classed "high Barrier." This division of the twenty-four delegates resulted in an even split with twelve high and twelve low Barrier members. In like manner the distribution of nominations for each of the seventeen sociometric items was analyzed. Chi-square tests were run for the Barrier distribution against each of the seventeen sociometric items, once for the first administration on the fifth day of the conference and again for the second series of nominations made on the tenth conference day.

TABLE 7:4   COMPARISON OF HIGH AND LOW BARRIER MEMBERS ON THE FIRST ADMINISTRATION (5TH DAY) OF THE GROUP BEHAVIOR QUESTIONNAIRE

Item	No. of High Barrier Members Receiving Nominations		No. of Low Barrier Members Receiving Nominations		χ^2	P (One-Tailed Test)
	Above Median	Below Median	Above Median	Below Median		
1. Influence others most	6	6	5	7	0	—
2. Influence others least	4	8	7	5	1.5	.11
3. Members who clash most	7	5	7	5	0	—
4. Members most accepted by group	9	3	7	5	.75	—
5. Most protective of others	7	5	5	7	.67	—
6. Operate independently of process analyst	8	4	5	7	1.5	.11
7. Most dependent on process analyst	6	6	8	4	0	—
9. Group goals above personal goals	7	5	6	6	0	—
10. Personal goals above group goals	7	5	6	6	0	—
11. Greatest desire to accomplish something	6	6	6	6	.67	—
13. Avoid conflict	7	5	5	7	.67	—
15. Withdraw when differences appear	7	5	5	7	.67	—
16. Most active in resolving differences	8	4	5	7	1.5	.11
18. Most want warm friendly group	10	2	5	7	2.8	.05[a]
20. Keep group "on the ball"	7	5	5	7	.67	—
21. Members talk to most	7	5	4	8	1.5	.11
22. Members talk to least	5	7	8	4	1.5	.11

[a] With Yates correction.

Tables 7:4 and 7:5 present the results of these analyses for the fifth and tenth day questionnaires respectively. The first interesting finding to be noted is that, as would be expected, the nominations made on the tenth day of the conference produce much more differentiation than those on the fifth day. On the fifth day, when presumably the members had hardly got to know each other, only six of the seventeen items even ap-

TABLE 7:5   COMPARISON OF HIGH AND LOW BARRIER MEMBERS ON THE SECOND ADMINISTRATION (10TH DAY) OF THE GROUP BEHAVIOR QUESTIONNAIRE

Item	No. of High Barrier Members Receiving Nominations		No. of Low Barrier Members Receiving Nominations		χ^2	P (One-Tailed Test)
	Above Median	Below Median	Above Median	Below Median		
1. Influence others most	6	6	6	6	0	—
2. Influence others least	5	7	7	5	.67	—
3. Members who clash most	4	8	8	4	2.7	.05
4. Members most accepted by group	10	2	4	8	6.2	.01
5. Most protective of others	8	4	7	5	.18	—
6. Operate independently of process analyst	8	4	3	9	4.2	.02
7. Most dependent on process analyst	4	8	8	4	2.7	.05
9. Group goals above personal goals	7	5	3	9	2.7	.05
10. Personal goals above group goals	4	8	8	4	2.7	.05
11. Greatest desire to accomplish something	6	6	9	3	.71	—
13. Avoid conflict	5	7	8	4	1.5	.11
15. Withdraw when differences appear	6	6	6	6	0	—
16. Most active in resolving differences	7	5	3	9	2.7	.05
18. Most want a warm, friendly group	9	3	3	9	6.0	.01
20. Keep group "on the ball"	6	6	6	6	0	—
21. Members talk to most	4	8	4	8	0	—
22. Members talk to least	6	6	8	4	.69	—

proach significant differentiation in respect to Barrier score. By the tenth day, however, when presumably consistent differences in behavioral patterns had had time to emerge, nine of the seventeen items show themselves able to distinguish high and low Barrier members. Several of these chi-square values are significant at or beyond the .01 per cent level of confidence.

Secondly, it will be noted that all the items on which high and low Barrier members are differentiated significantly, or where the differentiation approaches significance (.10), the direction of the difference in number of nominations received is in line with the hypothesis. There are no significant reversals of hypotheses occurring.

When all the limitations of the present study are considered, the emergence of these positive findings appears all the more significant. For example, the delegates attending the Laboratory represented a highly select group of subjects. Some of them had had considerable exposure to the Rorschach test and they could have been handicapped in giving a spontaneous record. In spite of the presence of such a potentially limiting factor in the production of Barrier responses, a representative and varied range of scores was obtained. Most important, we were able to predict in advance from these scores some significant aspects of group behavior.

It is true that, considered separately, these four experiments with group behavior fall short of the ideal goals sought in respect to strict rigor and levels of statistical significance, yet the over-all pattern emerging from these studies is impressive. In effect we have successfully pursued the relationship of Barrier score to group behavior through four successive and separate populations. It appears that the pattern of group behavior characterizing the high Barrier members in the present study closely approximates the behavioral pattern found in the previous studies. Thus, high Barrier members in the present study are nominated as being better able to function independently of authority figures (in this case the group trainer). On the other hand, as we predicted, low Barrier delegates receive the greater number of nominations for "showing the strongest need for direction and support from the process analyst."

Blake and Mouton (37) describe the possible degree of reliance on this authority figure in the following manner: "The training situation provides ample opportunity for expression of personal needs in the area of authority relationships. Since the trainer does not 'lead' in the conventional sense, those who want more direction easily can seek it, for example, through direct pleas to the trainer for help. . . ." The high Barrier members apparently rely more on their own goals and objectives; what we have referred to as the self-steering ability of the high Barrier personnel presumably aids in the independent conducting of their group activity. A consistent finding in these studies has been the observation that high Barrier members with a kind of built-in system of objectives and goals are less inclined to seek external aid and cues in determining behavior. Thus, high Barrier members turn less to outside rules and regulations in seeking to conduct themselves. Failure to solicit aid from authority figures who traditionally "give the answer" is apparently another example of this self-direction.

It is also interesting that, although our prediction concerning the most and least influential group members was not substantiated, the trend is in keeping with the prediction. Low Barrier members tend to receive more nominations as being the least influential group members. This would appear to be in keeping with their reliance on the process analyst. That is, since they are seen as being dependent on the group authority figure, whatever influence they have in the group is in a sense "borrowed influence."

In general the high Barrier members are more frequently nominated as behaving in a free and democratic manner, in contrast to the low Barrier subjects. In line with our prediction, high Barrier scorers are seen as setting group goals above personal goals in conducting the training group activities. In exact opposition are the low Barrier members who receive significantly more nominations for seeking after personal goals in carrying out the group meetings. High Barrier members receive an exceptionally high number of nominations for being active in promoting a warm and friendly group atmosphere. Probably as a consequence of such behavior they also receive the larger number of nominations for being accepted by the group. This is exactly the finding from the three earlier studies in which high Barrier members were described as the more warm and friendly in their group interactions. Blake and Mouton (37) refer to this inclination to protect and support others and to help in the resolution of differences as "maintenance aspects" of group behavior. They consider such behavior a common factor in groups "achieving maximum use of their resources in joint problem solving."

In respect to the present study, however, it is obvious that high Barrier members do not simply want to keep the group friendly at any cost, to the point, for example, of avoiding topics that might be emotionally laden. As in the case of the college groups studied, high Barrier members are not seen as withdrawing whenever conflictual topics arise. It is the low Barrier scorer who receives the greater number of nominations for this sort of withdrawing behavior. High Barrier members have previously been found ready to plunge into a discussion of difficult topics centering about hostility and other personalized feelings. Possibly the high Barrier person has been more successful in establishing controls over his impulses and feels safer in discussing such topics in contrast to the low Barrier individual who has relatively weaker means of containing his feelings and is concerned that they may "get away from him." In general it is our feeling that the results of this additional validation study demonstrate forcefully the pervasive influence of the Barrier concept on individual behavior as displayed in groups.

APPLICATION OF BODY-IMAGE
TO GROUP PSYCHOTHERAPY

INTRODUCTION AND HYPOTHESES

Encouraged by the success experienced in the previously described studies, we felt it was desirable to extend the application of boundary concepts even further in exploring group interaction. The groups studied had comprised a normal (i.e., college) population. Could the correlations found between body-image characteristics and the nature of group interaction be extended to groups composed of members from a different population and organized for different purposes? It was decided to examine the relationship of the Barrier score to various aspects of behavior in a group-therapy situation. Although an extensive literature exists for group psychotherapy, actually little is known concerning the selection of subjects for group therapy, and certainly no one has experienced any significant degree of success in predicting the behavior of individuals once introduced into a group. For example, group psychotherapists have, no doubt, introduced individuals to group therapy with the expectation, on the basis of their individual personality characteristics, that these persons would lead and stimulate a group, only to find them struck dumb within the group. Other less promising individuals blossom forth in a group while remaining awkward and anxious in an individual, face-to-face relationship.

In view of the success gained in the preceding studies in predicting certain aspects of small-group behavior from body image, it seemed worth while to explore the same relationships in group psychotherapy. We focused on two questions: (1) Would boundary definiteness be related to the degree to which an individual was active or took leadership in the group-therapy situation? (2) Would boundary definiteness be found related to ability to empathize or sympathize with the feelings and attitudes of others as they were expressed in group psychotherapy? If the findings concerning body image and small-group behavior in a normal, college population have any degree of generality, we expected to find that high Barrier patients would be rated as highly active in group participation. We expected that, in contrast to low Barrier therapy cases, the high Barrier members would take the initiative in urging the group members to examine their personal feelings and attitudes. In addition, we hypothesized that high Barrier members would show themselves to be more understanding and sympathetic concerning the expressed feelings of others in the group.

METHODOLOGY AND SUBJECTS

We were very fortunate, in our search for a population undergoing group psychotherapeutic treatment, to obtain the Rorschach records of twenty-three patients being treated in this manner by a psychiatrist* in private practice. Eleven men and twelve women comprised the twenty-three patients on whom Rorschach records were available. Individual Rorschach records had been obtained prior to treatment. A few members of the group at times had also received individual psychotherapy, but group therapy constituted the primary treatment. The twenty-three patients were selected from a larger population of forty-five patients in group treatment. These forty-five patients were members of five different therapy groups conducted by the psychiatrist in his private practice. The psychiatrist was asked to select from each of the five groups the two patients who ranked highest and the two ranking lowest on the following two behavior variables: (1) *Group Activity.* This variable referred to the degree to which a patient took the lead in getting the group to deal with personal problems and to encourage others to become active in investigating themselves and "working things out." (2) *Humanitarianism.* This variable had to do with the degree of interest and concern demonstated for the feelings of other group members.

The psychiatrist made these ratings without knowledge of the Rorschach records. In selecting patients at the extremes on the first variable (Group Activity), he picked out eighteen patients on whom Rorschachs were available. Two other nominations had not taken the Rorschach and so could not be included in the analysis. On the second variable (Humanitarianism), fifteen patients with Rorschachs were selected by the psychiatrist. In this case three other nominations had no Rorschach and in one of the therapy groups he was able to nominate only two members instead of four. The records were scored by the authors for Barrier responses, the total number of responses being restricted in the usual manner.

TABLE 7:6   COMPARISON OF BARRIER SCORE WITH RANKING ON GROUP
ACTIVITY

	Most Active	*Least Active*
Barrier Score Five or More	8	2
Barrier Score Less than Five	1	7

Patients scoring above and below the median on Barrier score were then compared as to their ranking on Group Activity and Humanitari-

---

* We are indebted to Dr. David Mendell, psychiatrist, Houston, Texas, for making available these data and for his ratings of the patients.

anism. Because of the small numbers involved, these results cannot be viewed with any degree of finality and are to be regarded only as trends indicating the direction for future research. Table 7:6 presents the findings in respect to the ratings on the Group Activity variable. In this case it is of interest that eight high Barrier patients were rated high on Group Activity whereas only two high Barrier patients were ranked low on Group Activity. Only one patient with a low Barrier score was rated as an active leader, whereas seven with low Barrier scores were seen as inactive by the group therapist. Analysis of these findings yields a chi-square value of 5.6, significant at the .02 level of confidence, after applying the Yates correction formula for discontinuity of data. Thus, even though the small numbers involved preclude any final estimate of the stability of these findings, the results are encouraging in being in the predicted direction, namely that the high Barrier members are rated as being more active in promoting group discussion than low Barrier members.

TABLE 7:7   COMPARISON OF BARRIER SCORE WITH RANKING ON HU-
MANITARIANISM

	Most Active	*Least Active*
Barrier Score Five or More	6	3
Barrier Score Less than Five	2	4

On the Humanitarianism variable the group therapist was able to select only fifteen patients on whom Rorschachs were available as being clearly high or low in demonstrating sympathy and understanding of others in the group sessions. As will be noted from Table 7:7, he selected six high Barrier members as being highly sympathetic and empathic and three high Barrier patients as being ranked low. Two low Barrier patients were rated high and four were rated low on Humanitarianism. These differences do not yield a chi-square value attaining statistical significance. Again the numbers are so small as to preclude any final statement and in this case the results are but slightly in the predicted direction. The median Barrier score for the high-rated members, however, is five, and for the low-rated patients, only three. Thus there is a tendency for high Barrier patients to be seen as demonstrating a greater Humanitarian philosophy in group discussion than for low Barrier members to do so, as was predicted.

The results of this preliminary and exploratory study attempting to extend to group psychotherapy the original findings concerning body image and small-group behavior can only be viewed as tentative. For one thing, the number of subjects studied was small and on only one of the two variables to be predicted, that of active leadership, were the differences significant. Then, too, these patients had been in group therapy for varying lengths of time and the effects of this experience on their behavior at the time of the ratings is not known. It is interesting and provocative, however, that in spite of these acknowledged limitations and reservations, the trend in relationship between body image and group behavior originally investigated in a normal college group continues to appear in a more select group and one meeting for a highly special purpose. The degree of success encountered in spite of these limitations points up promise for further study on a larger scale.

If these preliminary findings can be substantiated by further research, the implications for group therapy should be far reaching. For example, it may prove highly beneficial to utilize in group therapy at least one high Barrier individual as a sort of benevolent prodder and group catalyst. It would be highly profitable to predict in advance individuals who will become active in a positive and nondestructive manner in goading a group into introspective activity. The fact should not be overlooked, also, that group therapy needs followers as well as leaders, active participants as well as less verbose members, for discussion to flow freely. Perhaps the present findings mean that the high and low Barrier members tend to complement each other in group activity. The low Barrier members, as has been suggested in this chapter, rely on external figures to guide them. In this sense they probably welcome the sympathetic prodding afforded by the more active high Barrier members. One might also speculate that the high Barrier personnel are aided in this mutually complementary process by having in the same group more passive and receptive members. The entire process of group therapy is, of course, far more complex than has been outlined here. Possibly one aspect pertaining to the facilitation of the group process, however, is this matter of the proper admixture of group members. Sympathetic, understanding, yet firm and active members certainly provide a strong backbone for group interaction. Further investigation may also demonstrate that more passive members tend to respond to this kind of leadership by themselves becoming more responsive and active in the group.

CHAPTER EIGHT

....

The Role of Body Image in the Psychoneuroses and Psychoses

GENERAL BACKGROUND

IN CHAPTER 1, covering a survey of the historical development of the body-image concept, reference was made to the application of body image to the study of the psychoneuroses and the psychoses. It was noted that several writers (10, 56, 268) have made specific reference to the great profusion of strange and unusual body delusions and complaints accompanying severe neuroses and psychoses. Fenichel (92), in fact, held that various distortions in body image were usually the earliest heralds of schizophrenic regression. Such distortions as multiple hypochondriacal complaints, bizarre reports of body function, and feelings of depersonalization or alienation of one's body are among the most common of these symptoms in severe mental illness. This preoccupation with body function and the frequent reporting of perceived gross changes in body structure serve as adequate testimony to the radical shifts taking place in the body image as these illnesses develop. Both the intensity and near universality of these kinds of body-image phenomena in mental illness raise the question as to the nature of the relationship between body image and degree of emotional discord. For example, does an unstable body image precede mental illness or does it appear as a consequence? The study to be described in this chapter does not undertake to provide a definitive answer to this point, but one would conjecture that probably some kind of reciprocal relationship exists between degree of body-image boundary definiteness and degree of emotional illness. That is, persons with less definite boundaries may be more vulnerable to a neurosis or psychosis. In the event of trauma such individuals perhaps react more severely with further regression which, in turn, results in even greater uncertainty about the body image.

In order to gain more perspective as to the prevalence of altered body-image reports in severe psychiatric illness, it will prove fruitful to examine some of the body sensations and ideas associated with schizophrenia. Bleuler's (38) classic text offers some of the most dramatic and

230

vivid body-image distortions occurring in schizophrenic illnesses. For example, Bleuler (p. 100 f.) writes:

> The hallucinations of bodily sensations present such a kaleidoscopic multiplicity that no description could possibly do justice to them. Any organ can be the seat of the most severe pain. The scalp can become so sensitive that the slightest touch of the hair may produce terrible pain. . . . The patients are beaten and burnt, they are pierced by red-hot needles, daggers, or spears; their arms are being wrenched out; their heads are being bent backwards; their legs are being made smaller; their eyes are being pulled out so that in the mirror it looks like they are entirely out of their sockets; their head is being squeezed together; their bodies have become like accordians, being pulled out and then again pressed together.

In connection with the somatic delusions in schizophrenia Bleuler (p. 118) also has this to say: "The bodily 'influencing' constitutes an especially unbearable torture for these patients. The physician stabs their eyes with a 'knife-voice.' They are dissected, beaten, electrocuted, their brain is sawn to pieces, their muscles are stiffened. . . . A woman patient is told that her flesh would make delicious veal chops, which are then devoured by wolves. Their sexual organs are cut off. . . ."

It is interesting to note that one central theme runs through all these bizarre body-image fantasies: a theme having to do with the violation of the body boundaries. The boundaries are either obliterated or become so plastic and vague as to be worthless either as a defense against all the perceived threats or as a reference point to be used in distinguishing self from the outer world. In terms of the present study these strange fantasies suggest severe alteration of the body barrier and constant preoccupation with the penetration of the body barrier and periphery. Certainly such tortured fantasies reveal a fear that the body has become defenseless and open to attack.

Despite such general recognition of the importance and prevalence of these unusual body-image fantasies and of such body attitudes as those revealed in the phenomenon of depersonalization, for example, no methodical investigation has been reported on the role of body image in the neuroses and psychoses. In addition, as was reported in Chapter 1, only a few isolated studies have attempted to apply to neurotic and psychotic groups some of the more recently developed body-image measures based on such techniques as aniseikonic lens distortions or word associations. This paucity of research into the role of body image in severe psychiatric illness prompted the authors to apply the Barrier and Penetration of Boundary indices to neurotic and schizophrenic groups.

A word is in order regarding our decision to include the Penetration of Boundary score in the analysis of the boundary characteristics of these groups. We have not used it in any of our work with normal groups because we have been unsure of its meaning and also because its occurrence is confined to an extremely narrow range in such a population. However, we felt that it might be fruitfully applied within the neurotic-schizophrenic range for two reasons: (1) Preliminary observations indicated that a much wider range of scores occurred in neurotic and schizophrenic groups than in normal groups. (2) There seemed to be a striking analogy between the extremeness of the body disruption expressed in many of the terms that could be scored as Penetration of Boundary (e.g., "body torn open," "bullet smashing flesh") and the radical body-image distortions ("my eyes are being pulled out") reported to occur in disturbed individuals.

HYPOTHESES

Our survey of the literature relating to somatic delusions in mental illness left no doubt that body-image alterations commonly occur in schizophrenia and to a lesser extent in the neuroses. Such alterations appear to take the form of a lessening of the definiteness of the body boundaries. As the boundaries between the self and the outer world become more diffuse, a corresponding plasticity or even fluidity in the body-image boundaries should be found. In terms of the present study it was hypothesized that this loss of boundary definiteness would take two forms. On the one hand it seemed logical to expect that in a schizophrenic group where the boundaries between self and outer world become diffuse or largely obliterated, there would be little evidence of a strong, external barrier or boundary. It was predicted that this loss of boundary definiteness would be revealed in low Barrier scores as compared with a neurotic or normal population. To a lesser extent we anticipated that a neurotic group would be distinguished from a normal sample in also showing significantly lower Barrier scores.

It was also predicted that loss of boundary definiteness would be revealed in significantly higher Penetration scores in the schizophrenic group as compared to the neurotic and normal groups. It was hypothesized that to a lesser degree the neurotic group would exceed normal subjects on Penetration scores.

An entirely different line of speculation led to a third hypothesis concerning the Barrier score in a special subgroup of the psychoses. This hypothesis had to do with the role of Barrier score in a group diagnosed as schizophrenia, paranoid type. Theoretically, at least, the classical paranoid patient presents not a breakdown of boundaries but rather an abnormally well-developed system of boundaries. Reich (239) has referred to the hard armoring of the compulsive, paranoid character. Not only did he have in mind the psychological armoring of the paranoid character against the outer world, but he also referred to a literal physical rigidity of the paranoid. Fenichel (92) also suggests the hardness in the nature of the paranoid when he refers to the "encapsulation of the pathological process" by the rigorous systematization of the thinking and life style of the paranoid.

Following this line of reasoning, it was anticipated that a group diagnosed as schizophrenia, paranoid type would score unusually high on the Barrier index in comparison with other psychotic groups. In this case it was speculated that abnormally high Barrier scores would be reflecting the unusual degree of concern of this group with creating and maintaining a rigorous armor against the outer world. Compared to a group diagnosed as schizophrenia, undifferentiated type, it was predicted that the paranoid group would score significantly higher on the Barrier index. Ideally, in order to test this hypothesis, a group usually referred to in terms of *classical paranoia* should have been utilized. Traditionally such individuals demonstrate as their sole symptom a rigorous delusional system and in all other respects appear to be intact and well integrated. Such cases are very rare, however, and it proved necessary in this study to employ the more common category of schizophrenia, paranoid type.

SUBJECTS AND METHODOLOGY

The Rorschach records of forty male veteran patients diagnosed by the psychiatric staff of the Houston VA Hospital as psychoneurosis, anxiety reaction, were scored for the Barrier and Penetration indices. The primary factors leading to the anxiety reaction diagnosis were: (1) Presence of generalized anxiety revealed in such symptoms as tension, insomnia, restlessness, etc. (2) Absence of other specific neurotic symptoms, such as conversion manifestations, tics, or compulsions and obsessions.

The undifferentiated schizophrenic group comprised thirty male veterans and ten female patients of the Elgin Illinois State Hospital. As before, the Rorschach records were scored for the two body-image indices. Inclusion in the group diagnosed schizophrenia, undifferentiated type, relied upon: (1) Symptoms indicative of a psychosis such as disorientation for time, place, or person, hallucinations, difficulty in thinking, poor social history, flattened affect, vague somatic delusions, etc. (2) Absence of such specific signs of psychosis as catatonic stupor or well-systematized delusions.

A second psychotic population of twenty-eight male veteran patients and twelve female state hospital (Elgin, Illinois) patients with the diagnosis schizophrenia, paranoid type, was also studied. Barrier and Penetration scores were obtained from their Rorschach records. This group was distinct from the undifferentiated schizophrenic group in that in each case some kind of delusional pattern was present of varying degrees of systematization.

The group of normal subjects used for comparison in this study was originally collected by Dr. Samuel J. Beck° in his normative study of the Rorschach. This was a group of thirty women and twenty men actively employed in business and industry in the Chicago area. Fourteen of the group were employed in a skilled trade, nineteen were semiskilled, and seventeen were in junior executive positions. This distribution of level of vocational skill approximates that comprising the neurotic and schizophrenic groups. The fifty individual Rorschach records were scored in the usual manner for the Barrier and Penetration of Boundary indices. Total number of responses per record was controlled in the manner previously described.

All four groups were roughly comparable in respect to age, education and socioeconomic status. The hospitalized groups were also comparable in respect to length of hospitalization, since all patients regardless of diagnosis were given the Rorschach early in their hospital stay as part of their initial evaluation. Only those psychotic patients giving at least ten responses on the Rorschach were included in the study. Care was taken to control the groups for total productivity on the Rorschach, as this could have affected the production of Barrier and Penetration scores. All records with more than twenty-five responses were reduced to this number in the manner described in previous chapters. The number of records varying in total responses between ten and twenty-five were kept roughly comparable among the four groups. In this manner it was possible to assure equivalent mean number of responses for each of the groups. The mean number of Rorschach responses for the normal group was 20, for the neurotic group 19.7, for the undifferentiated schizophrenic group 18.5, and 19.1 for the paranoids. These mean scores do not differ significantly. We may conclude, therefore, that differences in body-image scores among the four groups are not a function of variance in total productivity.

RESULTS

Table 8:1 presents the range, median scores, and chi-square analyses of the four subject groups in respect to Barrier scores. Table 8:2 presents the same information for the distribution of Penetration scores. In respect to the Barrier index it will be noted that in line with our original speculations there is a tendency for Barrier score to decrease as one proceeds from a normal or neurotic group to a psychotic population. However, in this case the normal group did not differ significantly from the paranoid

---

° We are deeply indebted to Dr. Beck for the use of his Rorschach data.

group and the difference in Barrier score between the normal subjects and undifferentiated schizophrenics, although in the predicted direction, also failed to attain a level of statistical significance. In comparison with the neurotic group the normal group did not differ significantly in respect to Barrier scores. In fact, as a group the neurotics tended to score slightly higher than the normals on Barrier. The neurotic group does exceed by a significant margin both psychotic groups, as do the combined normal and neurotic groups. The most significant differentiation in Barrier score would appear to occur between the normal-neurotic groups on the one hand and the combined psychotic groups on the other. The presence of a psychosis appears to be the depressant factor in respect to Barrier score.

TABLE 8:1 BARRIER SCORE DISTRIBUTION FOR THE FOUR SUBJECT GROUPS

Groups	N	Median Barrier Score	Range of Barrier Scores	% Above Median Total Group	χ^2	P
Normals a	50	3	0–6	56	a vs. b = 1.3	—
					a vs. c = 0.0	—
Neurotics b	40	3	0–9	73	a vs. d = 1.6	—
					b vs. c = 5.2	.02
Undiff. Schiz. c	40	2	0–6	48	b vs. d = 7.4	.01
					c vs. d = 2.1	—
Paranoids d	40	2	0–10	43	ab vs. cd = 5.7	.02

Our speculation that a special subgroup of paranoid schizophrenics would reflect their hardness-of-life style in relatively high Barrier scores was not borne out by the data. Compared as a group to an undifferentiated psychotic group they do not differ significantly in respect to Barrier score. However, this failure of the Barrier index to differentiate the groups may be a function of the psychiatric diagnosis. That is, patients with varying degrees of paranoid symptomatology were included in the total sample of paranoids. Perhaps more rigid selection criteria for this group would have resulted in support of the hypothesis. This possibility gains some support in the fact that within the paranoid groups eleven patients made Barrier scores of five or more. Only four members of the undifferentiated schizophrenic group scored this high. When the psychiatrists who had made the diagnoses were questioned concerning the eleven high-scoring paranoids, they were of the opinion that these eleven cases most nearly represented the "classical paranoid." This is a finding which, if substantiated by further data, would tend to validate the original speculations concerning the body image of the paranoid.

TABLE 8:2   PENETRATION SCORE DISTRIBUTION FOR THE FOUR SUBJECT GROUPS

Groups	N	Median Penetration Score	Range of Penetration Scores	% Above Median Total Group	χ^2			P
Normals *a*	50	1	0–5	32	*a*	vs. *b* =	0	—
					a	vs. *c* =	8.8	.01
Neurotics *b*	40	2	0–5	28	*a*	vs. *d* =	3.8	.05
					b	vs. *c* =	8.5	.01
Undiff. Schiz. *c*	40	4	0–9	65	*b*	vs. *d* =	5.2	.02
					c	vs. *d* =	1.3	—
Paranoids *d*	40	3	0–10	53	*ab*	vs. *cd* =	13.7	.001

Table 8:2 presents the analysis of the Penetration of Boundary score distributions. It will be noted that in this case, as was predicted, a very nice continuum of Penetration scores is obtained as one proceeds from the normal, through the neurotic and two psychotic groups. The median Penetration score shows an increment of one for each succeeding group. However, in the case of the normal versus neurotic groups, this is not a significant increase in score. Both the normal and neurotic groups make significantly fewer Penetration scores than either of the psychotic groups. This is in keeping with our predictions. The psychotic groups do not differ from one another on the Penetration index, a finding which again fails to substantiate our speculations about the paranoid group. We had originally predicted low Penetration scores for the paranoids on the basis of a theory having to do with a "hard" life style. Again, though, there is a tendency for some of the paranoids to conform to our hypothesis and give low Penetration scores while making high Barrier scores. Seven of the eleven paranoids who made unusually high Barrier scores made scores of only zero or one on Penetration. These are the same patients said by the diagnosing psychiatrists to approximate the classical paranoid. Further investigation with a carefully selected paranoid group will be needed in order to settle the question raised by our hypothesis.

The combined neurotic and normal groups differ very significantly from the combined psychotic groups in giving much lower Penetration scores. As in the case of the Barrier score findings, a psychosis appears to be the distinguishing factor. Psychosis appears to elevate the Penetration score significantly.

QUALITATIVE ANALYSIS OF THE PENETRATION SCORES

Before proceeding to a discussion of these interesting findings, it will be fruitful to digress momentarily and examine more closely the actual content of the Penetration of Boundary scores made by the combined psychotic groups versus the combined normal and neurotic groups. Upon scoring the Rorschach records of the psychotic groups for Penetration responses, it became at once apparent to the authors that the high Penetration scores obtained resulted from a very special series of fantasies. These fantasies are unique in our experience in comparison with those obtained from all other populations studied. The psychotic groups were found to produce a great many Penetration responses having to do with a literal disruption, deterioration, and violation of the body boundaries. These responses are unique in their frequency, in their literal disruptive quality, and in the primitive, uncontrolled feeling they convey.

Only by actually quoting at some length a sample of these unusual responses can a true appreciation of their uniqueness be gained. The following are typical Penetration responses taken at random from many different psychotic records: "a bloody, dripping nose"; "a split womb"; "part of a bat cut out and bleeding"; "a bursting disc in the backbone"; "a vaccination scar cut open to let out the poison"; "butchered and bleeding calves"; "a rotted body"; "a circumcised penis"; "a body torn open"; "a hemorrhaging body"; and "a scalped head."

A count was made for the combined normal and neurotic groups and the combined psychotic groups of all those responses specifically referring to the destruction of the body. Only responses having to do with the literal violation of the body, human or animal, were included. For the purposes of this analysis, the more symbolic Penetration responses, such as X-rays or open mouths, and all other Penetration responses, such as described in the scoring manual reproduced in Chapter 2, were ignored.

The combined psychotic groups totaling eighty cases yielded ninety-three such responses, or an average of better than one unusual body-disintegration fantasy per record. The undifferentiated schizophrenic group yielded fifty-nine of these responses and the paranoids thirty-four. The combined normal and neurotic groups, equaling ninety cases, gave a total of only ten such responses. Nine of these responses came from the neurotic group and only one occurred in the normal group. Chi-square analysis of these differences, of course, proves them to be significant far beyond chance expectancy. The neurotic group and, to a lesser extent, the normal group give other kinds of Penetration responses, referring especially to inanimate objects. They fail to give, however, these highly unique, extremely literal fantasies having to do with the disruption and disintegration of the body boundaries, animal or human.

DISCUSSION

The foregoing results suggest that in the case of the psychoses and, to a lesser extent, the psychoneuroses, a definite shift in body image occurs. This shift primarily takes the form of a loss and destruction of the body-image boundaries. This is especially true of the very unique dissolution of body boundaries revealed in the psychotic groups by their frequent reference to literal insult to the body periphery. One is at once struck by the similarity of these unique Penetration responses with the actual somatic delusions and complaints described by Bleuler (38). Does it not appear highly likely that in both instances the thing being expressed is the bewilderment and confusion experienced by the schizophrenic at his loss of reality contact, his loss of boundaries between self and outer world?

We have already referred in earlier chapters, especially in Chapter 1, to the close relationship between ego and body image. It has been pointed out, for example, that Freud held the ego to be first a bodily thing. Fenichel (92, p. 418) writes on this point: "The body 'image' is the nucleus of the ego. The hypochondriacal sensations at the beginning of schizophrenia show that, with the regressive alteration of the ego, this nucleus appears once again and is altered." Many other writers have seen the break with reality experienced in schizophrenia as basically due to an increasing difficulty to distinguish the limits and boundaries of one's own ego. Werner (335, p. 415), for example, puts it this way:

> Reality, which represents characteristically independent existence for the normal person, is here known (in schizophrenia) from a highly egocentric standpoint; the outer world stands in a peculiarly intimate contact with the ego. A female patient describes this contiguity very clearly. She 'transmits' her visual and auditory senses to things, and in this way penetrates into them. Her eyes are directed outward and touch things directly; upon looking at a landscape, for example, she carries away with her some of the actual material of which it is constituted. This close relation between subject and object in the case of other patients expresses itself in such a way that they influence the outer world with their own bodies and their bodily movements.

This last reference by Werner points up the significant loss in distance and in distinction between the body ego and external reality in psychosis. Werner referred to this as an "egomorphic world relation." One could as well call it a "somatomorphic" relation since, as the data of this chapter indicate, in the psychoses and to a lesser extent in the neuroses, an altered body image occurs. This alteration assumes the form especially of the substitution of fluid and plastic body boundaries for boundaries once presumably firm and definite. If we assume that the schizophrenic is attempting to anchor his perceptions and sensations to this vague, plastic body boundary, the distortions and misperceptions occurring become more understandable.

Of course these findings can be interpreted in different ways and at different levels. What we choose to call indefinite body boundaries might also be seen simply as a reflection of the degree of loss of control so typically encountered in the psychoses. Or one could interpret the unusual Penetration fantasies as reflecting merely the confusion and turmoil which the schizophrenic is experiencing. But why is this expressed so literally in body terms? Whether we view the unusual Penetration responses as loss of control in one theoretical framework or self-concept in another, the problem still confronts us as to why fantasies having to do with body disruption accompany ego regression.

It appears to the authors that Freud's concept of the ego as primarily a body ego offers the most reasonable explanation. Freud erected a complete theoretical framework, the psychosexual theory of personality development, oriented at every level around the central problem as to what is happening to the child's body. The perception of varying muscle tensions and gratifying sensations in succeeding body areas comprise one of the cornerstones of this whole theory. Presumably gratification of the tensions arising in the oral, anal, and genital areas in the different developmental phases leads to positive, "good," feelings on the part of the infant for his body.

Psychoanalytic writers (91, 92) refer to such positive body feelings in varying terms, "oceanic feeling," "omnipotence," and "high self-esteem." Anxiety, panic, and "loss of self-esteem" are some of the negative feelings following failure to gratify tensions. The close connection here between perception of body feelings and attribution of ego feelings is important. Presumably a "good" body feeling precedes a "good" or adequate degree of ego awareness. Control of ego or self must probably be first established through control of body. This is exactly the point made by Bettelheim (33) on the basis of extensive therapeutic efforts with schizophrenic children. He makes it clear (p. 106) that he considers integrity of body image a prerequisite to integrity of ego when he writes: "A child who is insecure only about how he will stack up in general during the day is less disturbed than a child who is also worried about his body. It would seem that losing relative control over reality is a less far-reaching step in personal disintegration than losing control over one's body, which is more fundamental and therefore much more frightening. In brief, a child who has at least been able to establish control over his bodily functions is better off than a child who is not even adequate in that area."

The psychoanalytic theory of erotegenic zones and personality correlates would appear to be based primarily on very fundamental body attitudes. The entire sequence of oral, anal, and genital periods of development is predicted on the nature of the handling of the child's body by important figures in his life and the child's perception of this handling. Is it not possible that adequate gratification of the tensions arising in these successive levels forms the basis for a later and more generalized feeling of total body adequacy? In other words, perhaps final confidence in the integrity of one's body boundaries is contingent on previous satisfactory socialization experiences with each body area.

In schizophrenia and to a much lesser extent in the neuroses, there appears to be a return to preoccupation with this fundamental layer of the ego, the body. It seems especially true that the regression occurring in schizophrenia revives all the anxieties and doubts about the "good" and "bad" body feelings prevalent originally much earlier in life. The unique and frequently given Penetration responses of schizophrenics that have been described point up the feelings of helplessness, panic, and anxiety about the body which were perhaps also experienced in infancy or childhood. The lowered Barrier scores also found in the schizophrenic groups complement this picture. The boundary lines are thin or even nonexistent. No defensive periphery is available. All of the "bad," helpless feelings of the most archaic stages of ego development seem to have returned.

IMPLICATIONS FOR TREATMENT

These findings concerning the extremely tenuous body barriers of psychotic groups would seem to point the way toward special treatment efforts. If one of the major areas of confusion to the schizophrenic involves the limits of his own body, would not any efforts directed at attempting to redefine and reidentify these limits prove valuable? Further, if regression has been extreme, would not some definition of body limits necessarily precede other attempts at ego building and strengthening? If, as Freud, Fenichel, and others have theorized, the ego is basically a "body thing," it would seem that treatment efforts should touch on the body variable. What could be more comforting and reassuring to a person who feels that his body has lost all logical proportions and is being subjected to the most tortuous ordeals, than to be confronted with concrete evidence to the contrary? This point appears to have been recognized explicitly by some treatment ventures, implicitly by others.

For example, is it not possible that the logic implicit in such standard treatment methods as sedative tubs and wet packs involves this matter of emphasizing for the patient the periphery of his body? Physiotherapy and packs are very effective in calming most disturbed patients. Both methods provide maximum stimulation of nearly the entire body surface. Perhaps this widespread and intense stimulation of the body surface serves to bring back into focus for the patient his real body limits. Possibly the greater degree of control demonstrated by most disturbed patients following physiotherapy stems from this increased awareness of the reality of a firm anchor point, the substance of their own bodies.

Another common observation in schizophrenia is the loss of interest shown by the patient in his external appearance. Typically the schizophrenic neglects to dress neatly, to wash carefully, or to comb his hair, or to shave. Cosmetics and hair styles are neglected by female patients. Could it be that patients lose interest in this aspect of their bodies because these body areas have become alien to them? Perhaps since they are no longer certain about the definite quality of the body boundaries there is no longer need to "keep up appearances." Some therapists seem to have recognized this possibility and seek to restore a degree of confidence on the patient's part by providing fancy toilet facilities and beauty-shop aids. Perhaps being urged to shave, dress, or otherwise decorate oneself serves once again to sharpen the schizophrenic's blurred boundaries.

There are therapists who have formalized this body approach to the treatment of schizophrenic and severely neurotic patients. Reich (238), for example, has probably been foremost in the laying down of a theoretical framework concerning treatment in which the role of body-image variables assumes major importance. He repeatedly points out the necessity of utilizing body movements, muscle tensions, and body concepts in the therapeutic session. For example, with some neurotic patients he indicates that he gains release of bound up fantasies and reminiscences through relaxation of various muscle areas of the patient. In so doing he may be presumed to demonstrate the controlling influence over thinking and other ego functioning exerted by excessively defined body limits. Further, he seeks to demonstrate in the treatment of schizophrenics the return of ego control with the reestablishment of confused body boundaries.

Sechehaye (275) has reported on the intensive analysis of a severely regressed schizophrenic adolescent girl. It is of interest here that early in her psychosis the adolescent girl was reported to have eaten rust off iron fences in order to "become stiff like iron" and to have sucked stones to "become cold and hard." At the same time she entertained delusions that houses would crumble and crush her and that her own body was becoming smaller and would eventually disappear entirely. These latter fears surely reflect her loss of body boundaries or the imminent collapse of her body boundaries. Sucking rust and stones in order to be hard certainly sound like attempts to redefine and reestablish these boundaries. It is also important to point out that in treatment a very literal use was made by Sechehaye of various aspects of the girl's body and, indeed, also of the therapist's body. Sechehaye relates that real progress in therapy was achieved only when she understood some of the patient's symbolic language. For example, she eventually recognized at one point in the therapy that the girl's talk about apples actually represented a symbolic expression of her wish for closeness to mother. At this point Sechehaye urged the patient to eat pieces of apple at her (the therapist's) breast. Sechehaye feels that communication between the two of them was enhanced by this "symbolic realization." One might also speculate that in offering the reality of her own body to the patient the therapist was aiding in reestablishing the reality to the patient of the mother's body. In this case the reality of the therapist's body boundaries perhaps served as adequate substitute for the patient's own vague boundaries. Sechehaye also refers to the importance of bath taking at this time as a part of the treatment. Baths helped to emphasize for the patient the goodness and cleanliness of her body. At times the therapist would underline this point by saying directly (p. 79): "How clean you are today! How this lovely body is growing strong!" This was followed by massage treatments and at the patient's request camphorated alcohol rubs "to strengthen herself."

It is important for us to note that all these maneuvers were intended to emphasize the strength, goodness, and definiteness of the girl's body, especially very literally, her body boundaries. In such a severely regressed case, treatment must perhaps begin at the most elementary level. Only by first building up the adequacy and reality of the body can the ego begin again to develop and to strengthen. Sechehaye explains the success of her therapy as due largely to her ability to recognize the "magic presymbolic" mode of communication used by the patient. She feels that her recognition of the symbolic meanings of the patient's gestures and movements, "symbolic realization," enhanced the treatment. We might add also that Sechehaye, although not stating so explicitly, was implicitly utilizing in this process the patient's body as a starting point in treatment. By fortifying and strengthening the patient's body through the various means already described, she was beginning at the most primitive level the re-education of the patient's ego.

Treatment of schizophrenic children at the Children's Memorial Hospital in Montreal has at times involved application of body identification according to Rabinovitch (236). Disturbed children who have lost or who have never developed adequate reality contacts are aided in establishing differentiation between themselves and the outer world by identifying various parts of their body viewed in a mirror. As a therapist assists them in describing and identifying their own body parts, the real limits of the child's body are reawakened, and this, in turn, leads to greater stabilization of ego limits.

Bettelheim (33) has described in detail his interesting work with severely disturbed children. He emphasizes the central role played by body attitudes, fears, and anxieties in children's illnesses. In a great many different ways his counselors utilize body concepts in dealing with these children. In some instances simple praise and reassurance of proper body functioning is effective. At other times active physical exertion produces confidence in body adequacy. Bettelheim diagrams very clearly the close relation between adequate body and adequate ego in these children. On awakening, for example, some children can only begin the day after a careful inventory of their bodies to assure their integrity. Some children put their bodies to severe tests of endurance which, if passed, encourage them concerning their total adequacy.

Cutner (74) also has written of what she terms "body experiments" in the analytic treatment of schizophrenics. In much the same manner as Reich, she requires the patient early in treatment to focus his attention on his body and to introspect concerning the various bodily sensations he is currently experiencing. This technique appears to have been especially valuable in the reported case of a schizophrenic young woman who revealed many bizarre body delusions involving dissolution of her body in various ways. Cutner (p. 67) writes of this method of body experimentation: ". . . even the first attempts (with body experiments) engender a new kind of concentration and, in this particular case, provided a first reconnexion of the patient with her body. At this early stage (of treatment), greater awareness had been achieved not only of those parts which previously ached, but the whole of the body, feet, neck, head, etc., could now be felt by the patient as 'hers.'" Here we have another example of the value of emphasizing to the schizophrenic patient the reality and existence of his own body. The important point would seem to be that with the return of the substance of his own body, the schizophrenic patient can then generalize this body reality to the area of ego reality. Only with a firm anchor in the nature of a well-defined body image can there be developed a mature and integrated ego structure.

ALTERATION OF BODY IMAGE
FOLLOWING PSYCHOTHERAPY

The data presented up to this point suggest that with increasing severity of emotional illness, loosening of body-image boundaries becomes more pronounced. This inference is drawn, however, from differences in degree of body-image boundary definiteness among contrasting diagnostic groups. So far it has not been possible to demonstrate increasing fluidity of body image within the *same* individaul as he progresses from a normal to a neurotic or psychotic state. Since it would have been extremely difficult to gather any sizable number of records on the same persons first under normal conditions and secondly when these subjects had become psychotic, an alternative plan was adopted. We reasoned that persons diagnosed as being neurotic or psychotic who entered prolonged psychotherapy should demonstrate an alteration in body image. Originally diffuse and indefinite body-image boundaries should tend to become better integrated with progress in therapy. In other words, we set out to demonstrate that within the same individual a shift in body image would be found to accompany change in degree of ego integrity. Specifically, we predicted that Barrier scores obtained at the outset of treatment would be found to have increased at the conclusion of successful psychotherapy. Conversely, we expected the Penetration score to decrease for the same individual following therapy.

The therapist in each case was asked to make simply a gross evaluation of the patient's progress in therapy, that is, to state whether he was improved, unchanged, or worse. We were fortunate in obtaining the Rorschach records on twenty-five patients who had received prolonged psychotherapy, both individual and group. Fifteen of these patients received treatment from a psychiatrist* in private practice. The ten other patients were seen in individual therapy for periods varying from six months to a year at the Houston VA Hospital. All fifteen of the patients treated in private practice had received approximately two years of analytically oriented psychotherapy and all had shown some degree of improvement. Of the ten VA cases, four had improved following therapy and six were said to be worse or unchanged. In respect to diagnosis, the twenty-five patients all fell approximately within the general category of anxiety neurosis. Rorschach records were obtained on each patient before treatment was instituted; and a second Rorschach was obtained at, or near, the conclusion of therapy. The records were scored in the usual manner for Barrier and Penetration responses. The total number of responses was

---

* We are indebted to Dr. David Mendell who conducted the therapy with these 15 cases.

equalized for each patient on the two records obtained by reducing the total number of responses on the larger record to that of the smaller whenever the first and second Rorschachs varied in productivity.

Nineteen of the twenty-five patients were rated as improved following psychotherapy. Of these nineteen improved patients, eight made both higher Barrier *and* lower Penetration scores from first to second testing. Furthermore, nine other patients, also rated as improved in over-all adjustment, showed either an increase in Barrier score or a decrease in Penetration score on the second testing. The remaining two patients receiving an improved rating made identical body-image scores on both tests. Six patients in the total group were rated as unchanged or worse following therapy. Four of these patients had unchanged Barrier and Penetration scores on the second as compared to the first testing. One patient increased only on Penetration score and one patient made a higher Barrier score on the second testing (while also increasing his Penetration score).

Although these results must be viewed with caution because of the many uncontrolled factors, one can at least say that an alteration in body image is found to correlate with change in over-all ego integrity within the same individual over a period of time. Most of the patients studied revealed a shift toward greater definiteness of body-image boundaries, as defined by either one or the other of the body-image scores, following rated improvement in adjustment.

These results complement those already obtained in studying boundary definiteness in different psychiatric groups. In the one instance we have shown a loosening of body-image boundaries to accompany increasing mental illness. In the other instance a reversal of the loosening process in the direction of more intact boundaries has been found to correlate with improvement in total adjustment.

PART THREE

Development of Body-Image Boundaries

....

CHAPTER NINE

Family Patterns and Body-Image Variations

THE DATA to be reviewed in this chapter are primarily concerned with the question of whether the individual's experiences with his parents have an influence upon his body-image boundaries. Do the characteristics of one's parents and the reactions one has to these characteristics play a part in the formation of boundary concepts? This question has already been partially touched upon in Chapter 3 where results are reported concerning the relationship of the Barrier score to the definiteness of the individual's concept of the parental figures as defined in the Thematic Apperception Test.

It was shown that high Barrier persons tend to have a more definite concept of the parental figures than do low Barrier persons. Those individuals with definite boundaries were likely to describe parental figures in the TAT with phrases that crystallized into perceptible portraits. Whether the portrait was favorable or unfavorable, it had specific attributes. Individuals with indefinite boundaries were inclined to depict parental figures in the TAT in such a manner that they were blurred or reduced to ineffectual nonentity roles. Consistent differences in this respect between persons with high Barrier scores and persons with low Barrier scores were obtained in an original experimental group and in a subsequent cross-validation group. It seemed logical to reason on the basis of such data that the degree of definiteness of an individual's boundaries might be a function of the models his parents had provided for him. It appeared that the formation of definite boundaries required that one have parents who stood for certain definite values and ways of doing things. Indefinite boundaries could be considered to evolve out of interaction with parents who were hazy models and who therefore had little to contribute toward the building up of a well-differentiated identity.

Although these differences between high and low Barrier subjects relative to definiteness of parental images were statistically significant and also apparently meaningful, the fact remained that one could not be sure about what they really represented. One could argue that the differences in parental images observable in the TAT were actually a reflection of corresponding differences in the real life traits and characteristics of the parental figures. But one could argue, too, that persons with definite boundaries would in general be more likely than those with indefinite boundaries to structure the vague TAT pictorial representations in a definite and forceful manner. Thus the degree of definiteness assigned to TAT parental figures might be considered to be the result of the degree to which one is inclined to organize unstructured material in a definite fashion, rather than to be a reflection of how one experienced one's parents.

It became apparent to us that the best way to get some reliable information about the parents of individuals differing in body-image boundary definiteness would be to make observations of such parents themselves. We were fortunately able to do so by analyzing a body of data collected by Fisher and Mendell (103, 216) in the course of a project concerned with the personality similarities among family members. This study involved patients who had come to a private psychiatrist for treatment. The patients and a sample of their close kin (e.g., spouse, children) were evaluated on an individual basis by means of the Rorschach test and nine TAT cards (1, 2, 5, 6BM, 7BM, 6GF, 7GF, 13G, 17BM). The number of close kin tested in each family varied considerably. In some only the spouse was studied, whereas in another the spouse, the children, the parents, and even sibs were included in the evaluation.

The Barrier score was determined for each individual, with all protocols over twenty-five responses limited to twenty-five in the usual manner. Data were available for sixty-seven husband-wife pairs, fifty-six mother-child pairs, and thirty-eight father-child pairs. Some comment is called for concerning the selective nature of this sample. Certainly one cannot characterize it as a normal sample. It is made up partially of people who were sufficiently uncomfortable that they sought psychiatric help and partially of their kin who would, under the circumstances, be presumed to be more than ordinarily troubled. The individuals who were actually patients make up about one-fourth of the group. The selectivity of the group is further increased by the fact that it is composed primarily of middle-class people. Therefore, any conclusions that may be drawn from the data are circumscribed by the sampling bias. In partial defense of our use of data from such a biased sample, it may be pointed out that it is almost impossible to get the various members of normal families to submit to the considerable inconvenience of taking psychological tests. They do not have the press of anxiety which prompts the psychiatric patient and his family to respond in an ego-involved manner to the tests as one phase of a total treatment process which will be relieving.

BODY-IMAGE SIMILARITIES AMONG FAMILY MEMBERS

One of the first questions that came to mind in approaching the data was whether kin would manifest similarities in body-image characteristics. If one found positive correlations between parents and their children, this would have special theoretical implications because it would support the position that the child learns to structure his boundaries in terms of models implicit in the parents' behavior. The analysis of the data was carried out in the following fashion. First, all the family members were categorized into one of four groupings: mother, father, adolescent child (ages 11–17), and young child (ages 4–10). Then, rank-order correlations were determined between the Barrier scores of each category and each of the other categories. In addition, the average of the Barrier scores of the two parents in each family was correlated with the scores of their children. It was necessary to eliminate from 10 to 20 per cent of the subjects frrom the correlational analysis because the number of Rorschach responses they had given was very discrepantly lower than that of their family members, and therefore their Barrier scores could not logically be compared. It would, for example, not be very meaningful to compare the Barrier score of a parent based on a record of ten responses with the Barrier score of a child based on twenty-five responses.

TABLE 9:1 RHO CORRELATIONS OF BARRIER SCORES OF FAMILY MEM-
BERS OF DIFFERENT LEVELS OF RELATIONSHIP

Groups Correlated	Rho	Significance Level
Father vs. mother (N = 54)	.25	.10–.05
Father vs. adolescent children (N = 16)	−.31	Not significant
Mother vs. adolescent children (N = 20)	.37	Not significant
Average of father and mother vs. adolescent children (N = 16)	.42	.10–.05
Father vs. young children (N = 19)	.30	Not significant
Mother vs. young children (N = 19)	.33	Not significant
Average of father and mother vs. young children (N = 19)	.17	Not significant

Table 9:1 indicates the results obtained in the correlational analysis of the Barrier scores of the family members. There is a low but significantly positive relationship (.25) between the Barrier scores of the mothers and fathers. Two of three correlations involving the relationship of the Barrier scores of parents to those of adolescent children are positive; and one of these correlations is of borderline significance (.10–.05). All three of the correlations which have to do with relating the parental Barrier scores to those of the younger children are positive, but none are statistically significant.

What can one say on the basis of such results? It would appear that there is a significant similarity between the Barrier scores of the spouses in each family. Also, it would appear that there is a tendency for the Barrier scores of children to resemble those of their parents. The fact that there is a tendency for the Barrier scores of parents and their children to be positively correlated is congruent with the position that the parent does somehow provide a model which influences the body-image boundaries of his child. It is clear from the smallness of the correlations involved, however, that the degree of definiteness of the child's boundaries cannot be accounted for in any simple straightforward fashion in terms of the boundary characteristics of his parents. It is, of course, possible that the literal boundary characteristics of the parents do have a large influence on the child's boundaries, but that the influence is the resultant of interaction patterns which would not be picked up by the methods of data analysis available in this instance. For example, it is possible that the child's boundaries are highly influenced by the definiteness of the boundaries of the parent with whom he has the greatest psychological closeness. Thus in some instances the most influential figure might be a father and in other instances it might be a mother. But a simple correlation of the Barrier scores of children with those of their mothers or fathers (or an average of mother and father scores) could not test such a complicated possibility.

The correlation found between the Barrier scores of spouses could be interpreted as a function of selective mating or as the result of having lived together and having exerted significant influence one upon the other. That is, the similarity in spouses might be the result of a selective process which is such that individuals who possess an equivalent degree of boundary definiteness tend to pair off with each other. Or it might be the result of the intimate interaction process which occurs following marriage. Inspection of the data indicates, however, that the size of the Barrier score correlation for spouses married for short periods (one year or less) is not less than for spouses married many years. This result favors the selective-mating explanation.

It is interesting to note that the general level of correlation of the Barrier scores among family members falls into the same range of correlations found between family members for other partially comparable psychological measures. Roff (251), in reviewing the pertinent literature in this area, reports that correlations between fathers and sons for a wide variety of the Strong Vocational Interest scales have in three separate studies averaged out respectively to .29, .35, and .19. He indicates that in one study of 110 husband-wife pairs, the correlations of their Bernreuter subscale scores were of the following order: .19, .11, .16, .23. In still another study the Minnesota Multiphasic scores of family members were compared. For the M-F scale the correlation between fathers and sons was .31 and for mothers and daughters it was .27. Correlations for the other Multiphasic scales averaged .11 between fathers and sons and .12 between mothers and daughters.

DIFFERENCES IN PERSONALITY FUNCTIONING BETWEEN PARENTS OF DEFINITE-BOUNDARY CHILDREN AND PARENTS OF INDEFINITE-BOUNDARY CHILDREN

There were available Rorschach and Thematic Apperception Test data concerning each of the parents of the definite- and indefinite-boundary children. The problem was to analyze this data to determine if there were differences in personality functioning between parents of the two categories of children. Could differences in personality defenses and basic attitudes be shown to exist between the two groups of parents? If so, they would provide clues concerning how parent-child interactions affect body-image boundary formation in the child.

RORSCHACH DATA

First, let us consider how the Rorschach record of each parent was analyzed. It was decided to restrict the analysis to two broad measures which may be derived in a configurational and yet objective fashion from the Rorschach protocal. These two measures are the Fisher Maladjustment score and the Fisher Rigidity score (97). The Maladjustment score attempts to evaluate the degree to which the individual shows signs of personality malfunctioning and disorganization in his responses. It is not based on any one or two Rorschach variables but rather upon the patterned interrelationship of a whole range of variables. It assumes that normal functioning is characterized by certain optimum ratios among various Rorschach variables; and penalty weights are assigned for deviations from such optimum ratios. For example, there are standards concerning the number of movement responses that should occur in a record of a given length or the ratio of controlled color responses to uncontrolled color responses that should occur. A total score is derived for each individual which indicates the degree to which his Rorschach record departs from the ideal standard. This measure has been used in a considerable number of studies and has proved itself able to predict various kinds of maladjustive behavior.

Thetford and De Vos (313) have successfully cross-validated Fisher's findings that it significantly differentiates normals, neurotics, and schizophrenics. Fine, Fulkerson, and Phillips (94) have shown that it significantly distinguishes between normal persons who have been successful in their social attainment and those who have been unsuccessful in this respect. Fisher (97A) has found it to be significantly correlated with tendencies to deal with hostile impulses maladaptively. Friedman (114) reports that it is significantly correlated with positiveness of self-concept as inferred from the level of aspiration behavior. Bindman (36) indicates that in terms of measures derived from the Brownfain Self Concept Test, persons with high self-esteem obtain significantly lower Fisher Maladjustment scores than do persons with low self-esteem. Fisher (96) has shown that the test-retest reliability of the Maladjustment score is high even when the first test is administered under unusual stressful conditions.

The Rigidity score has been described as follows (97, p. 9):

> The Rorschach measure of personality rigidity is based on a variety of Rorschach signs which clinically have been found to characterize persons who are habitually constricted and who find it necessary to deal with the environment with an unusual amount of guarded caution. Quite literally, these signs are derived from indicators of the degree to which individuals limit the range and character of their responses to the Rorschach ink blots. Thus, limitation in the use of color in perceptions; restriction of percepts to one class of objects (e.g., animals); and very delayed reaction times are illustrative of what is considered rigid or restricted behavior in the Rorschach test.

The total Rigidity score of an individual is equal to the sum of the penalty weights he incurs for such forms of response limitation. One finds quite a number of reports in the literature which support the validity of the Rigidity score. Becker (19) indicates that it is significantly correlated with an aniseikonic-lens measure of rigidity. Johnson and Stern (157) report that it is similarly correlated with still another perceptual measure of rigidity based on response to intermittent photic stimulation. Roman (252) found it meaningfully linked with degree of authoritarianism, as defined by the F-scale. De Vos (82) found clear differences in the Rigidity scores of various groups of Japanese-Americans and felt that these differences logically corresponded to variations in their cultural backgrounds.

The Maladjustment and Rigidity scores were singled out by us because they get at two of the broad dimensions which most often are mentioned in discussions regarding parent-child interactions. There is much in current psychodynamic theory which implies that two factors of paramount importance in the child's personality development are the soundness of the personalities of his parents and the over-all restrictiveness of their life orientation. The child's "security," "ego strength," "emotional stability," and other related aspects of his personality are frequently traced to the degree of maladjustment shown by his parents. The child's "flexibility," "rigidity of character structure," "superego strictness," and other analogous characteristics are often attributed to how narrow and rigid his parents were. In any case, it appeared to us that the Maladjustment and Rigidity scores would be indices to broad and important aspects of the personality functioning of the parents of the high Barrier and low Barrier children.

When a tabulation was made of the parents of individuals who clearly had high or low Barrier scores, it was found that the population available for analysis was quite limited. There were eight females and eleven males in the high Barrier group whose parents had been studied. Of this group eight were adults, eight were adolescents, and three were children at the time of the study. The Rorschachs of the nineteen mothers of these individuals were available; but only fourteen of the fathers' Rorschachs had been secured. In the low Barrier group there were eight females and eight males whose parents had been given the Rorschach. Seven were adults, seven were adolescents, and two were children at the time they were tested. The Rorschachs of sixteen of the mothers and eleven of the fathers of these individuals had been obtained. It can be seen that in both groups the number of mothers studied does provide an adequate, if minimal, sample with which to work. But the number of fathers in the two groups is so limited as to prevent a really meaningful comparison of their Rorschach scores.

TABLE 9:2 LEVELS OF SIGNIFICANCE OF THE CHI-SQUARE COMPARISONS OF FISHER MALADJUSTMENT SCORES AND FISHER RIGIDITY SCORES OF PARENTS OF HIGH BARRIER CHILDREN AND PARENTS OF LOW BARRIER CHILDREN

Scores	Mothers with Highest Score	Significance Level	Fathers with Highest Score	Significance Level
Maladjustment	L.B.[a]	.01	L.B.	Not significant
Rigidity	L.B.	.05–.02	L.B.	Not significant

[a] L.B.—Parent of a low Barrier child.

Table 9:2 makes it clear that parents of low Barrier children tend to obtain higher Maladjustment and Rigidity scores than do parents of high Barrier children. It is true that the differences do not even approach significance in the instance of the fathers. However, the difference between the mothers for Maladjustment is significant at the .01 level; and the difference between them for Rigidity is significant at the .05–.02 level.

TABLE 9:3   MEAN FISHER MALADJUSTMENT AND RIGIDITY SCORES OF VARIOUS GROUPS

Group	Maladjustment	Rigidity
H.B.[a] mothers	25.8	26.4
L.B. mothers	43.1	36.4
H.B. fathers	35.0	22.0
L.B. fathers	36.1	33.4
Normals[b]	36.9	24.9
Hysterics[b]	59.7	44.3
Paranoid schizophrenics[b]	85.5	44.1

[a] H.B.—Parent of high Barrier child. L.B.—Parent of low Barrier child.

[b] Subjects evaluated by Fisher (97) as part of another study. The three groups consist entirely of women. The normal group is made up primarily of nurses in training and occupational-therapy students.

Table 9:3 contains the mean Maladjustment and Rigidity scores of the mother groups and father groups. In addition, it contains corresponding mean values for normal subjects, hysterics, and paranoid schizophrenics who were evaluated in a previous project (97). One notes that the same differences are present between mothers of high Barrier and low Barrier children and also between fathers of high Barrier and low Barrier children as appeared in terms of the results of the chi-square analysis. But it is of special interest to compare the values in the parental groups with the values of the normal group which had been studied in another setting. The mothers of high Barrier individuals have a lower mean Maladjustment score (25.8 versus 36.9) than this normal group; whereas the mothers of low Barrier individuals have a higher mean Maladjustment score (43.1 versus 36.9). Similarly, the mean Rigidity score of the mothers of high Barrier individuals is a fraction lower (24.6 versus 24.9) than that of the normal group, and the mean score of the mothers of low Barrier individuals is higher (36.4 versus 24.9) than that of the normal group. The mean differences involved in comparing the father groups with the normal group follow the same pattern, with the exception that fathers of low Barrier individuals have a lower Maladjustment mean than the normal group. The fact that all the mean scores of the parental groups are definitely lower than those of the hysteric and schizophrenic groups suggests that the sample is not too highly biased in the degree of its personality pathology and does fall somewhere in the normal range.

The results from the Rorschach data indicate that there are differences in personality functioning between parents of high and low Barrier persons. It would be more accurate to say that there are differences between the mothers of such persons, since the differentiation between the fathers appears only as a nonsignificant trend. In any case, one may say that the high and low Barrier individuals are distinguished from each other with respect to characteristics of at least one of their parental figures. The tendency toward greater maladjustment in the parental figures of the low Barrier individuals suggests that the low Barrier person is more likely than the high Barrier person to grow up in a family atmosphere characterized by instability, overtones of anxiety, insecurity about dealing with reality problems, and chronic tension. One may say, on the basis of the trend toward greater rigidity in the parental figures of the indefinite-boundary individuals, that the formative years of these indefinite-boundary persons were more likely than those of the definite-boundary persons to be marked by restrictiveness, a narrowed range of permissible behavior, and frustrating restraint which blocks outlets for relieving tension. Thus, one is left with an over-all impression that the low Barrier person grows up in a setting which is less secure and more frustrating than that in which the high Barrier person develops.

THEMATIC APPERCEPTION TEST DATA

The TAT data available for each of the parental figures were analyzed along three different lines:

(1) One level of analysis was concerned with degree of achievement orientation. That is, the question was whether the parents of high Barrier individuals manifested more high achievement themes in their TAT stories than the parents of low Barrier individuals. The same measure of High Achievement was used as is described in Chapter 3. It simply involves a count of all statements which refer to a story character's hoping for high achievement, working hard, or having attained high goals. This variable was selected for special study because high Barrier people have so prominently emerged in several studies as having higher aspiration levels than low Barrier people. The prominence of these differences suggested the possibility that somehow high aspiration attitudes on the part of the parental figures were fundamental to the formation of definite boundaries.

(2) A second level of analysis focused on reactions to card 2 of the TAT series. This is the only card which pictures a group of individuals that can be perceived as a family consisting of mother, father, and child. It is

frequently seen as such a family group. But there is a range of interpretations; and at another extreme there are individuals who not only do not see it as a family group but who insist that the three figures are strangers to each other. It was hypothesized that the manner in which an individual pictured the three figures would define his basic concept of family life. If he saw the figures as interacting members of a family group, he would be likely to seek such closeness in his own family life. If he conceived the figures as distant, however, and isolated from each other, he would tend to structure his own family role as if there could be no real communication and closeness. A two-category scoring system was devised for evaluating response to TAT card 2. A "close-family" category was designated for those stories which fulfilled the double criterion of explicitly referring to the three figures as members of the same family and indicating that at least two of the figures were interacting or influencing each other in some manner. Stories not fulfilling this criterion were classified in a "distant-family" category.

It was hypothesized that the parents of definite-boundary individuals would more often give "close-family" stories than would the parents of indefinite-boundary individuals. If one conceives of the body-image boundary-formation process as in large part being a function of models provided by the parental figures, it would follow that close communication between parent and child was a prerequisite to boundary definiteness. In the absence of such communication the parent could not provide an adequately well-defined model. One may think of indefinite boundaries as representing in many ways a failure in parent-child communication. It is assumed that without certain kinds of cues and guiding information from his parents, the child is seriously hampered in differentiating a body-image domain for himself.

(3) A third approach to the TAT data was attempted which is concerned with the broad dimension of completion and definiteness of response. Since there were findings (Chapter 3) that high Barrier persons were more likely than low Barrier persons to picture the parental figures as representing something definite and as pursuing clear-cut goals, the question presented itself whether one could actually detect analogous contrasting characteristics in the parents of definite- and indefinite-boundary persons. This question was translated into TAT terms by considering whether or not the two categories of parents would differ in their manner of constructing TAT stories. The greater the degree to which an individual has definite values and approaches life with a well-crystallized style, the more likely he is to leave a stamp of definiteness upon any task he undertakes, such as the creation of a TAT story. Therefore, if subjects are instructed to make up stories about a series of TAT pictures, it would be anticipated that those with the most definite, or crystallized orientation

would be most likely to impart to each story a directional sequence, a sense of completion. A scoring system was developed for evaluating this variable. Each story was classified as either "definite" or "indefinite." In order to be classified as "definite," the story had to state explicitly that someone was doing something or planning to do something. Furthermore, this action or intent attributed to story figures had to go beyond a superficial descriptive level and had to be embedded in a story plot. For example, a story would not be classified as "definite" if it consisted simply of a statement that someone was walking or sitting or looking. But it would be categorized as definite if a person in the story were walking someplace to get something, or sitting and waiting for someone to keep an appointment, or looking to see if a particular event had occurred. Each of the nine stories given by a subject were scored as either definite or indefinite.

TABLE 9:4   CHI-SQUARE ANALYSIS OF DIFFERENCES BETWEEN PARENTS OF HIGH BARRIER AND LOW BARRIER PERSONS FOR TAT MEASURES

TAT Measures	Mothers (N = 33)		Fathers (N = 26)	
	Group with Higher Score	Significance of Difference	Group with Higher Score	Significance of Difference
High aspiration	H.B.[a]	.06–.05	L.B.	None
Family closeness	H.B.	.05–.02	H.B.	None
Story definiteness	H.B.	.05–.02	N.D.	—

[a] H.B.—Parent of high Barrier individual. L.B.—Parent of low Barrier individual. N.D.—No difference.

Table 9:4 summarizes the results of the three lines of TAT analysis described above. One can see that in the instance of the mothers all three hypotheses are significantly supported. The mothers of high Barrier individuals exceed the mothers of low Barrier individuals in the number of High Aspiration themes produced, in the frequency with which they interpret card 2 as involving close family communication, and also in the frequency with which they make their stories definite. The results obtained with the fathers, however, are not consistent with the hypotheses. Thus it is the fathers of low Barrier persons who slightly exceed the fathers of high Barrier persons in number of High Aspiration themes produced. Also, there is no difference between the categories of fathers as far as story definiteness is concerned. Actually the two groups of fathers do not differ significantly for any of the TAT measures. The difference in the pattern of results found for the mothers and that found for the fathers is puzzling. It is possibly a function of the relatively smaller number of fathers involved. Perhaps it is a function of genuine differences in the influence that mothers, as contrasted to fathers, have upon the body-image formation process. The limitations of the data make it presently impossible to choose between the alternate explanations.

The significant differences in TAT scores that were observed between the mothers of high and low Barrier individuals may be considered to form a meaningful pattern. One may interpret both the elevated interest in achievement and the relatively marked inclination toward story definiteness on the part of the mothers of high Barrier persons as indicators, at different levels, of a forceful well-contoured way of behaving. The achievement motivation represents the energy aspect of this contoured forcefulness; and the story definiteness exemplifies how it gets expressed in a specific product. These results are certainly well in keeping with the fact that definite boundary persons have been found to picture their parents in the TAT with a more clear-cut specificity than do individuals with indefinite boundaries. The greater specificity of their TAT images apparently has some basis in reality.

The distinction shown in Table 9:4 between the two categories of mothers with reference to the family closeness score may be viewed as another facet of the difference in the sorts of models they provide for their children. It has already been demonstrated that the two classes of mothers differ in the degree to which they represent well-contoured models. But what the family closeness results suggest is that the greater definiteness of the behavior style of the high Barrier mothers as compared to that of the low Barrier mothers is further enhanced by a differential in the communicativeness of the two categories of mothers. To be a definite model for someone else one must not only stand for something definite but must also be motivated to serve as a model by engaging in intimate interaction with the other person. It would appear that the definite-boundary category of mothers is interested in such intimate association. However, the indefinite-boundary class of mothers seems to minimize even further its already quite hazy model contours by its relative lack of interest in intimate association with other family members.

It would be well at this point to integrate briefly the findings concerning the differing classes of parents which have emerged from the Rorschach and TAT. The indications from the Rorschach are that parents of high Barrier individuals are less maladjusted and less rigid than parents of low Barrier individuals. Perhaps it would be safer to say that this is true of the mothers, for the results concerning the fathers are not statistically significant. The results from the TAT suggest that the high Barrier category of mothers represents a more definite model and also one more easily communicated with than does the low Barrier category of mothers. If one adds up these results, it may be said that low Barrier persons are exposed to a family atmosphere that not only provides few definite and well-contoured identification models but also one which is characterized by relatively high insecurity and inappropriate rigidity. One might characterize this family atmosphere as maximizing the uncertainty, the irrationality, and the lack of meaningful structure in the world. It is an apparent fact, and also one verified by studies of perception under unstructured conditions, that the process of setting up boundaries or working out definitions is made maximally difficult under such uncertain conditions.

SOME QUALITATIVE OBSERVATIONS CONCERNING THE ATTITUDES OF HIGH AND LOW BARRIER INDIVIDUALS TOWARD THE PARENTAL FIGURES

There were available detailed clinical evaluations of the Rorschach and TAT data which had been secured from the various family members. These evaluations had all been written by one of the authors° (Fisher) purely on the basis of the test results and without any other information about the individuals involved except their ages, family constellations, and occupations. In each evaluation there was a section devoted to an analysis of the individual's apparent concept or image of his mother and father. It was considered that some interesting clues concerning relationship of the Barrier score to modes of interaction with the parents might be found from a study of the descriptions of the parental images. Such clues would be purely qualitative, but still might provide leads for future research in this area.

The clinical reports concerning twenty high Barrier persons and twenty low Barrier persons (equal sex ratio) were randomly selected, and all statements concerning attitudes toward the parental figures were abstracted. A review of these abstracted statements revealed only one major difference between the low Barrier and high Barrier subjects. The low Barrier subjects were more often described as conceiving of their parents as threatening, destructive, and disrupting. They were more often referred to as fearing and expecting to be hurt by their parents. A tabulation was made of the reports in which there was an explicit reference to the mother figure as a threatening, fear-inspiring person. The same was done with respect to father figures. It was found that a significantly greater number of mother figures and also father figures were described in this fashion in the low Barrier group than in the high Barrier group. For the mother figure references the chi-square difference was significant at the .01 level; and for the father figure references also the difference was significant at the .01

° The possibility that these reports were contaminated by the writer's theoretical expectations were minimized by two factors. First, most of the reports were written a number of years ago before formal research on the body-image problem had been undertaken. Secondly, the writer had no knowledge of the Barrier scores of the children of these parents at the time he wrote the reports.

level. It would probably clarify the results if a few examples were quoted from the reports of low Barrier subjects of descriptive statements emphasizing the threatening manner in which the parents were experienced.

"She sees her mother as the most dangerous force in her life. She sees herself as engaged in a bitter contest with her and believes that the loser will be completely eliminated from the picture."

"She unconsciously sees her father as an aggressive penetrating person who could get pretty rough. In her projective responses she reveals great fear of him. She sensed that he liked to disturb people. . . ."

"He feels mistreated by mother. He literally feels engulfed by her. . . . He finds it hard to devise ways of defending himself against mother's attacks. She looms as a tough opponent for him."

This material derived from a clinical level analysis of the tests is interesting because it adds further perspective to the results obtained from more objective data. Although it was clear from previously described data that the low Barrier individuals had more insecure and more confused relationships with their parents than did the high Barrier individuals, there was nothing to indicate how threatening and attacking they might perceive their parents to be. One gets the impression that in the case of the low Barrier person, it is often not simply a matter of having a poorly structured mode of interaction with the parents, but of experiencing them as opposed to one's growth and development. It is, perhaps, as if the parents represented antagonistic strangers who blocked individuality. If the low Barrier person does, indeed, experience his parents in this fashion, it means that when his boundaries were evolving they were under constant attack. He not only did not receive positive material with which to build boundaries, but was subjected to conditions which breached the boundaries he did manage to erect somewhat on his own. These ideas are at present only slightly better than speculations and need to be studied more systematically.

....

CHAPTER TEN

Sex Differences in Barrier Score Among Children, Middle-Class American Adults, and Adults of Other Cultures

SEX DIFFERENCES AMONG CHILDREN

IN ATTEMPTING to understand fully the development of such a basic variable as that of body-image boundaries, one should, of course, begin at the beginning. Presumably a laying down of the foundations of one's body image gets under way very early in life, very probably by the age of six months (150). Unfortunately, the measurement of such a complex variable as body image must await the development of complex modes of communication on the part of an individual being studied. Even the most elementary kind of intelligence or personality testing must rely to some extent on verbal communication. In the case of Rorschach administration, although some authorities have managed to provide a semblance of norms as early as two years of age, anything representing a valid and reliable record probably awaits the advent of the school years, or at the least, the immediate preschool years. Not only are the extremely young handicapped in responding to the Rorschach by limited verbal expression, but what is even more important, the necessary varieties of experiences and events have as yet not taken place to provide a storehouse of information in responding to vague ink blots.

It was impossible to investigate the production of Barrier responses during the earliest formative years. Furthermore, a developmental study was rendered hazardous because it is a consistent finding in developmental studies of the Rorschach that a greatly expanded response total occurs with advancement in chronological age. Thus the significance of any shift in Barrier score with change in chronological age would be obscured by the over-all increase in productivity. We did decide to investigate the Barrier score in children from another viewpoint, however. We focused on the differences in Barrier score between the sexes at various age levels. The primary purpose was simply to ascertain whether boys and girls at various age levels differed significantly in respect to Barrier score. Secondly, we were interested in comparing any differences found with those reported by other studies in the literature which have dealt with sex differences in children relative to various personality variables.

SUBJECTS AND METHODOLOGY

In seeking to obtain Rorschach records on normal children at various age levels, we were fortunate in being able to use the normative records collected by Ames (9), Beck (314), and Swift (305).* From these combined sources we were able to obtain the records on ninety-eight boys and girls in the age range of 5–7 years; seventy-two records were available on children at ages 8–10; eighty-two Rorschachs were collected at the age range 10–13; and sixty were records of the ages 13–17. These particular age groupings were dictated by available data. Ideally, a representative sampling at each age level should have been studied, but in this case there were not enough records to make such an analysis. Records on ten boys at age four were not used, because no comparable Rorschachs for girls at this age could be obtained.

The Ames, Swift, and Beck groups constitute a fairly representative cross section in respect to socioeconomic status and intelligence. The Ames sampling was drawn from urban areas of Connecticut and was described as being of above-average IQ and from above-average social status. Approximately half the Ames sample was being followed as part of a longitudinal study on child development by the Yale Child Development Clinic. The Swift group represented children from Iowa nursery schools and was reported as of superior intelligence. The Beck sample was drawn from the public schools in the Chicago area and was described as being within the normal range of intelligence. Thus, each subsample contributes unique characteristics which combine to result in a fairly acceptable diverse cross section of normal children.

The Rorschach records were scored for Barrier and Penetration of Boundary responses. All records with more than twenty-five responses were reduced to that number in the usual manner.

RESULTS AND DISCUSSION

In Table 10:1 the results of the analyses of Barrier score for the various age groups are presented. As was expected, there is a steady and significant increase in total Rorschach productivity for each successive age group, a fact which renders hazardous any comparison of Barrier scores for different age groups. Within each age grouping the sexes are not distinguished by any significant difference in total response to the Rorschach.

---

* We are grateful to Drs. L. B. Ames, S. J. Beck, and J. W. Swift for the use of these Rorschach data.

We can conclude, therefore, that differences in Barrier score between the sexes is not a function of difference in total Rorschach response.

TABLE 10:1 COMPARISON OF BARRIER SCORE FOR BOYS VS. GIRLS

Age Groups	N	Median R	Range R	Median Barrier Scores	Range Barrier Scores	% Above Median Barrier Scores for Total Group	χ^2	P
Boys 5–7	46	12	8–25	1	0–6	33	5.2	.02
Girls 5–7	52	12	7–25	2	0–7	56		
Boys 8–10	37	15	5–25	2	0–5	57	0.0	—
Girls 8–10	35	14	10–25	2	0–5	52		
Boys 10–13	40	16	8–25	2	1–6	68	4.2	.02–.05
Girls 10–13	42	16	5–25	1	0–7	45		
Boys 13–17	30	25	12–25	2	0–6	50	0.0	—
Girls 13–17	30	25	10–25	2	0–7	52		

It will be noted that at two of the four age ranges studied the sexes differ significantly in respect to Barrier score. At ages 5–7 girls produce significantly more Barrier responses than boys, but at ages 10–13, this situation is reversed. It should also be mentioned that too few cases at some of the age levels in the three samplings prevented a separate analysis of Barrier score for the Ames, Beck, and Swift data. However, for the age groups 5–7 enough records were available for a separate analysis. Here the trend is consistent for all three populations studied; namely, in the Ames, Beck, and Swift samples, girls consistently exceed boys in Barrier production.

One further amplification of the findings should be made. For age group 5–7, boys give significantly more Penetration responses (.01 level of confidence) than do girls. This is true both for the analysis of the combined samples and for each of the three populations analyzed separately. At all other age ranges studied no significant sex differences in Penetration score was observed.

The most interesting aspect to these findings is the significant reversal in trend in respect to Barrier score encountered at age levels 5–7 versus

10–13. First girls to a significant degree exceed boys on Barrier score, and then at the later age period the sexes reverse position in regard to Barrier score. Between these two age ranges, at the 8–10 year level and beyond 13 in the adolescent years, no sex differences for Barrier score are found.

In attempting to understand these findings and to fit them into some logical frame of reference, we were struck by similar findings in other studies having to do with sex differences among children on a number of personality variables. The striking thing about these other studies is that in each case a significant reversal in the variable under investigation occurs between the sexes at approximately the same age levels as those investigated in the present study. For example, Friedman (116) investigated directly the identification process and the degree of what he termed "castration anxiety" occurring in children at the same age levels as those used in the present study. In a novel fashion he applied projective story- and picture-completion tests to children. One phase of the study involved having children complete an incomplete fable. One fable, for example, had to do with a monkey and the loss or retention of his tail following a series of events. Each child was asked to complete the fable about the monkey and his tail. Friedman concluded that to avoid or overlook the loss of the projection (monkey's tail) in completing the fable implied a good deal of anxiety on the part of the child about possible damage to his own body or loss of his own body members (castration anxiety). He found, for example, that children who omitted reference to loss of the monkey's tail also blocked a great deal in the general process of completing the fable. Most interesting of all was his finding that significantly more boys than girls at ages 5–7 omit reference to the lost body member. In other words, at this age level boys demonstrate significantly more castration anxiety than do girls. But by ages 11–12 this situation is exactly reversed and girls in the Friedman study now exceed boys in avoiding reference to body loss.

This reversal in trend concerning anxiety about what is presumed to be the integrity of one's body parallels exactly the finding in the present study in respect to Barrier score. Also, it should be mentioned that Friedman found for ages 8–9 no differences between the sexes in tendency to omit reference to loss of a projection of the body. In the present study there were no sex differences in Barrier score at the age range 8–10. Friedman interpreted the reversal in trend for castration anxiety among boys versus girls as verifying psychoanalytic hypotheses about the Oedipus complex and the process of taking on of a sex role for boys versus girls. He pointed out that at ages 5–6 boys, in general, are still under the influence of castration fears and are in the midst of the turmoil aroused by attempts at resolution of the Oedipus complex. Friedman reasoned that boys' anxiety is revealed by avoidance of thinking about possible loss of body part. In contrast, girls, although their own castration fears have not been fully dispelled at this age, do reflect significantly less anxiety at this period. Presumably girls have already passed the height of their turmoil over Oedipal problems by age six, since there seems to be general agreement that girls do precede boys in their Oedipal resolution. However, girls on the average also enter puberty earlier than boys; and in Friedman's study, they apparently revealed their relatively earlier re-aroused anxiety by avoiding reference to loss of body parts at ages 11–12 to a greater degree than did the boys. Friedman also made the point that the sexes do not differ in respect to anxiety over possible body disruption at the age level 8–9. He reasons that this period, in analytic theory the "latency period," represents a lull in anxiety over Oedipal problems and the acquisition of a sex role. Consequently neither sex during these years is seriously, actively disturbed about sex role, sex identity, or body integrity.

Other investigators, too, have found sex differences in children in respect to body-image variables. Katcher and Levin (166) demonstrated that there is a differential in the degree to which girls versus boys make realistic estimations of their own body size. Children were asked to select from a triad of schematic body parts—heads, torsos, and legs—one of each part most like his own size. Each triad consisted of three sizes of each part; a large, medium, and small size. For our purpose, the interesting finding was that girls tended at an earlier age than boys to select body sizes more realistically, that is, corresponding more to their own body size (small). Significantly, the age group of girls 4–6 years that showed this tendency corresponds roughly with our age range 5–7 years, where girls exceeded boys on Barrier score. This finding would seem to complement the results on Barrier score for this age range. That is, our reasoning has been that girls, in contrast to boys, are in the main less confused at this point concerning the limits of their own boundaries. To find that they are more realistic in estimating their own body size would seem to be congruent with this idea.

In another study by Swensen and Newton (304), the Draw-A-Person Test was used as a technique in tracing the development of sexual differentiation in children. At age six girls were found to exceed boys in their tendency to draw spontaneously a like-sex figure first. Also, girls tended to differentiate between the sexes better than boys at this age. By this the authors meant that girls adorn their drawings with more recognizably feminine features than do the boys with masculine features. Not until the age of thirteen did boys as a group attain the level of sexual differentiation enjoyed by the girls. The authors did not discuss the significance of these findings. The usual interpretation as to the meaning of the spontaneous choice of a like-sex figure, however, is that it represents a relatively satisfied and secure attitude toward one's own sex role and identification. On the other hand, preference for the opposite sex figure, at least among children, may represent some uncertainty and confusion about one's identity. The important thing about the findings of this study was that once again girls tended to indicate acceptance of a more clear and definite picture of their sex role and identity earlier than did boys.

This study has been duplicated in its essential features by Wieder and Noller (340) who also found that at ages 5–8 significantly more girls than boys draw like-sex figures first. Socioeconomic status was found to be unrelated to the nature of the figure drawings. Girls, besides drawing a like-sex figure first more frequently than boys, also tended to add more facial details and to draw full-face figures rather than profiles. Drawing of profiles is usually thought to represent a more evasive and "easier" approach to the task than the full-face drawing. These authors concluded that girls tended to identify earlier and in a more complete degree with their own sex role than did boys.

Machover (203) has reported some preliminary findings concerning the human figure drawings of 1,000 children from about ages 5–11. Writing about a sample of public school, nonparochial, middle-class children within this age range, she has this to say in interpreting their figure drawings (p. 87): "Throughout this age range we find that girls fare better than boys. The taming process is not so painful. They appear more comfortable with regulations and social defense, incorporating these in their body image early in life." She goes on to point out that this relative advantage of girls is disrupted by the advent of puberty and not until later adolescence do girls again regain their "self-esteem and efficiency."

To the authors it appeared that the similarity between the findings of the various studies which have been cited and the results we obtained must be more than coincidental. It would seem to be a fair statement to say that all these studies suggest a differential rate of acceptance of sex role and identification between boys and girls. We find that a lowered Barrier score accompanies those periods during which either sex is experiencing the most confusion and uncertainty about sex role and sex identity, or probably in a more general sense, confusion over the whole question of life goals, proper modes of behavior, and philosophy of life. Repeatedly in this book a relationship between Barrier score and degree of definiteness of one's role, of one's purpose and goals in life has been demonstrated. In examining both the results of the present study and similar findings concerning sex differences in children on various measures, it was our feeling that the area of commonality for all these studies has something to do with a reflection of the varying struggle of the sexes in seeking a well-defined life model. Sex differences in Barrier score among children seem to mirror differences in their degree of confusion and uncertainty over life goals and role standards at a particular phase in their socialization. This sex difference in Barrier score is found at those age points where a transition in roles for one of the sexes is in progress.

SEX DIFFERENCES IN BARRIER SCORE AMONG AMERICAN ADULTS

Normally in our study of the Barrier score in adult groups no sex differences have been found. None of the various college populations reported at different points in this volume yielded any sex differences in Barrier score. Further, a normal adult group collected by Beck,[*] consisting of thirty women and twenty men employed in industry in the Chicago area, failed to establish any sex differences in Barrier score.

Nor have we found any relationship between Barrier score and degree of masculinity-femininity in normal individuals in terms of a questionnaire type of scale. As part of a larger study concerning Barrier score and a host of independent measures, described in Chapter 4, responses of ninety-six male ROTC students at the University of Texas to the Masculinity-Femininity items of the MMPI scale were compared with their Barrier scores. Only a chance relationship was found by means of chi-square between M-F scores and the Barrier scores. In still another study a comparison was made of Barrier scores and degree of masculinity-femininity as measured by the Terman-Miles scale. Seventy-two male undergraduates were examined by King[†] and a completely chance relationship was found between Barrier score and the Terman-Miles M-F scale.

From the results of all these different studies, we emerge with the conclusion that no relationship between Barrier score and degree of masculinity-femininity, per se, has been established. We do not find any sex differences in Barrier score among children at those ages where turmoil over life goals and values is at a minimum. Adult men and women from middle-class American society do not differ on Barrier score. We do find, however, variation in Barrier score between the sexes in children at age points where one sex or the other experiences an upheaval of anxiety and confusion over methods and procedures in attaining life goals.

These findings suggested the general hypothesis that whenever sex differences occur in Barrier score, they represent differences in degree of

---

[*] This is a portion of the normative Rorschach records collected by Dr. S. J. Beck at the Spiegel Department Store. We are grateful to Dr. Beck for his permission to use these data.

[†] We are grateful to Dr. Stanley H. King, Research Associate, Graduate School of Public Health, University of Pittsburgh, for use of these data.

confusion and uncertainty over life goals and self-identity. Whenever sex differences in Barrier score are encountered, we would expect to find the sex group with the lowered Barrier scores to be the more anxious and confused over roles and identity. We would expect to find the group with lowered Barrier scores to be in some state of transition of roles, i.e., a period of major change in predominant modes of reaction and behavior.°

It should be noted that this hypothesis assumes that by adulthood in middle-class American society, men and women each in their own way have clarified to a similar degree their previous, more obscure life objectives. Presumably by adulthood each sex has worked out in its own way a system of values and roles which are of relatively equal definiteness. Accordingly, we ordinarily find no sex differences in Barrier response in adults.

It is only fair to note that this assumption does not find support in all areas of theoretical discussion concerning the establishment of the sexual and social roles of the two sexes. Most analytic writers, for example, are inclined to give women much the worse of this struggle in effecting life orientation. A sort of inherent, almost biological inferiority is ascribed to women by most of the earlier analytic theorists. More recently, however, other authors, such as Thompson (314A) or Parsons and Bales (232), have attacked the Victorian attitudes concerning the supposed inferiority of women. Parsons and Bales, who have written extensively concerning role differentiation, conclude that American middle-class society most closely attains the epitome of equalization of role opportunity. On this point they write (p. 339):

> From certain points of view the American middle-class family approaches most clearly to equal allocation of instrumental and expressive activities. The universalistic value schema (in which women are "just as good as" men) coupled with the general attitude toward the explicit expression of authority ("I'm agin it") apparently constitutes the limiting case of no differentiation (of roles) at all.

° One bit of data which offers some support to this hypothesis should be noted. One of the authors (61) examined three adult males who had demonstrated a lifelong inability to establish any fixed pattern of roles or purpose in life. So thoroughly mixed up about their entire identity were these individuals, that they had finally dramatized their confusion in acts of self-castration. The individuals in this group had from a very early age been unusually dissatisfied and uncertain not only about their sexual identity but also about their goals and entire philosophy of life. The final desperate act of self-castration merely highlighted their confusion. The interesting point to be noted here is that Rorschach tests, administered to these individuals long before the self-castration, revealed a total absence of Barrier score together with abnormally high Penetration scores. Unfortunately, only three cases could be included in this study and the question remains open as to how typical of such cases these findings may be. However, complete absence of Barrier score is an unusual finding. It is interesting that it occurs here in individuals who are so thoroughly confused about their identity and whole philosophy of life.

SOME FINDINGS CONCERNING ADULT SEX DIFFER-ENCES IN BARRIER SCORE IN JAPANESE AND JAPANESE-AMERICAN CULTURES

The point has been suggested that Barrier score is in some way related to the degree of certitude one has about how to make one's way in life. Masculinity or femininity, as such, seems to have no special significance for Barrier score. But the sexes do differ on Barrier score at age points where some transition phenomenon is making a relatively greater impact upon one sex than the other. Thus, at those periods in childhood which appear to be focal points of unrest, crisis periods of anxiety about one's entire identity, Barrier score sex differences are found.

The point has also been made that adult, middle-class American populations yield no Barrier-score sex differences. Presumably the major and important decisions have been made concerning the basic modes of adjustment by adulthood. But what if Barrier score were studied in a culture or subculture where the patterns of behavior for the sexes were *actually* in a state of transition? Suppose a culture could be studied which provided an opportunity for examining adult members whose roles were in varying degrees of change? Would we not find sex differences for Barrier score? On the basis of our findings up to this point, we would be inclined to predict sex differences in Barrier score in adults who had grown up in a cultural setting which did not provide equally good definitions of roles for the two sexes.

An opportunity to test such a prediction was made possible through the efforts and cooperation of George De Vos.° He had collected Rorschach records of native village Japanese and immigrant (Issei) and American-born Japanese (Nisei). This data collection was part of a larger, interdisciplinary study concerned with the relationship of the process of acculturation to prevalent patterns of personality.

We selected these three different Japanese groups for study since they appeared to offer an excellent opportunity to compare the effect on Barrier score of a transition in roles for the two sexes. The native village Japanese, of course, have centuries of tradition and ceremony behind them by which the roles of men and women have become fixed and defined. One would not expect to find sex difference in Barrier score in such a stable culture. Also, to nearly the same degree, the sex role traditions of the Issei would tend to be stable. At least the adult Issei were exposed during their formative years to the same rigid behavior patterns and training of roles as the village groups. Therefore we did not expect to find sex dif-

---

° We are indebted to Dr. De Vos for the use of these data.

ferences in Barrier score in this sample. But the American-born Japanese (Nisei) as a group present an altogether different situation. Rather than attempting to adhere to the concepts of a native homeland, the young men and women comprising the Nisei group struggle to readapt their way of life to correspond to the demands of contemporary middle-class America. As will be brought out in discussing our findings, several investigators have called attention to the transition in roles necessary among the Nisei in becoming acculturated.

There were available thirty-seven Rorschach records on native village Japanese, fifty records for Issei or Japanese-born, and fifty records for Nisei or American-born Japanese. A description of the careful sampling procedures used and a detailed description of these subject groups may be found in De Vos's monograph (82). These records were scored in the usual manner for Barrier responses.

The incidence of Barrier score for the sexes in these three groups is listed in Table 10:2. It will be noted that the three groups differ significantly from each other in regard to total responses given on the Rorschach. The village group produce significantly fewer responses than do the Issei or Nisei, and the Issei give significantly fewer responses than the Nisei. For this reason no comparison can be made for Barrier score among the three groups. Within each group, however, no significant difference in total productivity occurs between the sexes. Of course, there are other factors which are not equated among the three groups, as for example, educational status. The Nisei as a group far exceed either the village or Issei populations on educational attainment. However, within each group factors of age and education are equated for the sexes.

Inspection of Table 10:2 reveals that in both the village and Issei groups no sex differences for Barrier score are observed. In line with our expectations, however, the Nisei sample reveals women to score significantly higher than the Nisei men on Barrier. In other words, in a subculture which is in a state of high transition, a sex difference for Barrier score is found. In line with our original ideas in pursuing this study, it will now be of interest to examine the nature of the general life patterns of the village, Issei, and Nisei groups. Is it possible to point out differential areas of conflict and confusion concerning values, goals, and general life orientation among Nisei men and women which will explain their differences in Barrier scores? On the basis of our original thinking about this, we would expect the Nisei women to make the transition in roles from the tradition-bound native Japanese culture to the American culture in a smoother and less confused style than do the Nisei men. As already indicated, in the case of the village group and of the Issei men and women with centuries of tradition and custom giving firm outline to the respective roles of Japanese men and women, we would expect to find little confusion on the part of either sex over expected modes of behavior. Each sex in its own way would presumably have well-defined and, in fact, rigid patterns of behavior worked out. We are not proposing that the sex roles do not differ in Japan. We are not contending that neither sex holds a dominant position nor that neither sex enjoys a favored way of life. Undoubtedly the sexes do differ on these important

TABLE 10:2 COMPARISON OF JAPANESE VILLAGE, ISSEI AND NISEI MEN VS. WOMEN ON BARRIER SCORE [a]

Group	N	Range R	Median R	Median Barrier Score	% Above Median Barrier Score for Total Group	χ^2	P
Village men	16	10–25	13	2	25		
Village women	21	8–25	13	2	47	1.4	—
Issei men	26	10–25	18	1	42		
Issei women	24	11–25	16	1	40	—	—
Nisei men	25	12–25	25	3	40		
Nisei women	25	13–25	25	4	68	4.0	.02–.05

[a] Issei refers to Japanese-born immigrants, Nisei to American-born Japanese.

variables. Our point is that whatever roles have been elaborated for the sexes, these are well-defined and clear-cut in the Japanese village and Issei populations. On the other hand, in the Nisei population, the whole pattern of traditional social roles is overthrown and adjustment to entirely new ways of life must be worked out.

It would be helpful in evaluating the relative stability of the roles played by men versus women in Japanese and Japanese-American cultures to examine the writings of other investigators. There appears to be common agreement concerning the inflexibility and rigidity of the basic philosophy of life of the native Japanese culture. Benedict (26), De Vos (81), and Embree (85), for example, all stress the intense respect for authority, the personal submergence of individual goals, and the heavy sense of obligation and duty to one's family and country instilled in both sexes by adulthood. De Vos (81) refers to the inflexibility of the social roles of village and Issei men and women. A concept of the orderly hierarchy of things appears to dictate to a large extent interpersonal relations. Embree (85) has written at length of life in a rural Japanese village and at various points refers to "the sharp social division of the sexes that lasts until old age." Repeatedly he illustrates how a majority of the major life decisions of both men and women are made, not on the basis of individual choice, but are dictated by custom and family expectation. There are sharply defined differences in the social roles of the sexes, and the over-all rigidity of the roles for each sex makes for a feeling of inevitability of one's role, whether male or female.

In contrast, the Nisei struggle through the process of acculturation and demonstrate, in their efforts to divorce themselves from Japanese tradition, a sharp transition in patterns of behavior. De Vos (81), Caudill (59), Benedict (26), and other writers seem to feel that in making this transition Nisei women have the better of it compared to the Nisei men. De Vos points out that the Nisei as a group appear much more flexible in contrast to the social rigidity of the village Japanese and the Issei, exposed as the latter groups were in their formative years to the tradition-bound customs of the homeland. In analyzing the relative degree of response of Nisei men and women to the freedom of opportunity for individual development in middle-class America, De Vos has this to say (82, p. 83):

> The differences (in Rorschach responses) noted between the Nisei men and Nisei women suggest some differences in acculturation which seem influenced by social sex role. The Nisei women definitely seem, according to behavioral evidence as well as the results reported above (on Rorschach tests), to be more acculturated than the men. The more pressing economic responsibility of the men may be a factor, or, possibly the totally different conception of women between cultures such as the Japanese and American way, account for the radical shift in some fashion.

In other words, for reasons not yet spelled out, from De Vos's data we can argue that Nisei women, who in our sample significantly exceed Nisei men on Barrier score, enjoy the more clearly defined and less confused behavioral patterns in meeting the demands of middle-class American society.

Caudill (59), on the basis of his research using the TAT with Issei and Nisei groups, reached similar conclusions to those of De Vos in describing the changing roles of Nisei men and women in facing the challenge of Western culture. He pointed to the stability and relatively fixed nature of the roles of the sexes in Issei culture. Even though females are taught to be submissive in Japanese culture, they are also taught that they must fulfill their obligations to family and country as thoroughly as do Issei men. Caudill, in fact, outlines for Japanese women a pattern of roles as thoroughly well-delineated as those of Japanese men. He writes, on this point (p. 30): "This culture does not create weak women, it creates overly submissive women with great hidden strength." But in the case of the Nisei men and women he makes clear that there is a decided difference in the impact of Western culture on the relative stability of the roles of the two sexes. On the basis of TAT fantasies he concludes that Nisei women throw off their submissiveness and enter freely into the competitive struggle of middle-class American society. He sees Nisei women as in hostile competition with men and in rebellious opposition to the former passivity enforced by Issei parents. Nisei women now employ their strength to live in a society that neither requires nor rewards marked submissiveness to authority. In this aggressive struggle Nisei women presumably construct for themselves a rigorous and well-defined system of roles and patterns of behavior.

Nisei men, on the other hand, appear to be much more confused by Western culture. Caudill finds the Nisei men more reluctant to break with tradition and their Issei parents. As a consequence Nisei men lead an ambivalent role, afraid on the one hand to strive for middle-class American goals, because this represents for them a threatened loss of security of the traditions of home and entry into a frightening outer world. On the other hand, they are faced with parental and social demands that they make their way in the world. On the basis of his TAT findings, Caudill concludes that the Nisei men, in comparison with the Nisei women, feel more vulnerable to attack whenever they attempt to fulfill the American middle-class masculine role of competition and struggle.

To the authors it appears that the conclusions of both Caudill and De Vos concerning the relative degree of confusion on the part of the Nisei men in seeking a new way of life in Western culture tend to support our original hypotheses about the significance of adult sex differences in Barrier score. That is, we originally predicted a lowered Barrier score for that sex which as a group experienced a period of uncertainty over proper social roles. In the Nisei sample studied just such a significant sex difference in Barrier score was found. And as has been pointed out, other investigators indicate that for various reasons it is the Nisei men who experience much the greater confusion and ambivalence in coping with American customs, as compared with the Nisei women.

Of course, our conclusions must remain tentative. We have after all drawn from a small sample of Japanese and American-born Japanese.

Only further research on larger and carefully selected groups from still other contrasting cultures and subcultures can decide whether or not these speculations about the relationship between Barrier score and degree of delineation of social roles of adult men and women are justified.

....

CHAPTER ELEVEN

Cultural Differences in Boundary Characteristics

INTRODUCTION AND PROCEDURE

As was shown at an earlier point (Chapter 9), there are significant relationships between the boundary characteristics of individuals and certain attributes of their parents. It can be said with some assurance that the manner in which the parent conducts himself toward his child affects the kind of body-image boundary the child will develop. One may conceptualize the boundary-formation process as a function of the way in which the whole socialization sequence is structured. If one takes this view, the beguiling thought then arises that there ought to be contrasts in the boundary attributes of unlike cultures. That is, since the socialization procedures among various cultures are often radically divergent, it should be possible to find correlated differences in body-image boundary definiteness. Were such to be demonstrated, it would add even further support to the view that degree of boundary definiteness is a function of socialization pattern. Also, it would possibly add another dimension to those already available which one can use in describing differences among cultures.

In approaching the task of exploring cultural differences in body-image boundary definiteness, we had two choices. First of all, we could have studied the available anthropological data concerning a number of cultures and predicted from the data which cultures would tend toward boundary definiteness and which toward boundary indefiniteness. These hypotheses could then have been checked by determining the Barrier scores of Rorschach protocols obtained in the given cultures. An alternative was to begin by determining the Barrier scores of Rorschach protocols from various cultures and to relate empirical differences that might emerge to what was already known about these cultures. The latter of the two alternatives was chosen because neither of the authors was sufficiently versed in anthropology to have the detailed grasp of conditions in a range of cultures which would be necessary in order to formulate hypotheses concerning body-image boundary phenomena in those cultures. Of course, we realized that if we did find Barrier score differences among cultures by means of a sweep through a great variety of Rorschachs, we would be exposed to the temptation of picking and choosing from what was known about the cultures in question in order to rationalize and explain such differences. This realization made it clear that our work in this area could be considered only as a search for leads and hypotheses that would require future validation.

A survey of the pertinent literature indicated that Rorschach records had already been collected in numerous cultures. Hundreds of protocols have been secured throughout the world (141, 315, 149). The problem of gaining access to some of these protocols was fortunately simplified by a project carried out by Bert Kaplan (164). He had, with the support of the National Research Council, obtained Rorschach records collected by many anthropologists in the course of their field work and reproduced them in a published series of microcards. In this series were Rorschachs that embraced such a diversity of peoples as North American Indians, Haitians, and Hindus. Our intent was to determine the median Barrier score of the records from a number of these groups and to test whether there were significant differences among them.

At first, this seemed like a rather straightforward task that could be accomplished without too much difficulty. We soon learned, however, about the complications which have beset all investigators who have tried to use data from the Rorschach in understanding and comparing cultures (149, 141). These complications have usually centered about two prime issues: (1) The representativeness of the Rorschach sample; (2) the conditions under which the test was administered. For us there was the additional complication that cultural groups differed considerably in their response productivity and that the Barrier score is significantly a function of response total. There follows now a brief scanning of how we dealt with these methodological difficulties.

The problem of the representativeness of the Rorschach sample secured in any given culture is at present almost an insurmountable one. Anthropologists who have administered the Rorschach in the course of their stay in a particular group have rarely taken more than 150 protocols and most have taken less than 100. In terms of the total population of the average culture, a sample of this size is of minute proportions. Furthermore, one can rarely be sure that the anthropologist did not operate on the basis of some selective bias in arranging for his test population. As horrendous as the problem may sound, it is interesting that several published Rorschach analyses of culture-personality patterns have correlated well with other sorts of data concerning the cultures in question (141, 315). Our attitude concerning this problem has been to ignore it. That is, we have made no attempt to evaluate the representativeness of the

Rorschach samples available to us. Since our mission was primarily one of hypothesis development, we assumed that any irregularities introduced by sampling could be checked in later validation studies. The one control measure we did introduce was to confine our analysis (with a few exceptions) to male subjects. This was necessary because many of the Rorschach culture samples available on microcards to us consisted primarily of men.

A second major question that arose concerning the Rorschach data collected in various cultures was whether differences in instructions, physical setting, and in subject motivation could conceivably have large effects. One finds that some field workers administered the Rorschach in their own houses, others in the homes of their subjects, and still others by the roadside. A number of workers have paid their subjects; others have cajoled and enticed individuals into taking the test; and still others were fortunate to have eagerly cooperative subjects. Our method of dealing with this issue has been to use only those records in which the subject did not verbalize inordinate resistance. Furthermore, we have used only records which contain at least ten responses and have assumed that this would represent a minimum behavioral token of involvement in the test.

A third problem in using the collected Rorschach protocols had to do with the large differences in median response total for the various cultures. The median response total in some cultures was fifteen; in others it was as much as twenty-five. We solved this problem by extracting from each available cultural sample only those records which could be matched in response total to those from all the other samples. An equal proportion of high and low response total records were pulled out that would result in a median response total in the range 19–20. This selective process resulted in the usable sample from each culture being limited to a rather small number of records. But while this limited the size of the samples, it insured that they were as comparable as possible with regard to response total.

Rorschach records from the following cultural groups were selected for the Barrier score analysis:

Bhils of India	Navaho Indians
Hindus of India	Zuni Indians
Haitians	Tuscarora Indians

In addition, three groups from the United States were included. One of these groups was collected by Beck (18A) in Chicago. Although selective in some respects, this Chicago sample consists of individuals distributed through lower- and middle-class occupational categories and is grossly representative of these categories in the Chicago population. A second group consisted of college students in an introductory psychology class at the University of Washington to whom Steisel (291) had individually administered the Rorschach test. A third group was made up of a variety of undergraduate students at Western Reserve University who had been individually tested with the Rorschach by Cheatham (60). These college groups were chosen randomly from the various college groups available to us in our file of college populations. The Beck group and the two college groups provided two somewhat contrasting samples from United States culture to compare with the samples from the other cultures; but they were, of course, biased samples so far as response total is concerned.

ANALYSIS OF BARRIER SCORE DIFFERENCES

The results in Table 11:1 do suggest the existence of Barrier score differences among the cultural groups evaluated. The Bhil group of India

TABLE 11:1   BARRIER SCORES OF CULTURAL GROUPS

Group	Response Total Median	Barrier Score Median
Bhil (India) (N = 21)	18	4
Navaho (Indians of Southwest U. S.) (N = 24)	19	3
Zuni (Indians of Southwest U. S.) (N = 28)	19	3
Tuscarora (Indians of Northeast U. S.) (N = 23)	18	3
Hindu (India) (N = 24)	19	2
Haitian[a] (N = 21)	20	2
U. S. Chicago sample (N = 21)	22[b]	2
U. S. College sample (Washington) (N = 18)	23	2
U. S. College sample (Ohio) (N = 23)	21	2

[a] It was necessary to include seven women in this group in order to make up an adequate sample.

[b] Despite our best efforts, we could not obtain enough college records with a limited number of responses so that the median response total in each U. S. college group would be as low as the medians of the other cultural samples.

has the highest score. Next in succession are the Navaho, Zuni, and Tuscarora. The lowest Barrier scores are obtained by the Hindu, Haitian, and three United States groups. Chi-square tests were run on the significance of the differences between the groups. As pointed up by Table 11:2, the Bhil group tends to be significantly higher than all the other

TABLE 11:2   CHI-SQUARE TESTS OF DIFFERENCES IN BARRIER SCORES
AMONG CULTURAL GROUPS

Groups	*Group with Higher Score*	*Significance Level of Difference*
Bhil vs.		
Navaho	Bhil	.10–.05
Zuni	Bhil	Not significant
Tuscarora	Bhil	.10–.05
Hindu	Bhil	.10–.05
Haitian	Bhil	.10–.05
U. S. Chicago sample	Bhil	.001
U. S. College sample (Washington)	Bhil	.001
U. S. College sample (Ohio)	Bhil	.02–.01
Navaho vs.		
Hindu	Navaho	Not significant
Haitian	Navaho	.10–.05
Tuscarora	Navaho	Not significant
U. S. Chicago sample	Navaho	.10–.05
U. S. College sample (Washington)	Navaho	.10–.05
U. S. College sample (Ohio)	Navaho	.30
Zuni vs.		
Hindu	Zuni	Not significant
Haitian	Zuni	.10–.05
Tuscarora	Zuni	Not significant
U. S. Chicago sample	Zuni	.02–.01
U. S. College sample (Washington)	Zuni	.10–.05
U. S. College sample (Ohio)	Zuni	.20–.10
Bhil + Navaho + Zuni vs. Haitian + three U. S. samples	Bhil + Navaho + Zuni	.01

groups except the Zuni. The Navaho and Zuni tend to be significantly higher than the Haitians and the three United States groups. They do not exceed the Hindus or Tuscarora significantly. When the combined (Bhil + Navaho + Zuni) group is contrasted with the combined (Haitian + three United States samples) group, the latter proves to be significantly lower in Barrier score. It should be noted that the Hindu and Tuscarora groups are somewhat intermediate between the Navaho and Zuni, on the one hand, and the Haitian and United States samples on the other hand. Because their position is clear only relative to the Bhil group, they have been excluded from the detailed analysis which follows concerning the Barrier score differences obtained.

The Barrier score results indicate a rough division of the various cultural groups into two categories. In one category are the Bhil, Navaho,* and Zuni groups which seem to have relatively definite body-image boundaries. In the other category are the Haitian, the United States Chicago sample, and two United States college sample groups which apparently have relatively indefinite boundaries. The question arises as to whether this split corresponds to other differentiations between these groups that have been observed. One is, of course, immediately struck by the fact that all the United States samples are in the indefinite-boundary category. They manifest relatively low Barrier scores despite the fact that their median response totals are higher than those of the other groups. The presence of the Haitian group in the same category with the United States groups is superficially puzzling until it is noted that about two-thirds of the selected sample consist of well-educated members of the elite upper class of Haitian society who have, by and large, been brought up in a Western tradition (French literary tradition) which in its basic assumptions is probably not radically different from that prevailing in the United States.† Thus, all the groups in the low Barrier score category are comprised mainly of individuals who were reared in the spirit of modern Western civilization. All three groups in the high Barrier classification, however, represent cultures with rather unique characteristics and values quite different from those prevalent in modern Western civilization.

As was earlier indicated, the level at which we planned to explore in our attempts to gain insight into the factors underlying the division of the cultures upon the basis of Barrier scores was dictated by the results that had emerged from our family studies. These results had made it clear that parental attitudes and parental patterns of behavior exert a significant effect upon the character of the child's body-image boundaries. It therefore seemed logical to examine the difference between the bloc of definite-boundary cultures and the bloc of indefinite-boundary cultures in terms of parental attitudes, practices, and values. Could one find similarities in the style of child rearing of the cultures in a given

---

* It is interesting that when Friedman (115) analyzed the content of stories from the mythology of eight different American Indian groups in terms of McClelland's *n* Achievement measure, he found the Navaho to be highest in *n* Achievement. In view of the positive correlations we have in general observed between Barrier score and achievement level, one may consider the fact that the Navaho are in the high Barrier category as indirectly supported by Friedman's results.

† Actually, the amount of specific data available concerning the life pattern in the elite Haitian group is limited. There are strong suggestions from observations made by Bourguignon (44), however, that this life pattern leans far in the Western direction.

bloc, and would this style contrast with that typical of cultures in the other bloc?

Our survey of the available data concerning the cultures involved led us to propose two hypotheses to account for the observed body-image boundary differences.

The first of these hypotheses has to do with degree of tolerance for impulse expression. It appears to us that the high Barrier cultures provide considerably more freedom for the developing child to indulge his impulses than do the low Barrier cultures. For example, there seems to be much less restraint on direct relief of body tensions in the Bhil and Navaho groups (especially during the developmental years) than in the general culture of the United States. It is conjectured that the more a parent denies impulse outlets to his child the more likely are their interrelationships to become antagonistic, and therefore the less likely they are to work out a satisfactory equilibrium between themselves. The absence of such an equilibrium would seem to minimize the possibility of the child's communicating closely with the parent in a manner required to experience him as a consistent model. The parent would therefore be psychologically less available to supply the sort of patterned model that seems to be necessary for the formation of definite body-image boundaries.

A second hypothesis concerning the boundary differences between the blocs relates to the clearness of definition of the standards and values in the cultures. It is proposed that the definite-boundary cultures are characterized by rather well codified and noncontradictory belief systems; whereas the indefinite-boundary cultures are marked by multiple contradictory standards from which the individual makes his choice in a relativistic fashion. For instance, the average Zuni holds to a way of life and a view of things that conform to fairly simple patterns which are reiterated in ritual, folklore, and the behavioral example of his contemporaries (25, 127). But the average individual in most areas of the United States finds himself sharply exposed to multiple philosophies and widespread indecision as to what is right and wrong. Other things being equal, it is presumed that the parent who functions in a milieu in which standards are well ordered is more likely to be experienced by his child as representative of a definite way of life than is the parent who lives in a society with vaguely ordered standards. The parent in the well-ordered milieu would presumably be in the best position to supply the sharply contoured model that seems to be required for the formation of definite body-image boundaries.

There follows now an attempt to document the differences between the cultural groups which have been hypothesized above. This documentation will be confined mainly to the high Barrier groups because the pertinent facts about them are not widely known. It will be assumed, however, that it is not necessary to review the supporting data which point up the high degree of impulse restriction and vagueness of value standards which are currently characteristic of the way of life that basically embraces both the United States and the Haitian upper classes. Detailed studies and analyses of this modal life style which have dealt with the two issues in question may be found in the writings of Riesman (245), Fromm (117), Warner and Lunt (325), Ericson (86), West (337), Davis, Gardner, and Gardner (78), and Brody (49). The weight of the evidence is in favor of the viewpoint that the Western way of life usually involves early demands for self-regulation of oral, anal, and bladder tensions, the ordering of behavior to mechanistic time schedules, the long-term inhibition of straightforward hostility, the imposition of restraint upon sexual expression until late adolescence, and extended periods of formal schooling designed to inculcate complex patterns of training. The emphasis is upon blocking direct impulse outlets and learning, on the contrary, to secure release through tangential indirect channels.

Note what Whiting and Child have to say concerning this point on the basis of a systematic quantitative evaluation of socialization patterns in various cultures (339, p. 320):

> We have compared the child training practices of a group of midwestern urban middle-class families with those of our sample of primitive societies. We found that this American group is generally nonindulgent during infancy, in a hurry to start the training process (especially with respect to weaning and toilet training), and quite severe in the general socialization of their children.

Aside from this rather consistent generalized orientation toward control of impulses, however, the Western way of life is marked by the competition for dominance of multiple values, ideas, and philosophies.*

---

* Conflict concerning multiple values is particularly characteristic of the elite Haitians. Bourguigon says regarding this point (44, p. 320): "Haitian society contains a great many realistic conflict situations. The elite, unlike the masses, have no acceptable culturally patterned way of expressing aggression, such as through magic, or through accusing others of magic, which we find among the masses. They have no evil *vodun* priests, secret societies, and *zombies*, which present acceptable ways of localizing their fears for the masses. Nor do they have the gods of *vodun* to protect them. While in their childhood they became acquainted with *vodun* practices, tales, and proverbs, they were later forced to reject these. Insofar as they have rejected them and are nostalgic, they are ambivalent. While the child of the masses is permitted to grow up with the beliefs and world view he acquired in childhood, the elite individual must reject his childhood world view as he grows up. It is this discontinuity in the process of maturation which is shared by all members of the elite, which leads to the lack of integration which we find in their world view and thus to their characteristic ambivalence. As their class position and the accepted orientation of their elders pulls them toward the West, their childhood pulls them away from it."

Values seem to be in constant flux and often exist side by side with other values that are incongruously different. One generation may find itself adhering to standards which deviate grossly from the standards which were acceptable to the previous generation.

While impulse restraint and contradictions in values may be similarly observed in the Bhil, Navaho, and Zuni groups, they are of a far less extreme order. An initial demonstration of this point may be undertaken by reviewing some of the patterns characteristic of the Bhil culture.

BHIL CULTURE

The Bhils whose Rorschach protocols were analyzed for the Barrier variable live in Kotra Bhomat, Udaipur which is in northwestern India (164). They are located in a remote area which has long been regarded as dangerous because of the big game and because of their attitude toward travelers, who have customarily been regarded as prey for robbery. Only in the last ten years has there been a regular road to outside regions. The Bhils are the oldest surviving inhabitants of the area. More recent arrivals in India (e.g., Hindus) have regarded the Bhils as an inferior "monkey people."

The Bhils of Kotra Bhomat live in villages in which the houses are set wide apart. Their traditional crop is maize. Each household tries to build up a stock of goats, cattle, or buffalo. The tribe is divided into a number of exogamous patrilineal lineages. The wife usually goes to live in the husband's village. There is a headman in each village, but decisions on major matters are customarily arrived at by informal meetings of all the grown men. The headman secures conformance to his day-by-day decisions only if they are, by and large, endorsed by the majority of the group. Women have relatively high status. They are less downtrodden than are the wives of their neighboring Hindus. They work side by side with their husbands in the fields. If a wife develops a strong dislike for her husband, she is likely to come across a roving bachelor who will have a good chance of convincing her to run off.

The Bhils place minimum emphasis upon early control of body functions. Their children are nursed until they are about three years of age and typically are fed when they cry. Toilet training is "leisurely and unenforced." However, fathers and mothers are quite open in their aggressive expectations that beyond early infancy the children will learn to be self-supporting and "useful members of the family work-team." There is a good deal less of the emphasis on the sort of formal submissiveness expected by the Hindu parent in India, of his son. There is little privacy in the Bhil household and intercourse is witnessed early by the children. Carstairs indicates (164, p. 14), "There is a great deal of tolerated promiscuity among the young men and girls, with the provision that this must be carried on out of sight, in the jungle."

Apparently the Bhils enjoy working together. They cooperate in a variety of agricultural projects. Customarily five or six households will pool their efforts at the time of plowing or to dig a well or to dam a river for fishing. Carstairs refers to them as an expressive people who enjoy spontaneity and direct action. Some of his characterological descriptions of them should be cited:

> The writer can best give his impressions of Bhil personality by contrasting certain aspects of it with that of the orthodox Hindu. Perhaps the basic difference is one of sturdier ego-formation among the Bhils: they carry themselves with assurance, look you in the eye, do not conceal their feelings. [p. 15]
>
> The ability to show emotion unashamedly is apparent, also in Bhil dancing and singing, both of which are not rigidly formalized, as with the Hindus, but leave scope for impromptu innovations and individual self-expression. Every Bhil youth learns to play the flute and each one seems able to take a turn at beating the drums or singing when a dance group is in progress. [p. 14]
>
> The Bhils are in general much more free of restrictions and taboos than are the Hindus. They relish eating meat (even, in secret, the meat of the sacred cow) and drinking spirits, and above all they relish making love. Sex has none of the connotations of danger and sin and loss of manly powers which Hindus attribute to it: it is to be enjoyed. [p. 14]
>
> Bhils are remarkably resilient in the face of material hardship. They are optimistic not in the passive dependent way of Hindus, whose constant daydream is of a god-like figure appearing and giving them riches and kirdness all for nothing, but with the sentiment: "See, I have enough to eat today; I'm sure I'll manage to find something to eat to-morrow too." [p. 16]

Concepts of religion and magic are prominent in Bhil life. There are many household gods and also there are numerous shrines. When sickness occurs, the *devalo* (magician) is called and he makes use of healing rituals. Harmful events or misfortunes tend to be attributed to witchcraft, particularly on the part of some woman; and there are organized group means of detecting the witch and forcing her to cease her evil influence.

Over all, the available data concerning the Bhils depict them as a group in which spontaneous impulse expression is relatively permissible from an early age. At the same time, however, there are definite pressures upon the child to begin to learn at a particular time to become independent and to function as a member of the work team. Religion and magic play a prominent part in the culture and provide specific ritualistic means for dealing with hardships and anxiety-provoking events.

NAVAHO CULTURE

When we proceed to review some of the salient features of the Navaho way of life, we find that it likewise provides a picture of a pattern of culture that is less suppressive of impulses and more definite in its values than that typical of the United States and Haitian samples. The Navaho whose Rorschachs we evaluated were part of a Navaho community of about 650 living south of Gallup, New Mexico. It is a community whose fundamental tenets have not been radically altered by the outside white culture. Originally, the Navaho were roving hunters who lived in a marauding fashion. But following their military defeat in 1864 by United States forces, they turned mainly to herding and farming. They now live in scattered houses (hogans) and have no formal villages. Thompson (315, p. 258) has described them as making "an exceedingly vigorous, relatively spontaneous adjustment to life, and one which, while generating fear and anxiety, also dispels them to a considerable extent by means of obvious, familiar activities of a practical or a ceremonial nature. . . . The individual habitually functions according to a simple personal code which gives him security for a minimum price in terms of personal responsibility and discipline, so to speak, and which allows him free range outside the limits of well-defined family and ceremonial obligations."

Kluckhohn and Leighton (175, p. 115) say of them that they are, "distinguished among American Indians by the alacrity, if not the ease, with which they have adjusted to the impact of white culture while still retaining many native traits and preserving the framework of their own cultural organization."

Their concept of life and of the proper way to conduct oneself seems clearly crystallized. They have well-spelled-out definitions of what a good life should consist. Kluckhohn (174) reports, for example, that he collected independently from more than fifty men and women of varying ages their listing of the five or six persons whom they considered to approximate best the model of a "good man." These lists proved to be amazingly similar in their designations. That is, there was wide agreement as to the identity of the "good" men in the community.

Many of the basic principles of Navaho life are symbolized in ceremonials to which the group gives an important segment of its time. Kluckhohn (173) has calculated that men in the community give one productive day out of four to ceremonial activity. He indicates that ceremonials are a "focal point" of the transactions of Navaho society.

The child-rearing and socialization patterns of this society have been reported upon in detail by Kluckhohn (176). His accounts specifically underscore the fact that there is permissive acceptance of many kinds of impulse release, particularly during the early developmental years. Some quotations from these accounts follow:

> Except when the mother is seriously ill, a relationship of almost constant physical proximity between mother and child begins after the child's first bath and is unbroken until the child can walk. Night and day, wherever the mother goes, whatever she is doing, the baby is either being held by her or is within sight of her eye and almost always within reach of her hand. As soon as she is physically able, the mother herself responds to every manifestation of want or discomfort on the part of her child. Her usual first response whenever the child cries is to place it to her breast. If this fails to produce quiet the baby will be cleaned and dried, cuddled, talked to or sung to. (p. 475)
>
> Almost all training in the first two or three years of life is delayed, gradual and gentle. The positive side of child training in this period is mainly a matter of constant encouragement in the acquisition of language and other skills. (p. 478)
>
> Not until he can talk and understand is pressure put on a child to learn Navaho conventions of excretion. If a child who can walk and talk (or at least respond to speech) starts to urinate inside the hut, he is told to go outside to do this, and an older child will gently lead him out. (p. 483)
>
> In short, the two evacuation activities of the child are uniquely free from parental interference for a long time. Whatever may be the sensations associated with evacuation or retention of urine and feces, the processes are subject for some time to the impulses of the child, unmixed with parental punishment. The conflict between the child and its parents because of the discipline of cleanliness, which is so critical in child development among us, is postponed for at least a year and usually, for all practical purposes, for two years. (p. 484)
>
> Except for these restrictions as to modesty, the Navaho take sexuality from the very beginning of life as natural and permitted. They do not interfere with the toddler's exploration of the genital region or with so-called "infantile masturbation." Not only is no attention paid when children manipulate their own genitals, but the mother herself may stroke the naked genitals of a nursing child with her hand. Children not only use their hands freely but also rub themselves against brooms and sticks and indulge in other forms of autoerotic experiment. This acceptance of erotic pleasure from infancy on may be the central explanation of the fact that impotence in men and frigidity in women appears to be excessively rare among adults. (p. 478)
>
> Older persons are almost always quite tolerant of displays of

aggression (even blows with sticks and other objects) and temper tantrums. When a toddler has something taken from him or fails to get what he wants, he will scream, arch his back, brace himself, hold his breath, and be quite inconsolable until his elders give in (which they do more often than not) or somehow distract him. (p. 479)

The passages, quoted above from Kluckhohn's description of the infancy and early childhood of the Navaho, suggest that during this period there is great freedom in oral activities, in excretory and eliminative functions, in autoerotic exploration, and in expression of anger. Whiting and Child (339) indicate on the basis of quantitative ratings of the socialization procedures of a United States sample and a Navaho sample that the Navaho are significantly "more indulgent" over a wide area of behaviors.

It should be indicated, however, that the Navaho child is exposed to one type of restriction which the average United States child does not encounter. When he is about four or five months old, the Navaho child is strapped into a cradle which is carried on his mother's back. He is not completely separated from this cradle until he is about one year of age. Especially during the first six months he spends a great deal of his time in it, bound in a very restrictive fashion. This results in great limitation in his motor behavior and in some aspects of his sensory experiences. But Kluckhohn suggests that although cradling is a frustrating experience in some ways, it also seems to have advantages in increasing the child's sense of security by stabilizing his relationship with his mother and removing him from contact with tempting but dangerous objects in the environment.

Weaning is usually late and gradual for the average Navaho child and most often occurs after the birth of a sibling. But this weaning period signals the beginning of a new phase in which more exacting reality demands are made "for responsible behavior and for conformance to custom." The weaned child is assigned duties. He is given simple chores, such as bringing in sticks of wood for the fire. He is expected to refrain from certain forms of mischief and is scolded or mildly switched for his transgressions. Strong pressures are applied to help him become a contributing member of the economy. One is struck with the fact that there is a certain similarity between the Navaho socialization pattern and the pattern observed among the Bhils: of free expression and easy gratification followed by definite and aggressive reality demands.

It has been stated by some that the average adult Navaho is an unusually anxious person who operates at a high level of tension. Kluckhohn (176) has pointed out, for example, how widespread is the fear of witchcraft in the Navaho community. He refers also to the prevalence of moodiness, melancholia, and worry. Such observations are difficult to reconcile with the fact that the Navaho group falls within the high Barrier bloc. One would not expect an unusually elevated level of personal disturbance to characterize a high Barrier group. We have no ready explanation for this apparent discrepancy. However, it should be pointed out that in reality there has been no objective or quantified demonstration that the Navaho as a group are unusually anxious. Furthermore, it would seem to be too easy to exaggerate the import of such a highly visible phenomenon as fear of witchcraft which is a Navaho way of symbolizing anxiety and to forget about our own multiple anxiety manifestations that are less visible because of their rationalized façades.

ZUNI CULTURE

The third group in the high Barrier bloc are the Zuni. The Rorschach protocols for this group were obtained from a community of about 3,000 Zuni who live south of Gallup, New Mexico, in the same area as the Navaho, who have been described above. In this region the Zuni are the oldest inhabitants. They live by a long-established system of irrigation farming which is supplemented by stock-raising and by craft work. They spend the winters in the stone houses of their large central pueblo and during the agricultural season move to farming villages. The social structure is founded on the matrilocal household.

Published reports (127, 25) indicate that the infancy and early childhood of the average Zuni child are marked by the same opportunities for gratification and expression as have been described as typical of the Navaho. In discussing this point, Goldfrank (127, p. 252) quotes Cushing (73) as describing a Zuni infant in the following terms:

> She was the small "head of the household." All matters, however important, had to be calculated with reference to her. If she slept, the household duties had to be performed on tiptoe, or suspended. If she woke and howled, the mother or aunt would have to hold her, while "Old Ten" procured something bright-colored and waved it frantically before her. If she spoke, the whole family must be silent as the tomb, or else fear the indignation of three women and one man.

Goldfrank also notes that "while this treatment may have been somewhat excessive because the baby was a girl, there can be little doubt, if the whole literature on the subject is considered, that in the Pueblos infancy is characterized by great indulgence. . . ." However, at the same time there are data which suggest that the Zuni culture does quickly place special restrictions on the expression of hostility and aggressiveness. From early childhood quarreling even in play is discouraged. We shall not go into further detail about the first several years of the Zuni child's socialization, because in its main outlines it approximates the conditions of gratification and freedom found in Navaho child-rearing practices.

Once the Zuni child has passed the first few years of relatively great freedom, he is exposed to sharply increased demands for conformance to his culturally defined role. Goldfrank considers the Zuni to typify a group "where infant disciplines are weak and later disciplines are severe." A highly elaborate series of rituals, initiations, and threatening social sanctions are used to mold the developing child to almost universally accepted definitions of what is proper. One of the most typical things about Zuni culture is the exactness of its standards and the precision of its interlocking parts. There are customs, categories, and procedures for dealing in a highly specific fashion with most of the crises and problems that may confront a human being. Benedict gives us the flavor of the careful definition and formalization characteristic of the Zuni (25, p. 54):

> Their interest is centered upon their rich and complex ceremonial life. Their cults of the masked gods, of healing, of the sun, of the sacred fetishes, of war, of the dead, are formal and established bodies of ritual with priestly officials and calendric observances. No field of activity competes with ritual for foremost place in their attention. Probably most grown men among the western Pueblos give to it the greater part of their waking life. It requires the memorizing of an amount of word-perfect ritual that our less trained minds find staggering, and the performance of neatly dovetailed ceremonies that are chartered by the calendar and complexly interlock all the different cults and the governing body in endless formal procedure.

Benedict focuses on the fact that they live a middle way, rarely going to the extreme of severe denial of impulse expression or to the extreme of uncontrolled release of impulses. Their aim is to be moderate. Violence and orgiastic release are very rare. The moderate and well-defined attitude taken toward self-gratification in Zuni society is illustrated by their orientation toward sexuality, as described by Benedict (p. 115):

> The attitude toward sex in Zuni parallels certain standards we know in our civilization as Puritanical, but the contrasts are quite as striking as the parallels. The Puritan attitude toward sex flows from its identification as sin, and the Zuni have no sense of sin. Sin is unfamiliar to them, not only in sex, but in any experience. They do not suffer from guilt complexes, and they do not consider sex as a series of temptations to be resisted with painful efforts of the will. Chastity as a way of life is regarded with great disfavor and no one in their folktales is criticised more harshly than the girls who resist marriage in their youth. . . .

Pleasant relations between the sexes are merely one aspect of pleasant relations with human beings. . . . Sex is an incident in the happy life.

The cohesion and careful articulation of the Zuni culture is perhaps most apparent in the fact that even under the impact of modern United States life the Zuni have maintained their own style of life in a relatively unaltered fashion.

INTERPRETATIVE COMMENTS

The preceding survey of some of the behavior patterns of the groups in the high Barrier bloc indicates certain underlying similarities among them; but one would hardly suggest that they were uniformly alike. Indeed, they are very unlike each other in many ways. Obviously, for example, there is a marked difference between the values and goals of the Bhils who often rob travelers passing through their area and the Zunis who are opposed to predatory aggression. It would seem fair to say, however, that the three high Barrier groups are alike in that they all permit relatively greater impulse satisfaction during the first few years of life than does the modern Western mode of socialization. Furthermore, it would seem reasonable to say that the three high Barrier cultures provide the individual with more definite and less conflictual value models than does modern Western culture. As far as one can tell from the sort of data we have reviewed, the difference between the definite-boundary bloc and the indefinite-boundary bloc appears to be, at least partially, a function of the two contrasts in socialization conditions just cited. In any case, the results are suggestive enough to justify considerable more investigation along such lines.

One of the unexpected things that emerges from our analysis of the various cultures is an apparent difference between the definite-boundary bloc and the indefinite-boundary bloc in the ratio of demanding control imposed in early infancy versus that imposed in later stages of the socialization period. Thus, while the Bhils, Navaho, and Zuni permit relatively great gratification to the child during its early infancy, they tend to make quite exacting and reality-oriented demands upon the child following the easy gratification period. That is, once they begin independence training with the child, they begin to push him steadily and aggressively. They confront him with real life tasks and place clear-cut responsibilities upon him.

But it strikes us that modern Western culture proceeds in a manner which represents a reversal of this pattern. There the child in early infancy is subject to relatively stringent impulse control which limits gratification. But even though independence training is initiated early, it proceeds at a very slow uneven pace and the imposition of real life responsibilities tends to be delayed until adolescence. Whiting and Child (339, p. 94) voice a supportive viewpoint concerning this point on the basis of their analysis of socialization customs in a variety of cultures:

> Comparison between the United States and various primitive societies as to age of this training is not adequately given, however, by the beginning age alone. American customs are rather unusual in that independence training is completed at a very late age. Where many primitive societies expect their children to become very thoroughly independent in a short time, American parents require a high degree of continued dependence into adolescence and even early maturity.

It is possible, then, that we have a specific lead concerning the manner in which the sequence of socialization processes affect body-image boundary definiteness. The sequence which perhaps maximizes the chances of a culture producing definite-boundary individuals is one marked by an initial period of almost complete gratification that is in turn followed by a period in which training for adult responsibility proceeds forcefully and on the basis of immediate realistic issues. If this idea is correct, it is an oversimplification to relate the degree of boundary definiteness of an individual to any one limited dimension of his parents' behavior. It becomes necessary to deal with more complex levels of parental traits. One must think in terms of personality patterns that would lead the parent to provide high gratification of the child initially but then to impose well-defined standards and responsibilities in later developmental phases. Some parents might be able to permit early gratification, but be unable to be definite and realistic in later independence training. Other parents might be able to offer well-structured independence training beyond the earliest socialization period, but not have the flexibility to offer as high a level of spontaneous gratification initially.

One would conjecture that the parent most ideally suited to support the development of definite boundaries in his children would be one who had evolved a definite and clear value system oriented toward taking certain responsibilities and getting certain things done, but who, in the process of evolving such a system, had not had to sacrifice his own spontaneity and learn to fear free impulse release. It is probably true that parental definiteness is a prerequisite for the formation of firm boundaries in the child, but only if it is of a species of definiteness that does not have its roots in rigidity and a desire to keep things under excessively tight control.

One wonders about the general implications of the fact that the cultural groups representing modern Western tradition were those falling lowest on the boundary-definiteness scale. Does the fact that a culture becomes more complex and is therefore likely to be marked by a diversity of conflicting values and standards result inevitably in an average decrease of the definiteness of the body-image boundaries of its members? Does a society based on extreme division of labor set up de-individualizing conditions which minimize the development of definite body-image boundaries? In other words, we are raising the general question whether the things most characteristic of modern Western culture (e.g., size, complexity, division of labor, the use of machines that dwarf man) are not antithetical to firm boundary formation. Can most individuals in such a culture avoid the feeling that they are surrounded by forces so much greater than themselves that there is no real safety in the boundaries they can muster in their own behalf? We are, of course, speaking about the culture as a whole and in no way suggesting that there may not be important subcultures in which individual boundary definiteness is maximally fostered.*

CULTURAL DIFFERENCES IN BOUNDARY COMPOSITION

The fact that there seemed to be possible contrasts in the socialization practices of the high Barrier bloc versus the low Barrier bloc led us to wonder whether there might not be qualitative differences in the way that body-image boundaries were experienced in each bloc. We were inclined to guess that the individuals in the low Barrier cultures would have a more impersonal and artificial concept of their boundaries than

---

* In terms of our previous findings that the definite-boundary person tends to have a higher level of aspiration than the indefinite-boundary person, there is a paradoxical note about the fact that the U. S. samples should fall at the lower end of the cultural continuum of boundary definiteness. After all, U. S. culture would probably be thought of (in terms of current stereotypes) as showing more interest in go-getting achievement and task completion than would the Navaho or Zuni cultures. A few ideas about this apparent paradox come to mind. (1) It is apparent that the manner in which one measures achievement and goal attainment in different cultures varies considerably. For example, in the United States, achievement might be equated with the number of objects of a certain type that one had fashioned or the amount of money one had earned, but the measure of achievement among the Zuni might be based on the excellence one had attained in learning religious ceremonials. Relative to this frame of reference, the Zuni might on the average have higher achievement goals than the average U. S. individual. (2) It is conceivable that the advanced technology which the United States has evolved magnifies the immediate achievement of the culture as a whole, but that the energy output demanded of himself by the average U. S. individual is actually no greater or is perhaps even less than that demanded of himself by the average Zuni. Apropos of this point, it was shown in Chapter 5 that interest in things, physical science, and technology is more characteristic of low Barrier than high Barrier persons. Perhaps our culture has gained an exaggerated reputation for energy output because it contains an unusually high proportion of low Barrier persons whose focus of interest tends to lead to technological advantages that multiply productivity.

those in the high Barrier cultures. The mechanized and rather impersonally timed style of socialization in the low Barrier cultures seemed likely to encourage such an artificial concept. It would be as if the individual considered his best protection against the dangers of the world to be the powers associated with impersonal forces and objects rather than those associated with the strength of the living organism itself.

In seeking a way to study this possibility, the idea presented itself of analyzing for each culture the categories of content most contributing to the Barrier score. If one surveys the various kinds of Rorschach content which may be scored as Barrier, one notes that it embraces a wide diversity. It includes animals, costumes, containers, coverings, and so forth. A scheme was developed for categorizing this content into living things (e.g., animals) and nonliving things. It was necessary to limit the "living" category to animals because human percepts do not contribute to the Barrier score. A "nonliving" category was set up which was arbitrarily split into a subgrouping of responses referring to containerlike percepts (e.g., vase, basket, volcano, bay) and a second subgroup relating to clothes. It was anticipated that the low Barrier bloc would show a predominance of "nonliving" content and the high Barrier bloc a predominance of "living" content. Perhaps the point should be made here that all previous exploratory attempts to find analogous content differences among various United States groups that have been studied yielded essentially negative results.

There was tabulated for each group the total number of responses falling in the living and nonliving categories and these frequencies were converted to percentages. Table 11:3 establishes with clarity that there

TABLE 11:3 PERCENTAGE ANALYSIS OF SOME CONTENT CATEGORIES CONTRIBUTING TO THE BARRIER SCORE IN CULTURAL GROUPS

Group	Animal, %	Container, %	Clothes, %	Miscellaneous, %
Bhil (India)	61	21	18	0
Navaho	68	18	14	0
Zuni	54	23	18	5
Tuscarora	33	41	22	4
Hindu (India)	63	23	13	1
Haitian	24	52	24	0
U. S. Chicago sample	32	33	33	2
U. S. College sample (Washington)	31	36	33	0
U. S. College sample (Ohio)	34	34	32	0

are extremely large differences between the definite-boundary bloc and the indefinite-boundary bloc relative to the percentages of living versus nonliving content contributing to the Barrier score. Within the definite-boundary bloc one finds that living content constituted in the Bhil, Navaho, and Zuni groups 61 per cent, 68 per cent, and 54 per cent of their respective total Barrier scores. The living content percentages for the Haitian, United States Chicago sample, and two United States college samples were respectively 24, 32, 31, and 34. Thus, the definite-boundary bloc shows on the average twice as great a percentage of living Barrier content as does the indefinite-boundary bloc. When tests were made of the significance of the difference between the percentage of living content in each low Barrier group and the corresponding percentage in each high Barrier group, eight of the twelve tests were significant at least at the 5 per cent level and four fell in the .20–.10 range.

Therefore, one may say that our speculation about the low Barrier cultural groups experiencing their boundaries as relatively more artificial and impersonal than the high Barrier groups is supported by the findings. It might be argued that actually such cultures as the Navaho and Zuni produce so much living content because this category is derived entirely from animal percepts and they have a great deal of contact with animals in their daily life. This would imply that the occurrence of so many living percepts in their Barrier tabulations was not a function of the way they experienced their body-image boundaries, but rather a resultant of their fund of experience with animals. This position does not seem satisfactory to us, however, in view of the fact that impersonal containing things (e.g., pottery, irrigation ditches, stone walls and clothes) are just as commonly experienced aspects of daily living in these cultures as are animals. Theoretically, such groups as the Navaho and Zuni could for their Rorschach Barrier percepts draw upon multitudinous experiences with impersonal containing and covering objects. But they give a predominance of living percepts instead.

CONCLUDING NOTES

In general, our exploratory excursion into anthropological realms has been profitable. Some interesting trends have been uncovered which are sufficiently striking to justify further, more detailed, validating work along the same lines. Special mention should be made of the fact that viewing Barrier score variations from the perspective of diverse cultures added an increased range to our frame of reference about the relationship of boundary definiteness to socialization practices. It permitted us to formulate a new hypothesis which relates boundary definiteness not simply to specific classes of occurrences during socialization but also to their *sequence*. Despite the many obstacles one encounters in using test responses collected somewhat unsystematically in other cultures, it would appear that they can be meaningfully studied in a rough approximate fashion.

....

PART FOUR

Body-Image Boundaries and Body Reactivity

....

CHAPTER TWELVE

Relationship of Body-Image Boundaries to Site of Cancer*

THE RESEARCH to be reported in this chapter represents a somewhat radical extension of the psychosomatic work described in Chapters 2 and 3. It was established in these earlier chapters that high Barrier persons are likely to develop psychosomatic symptoms involving the exterior body layers (e.g., rheumatoid arthritis and neurodermatitis), whereas low Barrier persons are likely to develop symptoms in the body interior (e.g., stomach complaints and spastic colitis). The question we were led to consider was whether the site of development of cancer in the body might be similarly influenced by body-image factors. Might there be a significant relationship between degree of boundary definiteness and the occurrence of cancer in an exterior versus interior site? We were encouraged to think of psychological factors as playing a role in certain phases of the cancer development process by results described in a growing series of papers in this area. Since the content of these papers was a basic framework for the work we undertook relative to cancer phenomena, it is necessary to review some of the more important and significant of the findings.

Tarlau and Smalheiser (307) in a pioneering project found, by means of interview, Rorschach, and figure-drawing data, differences in some personality characteristics between women with cancer of the breast and women with cancer of the cervix. These researchers suggested that women with breast cancer were much less expressive of themselves sexually than women with cervix cancer. Bacon, Renneker, and Cutler (14), who studied women with breast cancer by means of interview techniques, have in a confirmatory manner pictured the breast-cancer patient as extremely repressed sexually. Furthermore, they indicated that women with breast cancer seem to be markedly inhibited about expressing aggression and tend to camouflage themselves with a façade of pleasantness.

---

* Large portions of this chapter appear in a previous paper by the writers: Relationship of Body Image to Site of Cancer, *Psychosomatic Medicine,* 18:304–305 (1956).

They were cautious about ascribing any causal significance to the relationships they found.

Reznikoff (241), who studied women with breast cancer by means of a questionnaire, the Thematic Apperception Test, and a sentence-completion test, found that they are different from control groups in several respects. He reports that they are more likely to have carried a heavy load of responsibility for the caring of younger siblings during childhood, that their marriages were less successful, and that they took more negative attitudes toward pregnancy and birth than did patients in control groups.

Stephenson and Grace (292) surveyed a group of women with cancer of the cervix by means of interview procedures. They found that women with cervical cancer are sexually less responsive and more poorly adjusted maritally than are women in a control cancer group. The control group consisted mainly of women with cancer of the stomach. These results certainly complicate the interpretation of the findings of Tarlau and Smalheiser who indicated that cervical-cancer patients are relatively less repressed sexually than women with breast cancer. Stephenson and Grace found further that Jewish women are significantly less likely to develop cervical cancer than are non-Jewish women.

Correlations of characterological data with cancer phenomena have been made by Trunnell (318), who finds clinically that patients with prostatic cancer tend to be "unusually tractable" and "eager to please." Cobb and Trunnell (65) have given a preliminary report concerning interview and projective test data obtained from patients with cancer of the thyroid. Their findings imply a greater tendency for those with cancer of the thyroid to turn hostility against themselves habitually than do patients in a control group with thyrotoxicosis.

A different type of contribution pertinent to this whole issue of the relationship of psychological factors to cancer has been made by Blumberg, West, and Ellis (39). They have explored, by means of interview and Minnesota Multiphasic test data, the question of host resistance to cancer. They have shown that there are significant personality-attitudinal differences between patients in whom cancer runs a rapid, progressive course despite treatment and those who respond to therapy with long remissions and long survival. The first group is described as "polite," "acquiescent," and unable to express aggression; whereas the second group is referred to as consisting of "more expressive and sometime bizarre personalities."

Theodore L. Clemens (123), who also investigated host resistance, has shown that there are differences in autonomic functioning between patients with fast-growing cancer and patients with slow-growing cancer. He states: "The fastest tumor activity group displayed a greater systolic blood pressure rise than the slowest group on six of seven time-samples following subcutaneous epinephrine injections. The fastest group also showed less systolic blood pressure decrease on all time-samples after subcutaneous Mecholyl injection than did the slowest group."

Meerlo (215) has taken a position based on clinical observation that emotionally catastrophic situations may trigger off cancer growth. He speculates that in some instances the site of cancer is determined by unconscious organ choice. In the same vein, Greene (131) has published clinical data to the effect that the factor which very frequently triggers off the appearance of lymphomas and leukemias in patients is an acute psychological stress. He cites the loss of support of an important life associate as a good example of this sort of stress. Le Shan (188) suggests that cancer is triggered off by the loss of important love objects.

MATERIAL AND METHODS

With this work as a background, it was decided to investigate the body-image fantasies of patients having cancer involving the exterior of the body and to compare them with the fantasies of patients with cancer affecting the internal organs. As a first exploratory step, the writers arranged with Dr. Beatrice Cobb of the psychology department of the M. D. Anderson Hospital and Tumor Clinic, in Houston, Texas, to remove all identifying data from the Rorschach records of a number of patients with exterior cancer and a number with interior cancer in order to determine whether we could correctly differentiate them on the basis of our body-image criteria. The kinds of Rorschach records available in her files dictated that the exterior group should consist of six patients with melanoma and that the interior group should consist of eleven patients with cancer of the cervix. In the process of sorting the Rorschach records of these patients, the writers knew only the number of exterior and interior cases present in the total group of seventeen records. On the basis of such a blind sorting, correct identification of all but two cases was made. This level of success is, of course, significantly better than chance. Thus the possibility was demonstrated of identifying exterior versus interior cancer sites on the basis of body-image data derived from a psychological frame of reference.

The next step in the study was to collect more cases in order to determine if the initial results obtained from the blind-sorting procedure would hold up in a formal comparison of these body-image scores in larger and more representative groups of exterior and interior cancer patients. The Rorschach records of a total of fifty-nine exterior cases and thirty interior cases were obtained. With but few exceptions, all these Rorschachs were secured from the M. D. Anderson Hospital and Tumor Clinic and were administered to patients by examiners° other than the writers. The exterior group consisted of one man with skin cancer, six women with melanomas, and fifty-two women with breast cancer. The interior group consisted of one woman and two men with cancer of the colon, two men with cancer of the lung, one man with cancer of the stomach, and twenty-four women with cancer of the cervix. The median age of the exterior group was fifty-two years and the median age of the interior group was fifty. Clearly, breast and cervix cases constituted the bulk of the experimental population. It should be made explicit that we considered the breast to be an organ located in the exterior body layers, and that we considered the cervix to occupy an interior body position. All patients in both groups had had either surgical or radiation treatment or both. But with few exceptions, the Rorschachs had not been administered until six months following treatment in order to allow any shock effects of the treatment to be dissipated.

RESULTS

Table 12:1 indicates that the exterior and interior groups were significantly differentiated by both the Barrier and Penetration of Boundary

TABLE 12:1   CHI-SQUARE ANALYSIS OF DIFFERENCES IN BODY-IMAGE
SCORES BETWEEN EXTERIOR CANCER PATIENTS AND INTERIOR CANCER
PATIENTS

Cancer	N	% Above Median Barrier Score[a]	% Above Median Penetration Score
Exterior	59	46	15
Interior	30	10	40
Chi-square		11.4	6.8
P		.001	.01

[a] As defined in the previous work with arthritics, the scores were categorized into 0–2 Barrier responses and 3 or more. The same cutting point was used for the Penetration of Boundary score.

scores. The exterior group exceeded the interior group in Barrier responses at the .001 level in terms of a chi-square test. Also, the interior group exceeded the exterior group in Penetration of Boundary responses† at the

---

° We are grateful to Dr. Beatrice Cobb, Dr. Jack Wheeler, and Dr. Alan Krasnoff for making these data available to us.

† Penetration of Boundary scores were included as part of the study because they have previously proved meaningful in dealing with body symptom phenomena.

.01 level in terms of a chi-square test. Here is further demonstration that the body-image concept has a meaningful relationship to the site of cancer. In order to rule out the possibility of differences in the total number of Rorschach responses given, a chi-square comparison was made of the distribution of the total number of Rorschach responses in each group. The distribution proved to be not statistically different.

Another step was taken to evaluate how well the Rorschach records of patients in the exterior group can be distinguished from Rorschachs of those with interior cancer. This involved a blind-sorting technique. The Rorschach records of five melanoma patients and of five randomly chosen cervix patients were presented without any identifying data to three clinical psychologists. These psychologists were told only that of the ten records five were exterior cancer cases and five interior cancer cases. Each psychologist was carefully instructed as to the Rorschach criteria used by the writers in distinguishing the exterior and interior body image; and then each was asked to sort the melanomas into one grouping and the cervix records into another grouping. One of the three psychologists completed the task without error. The other two each misplaced two of the ten cases. All in all, then, two different blind-sorting procedures and an objective body-image scoring technique indicated the existence of a meaningful link between site of cancer and the boundary dimension.

In the process of trying to interpret the results obtained, the question arises whether the differences in body-image indices between the two groups might simply be a reflection of the fact that each experienced pain and unusual sensations from different body areas. Is it possible that the patients in the exterior cancer group give high Barrier scores because they have had disturbing symptoms and traumatizing procedures involving their body exterior? Do the interior cancer patients give high Penetration of Boundary scores because they experience the pain of the interior cancer growth and because their bodies have been subjected to treatment procedures which literally are penetrating? In order to evaluate such possibilities, a study was made of a control group* consisting of twenty-eight patients (eleven women and seventeen men) who had had colostomies because of the presence of cancer. Their median age was fifty-nine years. The unique control function of this group grows out of the fact that Rorschach tests were not administered to its members until a period of roughly ten years had elapsed since performance of the colostomies. These were individuals who had had interior cancer, who had had very radical operations which involved the creation of an artificial body opening, and who had lived for ten years with the artificial opening and with the anxiety of a possible recurrence of cancer. If the impact

---

* Obtained from Dr. Morton Bard at the Memorial Center for Cancer and Allied Diseases in New York for whose cooperation we are indebted.

of the cancer symptom and its attendant sensations and anxieties determined the body-image scores, one would expect the individuals in this control group, who had lived with such sensations for ten years, to give significantly higher Penetration of Boundary scores than the patients in the interior group, who had on the average dealt with similar sensations for only about one year. When a chi-square test was made of the Penetration of Boundary score differences between the two groups, it was found that these differences did not even approach statistical significance. It is therefore quite unlikely that one can attribute the body-image differences between the exterior and interior groups to mere differential experiencing of the symptomatology itself. It should be noted that a chi-square comparison of the distributions of total number of Rorschach responses in the colostomy group and the interior group indicated that they were not statistically different.

DISCUSSION OF RESULTS

The findings support the general proposition that psychological factors do play a part in phases of the cancer process. They also support the specific proposition that the character of an individual's body-image boundaries may influence the body site at which he develops cancer. It would appear that the long-term psychological patterns associated with a given type of body-image boundary somehow create conditions which favor one body site over another as the focus for certain pathological events. They somehow sensitize or render susceptible certain general areas of the body to physical illness in time of stress and trauma. This relationship between boundary conditions and site of symptomatology has now been shown to hold true for an array of pathologies that includes rheumatoid arthritis, neurodermatitis, stomach difficulties, spastic colitis, and cancer. The inclusion of cancer in this array is not easy to accept because it is rarely conceptualized in any but physiological or biochemical terms. One is not accustomed to seeing psychological constructs introduced into consideration of cancer phenomena. To some degree this is a matter of *Zeitgeist;* for as Le Shan (189) points out, it was once quite fashionable in the latter part of the nineteenth century to take a psychological orientation toward the cancer problem. In any event, our position would be that whatever role one assigns to psychological factors relative to cancer phenomena, the underlying assumption is that such factors are represented at another level by biochemical and physiological variables.

CHAPTER THIRTEEN

....

An Approach to Physiological Reactivity in Terms of the Boundary Schema

THE FACT that boundary definiteness proved to be linked with body symptomatology raised the possibility that it might also be linked with more basic physiological variables. Symptomatology such as is manifested in rheumatoid arthritis or spastic colitis is after all a reflection of underlying physiological events. Thus the muscle and joint rigidity shown by the arthritic is actually the end result of a chain of complex physiological reactions. If it is assumed that one pattern of symptoms is typically the outcome of a given sequence of physiological events and that a second symptom pattern is the result of still another physiological sequence, it would follow that any variable which distinguished the two symptom patterns would at the same time be demonstrating a meaningful relationship to the underlying physiological events. The assumption that certain symptom patterns are a function of associated physiological reactivity patterns is supported by the work of Malmo and Shagass (257), Wolff (354), and others (165). They have demonstrated that special physiological regularities do typify body areas which are susceptible to certain classes of pathology. Therefore since the Barrier score significantly distinguished subjects relative to their susceptibility to body-exterior symptoms versus body-interior symptoms, it seemed logical to speculate that degree of boundary definiteness was somehow tied up with associated differential physiological response patterns which might be presumed to exist. The possibility that there might be a relationship between the Barrier dimension and modes of physiological response was an exciting one because there has been such limited success in finding psychological models that are meaningfully related to physiological models.

Indeed, before proceeding further it would be well to review° briefly some of the problems and complications which have marked attempts to

---

° Portions of the material that follows have been published in the *Psychological Review* 64:26–37 (1957) under the title, "An Approach to Physiological Reactivity in Terms of a Body-image Schema."

correlate psychological and physiological phenomena. On the operational side, it is now possible to measure a large number of physiological reactions in the body with considerable precision. One° may obtain an almost endless variety of indices of physiological reaction, such as blood pressure, heart rate, finger temperature, saliva output, GSR, and respiration rate. A problem that has confronted those (330, 331, 183, 261) who are interested in such indices is to find a schema which will permit a meaningful grouping or clustering of the indices. That is, if one obtains ten different measures of physiological reaction from each of a group of subjects, can one functionally equate certain of the measures and not simply treat them as if they were ten disparate variables? There has been a tendency in the past to lump together the separate measures and regard them grossly as an over-all index of emotionality (58, 240). This was based on the implicit assumption that emotional response is a diffuse unpatterned process, just a general stirring up of many physiological systems. It should be noted that this point of view was concerned mainly with what happens to the organism after it has been disturbed and its usual equilibrium has been upset. It has had relatively little to say about the pattern of physiological measures obtained from the undisturbed organism. It also has had little to say about the relationship of physiological measures to such psychological constructs as "personality" and "traits."

A more differentiated frame of reference which has been much used in analyzing physiological reactions has revolved about the difference between sympathetic and parasympathetic response. There are obvious anatomical and chemical reactivity differences within the autonomic system that lend themselves to the sympathetic versus parasympathetic distinction. In an oversimplified fashion one may conceptualize the sympathetic subsystem as functioning mainly with reference to threats to the individual, but the parasympathetic subsystem appears to function mainly to conserve and maintain supplies for the individual's needs and development. After Gaskell [cited in Little (200)] published his views regarding antagonistic innervation (sympathetic versus parasympathetic) of most internal organs, there developed an increasing interest in the use of the concept to explain a wide variety of phenomena. Attempts were made to classify various illnesses as being primarily due to sympathetic or parasympathetic dominance. That is, it was assumed that an ideal balance between the two should exist and that if one became dominant over the other this imbalance would lead to organ changes which would be pathological (200). Attempts were also made to apply this imbalance

---

° We wish to acknowledge special gratitude to Dr. Hebbel E. Hoff, Chairman, Department of Physiology, Baylor Medical College, for valuable criticisms and suggestions concerning some of the formulations in this chapter.

concept to persons without clinical symptoms. That is, it was assumed that one or the other subsystem might be somewhat dominant in normal individuals and cause them to develop certain personality tendencies (333). In addition, there were efforts to classify all known measures of physiological response as being indices primarily of sympathetic or parasympathetic activity. Generally there was little objective basis for most of the assumptions that were made regarding the relationship of the autonomic subsystems either to symptom patterns or to normal personality characteristics. There was even some vagueness about what kinds of physiological measures were specifically representative of one autonomic subsystem as contrasted to the other.

More recently, Wenger (334) and others (183, 58) have approached the problem of autonomic functioning with more quantitative and controlled methods than were previously used. Wenger indicates, on the basis of his analysis of the interrelations among many physiological variables in children and in adults, that an autonomic factor score can be extracted which expresses the degree of imbalance between sympathetic and parasympathetic functioning. He has found some evidence that the direction and degree of imbalance may be correlated with degree of personality disturbance and also with a number of normal personality variables. But the degree of relationship is low and variable. It is also noteworthy that he did not find it possible to differentiate patients with stomach ulcers from normal subjects on the basis of autonomic imbalance scores. This is an important point because there have been many attempts in the past (200, 195) to describe this and other psychosomatic syndromes in terms of sympathetic-parasympathetic imbalance. Wenger's inability to distinguish ulcer patients from normal subjects in terms of autonomic imbalance has been confirmed by Little (200). One of the most interesting aspects of Wenger's work is that he has not only shown the limitations of the sympathetic-parasympathetic concept but also has discovered other factors which are important in accounting for the variance found in an array of physiological measures. In his factor analysis of a wide range of physiological indices obtained from normal individuals under stress and nonstress conditions, Wenger isolated not only an autonomic factor but also other moderately well-defined factors. His results indicate that the problem of categorizing physiological reactivity is a very complicated one. Darrow (76, 77) and Cattell (58) have likewise found that arrays of physiological measures cannot meaningfully be accounted for in terms of one or two simple dimensions.

Malmo and Shagass (206, 207), Lacey (183, 184), Lewinsohn (195), and Wolff (354) have further complicated the problem of categorizing measures of physiological reactivity by their demonstration that subjects may display fairly consistent patterns of physiological reactivity which are uniquely individualistic. Their work has indicated that one individual may respond to a stress with maximal activation of a given physiological function, moderate activation of another function, and underactivation of still another function. A second individual, however, may show a hierarchy of activation quite the reverse in character. These patterns of response cannot be explained suitably in terms of gross concepts like "sympathetic" or "parasympathetic." Those who have noted these patterns have tried to associate them with personality constructs. It has been especially theorized that some of these patterns are correlated with the same constellations of forces that result in an individual's developing a psychosomatic symptom in one organ system rather than in another (207, 58), that is, that just as certain kinds of psychosomatic symptoms may be one of the products of a given style of personality defense, just so may an individual's pattern of physiological reactivity be significantly affected by his style of life. In both instances it is assumed that life experiences have fixated certain modes of body response, and that the psychosomatic symptom is simply a more extreme example of such fixation. Several investigators (354, 165, 240) have indeed demonstrated experimentally that there is a significant tendency for individuals to manifest their maximum physiological reactivity to a variety of stimuli in those body systems that also are the focus of psychosomatic symptomatology.

It is apparent from this brief review that the problem of relating psychological variables to physiological variables is still largely unsolved. There is need for new approaches and new frames of reference. The remainder of this chapter will be devoted to a new approach which was attempted in terms of boundary concepts. This approach is not intended to stand in opposition to other ways of conceptualizing physiological responses, but is offered for consideration as an additional dimension from which to view such response.

THE BOUNDARY FRAME OF REFERENCE AND DERIVED PREDICTIONS

The boundary approach to physiological reactivity was derived purely from the analogy suggested by the fact that definite body-image boundaries are linked with symptoms of the body exterior and indefinite boundaries with body-interior symptoms. As earlier indicated, it was assumed that this pattern of linkage really involved some kind of relationship between the boundary variable and underlying physiological events at the body sites manifesting symptoms. It seemed logical in terms of the work of Wolff (354) and Malmo and Shagass (207) to think of the "underlying physiological events" in terms of levels of activation and readiness to respond. The fact that a psychosomatic symptom appears at a given body site may be conceptualized as meaning that for some reason that site was in a high state of excitation or response readiness previous to the appearance of the stress which finally triggered it into a symptom reaction. With this conceptualization in mind, it was hypothesized that persons with definite body-image boundaries would manifest a reactivity pattern such that responses involving the outer body layers would be relatively high and those of the body interior low; whereas persons with indefinite boundaries would exhibit a pattern in which body-interior response is high and body-exterior response is low. The assumption is made that although a stream of excitation may be triggered by certain centers (e.g., the hypothalamus), there may be differential degrees of response to it in the body interior versus the body exterior.

A definition of what is meant by the terms *body exterior* and *body interior* is important at this point. *Body exterior* is here meant to include the skin, the striate musculature, and the vascular components of these two systems. *Body interior* is considered to include all the internal viscera. This definition of body exterior versus body interior is intended to have purely locational or geographic implications, and is not at all concerned with the embryonic origins of various body areas.

The idea that differences in physiological reactivity may be correlated not with conventionally defined organ systems or nervous-system division, but with local characteristics of different body areas derives support from an elaborate study carried out by Davis, Buchwald, and Frankmann (79). They investigated a whole gamut of physiological reactions in subjects under a variety of stimulus conditions and attempted to define the patterns that stood out. The patterns they found did not correspond to any of the usual modes of categorization in the literature. Indeed, they coined new terms to designate the observed patterns. In describing the concept they have evolved of what constitutes a pattern or system of physiological response to a stimulus, they say, ". . . it is evident that a system in this sense does not correspond with any organ system of the body nor yet with the gross structural divisions of the nervous system. The receptors, the neural structures, and the effectors involved are each activated by a prior element in the chain, and, except for the ultimate one, activate the next succeeding element. *Local characteristics** of the elements will determine the character of the action, transducing it from one sort of force to another." They say further, "one is tempted to compare the spreading to the propagation of waves in a homogenous medium—a better picture would be that of a branching network, which the nervous system actually is, with the possibility of transmission at any point being able to vary somewhat independently of that at another." The boundary schema proposes that the local variations in "transmission" may be mean-

---

* Italics ours.

ingfully considered in terms of a body-interior versus body-exterior differentiation.

The division of the body into an exterior response zone and an interior response zone makes sense not only in terms of the correlations of the Barrier score with site of body symptoms but also from the point of view of the difference in the way the individual might be considered to experience each zone. As pointed out in Chapter 3, the individual has rather contrasting psychological experiences with his body exterior as compared to his interior. His body exterior is that part of his body which serves as the contact point with the environment. It touches the outside world in contrast to the body interior which is protected by the body wall from direct outside contact. Furthermore, the individual can better visualize the exterior part of his body than the interior. He has a detailed image of his outer aspects, whereas the interior is something hazy or ill defined. But most important of all, the activities of the exterior body layers are much more subject to voluntary control than are those of the body interior. The individual can embellish or change the appearance of his skin; and he exerts controlling force over his striated musculature. His body interior, however, is influenced, by and large, by involuntary autonomic centers. Consequently it may be presumed that the body exterior comes to represent the realm of voluntary response and the body interior the realm of involuntary response.

In general, then, the body exterior would tend to be perceived by the individual as that area most specialized for dealing with the immediate environment. His body interior would represent an area removed from direct contact with the outer world and minimally involved in the immediate process of voluntary manipulation of that world. If one grants that such a contrast exists in the way individuals experience their exterior and interior body zones, it then becomes possible to offer a hypothesis concerning how the postulated relationship between boundary definiteness and the relative physiological responsiveness of each zone might arise.

The previous chapters have presented much data which indicate that the definite-boundary person is more motivated in the direction of voluntary control of the environment than is the indefinite-boundary person. The person with definite boundaries is relatively intensely concerned with achievement, independence, task completion, and aggressive self-expression. In a word, individuals with high Barrier scores place greater value on self-steering behavior than do individuals with low Barrier scores. Some evidence has been presented which indicates that this difference is a function of their having been reared by parents who differ in orientation toward achievement and getting things done. The parents (especially the mothers) of high Barrier persons seem to be more interested in achievement and attaining goals than are the parents of low Barrier persons. Thus, the high Barrier person grows up in an atmosphere in which there is unusual importance assigned to active volitional behavior. Since this is so, would it not follow that the high Barrier person would come to assign special importance to the voluntary or volitional zone of his body?

Support for this view is provided by the fact that high Barrier persons in reporting body sensations and feelings tend to emphasize those occurring in the striate musculature to a greater degree than do low Barrier persons. One might conceive of this special importance assigned to the striate musculature as carrying with it a set or pattern of preparatory activation. One might picture the voluntary zone of the high Barrier individual's body as being chronically in a relatively high state of preparatory activation and thus more likely than other body areas to be triggered into response by stimuli. Conversely, it may be conjectured that the low Barrier person grows up in an atmosphere in which self-steering is minimized and the surrender to persons and forces greater than oneself is encouraged. A set toward voluntary response is discouraged and so activation of the voluntary zone of the body is held to a minimum. Under these circumstances the body exterior is presumed to show relatively low reactivity.

We go further and suggest that such conditions result also in a high level of body-interior reactivity. As far as we can see, the assumption of this sort of reactivity reversal in the low Barrier individual carries with it a further assumption. This would be that the reactivity of the body interior will customarily tend to be relatively higher than that of the body exterior unless the individual's experiences have led him to assign a certain minimum degree of importance to the outer "volitional" sector of his body. One is postulating that excitation tends to flow predominantly into body-interior response until the exterior "volitional" body layers have been stimulated through certain socialization experiences to develop specific readiness to respond characteristics. Consequently conditions such as one might find in a low Barrier family that would not foster the importance of the "volitional" layers would permit the body-interior reaction dominance to persist.

Our first thought after formulating the boundary approach to physiological reactivity was that, if it was meaningful, it should permit one to make predictions about physiological phenomena that would have some support from past observations and research. Three categories of predictions were formulated which might be evaluated in the light of past work:

(1) It would be assumed that past observations would have uncovered reaction patterns which are linked with body exterior in distinction to

body interior. Further, one would anticipate that those who had intensively studied various sorts of body reactivity phenomena would have found the body-exterior versus body-interior differentiation to be a meaningful theoretical framework.

(2) When varied physiological measures are obtained from individuals who have psychosomatic symptoms involving the body interior, these measures should indicate high reactivity of body-interior sectors. One would also expect such individuals to show low reactivity of body-exterior areas. Conversely, those with body-exterior symptoms should manifest high reactivity of the body exterior. This second prediction is derived from the idea that those who have exterior body symptoms are indicating the unusual importance of the barrier quality of their body exterior and thus their relatively greater tendency to maximize reactions in this sector of the body rather than the body interior. But those with interior symptoms are assumed to assign less importance to the body exterior and more importance to the body interior.

(3) Those who manifest unusually high physiological reactivity in the exterior body layers should have a more active and aspiring attitude toward life than those who do not show high reactivity in the body exterior. This prediction is based on the finding (Chapter 3) that in a normal group those who emphasize the importance of the body exterior express a relatively high level of aspiration.

ANALYSIS OF PAST RELEVANT RESEARCH

In connection with the first hypothesis, we have searched the literature widely for conceptual models developed by others to explain their observations of physiological reaction patterns which would correspond to the body-exterior versus body-interior schema postulated by us. There are several such models worth noting.

Burton and Edholm (55) in their recent book, *Man in a Cold Environment,* report a diversity of data concerning the manner in which the body adjusts to sharp temperature changes and how it maintains long-term temperature homeostasis. In the process of schematizing the various observed temperature-regulating mechanisms, they arrived at a formulation analogous to the exterior versus interior concept:

> The temperature of the deep tissues, the brain, the heart and
> abdominal viscera such as the liver is not exactly the same. . . .
> These are close enough to uniformity and constancy to justify the
> simplifying concept of a central deep "core" of the body of uniform,
> regulated temperature, surrounded by a "shell" or cooler peripheral
> tissues, whose temperature moreover is dependent on that of the
> environment as well as on physiological factors. Indeed, the home-

othermy of the "core" is accomplished, in great measure, by the adjustment of the temperature in the "shell."

That is, Burton and Edholm have perceived in the very complicated physiological processes involved in the body's adjustment to the changing temperatures of the surrounding environment a specialization in function that correlates with body exterior versus body interior.

Kleitman (171) has described a model having to do with levels of consciousness which is pertinent to the exterior-interior distinction. He has developed an "evolutionary theory of consciousness" based on a differentiation between the effects on consciousness of stimuli originating in the viscera and stimuli coming from more exterior sources, especially the proprioceptive end organs. He points out that in the newborn infant wakefulness (consciousness) occurs briefly every four or five hours and is related to afferent impulses from the viscera. Similarly he says of decorticate dogs, that they "almost invariably moved about for a few minutes after being fed, apparently because of afferent impulses from the colon resulting from the gastrocolic reflex. They would then defecate and immediately go to sleep" (p. 81). This kind of consciousness is described as "wakefulness of necessity." It is a function primarily of afferent impulses from the internal viscera. Kleitman indicates that with the myelinization of the afferent system in the child, the reactivity of the cortex to sensory stimuli increases. It becomes more capable of reacting to stimuli from without, particularly to impulses originating in the proprioceptive end organs. The development of the muscular system becomes a salient source of proprioceptive excitation which, in combination with other sensory impulses, leads to a higher level of consciousness.

Kleitman designates this higher level of consciousness as "wakefulness of choice." For our purposes, what is most interesting about this sharper form of consciousness is that it is strongly linked with the increasing potency of impulses originating in an important part of the outer body layers (e.g., the muscle-proprioceptive system). In summary of Kleitman's views, one may say that he associates a first lower level of consciousness with the individual's inability to react to little more than to impulses originating in the viscera of the body interior. He regards later and higher forms of consciousness as a function of increasing reactivity to sensory stimuli from without, particularly those involved in proprioception.

Lorr, Rubenstein, and Jenkins (201) factor analyzed ratings made by psychotherapists of 184 patients they were treating. These ratings concerned a wide range of behavior, including body complaints. The ratings of the body complaints clustered into three different factors. One factor was labeled a "factor of endodermal dysfunction" and involved complaints relating mainly to the upper and lower portions of the endodermal tube (e.g., gastrointestinal symptoms). A second factor involved complaints of "mesodermal origin." It included mainly symptoms which were "anergic, respiratory, and cardiovascular." The third factor was of a "cerebrotonic" order and particularly included skin complaints. This pattern of clusters which emerged is obviously one which conceptualizes body complaints and body symptoms as occurring in layerlike fashion, with inner layers roughly distinguished from outer layers. It too shows certain analogies to the body-interior versus body-exterior model.

Some of the more recent advances in our knowledge of the secretions produced by the adrenal medulla also lend support to the interior versus exterior concept of body response. Gellhorn (122) indicates that it is now well established that the adrenal medulla secretes not only adrenaline but also noradrenaline. Funkenstein (117A) reviews data indicating support for the idea that there are specifically differentiated adrenaline-secreting and noradrenaline-secreting cells in the adrenal medulla. He refers also to a specific innervation of these cells and to a differentiated hypothalamic representation for the corresponding secretory nerves. Adrenaline and noradrenaline produce different effects physiologically. Noradrenaline tends to cause moderate increase in systolic blood pressure, more marked increase in diastolic blood pressure, and a *decrease* in cardiac activity. Adrenaline acts more forcefully in increasing cardiac output, whereas noradrenaline produces some of its most marked effects in terms of increased peripheral resistance. Apropos of this point, Goldenberg, as cited in (117A), found that intravenous noradrenaline led to increased blood pressure mainly as the result of increased peripheral resistance, whereas, intravenous adrenaline stimulated a rise in blood pressure chiefly by means of an increased cardiac output. The accumulating data concerning adrenaline and noradrenaline suggest that their differential physiological effects fall into a pattern congruent with a body-exterior versus body-interior differentiation.

More recently Funkenstein, King, and Drolette (117A) have demonstrated that a predominance of either the adrenaline or noradrenaline response in a stressful situation is correlated with certain patterns of behavioral response. They studied sixty-nine students exposed to a stressful frustrating situation and classified their reactions into three primary categories. The first category was "anger out" and directed toward the experimenter who was producing the frustration. The second category was "anger in" and involved self-attack and self-criticism. The third category was "anxiety" and involved feelings of apprehension and fright. Significantly it was demonstrated that the anger-out group tended to show noradrenaline patterns of reaction. The anger-in and anxiety groups showed adrenaline patterns of response. Such data indicate that not only do adrenaline and noradrenaline produce physiological effects with a differential area of body response, but also that this differentiation is meaningfully linked with a difference in overt emotional behavior that is psychologically meaningful.

Anticipating a later point in this chapter, it should be pointed out that the linkage of anger-out with the noradrenaline response and the linkage of anger-in and anxiety with an adrenaline response is just what one would anticipate from the body-image schema that has been proposed. That is, we have shown in our previous work that individuals who emphasize the body exterior, as contrasted with those who emphasize the body interior, have a higher level of aspiration and a more active forceful approach to situations. It is therefore noteworthy that the subjects in the study carried out by Funkenstein and King who show a noradrenaline pattern of response (i.e., emphasis on peripheral reaction) are those who deal with the frustration directly by expressing their anger outwardly. However, the subjects manifesting the adrenaline pattern (where the response is relatively more interior) show less ability to deal with their feelings of frustration actively and tend to express them more in self-criticism and generalized anxiety.

Kubie (182) has been very explicit in differentiating the organs of the body into those which he calls "organs which implement our relationships to the external environment" and those he labels "organs of internal economy." The organs in the first group are "innervated predominantly by the somatomuscular and somatosensory apparatus." They represent that part of the individual which is most consciously directed. The second grouping of organs, however, "lies deep within the interior of the body and consequently are hidden from the individual's capacity for direct knowledge of himself. Furthermore, even though some of these organs have indirect connections with the outside world, our subjective awareness of them is absent or limited." Kubie associates disorders usually referred to as *conversion hysterias* with the external organ system, and he associates disorders called *organ neuroses* with the internal organ system.

Wenger (344) in the course of a factor analysis of a variety of physiological measures obtained from adults found a factor which he designates as "representing certain functions of the skin and peripheral blood vessels." Similarly, Sanford (261) studied a group of children and adolescents with a battery of physiological and personality measures. His analysis of the intercorrelations among the physiological measures revealed "a syndrome—consisting of flushing, sweating, skin stroking intensity, odor, acne, and palpable thyroid." That is, there was a clustering of variables having mainly to do with skin appearance and skin responsivity.

The second deduction that was made from the body-image schema involved the relationship of site of psychosomatic symptom to pattern of physiological reactivity. This deduction finds some confirmation in past work. It should be specified that, in order to keep the distinction between body exterior and body interior as clear as possible, measures of exterior body functioning will be restricted to GSR, muscle-action potential, and direct methods for evaluating vasoconstriction and vasodilation of the peripheral blood vessels. Measures of interior body functioning will be restricted mainly to heart performance and measures of changes in the stomach and colon.

Since intestinal disturbances and stomach ulcers are interior symptoms, one would predict in terms of the exterior versus interior body-image schema that subjects with such symptoms would show heightened reactivity relative to body-interior measures. Karush, Hiatt, and Daniels (165) investigated a variety of physiological responses manifested by six ulcerative colitis patients during psychotherapy interviews. They obtained measures of colon reaction, salivary flow, and peripheral vascular changes. There was clear indication that specific stressful material elicited in the course of the therapy produced correlated colonic responses in the colitis patient. But the salivary responses and the vascular bed responses (exterior) did not show meaningful correlations with the stressful therapy material. These patients with an interior symptom showed their most specific physiological responses to stress in terms of an interior reaction.

Lewinsohn (195) obtained a series of physiological measures from patients with duodenal ulcers, patients with essential hypertension, psychiatric patients in whom muscular tension was the outstanding clinical symptom, and a control group of patients with hernia, hemorrhoids, and similar difficulties. One of his clearest findings, which he could not explain, was that the absolute skin resistance of the ulcer group was significantly greater than that of the control group. This relative inactivity of the skin layer (sweat glands) in the ulcer patient corresponds to the minimizing of the body exterior which one would predict in terms of the body-image schema. It is perhaps confusing that high skin resistance is equated with inactivity of the skin layer. However, this formulation is based on the assumption that lowered resistance is directly or indirectly a function of the degree of activity of the sweat glands. Lowered skin resistance represents active response of anatomical "units" in the skin layer.

Van der Valk and Groen (320) have also found the skin resistance of patients with peptic ulcer to be high. Another of Lewinsohn's (195) most clear-cut findings was that patients with muscle-tension symptoms show more finger tremor under stress conditions than the control group and also that they are characterized by a significantly lower heart rate than any of the other groups. These individuals whose clinical symptom is most obviously focused in the outer layers of the body (musculature) show a high level of reactivity in the musculature (exterior) and a low level of activity in terms of an interior measure.

Little (200) in a study of peptic ulcer patients found that they were higher in dermographia persistence than a control group. That is, their peripheral vessels manifested less tone (and so may be assumed to have been less active) than did those of the control subjects. It should be acknowledged that, on the contrary, Wenger (334) found that a group of asthmatics (interior symptom) had significantly lower dermographia persistence (i.e., higher vessel tone) than normal subjects. Little (200) also demonstrated that ulcer patients had a significantly shorter heart period than a control group. That is, as would be predicted, they showed a relatively higher rate of response with an interior organ. Another interesting finding is reported by Little which points up the potential explanatory value of the exterior versus interior concept. He evaluated the effects of vagotomy on the physiological reactivity of a group of ulcer patients and compared the shifts occurring from the preoperative to the postoperative period with those changes in physiological reactivity occuring in a control group of other surgical patients from the preoperative to postoperative period. He compared the two groups in this fashion:

> Both the control and experimental groups showed a drop in arterial pressure after operation, yet the mechanisms that produced this drop seem to be different in the two groups. In the controls, peripheral vasodilation as indicated by increased Finger Temperature and decreased Dermographia Latency was the most relevant factor since the heart rate remained approximately constant. In the experimental group, however, there was an increased peripheral resistance, yet the blood pressure dropped in spite of it. In this group, the lowered heart rate is apparently the determining element. . . .

That is, following the cessation of the severe stress associated with the operation, both groups expressed their readjustment to the diminished stress by a drop in blood pressure. In the ulcer group, however, the readjustment took place in terms of an interior organ, whereas in the control group the readjustment was more peripheral in character. This trend in the ulcer group was nicely congruent with the interior emphasis that had been postulated from the body-image schema.

Graham (354) evaluated the specificity of skin reaction of a group of patients with psychosomatic skin disorders (exterior symptom). He compared their skin reactions to those manifested by a control group in which skin disorders were absent. He noted that twenty-three or twenty-four of the patients with skin difficulties responded with some whealing to histamine or to pilocarpine. A physiological saline applied in the same way gave rise to whealing in only one patient. In the twenty-five controls, there was a response to histamine in only six and a response to pilocarpine in three instances. Thus the individuals with the skin difficulties (exterior) showed a relatively greater body-exterior response than a normal group to a specific physiological stress.

The third basic deduction derived from the body-image schema focused on the idea that those who show unusually high physiological reactivity in the outer body layers tend to be relatively high in level of aspiration, forcefulness, and drive to attain goals.

Seymour (279) reports findings which are definitely in this direction. He indicates that children who show high GSR responsiveness (exterior) are significantly more interested in achievement and are more forceful in their behavior than children who are low in reactivity. He further describes a study which demonstrated that adolescent boys who are perceived by their classmates as listless give relatively low GSR responses to certain kinds of stimuli. In another phase of his data he found that adolescent girls who are more daring and active in games gave a larger GSR response than the opposite kind of girl.

Cattell (58) describes a factor which is characterized by high responsivity in terms of one of our designated exterior measures (viz., GSR) and points out that this factor is psychologically associated with alertness, activity, and excitement. Low responsivity in this factor is correlated with sleepiness and passivity. Brown, as cited by Cattell (58), reports appreciable correlations of PGR with desire to excel. Cattell also describes a factor, which he labeled "Nervous Disposition," which involves low PGR resistance and large PGR deflection, and which at the behavioral level is linked with "alertness, hyperactivity." In the previously referred to study of Sanford's (261), in which a cluster of measures prominently involving skin responsivity was discovered, it was also found that this cluster correlated positively with conscientious work and negatively with passive timidity.

In a somewhat different approach to the physiological responsivity problem, Wischner (346, 347) has recently found that a physiological response cluster based on two exterior type measures, GSR and muscle-action potential, is associated with alertness. Such data tend to affirm the idea that high physiological reactivity of the body exterior is correlated with alertness, striving, and active expressiveness.

The results of the analysis of the past literature seemed to offer considerable support for the body-exterior versus body-interior approach to physiological reactivity. They were sufficiently encouraging to stimulate a number of specific experimental studies of various physiological phenomena. The remainder of this chapter will be concerned with descriptions and interpretations of these studies.

SKIN SENSITIVITY

One of the first opportunities for evaluating some of the deductions concerning reactivity that were derived from the body-image schema presented itself in a body of data collected by Haber° (137). In the course of a project concerned with differences in gradients of tactile sensitivity in stumps of limbs that had suffered amputation and in normal intact limbs, Haber obtained various measures of tactile sensitivity from twenty-four male World War II veterans with unilateral above-elbow amputations. The sensitivity measures were based on threshold for light touch (modified von Frey hairs), two-point discrimination, and point localization. An individual Rorschach had also been administered to the subjects, and so it was possible to compute Barrier scores for each.

It was anticipated that there should be a positive correlation between degree of tactile sensitivity and degree of body-image boundary definiteness. This would be in line with the hypothesis that the more definite the boundaries the greater should be the responsiveness of the outer body layers. Rho correlations were determined for the relationship of the Barrier score to each of the three sensitivity measures for the intact limb and for the stump. The point localization and two-point discrimination threshold values from the intact limb correlated at a purely chance level with the Barrier score. However, a correlation of +.41 was found between Barrier scores and light-touch threshold values from the intact limb. This correlation, which is significant at the .05–.01 level, indicates that the more definite were the body-image boundaries, the greater was the sensitivity to light touch. Light-touch thresholds obtained from the stump correlated +.22 (not significant) with the Barrier score; but the correlations involving the other two sensitivity measures were of a chance order.

The results indicate in general what looks like a promising positive and consistent relationship between boundary definiteness and sensitivity to light touch. There is no sign of a relationship with two-point discrimination, however, or point localization in this respect. It is possible that these two measures do not correlate with the Barrier score because they are considerably a function of localization and spatial orientation factors and only minimally influenced by skin sensitivity itself. While the light-touch measure gives results which are supportive of the boundary frame of reference, they cannot be regarded as being much more than suggestive.

Parenthetically, a study carried out by Kepecs and Robin (170) is worth mentioning, in which it was analogously shown in an exploratory fashion that certain aspects of sensitivity may be linked with psychological factors. These two investigators observed the responses of five patients with

---

° We are indebted to Dr. William B. Haber for making these data available to us.

various dermatoses to the stroking of their skin with cotton wool over a two-minute period. They had previously found in a pilot study that reactions to stroking fell into five categories: (1) normal adaptation, with the initial tickle or itch sensation being replaced by touch; (2) failure to adapt, with tickle or itch persisting; (3) touch throughout; (4) irregular adaptation with fluctuation between tickle and itch; (5) partial adaptation, with a decline in itch or tickle. The reactions of the five patients in this respect were compared to what was known about their personality structures and attitudes. It appeared that those who tended to behave in an all-or-nothing fashion with people (e.g., by being overdefensive or excessively emotional) also gave all-or-nothing skin responses, either all touch or all itch-tickle. Patients who were better integrated psychologically and less extreme in their behavior manifested more skin responses of normal adaptation. There seemed to be a trend for patients who were most constricted and most self-punitive to respond with itch rather than tickle. This study has been cited because, although it is based on methods and procedures quite different from ours, it has paralleled our finding in so far as it indicates that skin reactivity may be meaningfully linked to psychological variables.

HEART RATE UNDER STRESS

A second exploratory attempt to evaluate the meaningfulness of the boundary approach to physiological reactivity was based on an analysis of heart rate under stress. It would be predicted in terms of boundary concepts that persons with definite boundaries would show relatively less heart response (interior) to stress than would persons with indefinite boundaries. It was possible to test this prediction by examining some data collected by Herring* (149A) as part of a study of the relationship of an individual's personality characteristics to his physiological response while under the influence of anesthesia in the course of major surgery. The subjects were twenty-five male veterans with a mean age of thirty-one years. Each had been routinely admitted to a Veterans Administration hospital for surgery either for herniorrhaphy, hydrocelectomy, or varicotomy. Herring describes the operative setting in which the heart measures were obtained as follows (pp. 246–247):

> At 6:45 A.M. on the day of surgery the patient was given premedication consisting of 100 mg. of Demerol and 1/50 grain atropine. Research patients were always first on the surgical schedule and were taken to the surgical suite at 7:30 A.M. An anesthesiologist who had not previously seen the patient then administered the gen-

---

* We are grateful to Dr. Fred H. Herring for making it possible for us to analyze his data.

eral anesthesia. This consisted of the following for the first ten patients: Intravenous Pentothal (Abbott) drip to induce sleep, 1½ cm. Anectine chloride (Burroughs Wellcome) to aid in intubation, cyclopropane to induce anesthesia, and ether to maintain. The latter was in a CO_2 absorption system with rebreathing bag. Because of changes in operating procedures, anesthesia for the last fifteen patients was induced similarly except that nitrous oxide, oxygen, and ether ("GOE") constituted the agent in place of cyclopropane. . . . Surgery was started when the patient reached the second or third planes of third-stage anesthesia. Any surgical action from that time on which might have influenced patient response was recorded, along with the five-minute physiological readings. The surgical notes were obtained in order that manipulation of the patient's body might be evaluated in any changes of response. The continuous cardioscope was in operation during the patient's entire presence in the operating room, but written records of the heart activity were made only during the stressful periods of anesthesia (intubation and extubation) or upon noting abnormalities of cardiac response.

There was administered to each subject prior to surgery a battery of psychological tests which included the individual Rorschach. Therefore the Barrier score of each could be established. It should be added that it was necessary to reduce all records to twenty responses (two per card) in order to equate the response totals of the high and low Barrier subjects.

There were two appropriate heart-rate measures available against which to compare the Barrier score. One was maximum heart rate during the stress of surgery and the other was minimum heart rate. The boundary hypothesis would require that high Barrier scores be associated with low maximum and also low minimum rates and that low Barrier scores be associated with high maximum and high minimum rates. That is, definiteness of boundaries should be accompanied by relatively little heart responsivity and the converse should be true of individuals with indefinite boundaries. A rho correlation between Barrier score and heart rate maximum was of a chance order. However, the correlation between Barrier score (high Barrier = rank 1) and heart rate minimum (low minimum score = rank 1) was +.41 which is significant at the .05–.01 level. That is, subjects with the highest Barrier scores manifested the lowest minimum heart rate during surgery. Here again is a result which tends to corroborate the body-exterior versus body-interior approach to physiological reactivity.

There was one interesting finding worth reporting which incidentally emerged in the course of inspecting the relationship of the Barrier score to several other physiological measures that had been secured by Herring. A rho correlation of +.53 was obtained between Barrier score (rank 1 = high score) and basal metabolic rate (rank 1 = high metabolic rate). This correlation which is significant beyond the .01 level indicates that the more definite the boundaries, the higher the metabolic rate. At this point one cannot easily explain the correlation. It might be speculated that the relatively high-goal setting and goal-completion needs of the definite-boundary individual somehow result in a relatively high state of physiological mobilization that is reflected in the basal metabolism rate.

GENERAL REACTIVITY UNDER STRESS

PROCEDURES AND METHODS

A further opportunity to explore the predictions concerning physiological reactivity which were derived from the body-image schema was provided by data that Funkenstein, King,[*] and Drolette (117A) had collected. In the course of a study concerned with differences in physiological patterns associated with individual tendencies toward expression of anger outwardly versus inwardly, they obtained a number of physiological measures from subjects exposed to frustrating stress. Fortunately for us, the measures they secured were of sufficient variety to permit an evaluation of the body-interior versus body-exterior response tendencies in which we were specifically interested. Furthermore, they had administered the Rorschach to each subject and so Barrier scores could be determined from the protocols. Records over twenty-five responses were lowered to twenty-five by the usual reduction procedure.

The actual conditions under which Funkenstein, King, and Drolette collected the data can best be conveyed by quoting from their description of their experimental procedure (pp. 405–406):

> The subject was brought into the experimental room, familiar from previous nonfrustrating visits, and was asked to lie on a wooden table. He was allowed to rest for at least 20 minutes so that his blood pressure might reach a stable level. The experimenter then obtained two blood pressure and two ballistocardiograph readings at one-minute intervals.

Following these readings the experimenter presented a series of tasks to each subject involving rote memory for digits and also the solution of various arithmetic problems. The tasks were graded so as to permit initial success to be followed by increasing failure. It was the intent to create an extremely frustrating situation for the subject; and this was reinforced by the manner of the experimenter who was very overtly critical and disparaging of each new failure. At the end of the problem series, when

---

[*] We are grateful to Dr. Stanley H. King for making these data available to us.

the subject was usually at the height of his sense of frustration, the experimenter secured blood pressure and ballistocardiograph recordings.

The physiological measures which were derived by Funkenstein, King, and Drolette are described by them as follows (pp. 407–408):

> The systolic and diastolic blood pressures were taken by the cuff and auscultatory method, the ballistocardiographic readings with a Sanborn ballistocardiograph, a high frequency electromagnetic apparatus. Two readings were taken during basal conditions, as stated previously, and the third reading used was taken at the point during the stress-inducing situation which was noted. . . . The following six measures were used:
>
> By the Cuff and Auscultatory Method
> 1. Systolic blood pressure
> 2. Diastolic blood pressure
> By Ballistocardiograph
> 3. Pulse rate
> 4. Average height of the IJ wave in mm., using 8 IJ waves, provided the pulse was under 80, and using 6 seconds of time if the pulse was in excess of 80.
> 5. IJ × p—The average height of the IJ wave multiplied by the pulse rate per minute, as determined over the time span of the IJ waves utilized.
> 6. $\dfrac{\text{Mean pressure}}{\text{IJ} \times \text{p}}$—The mean blood pressure, divided by the
>
> height of the IJ wave in mm., multiplied by pulse. The height of the IJ wave was not divided by the time of the IJ wave because it was found that the time was so consistently the same in different individuals that it made no difference in the final calculations. *No interpretation as to the meaning of these ballistocardiographic measures was made. They were used entirely on an empirical basis as simple physiological variables.* Starr and Nickerson have related height of the IJ wave to the stroke volume of the heart and IJ × p to the cardiac output. From data so derived, they have then used Aperia's formula to calculate the over-all peripheral resistance.
>
> For each subject the mean of the two basal readings for each variable was obtained and the percentage change between this value and the physiological measurement obtained during the stress was calculated. All references to these cardiovascular measurements or calculations in this study will, therefore, concern only the percentage changes.

The subjects participating in the study were Harvard University students ranging in age from nineteen to twenty-four years. They were paid a fee for their participation. The results of the original study were based on sixty-nine subjects. For the purposes of the present analysis it was possible to obtain data concerning only fifty-four of these subjects. The data from the other fifteen subjects were not available because of loss of records and their exclusion was not due to any selective factor.

RESULTS AND CONCLUSIONS

Of the six measures available from the Funkenstein, King, and Drolette study, we were interested primarily in four, viz., pulse, IJ, IJ × p, and P/(IJ × p). Although we agreed with the view that the significance of these measures was far from clear, it did seem reasonable to assume that pulse, IJ, and IJ × p were mainly indices of heart behavior and that P/(IJ × p) was a rough index of peripheral resistance (degree of vasoconstriction of peripheral blood vessels). With such assumptions in mind, it was hypothesized that high Barrier persons should score low on pulse, IJ, and IJ × p (all are heart or interior measures) and high on P/(IJ × p), a measure of response in the exterior body layers. Low Barrier persons should show the converse reactivity pattern. No predictions were made regarding systolic or diastolic blood pressure because the "inner" versus "outer" sources of their variance did not seem clearly discernible. But their relationships to the Barrier score were examined for exploratory purposes.

TABLE 13:1   CHI-SQUARE ANALYSIS OF DIFFERENCES IN PHYSIOLOGICAL REACTIVITY BETWEEN HIGH AND LOW BARRIER SUBJECTS

Physiological Measure	Group Showing Greatest Reactivity	Level of Significance[b]	
		Two-tailed Test	One-tailed Test
Interior			
Pulse	L.B.[a]	.05–.01	.01
IJ	L.B.	.20–.10	.10–.05
IJ × p	L.B.	.20	.10
Exterior			
$\dfrac{P}{IJ \times p}$	H.B.	.20–.10	.10–.05
Miscellaneous			
Systolic	N.D.	—	—
Diastolic	N.D.	—	—

[a] H.B.—High Barrier subjects. L.B.—Low Barrier subjects. N.D.—No essential difference.

[b] The highly specific nature of the hypotheses being investigated seemed to justify consideration of a one-tailed test also.

Table 13:1 indicates that in terms of a chi-square analysis all the results relevant to the inner versus outer distinction were in the direction anticipated. Pulse rate, IJ (stroke volume), and IJ × p (cardiac output) were all higher in the low Barrier group than in the high Barrier group. The difference for pulse fell at the .01 level (one-tailed test) and for IJ × p at the .10 level. The difference for IJ fell at the .10–.05 significance level. Total peripheral resistance P/(IJ × p) which has been equated with body-exterior response was higher (.10–.05) in the high Barrier group than in the low Barrier group. There were no differences between the high and low Barrier subjects with respect to systolic or diastolic blood pressure.

This was the first collection of data in which we found it possible to show that high and low Barrier individuals differed not only relative to a physiological measure at one particular body level (viz., exterior and interior), but that they simultaneously went in opposing directions relative to measures from both body levels. It is true that the results were not highly significant, but they were certainly encouraging in terms of the fact that they appeared in an experimental setting not specifically designed to test the hypotheses in question.

SPECIFIC VALIDATION EXPERIMENT

INTRODUCTION AND PROCEDURE

The next portion of this chapter is concerned with the presentation of results from a study specifically designed to test the physiological reactivity hypotheses based on the body-image frame of reference. Although data were available which tended to support the hypotheses, it was apparent that more detailed and extensive validation was necessary in the form of an experiment designed to pinpoint the important variables involved. At the writers' suggestion, A. Davis (77A) undertook the setting up of such an experiment. The general objective was to isolate two groups of subjects differing clearly in their degree of boundary definiteness and then to obtain various measures of exterior and interior reactivity under conditions of both rest and stress. By means of this procedure it would be possible to deal straightforwardly with such issues as whether high and low Barrier individuals do indeed contrast in exterior versus interior reactivity, whether some exterior and interior measures more clearly demonstrate the hypothesized relationships than do others, and whether the clarity of the hypothesized patterns is a function of how generally aroused (rest level versus stress level) the individual is.

Subjects for the study were fifty undergraduate male students at the University of Houston with a mean age of twenty-two years. These subjects were selected on the basis of their Barrier scores from a larger pool of individuals. Originally the group Rorschach was administered by Davis to three different undergraduate psychology classes; and the writers determined from the protocols the Barrier scores of all the male students. Out of 280 Rorschachs obtained 171 were those of men. Of this number twenty-five were randomly chosen who tended toward the low Barrier extreme and twenty-five who were inclined toward the high Barrier extreme. Those in the low Barrier group were individuals with Barrier scores of 2 or less; and those in the high Barrier group had scores of 5 or more. This was a selective sample in that it excluded the 34 per cent of the male subjects whose Barrier scores fell in the range 3–4 (median = 3). The decision was made to use a sample weighted toward the extremes in order at this stage to test the reactivity hypotheses in a context which would maximize the phenomena under consideration. Davis further decided to restrict his sample to men in order to eliminate the complications that might result from sex differences which are difficult to control in the relatively small groups he was studying. The fifty subjects who had been chosen for one or the other of the experimental groups were contacted and offered five dollars each to participate in the experiment. Only two of the fifty declined to participate or did not keep their appointment once it had been made. They were replaced by reserve subjects with equivalent scores.

The following physiological measurement techniques were employed in the course of the experiment:

(1) Electromyogram (EMG). Recordings were obtained from two EEG electrodes placed 2 inches apart over the frontalis muscle of the left eye. Degree of response was expressed in an integral reading by a current integrator and analogue to decimal converter which rectified the current and summated the area under the graphed curve of the EMG potential.

(2) Ballistocardiograph. The instrument used was a critically damped accelerometer designed so that it was more sensitive than the Virgil Hill Electromagnetic Ballistocardiograph, but which gave the same wave-form characteristics.

(3) Galvanic Skin Resistance. A measure of skin resistance was secured by means of a balanced DC circuit which remained at 50 microamperes irrespective of the resistance of the subject. Since the current was constant, the voltage across the subject was an index of his resistance. Readings were taken from the left hand. The skin sites at which the electrodes were to be placed were vigorously rubbed and cleaned with zinc sulphate solution in order to control extraneous factors (e.g., dirt which might affect skin resistance).

(4) Blood Pressure. Both systolic and diastolic blood pressure were determined by the cuff and ausculatory method.

From the measurement techniques listed above the following specific indices of reactivity were abstracted:

(1) Body-interior response (ballistocardiograph measures)
  a. Pulse (p) or heart rate
  b. IJ(stroke volume)
  c. IJ × p (cardiac output)
(2) Body-exterior response
  a. Electromyogram
  b. GSR (resistance level)
  c. Total peripheral resistance, $BP_m/(IJ \times p)$, where BP_m equals the mean BP computed by averaging the systolic and diastolic blood pressures
(3) Exploratory measures
  a. Systolic blood pressure
  b. Diastolic blood pressure

All the interior measures were concerned with some aspect of cardiac function. Other indices of interior response (e.g., stomach motility) which were contemplated could not be employed because of the limitations of equipment available in the experimental situation. The exterior measures were more diversified and tapped response in skin, muscle, and the peripheral vascular system. Systolic and diastolic blood pressure were included in the array of physiological measures not only because they were needed to compute total peripheral resistance but also simply for exploratory purposes. It was, of course, specifically predicted that the high Barrier group would show significantly more reactivity for EMG, GSR, and total peripheral resistance than the low Barrier group. It was further predicted that the low Barrier group would manifest significantly greater responsivity in terms of heart rate, stroke volume, and cardiac output than the high Barrier group.

There follows now a detailed account of the procedure used in obtaining the physiological measures. After a subject came into the experimental room, he was told that he was to participate in a study concerned with the heart and it was indicated that the various pieces of equipment visible to him pertained to heart function in some way. He was then asked to lie down on a ½-inch horsehair pad on the floor, and a sandbag was put under his heels. The various electrodes were attached to him while the experimenter chatted casually about neutral topics. It was suggested to the subject that he just relax and he was allowed to lie quietly for twenty minutes. During the last ten minutes of the rest period, GSR resistance level readings were taken every minute, and the last reading was designated as representative of this period. Also, blood pressure was sampled three times during the final ten minutes of the rest phase, and the last value was considered to be the most representative. Following the twenty minutes of rest, two-minute records of EMG and of BCG were obtained. The next to the last eighth of this two-minute record was designated as the basis for evaluating EMG and BCG during the resting level. Immediately after this two-minute period another resting blood-pressure reading was secured which was averaged with the last of the previous blood pressures. Another GSR resistance value was also taken which was averaged with the last of the earlier GSR values.

TABLE 13:2 SCHEMATIC REPRESENTATION OF EXPERIMENTAL PROCEDURE

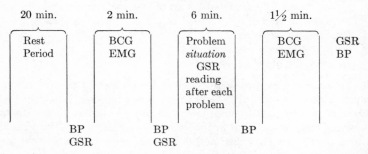

20 min.	2 min.	6 min.	1½ min.	
Rest Period	BCG EMG	Problem *situation* GSR reading after each problem	BCG EMG	GSR BP
	BP GSR	BP GSR	BP	

BCG—Ballistocardiograph. EMG—Electromyogram. GSR—Galvanic skin reflex. BP—Blood pressure.

A second phase of the procedure began when the subject was informed that a number of problems were to be presented to him in order to study the effects of problem-solving on heart action. Six arithmetic problems taken from the Wechsler-Bellevue Intelligence Scale were presented to him in a manner which was frustrating and which put him under stress. The first two problems presented to him were very easy, and even if he gave wrong answers he was told that he was right. Thus the problem-solving began in all instances with a taste of success. The next four problems were considerably harder and even the few subjects who occasionally arrived at a correct solution were told that they were wrong. The experimenter took an increasingly more hostile and exasperated attitude toward each succeeding failure by the subject. He made such remarks as, "These are getting too hard for you," and "This must not be your day." The impact of this sort of criticism was visibly disturbing in almost all instances. Subjects became irritable, anxious, and dejected. While a subject was working on the last of the six problems, a blood-pressure reading was taken, and was considered representative of the stress-period pressure. GSR resistance level was observed during the entire problem-solving period and the lowest value was designated as the stress-period response. When the subject had failed the last problem, one-and-one-half-minute runs of BCG and of EMG were obtained.

The second sixth of each of these runs was the basis for establishing the stress-level response for the respective measures involved.

RESULTS

The data were dealt with in terms of two different reference points. These reference points involved reactivity during rest and the difference between rest-level and stress-level reactivity, with this difference corrected for inequalities in resting-level base lines by regression analysis procedures suggested by Lacey (185). There follows now a survey[*] of the results obtained from analyzing the data in this fashion.

TABLE 13:3 SIGNIFICANCE OF DIFFERENCES BETWEEN HIGH BARRIER AND LOW BARRIER SUBJECTS FOR MEANS OF DIFFERENCES BETWEEN RESTING LEVEL AND STRESS LEVEL RESPONSE[a]

Measure	High Barrier Mean	Low Barrier Mean	Group with Higher Mean	Significance of "t"	
				Two-tailed	One-tailed
Exterior					
EMG	53.4	46.8	High barrier	.05–.01	.01
GSR	51.2	49.5	High barrier	.40–.30	.20–.15
Total peripheral resistance	51.7	47.5	High barrier	.20–.10	.10–.05
Interior					
Heart Rate	47.4	52.6	Low barrier	.05–.01	.01
IJ	47.9	53.1	Low barrier	.05–.01	.01
IJ × p	47.8	52.3	Low barrier	.05–.01	.01
Exploratory					
Systolic B.P.	45.9	53.7	Low barrier	.01	.001
Diastolic B.P.	48.7	51.3	Low barrier	.40–.30	.20–.15

[a] Each difference score was corrected for influence of the resting level by means of the following formula:

$$50 + 10 \frac{y_2 - x_2\, r x y}{1 - r_{xy2}}$$

As one looks over the total array of results, it is apparent that best support for the hypotheses may be found in the scores representing differences in responsivity between resting level and stress level. In Table 13:3 one finds that all the means of the difference scores for the body-exterior

[*] A more technically complete and detailed analysis of the results will be published elsewhere by Arville D. Davis, University of Texas.

TABLE 13:4   BISERIAL CORRELATIONS FOR THE TOTAL EXPERIMENTAL GROUP OF THE BARRIER SCORE WITH PHYSIOLOGICAL MEASURES REPRESENTATIVE OF RESTING LEVEL AND CORRECTED [a] DIFFERENCES BETWEEN RESTING AND STRESS LEVELS

Variables	Resting Level	Differences Between Rest and Stress Levels
Exterior		
Barrier vs. EMG	+.38 [b]	+.41
Barrier vs. GSR	+.19	+.10
Barrier vs. Peripheral resistance	−.05	+.26
Interior		
Barrier vs. Heart rate	−.25	−.33
Barrier vs. LJ	+.34	−.32
Barrier vs. IJ × p	+.17	−.28
Exploratory		
Barrier vs. Systolic B.P.	−.28	−.49
Barrier vs. Diastolic B.P.	−.13	−.16

[a] The difference scores were corrected for the influence of the resting level by means of the formula:

$$50 + 10 \frac{(Y_2 - X_2 \, rxy)}{\sqrt{1 - r_{xy^2}}}$$

[b] An r of .27 is required for the .05 level of significance and an r of .35 for the .01 significance level, in terms of a two-tailed test. With a one-tailed test, .21 and .19 fall at the .01–.15 level, respectively.

measures indicate relatively greater increased responsivity in the high Barrier group than in the low Barrier group. This is the direction of results which was predicted. That is, the definite-boundary subjects show a greater increment of reactivity in their exterior body layers under stress than do the indefinite-boundary subjects. For EMG the mean difference between the groups falls at the .01 level (one-tailed test). The mean difference for GSR is at the .20–.15 level; and the mean difference for total peripheral resistance lies at the .10–.05 level.

Even better results are shown in Table 13:3 concerning the increment of reactivity under stress for the two groups relative to the body-interior measures. The low Barrier group significantly exceeds (.01, one-tailed test) the high Barrier group in degree of increase of heart rate, IJ (stroke volume), and IJ × p (cardiac output). Thus the indefinite-boundary group proves itself to be relatively more reactive with a body-interior sector than the definite-boundary group.

In one section of Table 13:4 there is a listing of the biserial correlations having to do with the relationships of the Barrier score to the various

TABLE 13:5 MEAN STANDARD SCORE RESTING LEVELS OF PHYSIOLOGI-
CAL MEASURES IN HIGH AND IN LOW BARRIER GROUPS

Measure	High Barrier Mean	Low Barrier Mean	Group with Higher Mean	Significance of "t"	
				Two-tailed	One-tailed
Exterior					
EMG	53.1	46.9	H.B.[a]	.05–.01	.01
GSR	51.4	48.4	H.B.	.30–.20	.15–.10
Total peripheral resistance	49.2	51.0	N.D.	—	—
Interior					
Heart rate	48.0	52.0	L.B.	.20–.10	.10–.05
IJ	52.6	47.2	H.B.	.10–.05	.05–.01
IJ × p	51.1	48.9	N.D.	—	—
Exploratory					
Systolic B.P.	47.9	52.5	L.B.	.10	.05
Diastolic B.P.	48.9	51.1	N.D.	—	—

[a] H.B.—High Barrier. L.B.—Low Barrier. N.D.—No essential difference.

rest-level-stress-level increment scores in the total population of subjects
($N = 50$). A review of these correlations quickly points up the fact that
there is a reversal in the direction of relationship as one moves from body-
exterior measures to body-interior measures. The exterior measures are
all positively correlated with the Barrier score, whereas the interior
measures are all negatively correlated with it. The Barrier score is
correlated $+.41$ (.01 level) with EMG; $+.10$ (not significant) with
GSR; and $+.26$ (.05 level) with total peripheral resistance. But it is
correlated $-.33$ (.05) with heart rate; $-.32$ (.05) with IJ; and $-.28$
(.05) with IJ × p. Five of the six measures are significantly in the predicted direction. GSR is in the right direction but not significantly so.
This pattern of results may be translated to mean that the more definite the individual's body-image boundary the *greater* is the increment
in body-exterior response he manifests under stress. At the same time,
the more definite his body-image boundary the *less* is the increment he
shows under stress in body-interior response. One may say that in terms
of rest-level–stress-level difference scores the hypotheses are strongly
supported.

A further incidental analysis of the rest-level–stress-level difference
scores which was made should be described because it dramatizes the
contrast in the reaction patterns of the high Barrier and low Barrier
groups. The six difference score means in the high Barrier group were
ranked in descending order as to the indicated degree of increment of

reactivity. The same was done for the six means in the low Barrier group. Below are listed the results of this ranking.

	HIGH BARRIER		LOW BARRIER
Rank	*Physiological Measure*	*Rank*	*Physiological Measure*
1	EMG	1	IJ
2	Total peripheral resistance	2	Heart rate
3	GSR	3	IJ × p
4	IJ	4	GSR
5	IJ × p	5	Total peripheral resistance
6	Heart rate	6	EMG

The rho correlation of these two sets of rankings is −.83. What one notes is that in the high Barrier group greatest reactivity is indicated by the three measures of body-exterior response; whereas in the low Barrier group highest reactivity is associated with the three indices of body-interior response. It is striking that EMG occupies the highest rank position in the definite-boundary group and the lowest rank position in the indefinite-boundary group. Similarly, heart rate has the second highest rank in the indefinite-boundary group, but has the lowest rank in the definite-boundary group.

The results which were obtained from the separate analysis of resting-level response also tend to support the original hypotheses, but in a less clear-cut fashion.

Table 13:5 contains the mean reactivity scores that were obtained during the rest level. Two of the three mean differences between the Barrier groups for the body-exterior measures are in the predicted direction. The high Barrier group shows greater EMG reactivity (.01) and greater GSR reactivity (.15–.10). But there is no essential difference between the groups for total peripheral resistance. The results for the body-interior measures are conflicting. One finds that, as predicted, the low Barrier group manifests a greater heart rate (.10–.05) than the high Barrier group. But there is no real difference between the groups for IJ × p; and the difference for IJ is significantly (.05–.01) in the direction opposite to that predicted. The reason for this reversal of results for IJ is not at all clear. Scarborough (265) does report a slight, but not significant, negative correlation between IJ amplitude and heart rate in normal men. One might therefore speculate that conditions associated with the resting state in the present experiment were such as to maximize this negative relationship; and so the low Barrier subjects who manifested a relatively high heart rate tended toward low IJ amplitude. This is offered only in the way of a guess.

When one examines the correlations of Barrier score with the resting-level physiological measures for the total subject population (N = 50), the pattern appears in general like that seen in the analysis of mean differences between the groups. The Barrier score is correlated +.38(.001) with EMG and +.19(.05) with GSR; but it is not significantly correlated with total peripheral resistance. As far as body-interior measures are concerned, the Barrier score is correlated −.25(.05) with heart rate and +.34(.01) with IJ. The correlation with IJ × p is not significant.

Viewing the data as a whole, one would say that, of the body-exterior measures, EMG results fall best in line with the predictions about responsivity; the results from the total peripheral resistance measure are next most congruent; and those from PGR are least good. As far as the body-interior measures are concerned, heart rate tends to conform best to the hypotheses.

A word should be said about the exploratory findings pertaining to the blood-pressure measures. As indicated in Tables 13:3, 13:4, and 13:5, diastolic blood pressure is only minimally related to the Barrier score. Systolic blood pressure is highly related to the Barrier score, however. Thus it is significantly more elevated (.05) in the low Barrier group than in the high Barrier group during the resting level; and the increment of systolic pressure under stress is likewise greater in the low Barrier group. The correlation of Barrier score with systolic blood pressure in the total subject population (N = 50) is −.49 (.001). If one considers that a large part of the variance of the systolic pressure is probably a function of the energy output of the heart (interior sector), it becomes clear why it should behave like a body-interior measure. One would suppose that the reason diastolic pressure does not give the same results as the systolic measure is because a relatively larger part of its variance is a function of the degree of vasoconstriction of the blood vessels. Diastolic pressure reflects the energy output of the heart to a lesser degree and more circuitously than systolic pressure does.

If one compares the configuration of results from the measures recorded during the resting period with the pattern that emerges from the scores representing rest-level–stress-level increment, it is clear that the latter is more supportive of the basic hypotheses. One explanation that may be offered for this difference in the supportive value of the two sets of data has to do with the uniformity of the significance of the experimental situation to the various subjects at the time that their physiological responses were being recorded. It may be conjectured that the rest-level period had a greater diversity of meaning to the subjects than did the stress-level period and that as a result the rest measures are relatively more contaminated by uncontrolled attitudinal variables. During the rest level little was done in an active way to create a specific emotional set in the subject. It was simply hoped that by allowing him to lie still for a while and by carrying on light conversation with him he would relax. Probably a good many of the subjects did find this procedure reassuring and relaxing. It is likely, too, that there were quite a number who remained fearful and on edge. Thus the resting-level measures would represent samples of response from some subjects who at one extreme were quite relaxed and from others who at another extreme were somewhat scared. It is likely that the range of differences in the subjects' emotional states, however, was much narrowed during the stress period. At this time the experimenter set out in an active, aggressive, and standardized fashion to disturb and frustrate the subjects; and there is good reason to believe his tactics were very successful. He was trying to create a similar emotional response in each subject. His efforts probably decreased the range of over-all disturbance in the group in so far as it aroused all the subjects to at least a moderate degree of disturbance. One would assume that in narrowing this range a more controlled experimental situation was created than existed at the time the rest measures were obtained. This greater control would have increased the chances of testing the hypotheses in a straightforward manner.

It is our supposition that if rest-level conditions could be sufficiently standardized for a group of subjects, the body-exterior versus body-interior patterns would emerge with a clarity as great as that which we have found to hold true for the rest-level–stress-level difference scores. We consider that individuals manifest habitual ratios of body-exterior to body-interior reactivity in their everyday living. Of course, the results of the present study indicate that such habitual individual differences persist even at high states of emotional arousal. They are not obliterated by widespread arousal of the organism. The exterior versus interior pattern was, if anything, intensified rather than obliterated by the stress situation; and it may be presumed that the stress evoked a degree of alarm in many subjects comparable to that linked with Cannon's "emergency reaction."

The total aggregate of physiological reactivity results described in the present chapter places our hypotheses on a rather firm foundation. Evidence from several sources has been presented that individuals do differ with respect to the degree to which they respond with the body exterior as compared to the body interior and that such differences are linked with variations in body-image boundary definiteness. Having established this point, all kinds of interesting new vistas present themselves. One could, for example, systematically attack the whole problem of how differences in body-image boundary definiteness might get translated into differences in body-exterior versus body-interior reactivity, and then how such reactivity differences might in turn eventuate in the tendency for psychosomatic symptoms to occur selectively at exterior or interior body sites.

An example of another interesting research route would be to determine whether there are generalized differences in body-exterior versus body-interior reactivity in each sex at various age levels and to relate the findings to what we know about the average Barrier score and distinguishing socialization phenomena at such age levels. There are manifold other exploratory possibilities that could be cited.

It seems to us, however, that the most basic question that presents itself has to do with what organizations in the central nervous system correspond to the body-exterior versus interior reactivity distinction. How are patterns set up in the central nervous system which result in tendencies to send more activating signals to the body exterior than to the interior or more to the interior than to the exterior? Perhaps this question is most accessible to study in learning terms. What kinds of learning experiences are most likely to eventuate in given modes of central nervous system organization that favor specific ratios of activating signals to the body exterior versus the body interior? We have already tracked down, in some of our earlier described studies of families and contrasting cultures, a few of the categories of learning experiences which favor the development of definite versus indefinite body-image boundaries and which presumably would influence ratios of body-exterior response to body-interior response. But this is barely a beginning. A detailed study of the learning processes most relevant to this issue remains to be carried out.

We consider that the value to general personality theory of the physiological hypotheses we have formulated is much enhanced because they were derived from an organized series of psychological constructs. They grew out of a sequence of ideas about how people organize their experiences and become socialized. In this way a lever is provided for extending the complexity of the physiological concepts as further work increases the complexity of the underlying psychological constructs. An approach presents itself for systematically investigating physiological phenomena viewed not as empirical correlates of psychological events but rather as part of the total way in which the individual works out organized ways of dealing with the cultural milieu. But more specifically, since the formation of body-image boundaries seem to be such a fundamental aspect of the socialization process, the possibility presents itself that we may have found a new strategically important means for conceptualizing some of the physiological events which may be involved in establishing within the individual the norms of his culture. Extensive observations of body-image variations during the socialization cycle may provide data which would permit theory construction concerning certain of the physiological patterns which characterize this cycle.

AN EXPLORATORY APPRAISAL OF THE RELATIONSHIP OF THE BARRIER SCORE TO PERCENT-TIME ALPHA IN THE ELECTROENCEPHALOGRAM

The final portion of this chapter departs considerably from the level of conceptualization pursued in earlier sections. It is concerned not so much with the body-interior versus body-exterior reactivity correlates of degree of boundary definiteness as with brain event correlates. It represents an attempt to extend our physiological formulations to the level of brain functioning. As indicated earlier, it seemed to be a next logical step to try to elaborate the meaning of our physiological findings by relating them to central nervous system constructs. We decided quite arbitrarily to begin this effort by surveying the literature concerning electroencephalographic (EEG) findings. The intent was to note what correlates between personality attributes and EEG indices had been established which might provide leads for hypothesis development concerning the relationship of the Barrier score to such indices. Although EEG indices are admittedly very indirect and approximate measures, they represent one of the few practical means for obtaining information about brain processes in the intact functioning person.

We found five studies in the literature which seemed pertinent to our interests. These all suggested that the percent-time alpha of an individual was positively correlated with his degree of passivity. Saul, Davis, and Davis (263A) evaluated the personality attributes and EEG characteristics of a number of neurotic patients who were undergoing psychoanalytic therapy. They found that there was a trend for a passive personality orientation to be associated with a high alpha index (percent-time alpha) and an active forceful orientation to be associated with a low alpha index. The low alpha index was particularly linked with tendencies to be freely and aggressively self-expressive. Travis and Bennett (317A) reported, on the basis of a study of the Rorschach responses of individuals with high and low percent-time alpha, that high alpha index persons "possess a passive-receptive manner of organizing stimuli, and reflect the constrictive work of affective factors upon productivity." Rubin and Bowman (256) studied the alpha index and personality characteristics of 100 peptic ulcer patients. They established that a larger proportion of this group showed a high alpha index than did individuals in a normal group. They felt that the personality data, which had been obtained from interviews, indicated that the peptic ulcer patients were generally passive-dependent in their way of life. Moses (222B) studied another group of patients with stomach ulcers in a similar fashion by means of the EEG and interviews and arrived at essentially the same results. Rubin and Moses (256A) reported that a group of asthmatics was marked by a considerably higher alpha index than a normal group. They linked this finding with the assumption that asthmatics are basically very passive-dependent in their orientation. It should be noted that, although Sisson and Ellingson (285A) have criticized the five studies just cited as being methodologically unsound, it struck us that the consistent trend running through all of them could not be validly dismissed. There did seem to be a trend toward a positive correlation between percent-time alpha and passive reaction patterns.

Since our previous work linked passivity with indefinite body-image boundaries and striving activity with definite boundaries, we were led to speculate that the degree of boundary definiteness would be inversely related to percent-time alpha. That is, definite-boundary persons would be expected to show low percent-time alpha and indefinite-boundary persons to manifest high percent-time alpha.

An opportunity to check this hypothesis was provided by data collected by Travis and Bennett° (317A). They obtained Rorschach and EEG measures from a group of sixty-six normal adults. The EEG measures were obtained by means of an Offner, Type D, six-channel, ink-writing electro-encephalograph. During the recording period the subject sat alone with his eyes closed in a darkened room and was instructed to relax as though in preparation for sleep. The age range in the subject group was 19–45 years with a median of 25 years. Fifty-nine of the subjects were men and seven were women. The percent-time alpha of the EEG record of each subject had been determined; and all records with an alpha index over 50 were considered to be in the high index group and all below 50 in the low index group. We scored the Rorschach records for the Barrier variable. All records over 25 responses were reduced to 25 by the usual method. It was necessary to drop eight of the Rorschachs with the lowest response totals in the high alpha group from the data analysis in order to equalize the response total medians in the two alpha categories. The response total disparity between the groups had been described by Travis and Bennett who reported that the low alpha subjects had a significantly greater response total than the high alpha subjects. When the eight low response total cases were eliminated, there remained twenty-four cases in the high alpha index group and thirty-four in the low alpha group. The median response total in each group was 25.

A chi-square analysis of the Barrier score differences between the high and low alpha index groups yielded results very significantly in the predicted direction. The high alpha index group had a median Barrier score of 3 and the low alpha index group had a median Barrier score of 5. The difference is significant at the .001 level.

° We are indeed grateful to Dr. Clayton L. Bennett for making these data available to us.

Having demonstrated this link between body-image boundary definiteness and percent-time alpha, the question arises concerning its implications. How does it fit in with what is known about alpha and with what we already have found concerning the relationship of the Barrier score to other physiological variables? One finds upon consulting the pertinent literature, e.g., Ellingson (84A), Gellhorn (122), and Morruzi and Magoun (222A), that the alpha rhythm recorded by the EEG probably represents the optimal synchronization of the electrical activity of cortical elements. It is maximized in a state of relaxation or low alertness. But it is blocked or decreased by stimuli which alert the individual. As soon as the individual is placed in a situation which causes him to mobilize or to adopt a set of readiness, his alpha is blocked out (desynchronization). Decrease in alpha seems to be a regular correlate of the organism preparing itself for response. This fact is nicely congruent with the direction of the relationship between percent-time alpha and the Barrier score. A low alpha index may, in these terms, be viewed as representing a persistent tendency toward alertness and readiness for response; whereas a high index could be interpreted as indicating minimal tendency in the direction of such alertness. Thus, the high Barrier subjects (low percent-time alpha) would be typified by an EEG alertness pattern and the low Barrier subjects (high percent-time alpha) by an EEG pattern that corresponds to a low degree of preparatory self-activation. This pattern corresponds well with other differences in life style between the two Barrier groups which have been shown to exist by means of various techniques. It has been demonstrated that high Barrier individuals do keep themselves at a greater level of alertness than low Barrier individuals, in the sense that they are more mobilized for high aspiration, more intent upon the pursuit of goals to completion, and more actively dedicated to being self-steering.

There is good evidence (222A, 122) that blocking of the alpha rhythm is a function of stimulation of the brain-stem reticular formation (BSRF). Stimulation of the BSRF initiates a stream of impulses that activates the cortex via the hypothalamus and a diffuse thalamic system and thus blocks alpha.* This activation of the cortex actually represents but one phase of a generalized alertness process that is initiated by BSRF stimulation. The organism is mobilized and aroused to response readiness. The importance of the BSRF for maintaining an alert set is indicated by the fact that after its influence is removed by transection, the organism falls into a state of somnolence or unconsciousness from which it can only with difficulty be

---

* We are indebted to Dr. Donald B. Lindsley for comments which helped us to clarify our thinking concerning some of the brain mechanisms that might be involved in the correlation of the Barrier score with the alpha index.

even briefly stirred. The BSRF seems to be the brain region most involved in high alertness versus low alertness phenomena.

Since high Barrier individuals manifest an alpha pattern that corresponds to a high level of BSRF activation and the low Barrier individuals a pattern characteristic of low BSRF activation, the question arises whether there is some long-term contrast in the usual degree of BSRF arousal in the two Barrier groups. The differences in alpha index suggest that the BSRF in definite-boundary individuals is chronically more activated than the BSRF in indefinite-boundary individuals. If one postulates the existence of such a difference, the question arises concerning how it is brought about. How might the BSRF in the high Barrier group be influenced to a long-term higher level of activation than is characteristic of the low Barrier group?

One of the most likely explanations that presents itself is derived from the fact that we have demonstrated a significant difference in muscle tension between the high Barrier and low Barrier subjects. High Barrier individuals were found to have a more elevated level of striate muscle excitation than low Barrier individuals. It is postulated that this difference results in a persistent contrast in the amount of proprioceptive stimulation that feeds into the BSRF in the two boundary groups and therefore to a contrast in the level of activation of the BSRF in each group. That is, the greater the muscular activation that takes place, the more intense would be the resulting proprioceptive sensations evoked. There are indications that of all the various kinds of sensory impulses that may activate the BSRF, those of a proprioceptive type rank only second to pain in potency. Gellhorn notes (122, p. 186), "It seems that afferent impulses originating in the muscle spindles and quantitatively related to the intensity of the muscle tone determine to a great extent the excitability of the nervous system and thereby the state of wakefulness." Visceral sensations below the pain threshold apparently have much less activating influence upon the BSRF than do proprioceptive sensations (122). Thus, the relatively high level of proprioceptive arousal in the high Barrier group would lead to a relatively high degree of BSRF activation. However, the relatively high level of *body-interior* (e.g., heart) arousal that we have found to be characteristic of the low Barrier group would not have a similarly potent effect upon the BSRF. Of course, this formulation does not explain what neural mechanisms might be involved in the initiation and maintenance of the long-term differential levels of muscle excitation which have been noted and designated as contributing to differences in BSRF activation. It is possible that a specific level of muscle excitation is first initiated by processes in the BSRF under the influence of certain cortical centers. The feedback of resultant proprioceptive impulses to the BSRF and to cortical centers might then establish a self-perpetuating system of a given order.

PART FIVE

Conclusion

....

CHAPTER FOURTEEN

Theoretical Formulations

THE BOUNDARY DIMENSION

THE BODY-IMAGE boundary dimension has shown itself to have a powerful potential for predicting a wide range of behaviors. It has permitted prediction of such diverse phenomena as psychological adjustment to poliomyelitis, modes of interaction of members of small groups, and patterns of physiological reactivity. It is difficult to find other psychological constructs in the literature which have an equivalent range of meaningful application. The question arises as to why the body-image boundary concept has proved so useful. What are the factors implicit in it which contribute to its predictive variance?

Two main contributing variables may be distinguished. We consider, first of all, that one of the special properties of the Barrier score is that it measures an aspect of how the individual experiences his body. It provides data concerning the manner in which the individual conceptualizes his private body domain. This is a domain which, as we have seen, seems to be a significant frame of reference for making many judgments. From a knowledge of how a person has organized his perceptions of his body one has access to some of his basic feelings about himself as a separate entity. An individual's body is the one area in his experiential field which uniquely belongs to him and is the corporeal representation of his "base of operations" in the world. His concept of this base of operations must necessarily be significant in influencing how he conducts himself. For example, if he pictures this base as fragile, one would assume that he would be more likely to be timid in his life excursions than if he ascribes strength and solidity to it. It is the ability of the Barrier score to tap a level that involves such fundamental body attitudes, which is probably one of the principal sources of its value.

The second main factor which we consider to be contributing to its predictive variance is its linkage with boundary functions. That is, aside from its anchorage in a body model in general, it focuses particularly on the boundary characteristics of the model. It attempts to measure the state of affairs in a boundary region. As we see it, a boundary measure has unusual strategic import in predicting the behavior of an organism in the medium that surrounds it. It is at the boundary that the organism and the medium make contact. The boundary is the area of relatively highest interaction between the two. Therefore, observations made concerning this area of interaction are likely to contain a relatively higher percentage of valuable information about how the organism is responding to the medium than are observations concerning phenomena not related to the boundary process. We conceive of the Barrier score as an index which represents in condensed form the history of a long sequence of boundary transactions. The fact that the particular body-image score we developed had to do with a boundary level of functioning was actually quite accidental. The data from which the score was derived happened to be saturated with boundary implications. It is our feeling, most things being equal, that if we had formulated other types of body-image measures which did not sample boundary transactions, they would have proved to possess less predictive power than the Barrier score.

The importance of boundary phenomena has also been increasingly emphasized in other scientific disciplines (134). Boundary formulations are widely current in biology, sociology, and economics. Generally one gets the impression that there are relatively large returns from conceptualizing problems in boundary terms. But the application of a boundary frame of reference is fraught with complications which may not have been readily apparent in the work with the Barrier score which has been described.

Simply to define the boundary of a thing or a system is not always an easy matter and is often quite a complicated one. It is true that there is general agreement that a boundary represents a discontinuity between areas or a separation between things that are distinguishable. There are problems, however, in applying such definitions to phenomena in a clear-cut fashion. The zone of separation between two areas may be so gradual or hazy as to result in disagreement concerning the point at which a boundary may be said to exist. Often one has to content himself with a statistical boundary which provides only an approximation of a definition of the line of demarcation. Rapoport (134, p. 308) says concerning this point:

> If the distinguishability between the classes is not perfect, one may speak of a statistical boundary. What shall we call the edge of a forest? Obviously, what we agree to call by a given name is a matter of agreement. It is observed, for instance, that the density of trees in a certain area can be expressed as a continuous function on the surface where trees grow; we may agree to call the "edge" or the timber line, any imaginary curve such that the density of trees is above a certain specified value on one side of it and below on the other. Similarly, we can call the boundary of cloud an imagi-

nary surface where the density of condensed water vapor particles on one side is greater than some specified value, and less on the other. Similarly, if a social class in a society is characterized by the response which its members make in a particular situation, then unambiguous membership in a class is determined by the exclusive occurrence of a particular response. Those people who respond sometimes in one way and sometimes in another can be said to be in the *statistical boundary*, which can be more precisely defined by specifying the particular probability of response which is to be considered as the threshold of membership.

The difficulties encountered in identifying boundaries are even further enhanced by the fact that they may vary with time, with the position of the observer, and with the purpose of such identification.

Some of the particular problems that arise in the identification of boundaries having to do with psychological processes may be illustrated by analyzing a number of the connotations of the term *body-image boundary*. We have, by and large, side-stepped the problem of what line of demarcation is involved in the use of such a term and have fallen back on operational procedures. The only really specific definition that has been offered is operationally based on certain characteristics of ink-blot responses which have been shown to be significantly linked with classes of body experiences. If one inquires concerning what line of demarcation the term *body-image boundary* does indeed refer to, some confusing possibilities arise.

Is the body-image boundary a concept of a line of demarcation that literally adheres to the body-wall limits? Does one exclude the possibility that the body-image boundary might encompass the clothes which one habitually wears? Might the boundary extend out into a space area in the vicinity of an individual which is defined by the reach of his musculature? Is there the possibility that the body-image boundary may be experienced so that it includes only certain primary body sectors and excludes other important sectors? May the body-image boundary be extended so as to embrace areas quite distant from the individual?

All the possibilities suggested in these questions have been observed to occur. Observations of schizophrenics indicate that they may react to events at some distance as if such events were direct attacks upon their bodies. Patients with neurological syndromes may behave as if important areas of their bodies do not exist. The individual with an amputation may continue to experience his body boundary as extending out into space to include the area previously occupied by the missing member. The indications are that normal persons may experience analogous but less extreme versions of such body-image boundary contractions and expansions. It would therefore not be accurate to say that the body-image boundary adheres strictly to the limits of the body wall. Individuals may apparently vary considerably as to where they set the boundary. In terms of over-all averages, however, the body wall is probably a good representation of the locus of the body-image boundary. It is likely that the body wall is a primary reference point that serves to keep the boundary within certain limits. But it cannot be denied that a definition of the body-image boundary as residing at the body wall is, strictly speaking, somewhat of an arbitrary decision.

One should also consider that there may be large shifts in the site of the body-image boundary in the individual during his life span. It is doubtful that the first hazy boundaries developing in the young child would be associated with the body wall. Most of the meaningful body experiences at that time center on the mouth, stomach, and gut. Therefore, the boundary would tend to be experienced as encompassing an area somewhat interior to the actual body wall. It is conceivable that as the child grows older there is a differential rate at which the boundary approaches the body surface in various areas. At points of intensive contact with the world (e.g., mouth, anus, eyes) the boundary might early be set at the surface; but in other areas the boundary might be conceived as lying more within the interior. This presents a picture of a boundary which might have highly irregular contours. It is in the adult that the boundary probably reaches its maximum of regular contour at a locus identified with the body wall. There is the further possibility that, when the individual reaches a stage of advanced aging and experiences unpleasant changes in his outer appearance and a decline in body sensitivity, his body-image boundaries again retreat to more interior sites.

THE DERIVATION AND ELABORATION OF THE BODY-IMAGE BOUNDARY

Despite the mass of data we have accumulated concerning the Barrier score, we have had difficulty in developing a scheme or model which would satisfactorily trace the process whereby the body-image boundary arises and acquires properties of definiteness. An account of boundary development in terms of interaction with significant social figures is favored by the results of our studies of the relationship of the boundary attributes of children to the characteristics of their parents. Such a position is favored, too, by results suggesting that cultural differences in boundary attributes reflect contrasts in the socialization processes of the cultures involved. But the problem is to specify what mechanisms figure in the translation of socialization processes into the attributes of the body-image boundary.

The model we have chosen to represent how such translation occurs is

built around a framework of thought derived from Mead (214), Freud
(113), and Parsons and Bales (232). We start out with the general
postulate that the individual's personality structure is primarily the resultant of patterns of relationships he has had with key figures (e.g., mother,
father) in his life. Presumably, his experiences with various persons have
molding, shaping effect upon him which result in the emergence of recog-
nizable personality patterns. One of the prime assumptions in the separate
theories of Mead, Freud, and Parsons concerning personality formation
is that it revolves about an internalization process. It is assumed that
personality grows out of a process whereby the attitudes and characteristics of significant figures are somehow internalized and structured so as
to become functional directive systems within the individual. Freud pictured the unique articulations of each individual's "ego" and "superego"
structures as determined to an important extent by the sorts of objects
(e.g., parent models) he had "introjected." He indicated that many
parental values and prohibitions were "incorporated" and became resident
forces which guided behavior. Mead described the formation of "self"
(a term analogous to "personality") as dependent upon the individual's
making a part of himself the generalized attitudes of others toward himself.

It is worth quoting his summary account of this process (214, p. 158):

> I have pointed out, then, that there are two general stages in the
> full development of the self. At the first of these stages, the individ-
> ual's self is constituted simply by an organization of the particular
> attitudes of other individuals toward himself and toward one another
> in the specific social acts in which he participates with them. But
> at the second stage, in the full development of the individual's self,
> the self is constituted not only by an organization of these particular
> individual attitudes, but also by an organization of the social atti-
> tudes of the generalized other or the social group as a whole to
> which he belongs. These social or group attitudes are brought within
> the individual's field of direct experience, and are included as ele-
> ments in the structure or constitution of his self, in the same way
> that the attitudes of particular other individuals are; and the in-
> dividual arrives at them, or succeeds in taking them, by means of
> further organizing, and then generalizing, the attitudes of particular
> other individuals in terms of their organized social bearings and
> implications. So the self reaches its full development by organizing
> these individual attitudes of others into the organized social and
> group attitudes, and by thus becoming an individual reflection of the
> general systematic pattern of social or group behavior in which it
> and the others are all involved—a pattern which enters as a whole
> into the individual's experience in terms of these organized group
> attitudes which, through the mechanism of his central nervous sys-

tem, he takes toward himself, just as he takes the individual attitudes of others.

Parsons and Bales (232) have probably described the internalization basis of personality structure more systematically and elaborately than anyone else. They visualize personality growth as a function of the internalization of successively more complicated systems of relationships with various family members. The pattern of each relationship is literally duplicated in an interiorized system. Each interiorized system has properties which parallel the properties of the exterior relationship. Furthermore, as new relationships are interiorized their interactions and linkages result in patterned structures of some complexity. Parsons and Bales say (p. 54):

> . . . the primary structure of the human personality *as a system of action* is organized about the internalization of *systems* of social objects which originated as the role-units of the successive series of social systems in which the individual has come to be integrated in the course of his life history. His personality structure is thus in some sense a kind of "mirror-image" of the social structures he has experienced. . . .

Parsons and Bales continue (p. 56):

> . . . the internalized object must involve an organized pattern of the *meanings* which the external object has acquired. The accent here is both on *pattern*, i.e., *generalization* relative to any one specific percept of the object, and on *organization*, i.e., a structure of a plurality of different pattern components which have an orderly relation to each other. The significant external object, we assume, is an *actor in a role* vis-a-vis ego, an alter, conceived as a social object, or a collectivity. The organization of the internalized object then is an arrangement of patterns of meaning, with priorities and differentiation of aspects.

Parsons and Bales conceive of the interiorization process which results in socialization as beginning with the internalization of the simple isolated interaction system which the child experiences with his mother and proceeding to the internalization of highly complex systems that involve plural relationships with a number of family members (e.g., father and sibs) simultaneously. It should also be indicated that they picture the systems which have been interiorized as differing in such formal properties as degree of stability, degree of differentiation, and degree to which firmly bounded.

The nature of the internalization process is such as to place the individual's body in a unique position in his total perceptual field. There are factors growing out of the process which result in the body as an experienced object being psychologically "closer" to the collectivity of internalized systems that constitute the "I" or "self" than are objects exterior to the body. This, as we shall attempt to explain, results in the individual's perceptions of his body mirroring the characteristics of the internalized systems to a greater degree than do his perceptions of more exterior things.

Perhaps this point should be restated in another way. Certainly there is a wide range of data which demonstrate that the attributes one assigns to outside objects are significantly influenced by the organization of the central personality systems. Differences in personality organization have been shown to shape and distort one's perceptions of such diverse things as facial expression, passage of time, story themes, and ink blots. The position we are advancing is that as great as this shaping influence is upon the outside field, it is only a fraction of that exerted upon the manner in which the body is experienced. Indeed, we suggest that in many ways the body is experienced as an approximate replica of some of the basic internalized systems which constitute the "I" or "self."

A first step in delineating how such replication may occur is to clarify the basis for considering that the body is closer in the perceptual field to the central personality systems than are more exterior objects. It has been customary in past explanations of the unique properties of the body in the perceptual field to point out that only in this instance are there coincident with the usual sensory data various kinesthetic data which are localized in the same space. For example, Koffka says apropos of this point (178, pp. 328–329):

> If, then, the place of the visual body data coincides with the place of the other data belonging to the same part of the body ("coincides," of course, in behavioral space), then we should be able to apply our law of proximity to explain why the visual data are experienced with the Ego character, "my hand," "my leg," etc. For the local kinaesthetic processes, since in their entirety they help to organize the Ego, are not independent local events, but part events in a larger system of events. If then a visual datum is welded together with a kinaesthetic one, it must also of necessity become a part in a greater whole, i.e., it must be incorporated in the Ego system.

Within our frame of reference, we wish to suggest two primary reasons for the relatively intimate linkage of the body as an object with the central internalized systems that constitute the framework of the personality:

(1) First of all, the individual's body is actually one of the chief participants in some of the early relationships that are the prototypes of a number of the most basic introjects. The body as an object is importantly represented in the internalization matrix. The body object participates with unusual prominence in the matrix, and as such is indistinguishable from certain aspects of it. One can see how the individual's body comes to

occupy a highly significant role in the internalized systems if one considers that many of the early relationships from which some of these systems are derived revolve about reactions of the parental figures to the child's body. During the first few years of life the child experiences his parents mainly in terms of how they react to signals he gives them about his body sensations. Their attitudes toward him are expressed in how they go about satisfying his hunger sensations, how they pick him up and handle him, and how they try to regulate such body processes as excretion and defecation. The child's identity during this period is mainly a body identity. This is especially true of the primary interiorized system that is built up about the relationship of the child with the mother figure who devotes so much time to caring for his body. The system is built up about definitions and expectations arising out of mother's response to the varied expressed body needs of the child. Generally, the importance of the body as an object in the internalization matrix is enhanced not only by the primacy of its inclusion but also by the fact that it becomes a part of the extremely important (if not most important) systems which are based on interaction with the parental figures.

(2) A second reason that the body as an object is so closely linked with the central interiorized systems is that it is literally a container for these systems. The body is unique in the perceptual field in so far as it visibly demarcates an area of space which is identified with the sense of individuality that grows out of the organization of internalized systems. There is no other perceptual object which duplicates this function of visibly representing the spatial area in which the I or self resides. Would one not anticipate on this basis that the body would be experienced as psychologically in a highly intimate relationship to internalized objects and perhaps be only partially distinguishable from them? Would the body in this sense not be identified with the personality system to a greater degree than any more exterior object?

It is our position that, because the body is so uniquely close to and bound up with the internalized object systems, the manner in which it is experienced is to an unusual degree a replication of these systems. There are fairly well-verified data from work in the area of ego involvement which indicate that, as an object moves into greater psychological proximity to an individual, the probabilities increase that he will assign qualities to it associated with other objects he has interiorized. For example, if one passes an older man on the street whom one does not know, one is not likely to ascribe many qualities to him beyond those apparent from his immediate physical appearance. If this same older man is encountered as a boss or supervisor, however, the tendency is, as one gets closely involved with him, to judge him in terms of the qualities of some introjected object, like the father, and to act as if he had certain of the qualities ascribed to the father.

Similarly, the psychological proximity of the body to the internalized objects magnifies the probabilities that it will be experienced in a manner that mirrors the attributes of these objects. At one level, this sort of mirroring process might be illustrated in the frequently unrealistic complaint of the neurotic man that he has a small penis. He may experience his penis as small despite the fact that its size falls within the normal range. In working therapeutically with such an individual, we often discover that his distorted perception of the penis is a function of his viewing it in terms of an internalized system which involves a special sort of relationship between the father figure and himself. The core of this system is an interaction pattern between self and father which emphasizes smallness or inferiority of the self and superiority of the father. Somehow the penis becomes a focal representation for the characteristics of this system.

The idea that the attributes of interiorized systems are readily transformed into modes of body perception is supported, too, by the unusual frequency with which body-image distortions accompany neurotic and psychotic symptomatology or develop as a result of ego-involving stress. As soon as conditions arise which have significant distorting effects upon interior systems, these effects seem to be very quickly reflected in corresponding changes in how the body is experienced. This phenomenon is exemplified at one extreme by the schizophrenic who is spurred (by severe distortions arising in his interiorized assumptions about the intentions of others) to experience painful electric currents coursing through his body which are presumably inflicted upon him by persecutors. At a less extreme level the phenomenon is mirrored in the inclination of some individuals to highlight and dramatize sensations in the gastrointestinal tract when they find themselves in situations that activate the passivity aspects of certain interiorized systems.

We are mainly interested in the boundary aspect of the postulated duplicating relationship between body experience and internalized systems. After the fashion of Parsons and Bales, we conceptualize each interiorized system as possessing formal boundary properties. These boundary properties may be viewed as varying relative to the nature of the relationships that were the prototype for the system. For example, if an individual's interactions with the mother figure have been such that she had a series of meaningful, clear-cut, and stable expectations of him and he in turn developed similar patterns of expectations of her, one would assume that the interiorized system growing out of the relationship would have definite well-articulated boundaries. If, however, the mother's expectations have been experienced as not meaningful or as erratic and incon sistent, it would make for a poorly organized interior system with ill-defined boundaries. Degree of boundary definiteness of the system may be equated with the degree to which the relationship between the self and the prototype for the interiorization helped to make the world look meaningful and capable of being dealt with effectively. It is hypothesized that the qualities of the boundary one ascribes to one's body reflect the predominance of either poorly or well-bounded internalizations. It is suggested that the close involvement of the body object with the central personality systems results in the body-image boundary almost isomorphically mirroring the over-all boundary characteristics of these systems.

The importance we assign to the influence of internalizations upon the attributes of the body-image boundary is indirectly supported by the findings that the Barrier score manifests little relationship to indices which describe the actual structure or condition of the body. There is no correlation between the Barrier score and Sheldon's body-type classification. Also, persons who have experienced extreme body disablement from poliomyelitis do not differ in their Barrier scores from persons with mild or no polio involvement. Further, persons who have lived with colostomies for many years do not show greater boundary indefiniteness than comparable individuals who have not had colostomies. The implication of these findings is that within broad limits the manner in which an individual experiences his body-image boundaries is determined more by forces from inside than by the actual characteristics of his body. We have assumed that the inside forces stem from the characteristics of interiorized personality systems. Apropos of this point, it may be remembered that data were earlier reported which indicated that successful psychotherapeutic procedures tend to increase the degree of body-image boundary definiteness. The therapy techniques which were employed made no attempt to alter body appearance. But they did seek to introduce reorganization of certain interiorizations (e.g., concept of father figures); and one may assume that it was via such reorganization that changes in the body image were stimulated.

The idea presents itself that the body-image boundary corresponds in some ways to a screen on which is projected the individual's basic feelings about his safety in the world. It is a screen which he interposes between himself and outer situations and which he can carry with him at all times. It makes it possible for him to feel that he is not open and vulnerable to everything which occurs in his vicinity and that there is some dependable definiteness about his immediate behavioral space. This facilitates his viewing himself as existing in an environment in which the safety factor is fairly constant. He need not radically revise his concept of his vulnerability as he encounters new situations which vary in their degree of threat.

The body-image boundary probably does not reflect the state of immediate situations, but it is probably a fairly stable average of the past experiences out of which internalized systems were originally derived.

Thus the boundary may be conceptualized as playing an important role in maintaining homeostasis in the course of the individual's psychological transactions with the world. It is a projection of certain assumptions about life to an area of behavioral space which separates the individual from what is "out there." If experiences with primary figures have been meaningfully well contoured, the introjections representing these experiences will be of a like nature, and the body-image boundary will in turn reflect this quality. But if experiences with prototypes of introjections have emphasized the irrationality and inconsistency of the world, the individual does not have a basis for projecting a stabilizing image pattern onto the boundary.

Some of our data suggest that in the absence of a body-image boundary capable of supplying a minimum constancy in new situations, the individual finds it necessary to create exterior conditions which will artificially provide a substitute boundary. He seeks ways of supplementing his individual boundary. The behavior of low Barrier persons in small groups, which was earlier described, illustrates these supplementing tactics well. It was noted that in group situations low Barrier, as contrasted to high Barrier persons showed two special kinds of behavior: (1) they sought to structure the group so that one person would take the lead and relieve everyone else of responsibility; (2) they tended to embed group procedures and formulations in a context which emphasized a high degree of formality and of definition of relationships.

One may interpret these observations as meaning that the low Barrier persons were seeking to compensate for their inadequate boundaries by stabilizing the demands that could be made upon them from the outside. First of all, if it could be arranged for someone else to take the lead, this person would have to bear the threat of new experiences. These experiences, therefore, would make their impact upon his followers only in a secondhand fashion. He would thus constitute a boundary between his followers and outer stimuli. Likewise, the more the world can be defined in advance and the more that people are required to do things according to detailed formal rules, the more the immediate environment becomes a stabilized boundary region.

The high Barrier person has relatively limited need for such artificial boundaries. Because of the protective screen he carries with him, he is moderately impervious to the impact of even very threatening situations. He can experience himself as protected even in the midst of danger and is not likely to be flooded with disrupting anxiety. This is probably why high Barrier persons tend to perform better than low Barrier persons under stress conditions, whether the stress is produced in the psychological laboratory or is the result of contracting poliomyelitis.

Individuals whose body-image boundaries crumble catastrophically in the course of schizophrenic disorganization may manifest exaggerated extremes in their efforts to make the outside world substitute for their lost boundaries. They magically fill the world with objects that behave according to a fixed pattern and so provide themselves with an artificial boundary region. They can, for example, perseveratively see each new situation as part of a persecutory plot or as part of a grandiose scheme, but of course this only makes for a caricature of the sense of constancy that goes with definite boundaries. What is of intriguing interest is that often the delusionally projected figures who are seen in fixed fashion as populating the world seem to be duplicates of important interiorized objects. There are reports (92) based on intensive therapy with schizophrenics which suggest that the main figures in delusional systems duplicate important qualities of primary internalizations. Thus, the persecutory roles may duplicate interiorized aspects of the relationship with the father figure or the mother figure. If such duplication does indeed occur, it suggests that the same fundamental process is at work in the conversion of the outside world into a regulated boundary region as was postulated to occur in the process of assigning attributes to the body boundary.

It was originally hypothesized that the body-image boundary was designed to mirror qualities of introjections in such a way as to create some sense of constancy about the safety conditions of the world. That is, the boundary was considered to be a function in many ways of projected qualities of internalized objects. If, therefore, the schizophrenic magically fills his environs with the qualities of primary introjections when he tries to convert the "outside" into a boundary with constancy, he is paralleling the process by which the body-image boundaries are given substance. The schizophrenic's boundary-construction behavior would be then somewhat analogous to that involved in normal body-image boundary building, but extended into a behavioral space of far greater dimensions.

It may be conjectured that the body image represents one of the important realms in which constructs based on projection of qualities of introjections may be somewhat elaborately organized and distorted without significantly impairing reality testing. But when these distorted projections break out into the larger unrestricted areas of perception, they apparently result in serious reality alterations. The transition from distorted projection upon the body image to distorted projections upon the "outside" is nicely illustrated by the not uncommonly observed patient who manifests marked hypochondriac ideas and then gradually develops paranoid delusions. His hypochondriasis may be considered as representing an attempt to build a defensive construct within the confines of the body image; and the subsequent paranoid orientation signals the failure of this defensive maneuver. As long as his elaborations remain within the hypochondriac range, he can deal fairly adequately with most reality demands. With the shift of elaborations beyond this body-image realm, however, reality testing declines precipitously.

At quite another level, we have wondered about the consequences of possessing body-image boundaries that manifest qualities of unusually extreme definiteness. What are the implications of being bounded by a screen of this sort? Does such a screen simply provide a proportionate increase in the advantages that seem to be correlated with definite boundaries? Or does it somehow lead to consequences which have a negative effect upon functioning? Can one have body-image boundaries which are too definite?

Within the range of studies we have completed, there have been no significant indications of deficit in functioning being associated with extremely high Barrier scores. But we have made some qualitative observations which lead us to wonder whether a certain amount of boundary indefiniteness may not increase one's ability to understand and play the roles of others. Thus we have observed in a group of psychologists and anthropologists that although such individuals receive very high Barrier scores, they also tend to receive unusually high Penetration of Boundary scores. Since this is a group in which one would expect to find outstanding ability to empathize and identify with others, we are inclined to think of the elevated Barrier and Penetration of Boundary scores as indicating that such empathic ability is a function of possessing a boundary simultaneously definite and yet paradoxically easily penetrable. The implication would be that identifying with and understanding others in the manner that the psychologist or anthropologist does requires the security conditions that are correlated with definite boundaries and also requires the potential for boundary fluidity that seems to accompany a high Penetration of Boundary score. Presumably, a highly definite boundary without the potential for fluidity would interfere with role taking. This is, of course, only a guess. More systematic exploration of the problem would involve a detailed study of how the ratio of Barrier score to Penetration of Boundary score is linked to objective measures of empathic ability.

A FRAME OF REFERENCE CONCERNING THE RELATIONSHIP OF THE BODY-IMAGE BOUNDARY TO PATTERNS OF PHYSIOLOGICAL REACTIVITY

Data have already been cited in detail which support hypotheses linking degree of body-image boundary definiteness with patterns of physiological reactivity. It was shown that individuals with definite boundaries tend to manifest relatively high responsivity in the outer body layers and relatively low responsivity in the body interior. A converse pattern was found to characterize individuals with indefinite boundaries. An empirical explanation of the relationship was offered which was based on a sequence of ideas that goes as follows:

High Barrier persons grow up in a setting in which active, voluntary, reality-coping attitudes are emphasized. Such attitudes are relatively less emphasized in the families of low Barrier persons. Further, the exterior layers of the body (particularly the musculature) tend to be equated with voluntary, reality-coping behavior, whereas the body interior is equated with involuntary response. The orientation of the high Barrier persons is therefore translated into a persistently high level of activation of the exterior body layers. There is a set to respond with this region of the body which is manifested in a long-term pattern of preparatory excitation. The less aspiring, less active orientation of low Barrier persons results in a relatively low level of preparatory excitation in the exterior body layers and permits a high degree of excitation of the body interior. This last link in the sequence of ideas is based on the assumption that body-interior response will be dominant unless special excitation patterns are established on the exterior.

It is our intent at this point to formulate our physiological findings within a more systematic framework and to sketch in some detail the mechanisms whereby the boundary attributes find expression in physiological patterns. We may start with the assumption (already intensively discussed) that the degree of definiteness of the body-image boundary is a function of the over-all degree to which definite or indefinite boundaries typify the primary interiorized systems. The greater the number of systems which have definite boundaries, the greater the probability that the body-image boundary will be experienced as definite. It has been fairly clear in what we have said about introjected systems that each really consists of an aggregate of expectancies. This definition of an interiorized system in terms of expectancies is especially explicit in Parsons' work. From the point of view of such a definition, the interiorized mother object would be conceptualized as an aggregate built up of the expectancies that the mother had of the individual in question and also the expectancies that he had of her. The degree of definiteness of the boundary of this internalized system would be thought of as depending upon how definite and noncontradictory were the expectancies on both sides. If the mother were unclear in her expectations, or if her expectations were not meaningful relative to her child's expectancies, this would make for a poorly articulated and vaguely bounded introjection.

Our supposition is that, when the boundary attributes of the primary interiorizations are projected to the body-image boundary, the actual body locus identified with the boundary responds with a pattern of excitation equivalent to the boundary attributes. There are certainly data which indicate that responses in specific body areas may be correlated with psychological variables in this fashion. For example, it has been shown by Wolff (354) and others (165, 207) that if in the course of interviews one activates an individual's fantasies and attitudes about certain important figures in his life, such activation may be habitually linked with physiological responses in given body systems. One may also refer to a wide range of analogous clinical examples. The same pattern may be seen in the individual who develops pains in his stomach whenever his wife is not as supportive as he would like her to be, or in the individual who develops neurodermatitis when he finds himself in a hostile-dependent relationship with older male authority figures.

Little or nothing is known about the train of physiological events that occurs in the sequence from psychological variable to body reaction. One can only assume that the psychological variable is paralleled at another level by physiological patterns which initiate a chain of activation that eventuates in a response in a particular body area. We are suggesting that when the body-image boundary is identified with a body sector, special persistent excitation patterns are established there. How such excitation patterns would be set up and made to persist in various kinds of tissue we do not know. But we would like to offer a model concerning the manner in which excitation patterns that duplicate the body-image boundary attributes might be established in the striate musculature layer.

The model we have chosen is derived in good part from Floyd Allport's analysis (7) of the nature of "set" phenomena. Allport points out that wide areas of response are influenced by the existence of preceding expectancies. He says (p. 209):

> We do not usually perceive "out of the blue." Unless we are startled or confronted with an unexpected situation, there is behind our perceptions, as we go about our daily affairs, a background state of the body musculature that is more or less relevant to the objects we are about to perceive. This condition renders the perception, or for that matter any organized activity toward the object, more rapid and effective.

He conceives of a *set* as a persistent incipient stage of a behavior pattern. It is a readiness to respond in certain directions and is represented by increased excitation in given muscle groups. In describing the development of a set, Allport states (pp. 227–228):

> Some initial stimulus in the recent or more remote past has led *via* the central nervous connections to a motor response, as for

example, in limbs, hands, vocal organs, or the muscles of sensory accommodation. Proprioceptive stimulation in the muscles, tendons, or joints arising from that response starts impulses in afferent neurons leading back to the central nervous system. From there impulses produced or reinforced by this excitation flow out again into the musculature of the same effector organs. The contractions, so produced or reinforced, again set up proprioceptive backlash to the central nervous system—and so on. There is thus a circular process that can maintain itself for indefinite periods of time, that can, in a sense, become *independent* of time, until the internal condition of the organism or the environmental situation, changes.

Allport equates a set, or expectancy system, with a pattern that involves muscular response, proprioceptive feedback to the central nervous system which reinforces the excitation flow to the musculature, and then more proprioceptive feedback, and so forth.

As has been indicated, this model seems especially applicable to the problem of how the body-image boundary sets up patterns of excitation in the striate musculature. The bridge between this model and the body-image model described above is the concept of the *expectancy system.* We have defined the attributes of the body-image boundary in terms of a duplication of the boundary characteristics of internalized expectancy systems. A definite body-image boundary would reflect, then, the influence of many firmly bounded expectancy systems. We are postulating that when a body locus, such as the striate musculature, is identified with the body-image boundary, it becomes a target for stimulation patterns which represent the expectancies projected to the boundary.

One might compare this process to what happens when an individual expects something to happen with which he will have to cope by movement of some body part, such as his arm. The arm then becomes highlighted in his perceptual field and anticipatory excitation of the muscles occurs in preparation for the required movement. The arm becomes representative of the whole anticipatory pattern which has arisen. The body-image boundary is likewise a series of expectancies which, when projected to the striate muscle sheath, highlights the importance of that body sector in the perceptual field (largely unconsciously) and stimulates a pattern of increased muscle excitation that is so characteristic of anticipatory states. It is presumed that the more definite the expectancy systems underlying the body-image boundary, the more intense will be the level of anticipatory activation of the musculature. Apropos of the feedback model suggested by Floyd Allport, one may picture the persistent anticipatory activation of the musculature as eventually resulting in a relatively autonomous higher level of excitation in that body sector. Furthermore, it is supposed that such excitation results in a readiness to react which displaces the body interior from the response primacy we have assumed it to have had.

A word is now in order about the nature of the expectancies which are projected to the body-image boundary. These expectancies have been described as stemming from the kinds of relationships the individual has had with primary figures. As we see it, the individual learns from these relationships what can be expected from life, what problems and dangers there are in the world, and what his own effectiveness is in meeting the problems that confront him. The definiteness of his body-image boundary would be a function of the degree to which it was formed of expectancies that supported his ability to cope with whatever situations might arise. Such expectancies might be exemplified in the following kinds of paraphrased attitudes:

"I am sure that I can solve most important problems."

"I can respond to most people and know that in turn they will not respond in a way that will seriously hurt me."

"I usually am able to complete the things I undertake."

By screening himself with a boundary which consists of expectancies about his ability to make his way effectively as a relatively separate entity, the individual is able to create a world for himself in which it is safe to operate despite periodic wide fluctuations in the immediate situation.

We have described a crude model of how degree of body-image boundary definiteness might get translated into activation patterns in the musculature. But, as earlier indicated, we do not have any concrete ideas about how such translation might occur for the skin or other tissues. One can only note that "readiness to respond" and feedback properties are ascribed by physiologists to a wide range of organ systems. Allport, in a related vein, makes the following comment (7, p. 228):

> Though we have not included vestibular receptors, glandular activities, volumic or humoral changes in the blood system, or other sources of inner stimulation in our hypothesizing of the set and behavior cycle, there is no reason whatever for excluding them. The neurons also have their self-maintaining activities. In fact, the physiologists regard practically all kinds of tissues as having their "tone."

Our frame of reference is based on the idea that any tissue sector is capable to some extent of mirroring the sort of influence associated with the body-image boundary. Indeed, we hypothesize that factors which might lead to the association of the body-image boundary with a new body area would result in a new heightened excitation pattern in that area. Rather dramatic support for this hypothesis is provided by the work of Haber (138) with amputees. He significantly demonstrated that subsequent to amputation of the arm, the stump develops a degree of tactile sensitivity which is greater than that shown by the equivalent area on the other arm that has not suffered amputation. He demonstrated also that this new sensitivity approaches the relatively greater sensitivity usually characteristic of the hand itself. One may interpret these findings to mean that, as the result of the amputation, the body-image boundary in the arm area must be revised and becomes associated with the new limits set by the stump. Consequently, increased reactivity conditions are set up in the stump area which are reflected in an increase in tactile sensitivity; and so the new boundary manifests response characteristics like those of the old boundary.

Aside from such factors as amputation or gross mutilation which might necessitate revision of the body locus of the body-image boundary, another possibility comes to mind. One wonders if a similar sort of revision might not be encountered in the instance of schizophrenics who have been severely regressed for some time, since breakdown of the body-image boundary has been reported as a prominent aspect of such regression. If schizophrenic regression severely disrupts the body image for long periods, might this result in decrement or disappearance of excitation patterns in the body sectors linked with the body-image boundary?

This possibility could be put to the test by obtaining measures of body-exterior physiological reactivity from groups of schizophrenics that had been regressed for varying periods of time and by comparing their reactivity patterns with those of normal subjects and with each other. Support for the proposition would be indicated if it were found that the schizophrenics showed less reactivity in the exterior body layers (and more interior reactivity?) than did the normal individuals. It would be even more specifically supported if it were demonstrated that schizophrenics of longest duration manifested a smaller amount of exterior layer reactivity than schizophrenics of lesser duration.

The fact that a relationship has been significantly demonstrated to exist between body-image boundary definiteness and a pattern of physiological response (exterior reactivity versus interior reactivity) becomes a matter of generalized import if one accepts the view that the body-image boundary mirrors the properties of introjection systems. It means that a physiological pattern has been identified that duplicates the properties of a psychological system which has evolved out of certain specific socialization experiences. One then begins to wonder whether or not there may be other physiological response patterns which duplicate socialization patterns in our culture to a degree more highly specific than we have supposed possible.

The work of Funkenstein and King (117A) points in the same direction since it establishes a link between the way in which individuals have learned to channel their anger and the predominance of either adrenaline or noradrenaline reactivity patterns. Perhaps attempts should be made to find physiological patterns which duplicate such personality differentials as good versus poor ability to get along with authority figures, rigid versus nonrigid modes of relating to people, and simple versus complex [Barron (15)] ways of organizing experience. The results of our work indicate that an approach to physiological response at this level of conceptualization is entirely possible.

APPLICATION OF BOUNDARY CONCEPTS TO GROUP BEHAVIOR

We have theorized at some length about the relationship of boundary attributes to various aspects of individual behavior. In the interests of sketching a wider and more complete theoretical picture, it would seem helpful to speculate a bit about the relationship of boundary characteristics to group behavior. Sources of materials for such speculation are two-fold: (1) findings which were earlier cited concerning the behavior of small groups saturated with high Barrier versus low Barrier individuals; (2) findings concerning the behavior of individual high and low Barrier persons in group settings.

We may preface this discussion by indicating that it is our impression that unless the individual develops body-image boundaries of a certain minimum degree of definiteness, his relationships with people are somewhat restricted to attempts to duplicate patterns experienced in his association with such primary figures as mother and father. Without the security of a moderately definite boundary, the individual feels highly open and vulnerable to the dangers he perceives about him. Therefore he tries to establish contacts which will provide supplementary boundaries in the same manner that his contacts with the parental figures did. He seeks to relate to people in such a way that they will be screens between himself and the outside and will cushion the trauma of unexpected occurrences. This is, of course, the pattern typical of the parent-child prototype. It is probably only when the individual has the security that goes with definite boundaries that he feels free to look for relationships in which his aim is not primarily to find protection. With such security he may expand his goals to include contacts in which he actively offers things to others and establishes a reciprocal give-and-take pattern. The emphasis is then put less on being shielded and more on mutual stimulation and exchange.

Our formulations concerning the behavior of groups are meant to apply only to groups in which a considerable level of saturation of high or low Barrier persons has occurred. It is our premise that once a group has attained a certain saturation in this respect, a number of dimensions of its behavior become predictable. At present we have no data concerning the degree of saturation which must occur in different types of groups before they begin to show high Barrier or low Barrier consistencies. We hypothesize, however, that certain types of groups tend to attract a large proportion of indefinite-boundary persons and that other types are selectively interesting to definite boundary persons. Tendencies of this sort might fairly rapidly lead to high saturation with one of the categories of individuals as contrasted to the other category.

The idea that groups vary in their attractiveness to high and low Barrier persons is derived from the point of view that when groups are organized they differ in the extent to which they are implicitly intended to supplement the body-image boundaries of their members. Probably it is true that almost all groups serve to some extent as a bolstering screen between the individual and the "outside." The organization of the group, its rules and slogans, and its definitions of situations supply its members with a demarcated sector within which many stable expectancies can be established. During the time that an individual is embedded in a group, he is likely to be less dependent on his own body-image boundaries for reassurance that the world has a necessary minimum of limitation or predictability about it.

Despite the general boundary-demarcating function of most groups, however, one may distinguish sharp differences in how far they are dedicated to such a function. One may cite the following as examples of those probably providing high boundary support: a monastery community, the patient group living on a tuberculosis ward, many kinds of army groups, and certain types of political organizations. At the other extreme one would include such groups as those intended to train individuals for roles involving a great deal of individual initiative and those designed to act as a setting for intense individual competition. Our assumption is that persons with indefinite boundaries would seek out the boundary-supporting groups and that the definite-boundary persons would tend to be attracted to the less boundary-supportive groups. We would postulate further that, as the saturation of low Barrier persons mounted in a group which was attractive to them, an increasingly larger proportion of the group's time and energy would be directed into boundary-defining activities.

Let us now systematically review some hypotheses concerning the development and patterning of groups highly saturated with individuals belonging to one or the other of the boundary categories. Our first hypothesis is that, when groups are initially in the process of formation, the high Barrier group will establish a structure permitting its members to work together effectively more quickly than the low Barrier group. We noted that, when a number of high Barrier persons are asked to form a group for some purpose, they quickly create an informal organization that allows joint action. When the same request is made of low Barrier persons, however, they show more hesitancy about committing themselves to the group and find it necessary to spend a rather long period in working out the procedures whereby the group will function. They spend relatively much time in setting up hierarchies and rules before they are sufficiently integrated to act as a unit in pursuit of some goal. One wonders whether this difference may not reflect the contrasting importance that high and low Barrier persons attach to the formation of the group. The low Barrier person is probably inclined to view his participation in a new group in terms of what it will contribute to the serious project of bolstering his boundaries. He therefore does not want to commit himself too quickly to group relationships which he sees as having potentially great import. We assume the high Barrier individual views his immediate participation in a new group as of less basic import. He probably feels freer to enter into immediate working arrangements with other group members because he knows he can rather quickly withdraw without much resultant anxiety if he does not find the situation congruent with his own goals.

Still further, we suggest that once the preliminary stages of the formation of a new group have occurred, low Barrier groups tend to set up organizational structures which are more hierarchical and rigid than those found in high Barrier groups. This idea is supported by our observations that low Barrier groups are likely to be dominated by one or two persons who are set apart in a superior hierarchical category in so far as they are supposed to take the lead in devising rules and procedures for the others to follow. In high Barrier groups we have observed a more equalitarian pattern with most of the members participating in decision making and not waiting to be told what to do. The low Barrier group seems to become dedicated to maintaining a rigid constancy within its borders. One would conjecture that, as part of this need for constancy, the low Barrier group builds heavy barricadelike boundaries about itself. That is, it seeks to limit as far as possible the intrusion of outside influences which might disturb the constancy of the established group expectancies that serve to supplement individual body-image boundaries. Efforts to limit outside intrusion might take such forms as emphasizing the difference between those in the out-group and those in the in-group, admitting to the group only persons willing to promise conformance to a detailed code, and limiting interaction with other groups.

It would be anticipated that the greater the stresses in a situation which threaten a group's cohesion and its boundary-supplementing value, the greater would be the relative difference between the behavior of the high and low Barrier groups. The low Barrier group would be considered more vulnerable to stress, and more likely under stress to seek stabilization through a steeply accelerated tendency toward isolation and restricting proscriptions. We speculate that when a low Barrier group has found such stabilization methods inadequate to deal with disrupting stresses, it would be particularly inclined to convert surrounding areas into unrealistically controlled boundary regions. This unrealistic transformation of bordering sectors would be analogous to the behavior of the schizophrenic who substitutes delusionally controlled environs for his inadequate body-image boundary. Thus the low Barrier group might attempt to control its environs by such methods as making magical assumptions about neighboring groups or by attempting irrationally to incorporate these groups and imposing new detailed codes of conduct upon them.

It strikes us that a group which has unusual body-image boundary-supplementing functions would create an atmosphere tending to maximize the boundary indefiniteness of its separate members. The atmosphere of the group would discourage its members from building individual boundaries. A person growing up in this sort of group would be pressured to trust in the boundary implicit in the total group structure rather than to maximize the boundary identified with his own body limits. Conceivably, over a period of time, this process could result in a great decline in the body-image boundary definiteness of the average member of the group. One would suspect that a critical point might be reached when the average degree of individual boundary definiteness would fall below a certain level. At this critical point the anxiety of the group members would become too great to be cushioned and contained by the group's over-all mode of organization. The result would be the disintegration of the group; and the individual members would be forced to search for new groups in which to participate that could provide the necessary boundary-supplementing conditions.

An interesting parenthetical question that comes to mind is whether there is an ideal ratio of high Barrier to low Barrier individuals which maximizes group efficiency. A more meaningful way of phrasing this question is, "What are the ideal ratios for maximizing efficiency in given types of situations?" The ideal ratio for an Army unit or a factory work unit might be quite different from that for a team of researchers or a legislative body.

As earlier indicated, we have some data which suggest that high Barrier people tend not to work well in an authoritarian atmosphere such as is found in many Army units. An Army unit saturated with high Barrier persons might prove to be relatively balky and so demonstratively independent as to interfere with Army operational procedures. But a legislative body saturated with high Barrier people might provide a maximum number of sources of forcefully expressed ideas which would establish a basis for the formulation of policies. It is possible, of course, that, even in such a group, the saturation of high Barrier persons could become so high as to interfere with certain levels of functioning. At present one can only speculate about such points; but the potential payoff for research in this area seems good.

MISCELLANEOUS COMMENTS

We consider that our work has established for body-image concepts a more substantial place in personality theory. It is paradoxically true that we have almost taken the "body" out of "body image" by postulating that the body-image boundary does not really mirror the actual properties of the body surface, but that it is rather a representation of attitudes and expectancy systems which have been projected onto the body periphery. The fact remains, however, that some of our best predictive studies (e.g., psychosomatic and physiological) grew out of our assumption that the Barrier score could be conceptualized as indicating the degree to which the individual assigned certain attributes to his body.

Although we regard the Barrier score as having little to do with the actual physical appearance of the individual's body, we do regard it as a measure of important properties associated with the body as a social object. We consider the Barrier score to be supplying information about how the individual experiences a body region in terms of the attributes which have been assigned to it by the projection of interiorized expectancies. Within our frame of reference, body image is most meaningfully viewed at a level which takes off from the fact that the body has a special position in the perceptual field in so far as it is both a perceptual object and also intimately close to the central personality systems. We have assumed that it is this position of the body, intermediate between "outside" and "inside," which makes it a unique projection screen for patterns of attitudes; and we have concluded that the body image is formed of these projected attitudes.

An approach to body image in this manner does not, of course, rule out other levels of definition. For example, one might define body image in terms of the individual's verbal description of how he sees himself in the mirror. One could offer definitions which differed widely in the extent to which they equated body image with the individual's reaction to his actual physical appearance. Definitions might vary also with respect to the degree that an individual's body image would be equated with conscious feelings and attitudes as contrasted to more unconscious attitudes. Of course, any personality phenomenon may be defined at different levels; and indeed most have been. This obvious point is mentioned because one gets the impression that many researchers in the field of body image have tended to lose sight of the relativity of definition and have fretted because everyone will not agree on one that is uniform. In any case, the approach we have taken to body image and the results obtained from this approach indicate that there is an important place for body-image constructs in personality theory. It has been shown that the body-image boundary is a guiding reference point which continually influences the individual's orientation to the behavioral space about him.

The value of a line of research investigation lies not only in the immediate results it uncovers but also in the new kinds of problems it opens for study. Looking back over our work, we can see three such problem areas which have inviting possibilities.

(1) First of all, there is the question of how boundary-setting behavior in general is related to body-image boundary definiteness. It would seem profitable to construct various kinds of situations in which the individual's ways of establishing boundaries could be studied. One could observe such phenomena as the limits placed on autokinetic movement, the nature of the boundaries between categories developed in the course of conceptual sorting tasks, the degree to which fusion of contiguous figures occurs in an unstable field, and the characteristics of the borders erected in free-play construction scenes. Data derived from observations of this sort would indicate whether there are relationships between the body-image boundary variable and boundary-defining behavior as it is shown in specific areas and perhaps also as it might be conceived at a broad stylistic level that goes beyond specific areas (if there be such). A line of investigation of this sort might uncover a significant new organizational factor which is a function of the body-image boundary.

(2) As has been suggested at other points in the book, there appears to be a rich potential in pursuing a number of the physiological leads which have emerged. One would like to have answers to some of the following questions pertaining to the relationship of boundary definiteness to physiological reactivity:

a. At what age do individuals begin to show tendencies toward dominance of body-exterior reactivity over body-interior reactivity? Are there sex differences in this respect and are they correlated with sex differences in Barrier score?

b. Do conditions (e.g., schizophrenic regression) which produce disruption in body-image boundaries result in changes in the ratio of body-exterior reactivity to interior reactivity? If so, is the ratio restored when an individual recovers and is able to reintegrate himself?

c. What is the relationship between the degree to which one shows relatively high reactivity in the body-exterior versus the body-interior and the degree to which one is likely to develop psychosomatic symptoms at one or the other of these body sites?

d. How stable, over a range of situations, is the body-exterior versus body-interior difference in reactivity manifested by the average individual? Does it vary under conditions of high fatigue? Does it change under the influence of various drugs? Can it be distorted by hypnotic suggestion?

(3) A third area of research we should like to propose has to do with group behavior. We should be inclined to seek closure on such questions as the following:

a. To what degree must various types of groups be saturated with high or low Barrier individuals before they begin to behave in certain predictable directions?

b. Are there characteristic interaction patterns that appear when a high Barrier group is thrown into close proximity with a low Barrier group, or when two high Barrier groups make contact, or when two low Barrier groups become involved with each other?

c. Do stress conditions have more disorganizing effects on low Barrier groups than upon high Barrier groups? Are high Barrier groups more sensitive to certain kinds of stress than are low Barrier groups?

d. How do individual high Barrier or low Barrier persons behave when they find themselves part of a group consisting entirely of persons who have boundary characteristics quite opposite from their own?

The research possibilities that present themselves are truly varied and full of promise.

....

CHAPTER FIFTEEN

Reappraisal: A Review of
Developments from 1958 to 1967

THIS SUPPLEMENTARY chapter was written for the present edition of the book in order to review research developments pertinent to the Barrier score which have occurred since 1958.

Subsequent to the original publication of this book, a considerable literature was generated which sought to investigate the various hypotheses and formulations presented. Over twenty-five dissertations and a large number of research papers have appeared since 1958 which concern themselves with the Barrier score and related boundary phenomena. The question arises as to how the Barrier score has fared. To what degree have subsequent studies supported or not supported the original findings? The purpose of this new supplementary chapter is to present an overview of the principal trends to be found in publications dealing with the Barrier score from 1958 to 1967. Because the volume of the material involved is so great it will be necessary to focus upon highlights and major developments. A series of circumscribed topical areas will be considered.

THE SOURCE OF THE BARRIER RESPONSE

In 1958 various tentative kinds of evidence were available that the Barrier score reflects a pattern of body experience relating to differential prominence of exterior versus interior body sensations. But the evidence was circumstantial and there was puzzlement over the apparent fact that inkblot images could contain information about body experiences. Since that time several studies have been completed which give greater substance to the equation of the Barrier image with a specific dimension of body experience based upon the differential sensory vividness of boundary and nonboundary body sectors.

Fisher and Fisher (1964)* instituted a major effort, based on several

---

* The references cited in this section are presented in a separate bibliography beginning on page 433.

approaches, to demonstrate that the Barrier score is meaningfully related to actual body experiences. In a first group of studies they sought to test the proposition that the Barrier score would be positively correlated with a greater density of sensations from the boundary than nonboundary regions of one's body. They considered two samples of subjects ($N = 64$, $N = 51$) who were asked to report body sensations that occurred in two outer (skin, muscle) and two inner (heart, stomach) body sites during a five-minute period. In both samples the Barrier score was, as predicted, positively and significantly correlated with the excess of exterior over interior sensations reported. Two further samples ($N = 79, N = 20$) were also evaluated in which the Barrier score was related to the number of exterior minus the number of interior sensations reported in retrospective recall of a variety of emotional states (e.g., "When you are angry"; "When you are afraid"). Significant trends were found in both samples that the individual with definite boundaries is more inclined than the individual with vague boundaries to recall past emotional states as involving a higher proportion of exterior than interior body sensations.

In another phase of these studies the hypothesis was considered that the Barrier score would be positively related to the excess of exterior over interior "symptoms" or sensations experienced by individuals who swallowed a placebo which was presented as a "harmless" drug capable of affecting one's body in multiple ways. A sample consisting of forty-six men and seventy-two women was studied. The hypothesis was significantly supported in the male group but not in the female group.

A fourth aspect of the Fisher and Fisher project was based on the assumption that if selective perception of exterior versus interior body sensations chronically occurs, there will be an equivalent selectivity in one's recall of a series of verbal references to exterior and interior body sensations which had been learned. That is, a persisting contrast in an individual's pattern of exterior and interior sensory experiences could conceivably function as a paradigm influencing him to focus his attention differentially upon, and to assign differential importance to, verbal references to exterior and interior body sensations which were presented to him in the course of a learning task. Congruent with this expectation, it was found in two samples ($N = 48, N = 46$) that the Barrier score was positively and significantly correlated with the tendency to recall more words depicting exterior sensations (e.g., "muscle stiff," "skin cold") than interior sensations (e.g., "stomach pain," "heart beat") which had been previously learned from a list containing ten exterior and ten interior sensation phrases. The over-all results of the Fisher and Fisher studies indicated a spectrum of inter-relations between the Barrier score and body-experience variables. Boundary definiteness was meaningfully linked with present and retrospective reports of exterior versus interior body experiences; to a partial extent with the exterior versus interior pattern of "symptoms" induced by ingesting a placebo; and with selective memory for phrases depicting exterior versus interior sensations.

Cassell (1966) provided additional pertinent information by considering the relationship of the Barrier score to selective response to pictures of exterior and interior body regions presented tachistoscopically. He predicted that the more definite an individual's boundaries the more quickly he would recognize pictures of exterior sites (e.g., finger, forehead) and the less quickly he would recognize interior regions (e.g., heart, stomach). In a sample of 104 men and women the Barrier score was positively correlated with speed of perception of the exterior body areas. It was noted that men perceived internal organs at a significantly faster speed than women; and so the relation of this variable to Barrier was analyzed separately for each sex. With respect to the males, Barrier was significantly and negatively correlated, as predicted, with speed of perception of internal organs. But in the female group the results were of a chance order. Except for this result, the general tenor of the data indicated that the Barrier score could predict differential perceptual sensitivity to pictures of exterior and interior body sites.

The most direct attempt to appraise the body-experience context of the Barrier score is represented in the work of Fisher and Renik (1966), who reasoned that if the ratio of exterior to interior body sensations shapes the probability of producing a Barrier image, it should be possible to alter this probability by experimentally manipulating exterior versus interior awareness. A design was developed involving three groups of female subjects. One group (N = 20) was administered twenty-five cards of Form B of the Holtzman ink blots; subjected to fifteen minutes of body-concentration exercises designed to focus their attention upon their skin and muscle; and finally asked to respond to twenty-five cards of Form A of the Holtzman blots. A second group (N = 21) went through the same procedure, except that the body-concentration exercises were designed to focus attention upon interior sectors like the heart and stomach. A third group (N = 20) which served as a control had the same test-retest paradigm, but body-concentration exercises were replaced by a fifteen-minute interview about various preferences and experiences not referring to one's body. It was, of course, expected that the experimental condition involving a focus upon skin and muscle would increase Barrier; that the condition involving a focus upon body interior would decrease Barrier; and that the control situation would not alter it. The findings indicated that the exterior-focus group increased Barrier to a significantly greater extent than the interior-focus or control groups. While the interior-focus group showed a small decrease in Barrier, it was not significantly different from the change observed for the controls. The basic results indicated that a measurable change in Barrier responses could be induced by redirecting an individual's attention to specific body areas.

In a second study involving men ($N = 15$, $N = 15$, $N = 15$) and based on the same experimental design, Fisher and Renik° were able to duplicate the above findings.

It is apparent that body sensations and experiences do become incorporated into the projective images which are scored for Barrier qualities. Somehow, the projective image is sensitive to, and reflects, the relative prominence of exterior and interior body sensations. Indeed Fisher (1965) has generalized this proposition by showing that other kinds of body sensations find representation in projective responses. Thus, he reported that in two samples ($N = 102$, $N = 93$) the number of ink-blot responses with oral connotations which were produced correlated positively with degree of awareness of one's stomach. It was presumed that stomach awareness intruded into the process of constructing imaginative responses and stimulated the formation of oral images.

PSYCHOPHYSIOLOGICAL PATTERNS

Because the notion of the Barrier score evolved from observations of patients with body symptoms, it has been closely identified with certain psychophysiological concepts. On the basis of such observations, it had been originally proposed that those with definite boundaries would manifest greater physiological activation (or psychosomatic symptomatology) in outer than inner body sectors; whereas the obverse pattern was thought to hold true for those with indefinite boundaries. Several studies had, as of 1958, offered promising results in support of this model (e.g., Davis, 1960); but the findings were exploratory and not cross-validated in depth. Since 1958 there have been multiple publications concerned with testing aspects of the model. They will be briefly reviewed below.

Cleveland and Fisher (1960) and Fisher and Cleveland (1960) reported a replication of the original differences they observed in Barrier and Penetration scores between patients with rheumatoid arthritis and patients with stomach ulcers. Arthritics ($N = 26$) exceeded patients with stomach ulcers ($N = 34$) in Barrier responses and in turn were exceeded by them in Penetration responses. It was also found that the arthritics were characterized by a significantly lower heart rate (interior reactivity) and higher number of GSR responses (exterior reactivity) than the ulcer patients under stress conditions.

Williams (1962) evaluated arthritic ($N = 20$) and ulcer patients ($N = 20$) and reaffirmed that the former had higher Barrier and lower

---

° Unpublished data.

Penetration scores than the latter. In addition, he found significant trends for heart rate to be higher, and muscle potential lower, in ulcer as compared to arthritic patients under certain conditions. However, predicted differences in GSR were not observed.

Cleveland, Snyder, and Williams (1965) reported that a group of male rheumatoid arthritics (N = 18) had significantly higher Barrier and lower Penetration scores than a group of twenty male patients with ulcerative colitis or peptic ulcer. Similarly, they found in a second sample that male arthritics (N = 20) had significantly higher Barrier and lower Penetration scores than twenty males with peptic ulcers.

Schultz (1966) evaluated the differences in boundary attributes between twenty male patients with eczematoid dermatitis (outer symptom) and twenty males with duodenal ulcers. As predicted, the dermatitis group had significantly higher Barrier and lower Penetration scores than the ulcer group.

Cleveland, Reitman, and Brewer (1965) were able to detect significantly higher Barrier scores in a sample of thirty juvenile rheumatoid arthritics than in a sample of asthmatic children. Penetration differences were not significant.

Fitzgerald (1961) investigated children with Legg-Calve-Perthes (LCP) disease. This "disease," whose cause is unknown, results in damage to the hip joint which is perhaps analogous to some phenomena encountered in rheumatoid arthritis. Fitzgerald examined LCP from the perspective of the body-image boundary theory. He compared twenty children with LCP to fifteen controls. As hypothesized, the LCP children proved to have significantly higher boundary definiteness than the controls. Also, the LCP subjects as compared to the control subjects were significantly more motorically expressive and displayed relatively greater skill in performance than verbal tests (WISC).

There have been two studies to date which have failed to replicate the boundary distinction between patients with exterior as opposed to interior symptoms. First may be mentioned the work of Sherick (1964) who compared twenty-one male arthritics and twenty-one male patients with peptic ulcer symptoms and found no boundary differences. But one learns the following upon close scrutiny of this work: many of the ulcer patients were taking a tranquilizer; some of them were subsequently found not to have definite ulcer pathology; and many had been selected by means of a volunteering process differing from that used to select the arthritics. Since Cleveland (1960) has shown that tranquilizing medication may strengthen the boundary in disturbed patients, one can on this basis alone consider the experimental design employed by Sherick as faulty and inappropriate for making a fair test of the hypothesis. A second study failing to replicate was completed by Eigenbrode and Shipman (1960). They extracted from their clinical files the Rorschach protocols of fifty-four patients with "psychosomatic skin disorders" and twenty-five patients with internal disorders (e.g., stomach ulcer, genito-urinary disease). Their scorings for Barrier and Penetration revealed only chance differences between the two groups. One of the factors which may have contributed to this result is that there were included in the internal category a variety of symptoms (e.g., genito-urinary) which had not been conceptualized as internal in any previous studies.

In any case, it is a matter of interest that in a later, much more carefully controlled project Shipman, et al. (1964) found clear support for the exterior-interior reactivity model. They conducted a study of muscle tension, heart rate, and blood pressure in a group of patients ($N = 15$) hospitalized for depressive symptoms. Muscle potential was recorded simultaneously from seven different sites. Among a large number of psychological measures, the Barrier score was the best predictor of muscle-potential level. As anticipated by the exterior-interior model, not only was it significantly and positively correlated with muscle activation, but also negatively so with heart rate.

One of the most careful and decisive examinations of the exterior-interior reactivity issue has been presented by Armstrong (1964). He predicted that the Barrier score would be differentially related to conditionability of exterior versus interior autonomic responses. Choosing GSR as an exterior response and heart rate as an interior one, he designed a study in which normal subjects, consisting of an extreme high ($N = 20$) and an extreme low ($N = 20$) Barrier group, were conditioned to heart rate and GSR responses simultaneously by means of a partial reinforcement procedure. A shock which was the unconditioned stimulus was paired with a tone which was the conditioned stimulus. The high Barrier subjects evidenced significantly higher levels of GSR conditioning than the low Barrier subjects; but the obverse was found for heart rate conditioning. Interestingly, Armstrong discovered that it was difficult to produce any heart rate conditioning at all in the high Barrier group. A difference in outer versus inner reactivity related to boundary definiteness emerged sharply from the data.

Fisher (1959) appraised GSR and heart rate response with reference to Barrier in a group ($N = 30$) of adolescent girls. Recordings were secured during rest and stress. Barrier was significantly and positively correlated with GSR frequency and negatively so with heart rate during stress. During rest only a borderline positive correlation between Barrier and GSR frequency appeared.

In a sample of college girls ($N = 24$) Zimny (1965) was able to demonstrate that those in the highest one-third and those in the lowest one-third of the Barrier distribution differed significantly in skin resistance and heart rate in the directions required by the exterior-interior concept.

Cassell and Fisher (1963) predicted that degree of response to histamine introduced into the skin would be a function of Barrier. The skin, as a part of the body boundary, was expected to be more reactive in those with well-articulated than in those with vague boundaries. Skin reactivity was measured in terms of the redness and size of the wheal formation produced by the histamine. In a female sample (N = 45) the major hypothesis was supported, but not in a male sample (N = 55).

Malev (1961) extended the exploration of the exterior-interior hypothesis to normal children. His design involved thirty male six-year-old and thirty male eight-year-old subjects. The subjects' mothers were interviewed to ascertain the frequency with which each subject had been characterized by exterior versus interior symptoms. In addition, GSR, heart rate, and blood pressure were recorded from the subjects under conditions of rest and stress. The data indicated that at both ages six and eight the greater the boundary definiteness of the subjects the more likely they were to manifest a significant predominance of exterior over interior symptoms. Analysis of the physiological data demonstrated that in the six-year-old group heart rate was significantly negatively related to boundary definiteness, but GSR bore only a chance relationship to it. In the eight-year-old group, all the physiological measures proved to be positively correlated with boundary definiteness. This pattern differs from that characterizing adults; and it led Malev to question whether the physiological correlates of boundary definiteness may not systematically differ at certain age levels from those found in adults. However, he did point out further that the symptom patterns reported by mothers in both six- and eight-year-olds are correlated with the Barrier and Penetration scores in the same directions as they have been found to be in adults. He speculated on this basis that symptom reports by mothers about their children may be better indicators of long-term autonomic patterning than brief samples of physiological reactivity obtained in artificial laboratory situations.

It is also appropriate as part of this summary to point out the striking analogue between the exterior-interior model and a formulation advanced by Lacey which identifies environmental receptivity-nonreceptivity with specific physiological patterns. Lacey states (in Rubinstein and Parloff, 1959, p. 205):

> that skin conductance increase is excitatory, whereas increase of cardiac rate is inhibitory of . . . transaction of the organism with the environment. The pattern of response obtained when recording skin resistance and heart rate may reveal occasions when the individual is "open" to his environment and ready react to it, or conversely, when the individual is not "open" and indeed, instrumentally "rejects" the environment.

Lacey suggested on the basis of a review of experiments by Darrow (1929), Davis (1957), and Lacey (in Rubinstein and Parloff, 1959) that an attitude of being open and receptive to the world is accompanied by increased skin conductance and deceleration in heart rate, with the converse pattern typical of a closed unreceptive orientation. This formulation is obviously analogous to the inside-outside model which proposes contrasting levels of skin conductance and heart rate as boundary definiteness varies. Indeed, the analogy becomes even more precise if one considers that the definite boundary person (characterized by tendencies to high skin conductance and low heart rate) has already been found to be more "open" and less defensive in dealing with the environment than the indefinite boundary person.

Surveying the findings since 1958, one can say that the formulations regarding Barrier and exterior-interior reactivity have fared well. With minor exceptions, all studies employing physiological measurements have been congruent with expectation. This has been true in male and female groups, in patients with psychosomatic symptoms, in normal subjects, and in both adolescent and adult samples. Studies relying entirely on symptomatological indices have also conformed well to prediction. Two exceptions [viz., Sherick (1964) and Eigenbrode and Shipman (1960)] presenting negative evidence have been cited, but at least one of these is seriously defective in its experimental design.

RESPONSE TO STRESS

There was originally moderate documentation for the fact that a clearly articulated boundary permits an individual to deal efficiently with stress. Presumably, such a boundary provides one with a feeling of operating from a protected base and also indicates the possession of achievement and goal oriented traits and motivations—all of which would facilitate mastery of difficulty. The Barrier score seemed to be particularly able to predict an individual's ability to adjust to the serious disablement of his own body. For example, adequacy of adjustment to polio disablement and also amputation were positively linked with Barrier. Several studies since 1958 have been corroborative of such findings. Landau (1960) studied forty paraplegic men who had sustained traumatic spinal cord injuries. Ratings of these paraplegics by hospital personnel and also their responses to a sentence completion test were used as criteria of how well they had adjusted to their disablement. The Barrier and Penetration scores (as well as the Secord Homonym Test of Body Concern and Secord-Jourard Body Cathexis Test) were evaluated to determine their predictive efficiency with respect to the adjustment criteria. It was found that the higher the Barrier score the better the adjustment of the patient as defined by the rating measure and the sentence completion technique. The Penetration score had only a chance relationship to the criteria. The Homonym Test also tended to predict response to paraplegia, but less consistently than the Barrier score and at a lower level of significance. No association appeared between the Secord-Jourard Body Cathexis Test and the criteria. Incidentally, it was noted by Landau that the Barrier score was not related to the duration of time the patient has been disabled. This is congruent with previous studies already cited in which the Barrier score seemed not to be influenced either by the amount or duration of damage sustained by the body. It is pertinent too that Fisher (1959) has been able to show that the decline in appearance and physique accompanying advanced aging does not result in a decrease in Barrier responses.

Sieracki (1963) provided additional evidence of the ability of the Barrier score to predict adjustment to body disablement. His work embraced a group of men (N = 50), half of whom had sustained serious visible disabilities (e.g., amputation, paraplegia) and the other half nonvisible difficulties (e.g., rheumatic heart fever, tuberculosis). A variety of techniques (e.g., ratings, sentence completions) were used to determine how well each patient was able to accept and live with his disability. In both subgroups it was established that degree of acceptance of disability was positively and significantly correlated with Barrier. Once again, no relation was noted between Barrier and duration of illness.

A parallel problem involving anxiety about body mutilation was approached by Cormack (1966) in an unusual fashion. He made use of Wittreich's (1955) original observation that when one views objects through aniseikonic lenses, those which are most threatening are experienced as least distorted. For example, an amputee whose injury is presumably threatening to an observer was perceived through the lenses as less distorted than a normal non-mutilated person. Cormack investigated in a sample of men (N = 20) the relationship between Barrier and the amount of anxiety generated by viewing a life size mannikin with obvious mutilations. Anxiety was measured by comparing the power of lens required to produce a noticeable aniseikonically related alteration in the appearance of the mutilated mannikin with the lens power needed to produce such an alteration in a nonmutilated mannikin. A predicted negative correlation was found between Barrier and amount of anxiety revealed by the aniseikonic lens procedure. This relationship was detected by cubing each subject's Barrier score and plotting it against the threat criterion. It took the form of a hyperbola. Those with extreme low Barrier scores were highly threatened by the mutilation, but with increasing size of Barrier the threat rapidly diminished.

McConnell and Daston (1961) considered the responses of twenty-eight women to the stress occasioned by their own pregnancies. Subjects were seen twice, first during the eighth or ninth month of pregnancy and again three days after delivery. On the first occasion the subject was given the Rorschach; the Osgood Semantic Differential which consisted of seventeen pairs of adjectives (e.g., beautiful . . . ugly, hard . . . soft) to be applied to her own body; and an interview focused on how positively or negatively she experienced the pregnancy. On the second occasion only the Rorschach and the Osgood Semantic Differential were repeated. The favorableness with which subjects viewed their pregnancies turned out to be positively linked with their Barrier scores. Interestingly, it was also established that while the Barrier score did not shift from the first to the second testing, the Penetration score declined significantly during the same interval.

The decline in the Penetration score was interpreted as indicating that women feel considerable anxiety about the vulnerability of their bodies while they are pregnant, especially with reference to the literal penetration of its boundaries that occurs at the time of delivery, but that such body anxiety declines once the delivery experience has been successfully achieved. The fact that the Barrier score did not change was considered by McConnell and Daston to be congruent with past findings that it is relatively independent of actual alterations in the body itself. No correlations were found between the body-boundary scores and the Osgood scores (Evaluative, Potency, and Activity factors).

Pertinent to these pregnancy findings, insofar as they concern variables having to do with reproductive functions, are two other studies. Osofsky and Fisher (in press) used the Barrier score to predict the development of amenorrhea in a group of girls ($N = 66$) who had been subjected to the stress of leaving home and entering the freshman class of a nursing school. Each subject maintained a "menstrual calendar" for the first four months of school, and the Barrier score which was obtained at the outset of the school year was found to be negatively and significantly correlated with several indices indicating later delay or irregularity in menstrual functioning. Fisher and Bialos[*] obtained physicians' ratings of the amount of anxiety manifested by a sample of women ($N = 49$) while participating in a gynecological examination, which often has a stressful and embarrassing impact. Those with definite boundaries were rated as significantly less anxious than those with indefinite boundaries.

In earlier studies the Barrier score had also demonstrated itself to be positively correlated with the ability of normal subjects to tolerate stress when performing such tasks as mirror drawing and attempting to hold a rod steady under frustrating conditions. Relatedly, Brodie (1959) evaluated the Barrier score, among a variety of other measures (e.g., TAT puni-

---

[*] Unpublished study.

tiveness, authoritarianism, need achievement), as a predictor of response to two stress situations (delayed auditory feedback, holding a rod steady while being shocked). The response to stress was examined primarily in terms of the following dimensions which were judged from the subject's spontaneous behavior and recorded verbalizations as he performed the tasks: self-blame vs. blame of others for failure; emotional expressivity; aggressiveness vs. passivity; and tenacity in persevering at task goals. Brodie considered these dimensions to be rough and exploratory in nature. Thirty men and thirty women were studied. The Barrier score proved to be significantly linked with a number of the criteria measures, but the pattern of relationship was often inconsistent and difficult to interpret. It was negatively correlated (0.5 level in men and .07 level in total group) with emotional expressivity under stress. High Barrier subjects clustered at the end of the expressive continuum defined as "controlled" and "guarded," whereas low Barrier subjects were at the other extreme depicted as "impulsive" or "uninhibited." In relation to a second dimension, high Barrier subjects were inclined to be described as "unhappy" and "whining," with low Barrier subjects portrayed as "angry" and "assertive" (.02 level in men and .01 level in total group). High Barrier women tended to be more tenacious in completing the hand steadiness task under stress than low Barrier women (.08 level). High Barrier subjects rated the stress situations as more stressful than did the low barrier subjects (.05 level), but also evidenced a greater decline in the subjective sense of stress from the first stress task to the second (.05 level). These findings cannot readily be organized into a meaningful pattern. On the one hand, high Barrier subjects appear as more "unhappy" and "whining" and more concerned about the stressfulness of the experimental situation than the low Barrier subjects; but on the other hand they manifest a greater decline in anxiety during the total session; and in the female group they tend to stick more tenaciously to the assigned task. Finally, it is difficult to know where to classify the fact that the high Barrier subjects were more guarded and less impulsive than the low Barrier subjects. Clearly the Barrier score was related to a number of aspects of the subject's stress behavior. However, one cannot easily define what the data signify with respect to the stress tolerance of well and poorly bounded individuals. They are more descriptive of modes of emotional expression than of effectiveness of response in relationship to task goals.

Several other aspects of stress response have been appraised with respect to boundary definiteness. Shipman (1965), working with a neurotic sample (N = 40), discovered that the Barrier score was positively and significantly correlated with level of performance on the Stroop Color Naming Test, which is a measure of ability to maintain cognitive efficiency in the face of an intense distraction. Schultz (1966) found a more complex pattern of results when he determined the relationship in a sample of men ($N = 40$) between Barrier and efficiency in performing a Scrambled Words Test under two degrees of stress. Low Barrier subjects performed better than high Barrier subjects under slight stress, but the opposite held true for high stress. A third study by Nichols and Tursky (in press) predicted that the ability to tolerate stressful pain would be positively related to boundary definiteness. Thirty males were exposed to electric shocks of various intensities and were asked to judge when they became "uncomfortable" and "painful." Tolerance for shock was significantly correlated with Barrier in the predicted direction.

The findings outlined in this section indicate that Barrier is an excellent predictor of ability to cope with actual or threatened damage of one's body. Data presented by Landau (1960) and Sieracki (1963) are particularly convincing in this respect. There is also increasing reinforcement for the view that a clearly articulated boundary provides an advantage in dealing with stresses which are not a derivative of damage to one's body. But more work is needed not only to find more decisive support but also to clarify possible complexities related to the intensity of the stress, such as noted in the Schultz (1966) findings.

SOCIAL INTERACTION

The manner in which the individual feels his body to be differentiated from its environs has been shown to play a role in his style of social interaction. The Barrier score has been found to be positively related to the following behavioral variables in group situations; spontaneity and expressiveness; low dependence on the group leader; concern with promoting group goals; warmth and friendliness; and willingness to face up to hostility when it arises. A picture has emerged from previous work of the high Barrier person as more open and direct and sometimes more aggressive in his group dealings with others than the low Barrier person, but simultaneously striving harder to achieve group aims and cohesiveness.

Cleveland and Morton (1962) sought to cross-validate these findings by evaluating seventy VA psychiatric patients participating in a group oriented therapy program. In groups ranging from six to nine the patients interacted closely with each other (for a four-week period) in contexts designed to give them skills in dealing with certain classes of personal problems. Because of the close and extended interaction of the group members there was an unusually good opportunity for them to become acquainted with each other. In the final week of the four week interaction period they were asked to fill out a sociometric questionnaire devised by Blake and Mouton (1956) containing thirteen items, each of which requested two nominations for the group members who had been most or least characterized by specific behaviors. For example, there were inquiries as to which two most often put group goals above individual goals; which two most wanted the group to be warm and friendly; which two talked the most; and so forth. The nominations received by group members could then be related to the number of Barrier responses they had given to the Holtzman Ink Blots. The results were strongly supportive of previous findings in that nine of thirteen predictions were borne out. High Barrier subjects significantly exceeded low Barrier subjects in nominations for ability to influence the opinions of others; degree of acceptance by the group at large; ability to operate effectively without direction from the group leader; setting group goals above individual goals; desire to accomplish something; helping in the resolution of group differences; keeping the group "on the ball"; and being preferred as a recipient of discussion. The frequency of nomination was reversed for the sociometric item inquiring about those who put personal above group goals. Cleveland and Morton (p. 6) summarized these results as follows:

> High Barrier subjects receive the greater number of nominations for being the most influential group members, doing more to keep the group active and goal directed and operating without external support and guidance in the form of a leader. For the low Barrier members the results are not as clear. . . .

Ramer (1961) hypothesized that the high Barrier person would exceed the low Barrier person: (1) In initiating communications in an interpersonal situation; (2) In communicating committal, directive, and disagreeing statements rather than self-depreciating ones. These hypotheses were tested by studying ninety-six female subjects who were seen in groups of four in a setting in which each subject was isolated from the others behind board partitions. Instructions were given to write a story about a sequence of three pictures and then to communicate with a fictitious partner about the story by writing messages on slips of paper which would presumably be delivered by the experimenter. One-third of the subjects were given no responses to the messages they sent; another third were given negative, unfriendly replies from the fictitious partner; and the remaining third were given positive, rather friendly replies. Analysis of the data revealed that, as predicted, high Barrier subjects sent significantly more messages and more units of communication than the low Barrier subjects. A significant difference in the same direction occurred with respect to number of messages containing responses which are committal and orienting (defined by Bales categories) as opposed to those asking for opinion and orientation. There were non-significant but consistent tendencies for the Barrier score to be negatively related to such variables as number of self-depreciating or passive accepting messages but positively with the number of messages giving directions and suggestions. Also, borderline evidence was obtained that the "Barrier style of behavior" was most evident in a frustrating or threatening situation. Over-all, Ramer considered the majority of his hypotheses to have been confirmed or at least supported by the results.

Differences in degree of communicative expression in group situations between high and low Barrier subjects have also been observed by Hornstra and McPartland° to hold true in a schizophrenic population. They report that there are significant distinctions in the ward behavior of schizophrenic patients with relatively high and low Barrier scores. Patients with relatively high scores are rated by ward personnel as displaying behavior which is restless, acting out, and initiatory of interaction. This is in contrast to patients with lower Barrier scores who are depicted as showing "retarded and withdrawn behavior."

A provocative feature of the Cleveland and Morton (1962) paper referred to above was an evaluation of how well the Barrier score would anticipate the individual's ability to maintain his own views when opposed by group pressures. In previous work suggestibility showed a tendency to be inversely related to boundary definiteness. This had evidenced itself primarily in terms of the criterion of how far the individual could be influenced to change his judgments of autokinetic movement. In the Cleveland and Morton study subjects were asked to view a movie ("Twelve Angry Men") which narrated the deliberations of a jury in a murder case. The entire action focused on how the jury, which began with one vote for acquittal and the remainder for conviction, shifted eventually to a unanimous decision of "not guilty." Subjects were allowed to see the first twenty-five minutes of the film up to the point where the second ballot of the jury started. They had from the outset been provided with a chart which identified the jury members and instructed to familiarize themselves with their prejudices and mannerisms. When the film was stopped, they were told that by the end of the story the entire jury would have changed its vote to acquittal. They were asked to list the sequence in which they felt the various jurors would shift their vote. Having completed these rankings on an individual basis, they formed into small groups that were given the task of arriving at unanimous group decisions with regard to the same ranking procedure. Finally, when the group decision had been registered, they were requested again to make their own second individual rankings. It was possible to measure degree of suggestibility by determining how much each individual had been influenced by the group discussion to alter his second ranking in comparison with the first. Analysis of the data indi-

---

° R. K. Hornstra and T. S. McPartland, unpublished progress report entitled "The Relation of Behavioral Constellations to Drug Use," 1961, National Institute of Mental Health, Grant No. MY 3308.

cated that degree of apparent suggestibility was inversely and significantly related to the Barrier score.

A number of other reports bearing upon suggestibility and yielding behavior have appeared.

Mausner[*] (1961) constructed a situation in which subjects were to judge the numbers of dots on briefly exposed slides. At the same time that they were rendering their judgments they were receiving reports of the same phenomena from a partner. Although the partner's statements (in the form of numbers on a panel) seemed to emanate directly from him, they were actually controlled by the experimenter who changed them according to fixed schedules intended to contradict the subject's reports. Interview and questionnaire procedures were used to evaluate how each subject responded to the contradictions conveyed to him. It was found that the higher the Barrier score the greater the likelihood that the subject would consider his own judgments, rather than his partner's, to be correct. Furthermore, the Barrier score was positively linked with how satisfied the subject was with his own performance and negatively related to his anxiety, as manifested in the form of lengthened reaction time to the slides. Incidentally, the Barrier score was significantly and negatively related to the L (Lie) score on the MMPI. This was interpreted as meaning that the individual with definite boundaries has less need to present an exaggerated favorable picture of himself than does one who is vaguely bounded. Hammerschlag, et al. (1964) have since reaffirmed the finding concerning the L score.

There are two projects which are particularly convincing in their demonstration of the role of boundary articulation in yielding behavior. Dorsey (1965) observed degree of yielding in two samples of subjects (twenty-six women, forty-six men) who were asked to make judgments in an Asch type situation in which the experimenter's confederates tried to influence them in a given direction. In both samples the Barrier score was significantly and negatively correlated with amount of yielding displayed. Rothschild (in press) also studied yielding in an Asch type setting in a sample of forty-four men. His results significantly supported those of Dorsey.

Scanning the information concerned with the boundary and social interaction which has emerged since 1958, one finds encouraging consistency and support of previous formulations. Several studies have reaffirmed that the more articulated an individual's boundaries the greater the probability that he will seek to communicate with other group members and also that his communications will be direct and active rather than passive or self

---

[*] B. Mausner, unpublished progress report entitled "Experimental Studies of Social Interaction", 1961, National Institute of Mental Health, Grant No. M-2831.

depreciatory. The question whether suggestibility and yielding are a function of the state of the boundary has been considerably clarified by the Cleveland and Morton (1962), Dorsey (1965), and Rothschild (in press) studies. In all three instances negative correlations between Barrier and yielding modes of behavior were demonstrated.

PSYCHOPATHOLOGY

The Barrier and Penetration scores were found in our earlier work to have promise for discriminating schizophrenic from nonschizophrenic subjects. They did not distinguish between normals and neurotics, but roughly separated normals and neurotics (high Barrier, low Penetration) from schizophrenics (low Barrier, high Penetration). Of course, the association of vague body boundaries with schizophrenia had for some time been remarked upon by clinical observers (e.g., Schilder, 1935).

Among the first to explore psychopathology issues further after 1958 were Holtzman, et al. (1961). They applied their ink-blot series to a variety of normal and pathological groups and observed that the Barrier score was higher and the Penetration score lower in normal adult subjects than in chronic schizophrenics. However, only in the case of Penetration was the difference statistically significant. In addition, they factor analyzed the intercorrelations of twenty-three indices (including Barrier and Penetration) derived from the ink-blot test in sixteen different samples of subjects (e.g., children, normal adults, schizophrenics). They discovered that the Barrier score consistently loaded high on a factor which they associate with "well organized, ideational activity, good imaginative capacity, well differentiated ego boundaries, and awareness of conventional concepts" (p. 171). The Penetration score loaded high on several factors related to disturbance. It was particularly identified with indicators of immaturity, bodily preoccupation, and psychopathology. These factor analytic results tied the Barrier score to ego integration and the Penetration score to maladjustment. Subsequent studies [e.g., Holtzman, Gorham, and Moran (1964)] have supported Holtzman's et al. original work.

However, despite such findings and those earlier noted which seemed to be reassuring concerning the efficacy of Barrier in distinguishing those who are seriously disorganized, complicating reports began to appear. Jaskar and Reed (1963) compared a sample of female psychiatric patients (nineteen schizophrenic, eleven neurotic) with a control group of female hospital employees. They could find no differences in boundary definiteness between neurotics or schizophrenics or between either of these subgroups and the controls. Relatedly, while Reitman (1962) discerned a trend for the Barrier scores of a group of male neurotics ($N = 40$) to be higher than those of a group of male schizophrenics ($N = 40$), the difference did not attain statistical significance (although the schizophrenics were characterized by significantly higher Penetration scores than the neurotics). Even further, Fisher (1966) could find no significant differences in boundary definiteness between male neurotics ($N = 20$) and schizophrenics ($N = 45$); and actually turned up a difference between a sample of female neurotics ($N = 20$) and schizophrenics ($N = 46$) indicating that the latter had significantly higher Barrier than the former.

Another element was introduced into the picture by Conquest (1963) who contrasted the boundary attributes of paranoid and nonparanoid schizophrenics. He was stimulated to do this by the fact that our work had indicated a tendency (nonsignificant) for Barrier to be higher in paranoid than nonparanoid schizophrenics. His data showed that Barrier was significantly higher and Penetration lower in the paranoids than in the nonparanoids. In following up on this observation, Fisher (1964) discerned a borderline trend for paranoid schizophrenics ($N = 24$) to have higher Barrier scores than nonparanoids. When a combined Barrier minus Penetration score developed by Conquest was used, the difference became highly significant.

Reviewing the data just cited, Fisher (1966) concluded that boundary disorganization need not necessarily occur in the schizophrenic. Because this seemed to be especially true of the paranoid schizophrenic who is inclined to have a feeling of being special and a focal point of attention, the following hypothesis was formulated. When an individual who is caught up in a schizophrenic process constructs a new role which gives him a sense of importance, of individuality, and of prominence in the world, he is able to maintain a demarcating boundary between himself and others. The paranoid delusion with its new, somewhat grandiose definition of self somehow provides the security needed to maintain a feeling of being a bounded individual, even in the midst of severe personality disorganization. This view was tested by Fisher (1966) in a sample of forty-five male and forty-six female schizophrenics. It was reduced to two operational hypotheses: that the Barrier score would be positively associated with degree of paranoid symptomatology and also grandiosity. Lorr Inpatient Multidimensional Psychiatric ratings were obtained with the intent of using the Grandiose Expansiveness and Paranoid Projection scales. Analysis of the data indicated that patients diagnosed as paranoid ($N = 56$) had significantly higher Barrier scores than nonparanoids. But Barrier was not correlated with the Lorr Paranoid Projection ratings. The Barrier score in the female schizophrenic sample was, as predicted, positively and significantly correlated with Lorr Grandiose Expansiveness; and the same held true at a borderline level (p. 10) in the male sample. These results conformed rather well to expectation. They made it more tenable to consider seriously that there may be mechanisms whereby unrealistic and even bizarre assumptions about the world can serve to bolster and reinforce one's boundaries. In any case, it is apparent that schizophrenic disorganization does not necessarily involve boundary dissolution. Much remains to be done to clarify the conditions and modifiers which determine the state of the boundary in the psychotic individual.

Some inkling of the complexity of the problems involved in understanding boundary reorganization during schizophrenic breakdown is offered by the two following studies.

Cleveland (1960) explored the question of whether there would be changes in the boundary scores as schizophrenics recovered from the acute phases of their disorganization. Twenty-five male schizophrenics in VA hospitals were evaluated upon first entering the hospital with the Lorr Multidimensional Scale for Rating Psychiatric Patients. They were later evaluated again after five and thirteen weeks of treatment which typically consisted of a course of tranquilizers. A second criterion of the patient's response to treatment was the psychiatric decision whether to discharge him or continue his hospitalization upon the completion of the treatment plan. The Holtzman Ink Blots were administered to each patient pre-drug, and five and thirteen weeks after treatment had begun. A significant rho of .60 was found between decrement in Penetration scores (derived from the Holtzman blots) and decrement in the Lorr morbidity rating during the period from the onset of treatment to the fifth week. The rho for the same relationship from treatment onset to the thirteenth week was .61. There was also a significant tendency for patients judged capable of leaving the hospital to have declined in Penetration. This contrasted with non-discharged patients who were likely to have increased their Penetration scores. The Barrier score failed to be significantly related to any of the criteria of patient change.

A second phase of this study concerned forty-five acute hospitalized schizophrenic patients who had been administered the Rorschach on admission and again upon leaving the hospital. Each patient was also rated twice by two psychiatrists, once upon admission and again at time of discharge. When the boundary scores derived from Rorschach protocols were compared with the psychiatric ratings, it turned out that patients rated as improved or markedly improved showed a significant decline in Penetration. For Barrier the only significant change was an increase from first to second testing in the markedly improved group. Cleveland considered that his results demonstrated in the recovering schizophrenic patient a "dramatic firming up and defining of the body-image boundary" (pp. 259-260).

Cleveland and Sikes reported in one study (1966) that a sample of alcoholics (N = 70) who received intensive treatment, particularly group therapy, for a ninety-day period showed significantly lower Penetration scores from pre- to post-testing. No changes in Barrier were noted. However, in a second sample[*] (N = 146) of alcoholics exposed to the same ninety-day treatment program a significant increase in Barrier from pre- to post-testing was found. Penetration did not change.

Reitman and Cleveland (1964) studied the body-image changes in neurotic and schizophrenic patients in a VA hospital following a period of sensory isolation. Twenty neurotics and twenty schizophrenics were exposed individually to sensory isolation conditions (e.g., eyes covered, lying on foam rubber, white noise background) for as long as they would tolerate it, but up to a maximum of four hours. Holtzman Ink-blot tests, measures of tactile sensitivity, and estimates of body size were obtained before and after the isolation period. A special control group of twenty schizophrenics received the pre- and post-battery of tests, but with isolation not intervening. No changes in the scores of this group from pre- to post-evaluation were found. However, there were a number of significant changes in the two experimental groups. The neurotics were observed to have decreased Barrier and increased Penetration scores following isolation. The schizophrenics, in quite reverse fashion, obtained higher Barrier and lower Penetration scores. It was speculated that sensory isolation by minimizing stimulating input has a disruptive effect upon nonpsychotics which decreases boundary definiteness. But in the case of schizophrenics the sensory isolation seemed not to be disruptive. Indeed, it seemed to provide a uniform non-threatening pattern of stimuli which fostered reorganization and more realistic body boundaries. This latter finding was in keeping with several earlier reports (Azima and Cramer, 1956; Gibby, Adams, Carrera, 1960) concerning the therapeutic effects of isolation on schizophrenic symptomatology. It is important to note that the results obtained from the tactile threshold and body-size estimate tasks were similarly reversed for the two experimental groups and in a direction congruent with the concept that isolation produces boundary alteration. Thus, the schizophrenics showed increased tactile sensitivity and a decreased concept of body size following isolation; but the nonpsychotics showed no change in tactile sensitivity and an increased concept of body size. There are previous studies by Wapner, Werner, and Comalli (1958) which suggest that the pattern of changes with regard to body-size estimates in the schizophrenic group are related to increased awareness of the body periphery and those in the nonpsychotic group with lessened awareness of the periphery. It should be added that in estimating the sizes of nonself objects (e.g., twelve inches, baseball) the two groups did not

---

[*] Unpublished data.

shift their judgments from test to retest. Only judgments with regard to one's own body were sensitive to the sensory isolation effects.

One of the implications of this study is that although the boundaries of neurotics and schizophrenics may not differ grossly in definiteness, they are unlike in how they change under the impact of specific kinds of environmental inputs. What reinforces the boundary in one case produces weakening of the boundary in another. There may be other attributes of the boundary, aside from definiteness, which we will need to learn about in order to understand how boundary maintenance differs in well and poorly integrated persons.

There is one new line of research dealing with the boundary and disturbed behavior which has appeared since 1958. Several studies have asked whether the impulsive, delinquent individual has unusually poorly delineated boundaries. R. Fisher (in press) found that boys ($N = 46$) who were too impulsive to remain in regular school classrooms had significantly lower Barrier scores than normal boys ($N = 45$). Megargee (1965) was able to distinguish a sample of juvenile delinquents ($N = 75$) as having significantly lower Barrier scores than boys in several normal control groups. Indeed, those delinquents who had displayed the most "serious" threatening behavior ($N = 28$) had significantly lower Barrier scores than the remainder of the group. Leeds (1965) compared thirty male adolescent non-addicted delinquents, thirty male adolescent narcotic addicts, and thirty male adolescent normal controls. Both the delinquent and narcotic addict groups were characterized by significantly lower Barrier scores than the normals. The results of the three studies enumerated add up to a solid affirmation that delinquents have less differentiated boundaries than normal individuals. The fact that more consistent boundary differences have been detected between delinquents and normals than between schizophrenics and normals is surprising. No ready explanation offers itself except for the possibility that the delinquent's estrangement from society[*] and the fact that the culture does not have a valued role for him are sharply clear to him, whereas the schizophrenic can seek refuge in a delusion or a pattern of withdrawal which obscures his alienation and devalued status. Perhaps it is the open devaluation of one's individuality and personal importance which is particularly disruptive of self delineation and boundary maintenance.

---

[*] This possibility is pointed up by Miner and DeVos (1960) finding that urban Arabs who are conflicted about their identity produce significantly higher Penetration scores (.05 level) than oasis Arabs who have not yet been exposed to such extreme identity conflict. This, by the way, is confirmatory of our previous data which demonstrated that Japanese-American men who were struggling to adapt to United States life had less definite boundaries than native Japanese not beset by such identity problems.

DEVELOPMENTAL ASPECTS

There were scattered indications in our previous work that certain aspects of the developmental process were related to boundary attributes. But little has been done since 1958 to cast light on such developmental possibilities.

Fish (1960) has taken an exploratory look at the boundary correlates of several developmental parameters in children of different age levels. She applied an unvalidated multiple choice version of the usual Rorschach blot technique to measure Barrier and Penetration responses in boys at ages seven (N = 21), nine (N = 25) and eleven (N = 25). She also secured measures tapping such diverse variables as concept of time; resistance to perceiving aniseikonic-induced distortions in one's mirror image; concept of one's height; and ability to define the adult role. It should be specified that the last of the variables just cited was examined by means of tasks which required the subject to tell how you know "when you're grown up" and also to draw a human figure depicting how "you expect to be when you grow up." As noted in our previous studies, there were no progressive changes in boundary scores with age. It was ascertained, though, that the Barrier score was positively correlated with ability to represent adult qualities in figure drawings at age seven. Also, the Barrier score was positively correlated in seven- and nine-year-olds with a more "mature" mode of time perspective that involves the perception of future adult events as distant from, rather than close to, the present. The Barrier score was not meaningfully related to judgments of one's own height or to degree of distortion in self image induced by aniseikonic lenses. In general, it is interesting that despite the use of an untried method of Barrier measurement, the significant results which were obtained in relation to the Barrier score linked it positively with some indices of developmental maturity.

MISCELLANEOUS OBSERVATIONS

It would be helpful to those who might plan to work with the Barrier score to be brought up to date on a number of miscellaneous issues.

First of all, it has now been shown in diverse studies that Barrier and Penetration can be scored with high objectivity. There are at least nine instances which can be cited in which interscorer agreement has been in the high .80's and .90's [viz., Ramer (1961), Dorsey (1965), Allardice and Dole (1966), Eigenbrode and Shipman (1960), Leeds (1965), Sieracki (1963), Megargee (1965), Sherick (1964), and Bachelis (1965)].

A range of test-retest reliability values for Barrier has been obtained. They vary from .40 (Holtzman, et al., 1961) to .89 (McConnell and Daston,

1961). A total of seven test-retest studies have, to our knowledge, been completed. Of these, four have given coefficients above .80; one was .78; another .65; and one .40. The magnitudes of the values do not seem to be a function of the time interval intervening between test and retest. Over-all, the reliability findings are encouraging.

A final matter to be noted is that evidence has accumulated from several sources that female subjects tend to obtain larger Barrier scores than males. Fisher (1964), Hartley (1964), Jacobson (1965), Joyce Morton (1965), and Gail Gordon (1966) have reported significantly higher Barrier scores in females than males, both in adult and child populations. Fisher (1964) has tentatively conceptualized this difference, in the context of other body-image data, as indicating that the female in Western culture is more directly in communication with her body than the male and also has a greater sense of security about it.

CONCLUSIONS

With minor exceptions, the studies accomplished since 1958 have been consistent with the hypotheses and models first offered in this book concerning the body-image boundary. The new data have clarified the origins of the Barrier score as deriving from patterns of exterior-interior body experience. Further, they have demonstrated its formal psychometric adequacy as defined by scoring objectivity and test-retest reliability.

There has been particularly good substantiation of the fact that boundary variations are accompanied by certain patterns of physiological reactivity. Both in terms of psychosomatic symptoms and measures of autonomic response the bulk of the newly reported results indicate that the higher the degree of boundary definiteness the greater the tendency to channel excitation to skin and muscle and the less the tendency to do so at interior sites like the stomach and heart. These findings have appeared in adults, adolescents, and children and also in studies utilizing different designs and instrumentation. It is true that inconsistencies and complexities remain to be explained. For example, why do certain autonomic measures, such as GSR and blood pressure, differ in the direction of their correlation with the Barrier score in adults as opposed to children? We also need to learn a great deal more about the kinds of conditions (e.g., rest, stress, direction of attention) which are likely to maximize the correlation between Barrier and exterior-interior autonomic response differences. Of course, the even larger task remains of clarifying the mechanisms whereby body attitudes and body reactivity patterns become linked with each other. The concepts and data presented by Lacey (in Rubenstein and Parloff, 1959) concerning the relation between receptive and nonreceptive attitudes toward the environment and skin versus heart activation represent an important step in such clarification. A striking parallel exists between the physiological pattern manifested by the high Barrier individual who is communicative and prepared for interaction with others and the pattern described by Lacey as characterizing receptivity toward the environment. A similar parallel can be drawn between the physiological response pattern of the low Barrier individual and that associated by Lacey with a nonreceptive orientation.

It is a matter of import, too, that the accumulating results support the idea that certain aspects of autonomic reactivity can be understood within a body-image framework which conceptualizes the "place" or "geographical locale" at which response is measured as a significant factor. Previous conventional autonomic categories (e.g., sympathetic and parasympathetic) neglected such "geographic" possibilities.

There has been excellent corroboration of the fact that resiliency in the face of stress is likely to be greatest in those with well-articulated boundaries. This has shown up with such diverse stressors as the impact of mutilation or disablement of one's own body; painful shock stimuli; threatening representations of mutilation; having to separate oneself from home; and being confronted with difficult cognitive tasks while bombarded by distractions. Few, if any, previous psychological indices have predicted stress tolerance so consistently. As already indicated, one may speculatively attribute the resiliency that accompanies well-articulated boundaries to two variables: (1) If an individual possesses definite boundaries, this encourages him to have a sense of security about his "base of operations" (i.e., his body) which is reassuring and stabilizing in the midst of trouble. (2) There is sound evidence that the individual with well-defined boundaries is one who is achievement and goal oriented and highly motivated toward mastery of problems; and such traits count heavily in coping adequately with frustration and difficulty.

It is of related significance that the well-bounded individual has continued in more recent findings to be pictured as one who is effective in dealing and communicating with others. He seems to have an integrative role in small group contexts; and at the same time his behavior is independent and rather self directed. When confronted with situations in which others try to pressure or manipulate him, he takes a stand and has confidence in his own decisions. He is "self steering" and resistive of unreasonable control, but apparently willing to cooperate when he is a participant in small group interactions which he considers to be reasonable.

Such effective functioning in social interactions and the previously referred to "good adjustment" in the face of stresses that are associated with boundary differentiation in normal (nonpsychotic) persons could easily lead to the assumption that degree of psychopathology would be directly linked with Barrier. Previous findings seemed to point in this direction, but increasingly it is becoming obvious that this is not the case. It is possible for an individual to be clinically schizophrenic and yet maintain well-articulated boundaries. Exploratory efforts to understand this paradox have suggested that paranoid delusions or feelings of grandiosity may somehow supply a disorganized person with a sense of prominence and importance in the world which permit him to continue to experience himself as differentiated and bounded. The question remains whether a boundary so maintained is the equivalent of that found in nonpsychotics. The work of Rietman and Cleveland (1964) indicating quite opposite responses of the boundary to sensory deprivation in neurotics and schizophrenics implies that they are not equivalent. Clarification of this whole issue now stands out as one of the most potentially interesting and profitable tasks to be undertaken in future body-boundary research.

An unexpected and novel fact that has emerged from the newer studies is that the boundary scores are rather sensitive indicators of certain kinds of change in the individual. Cleveland (1960) detected significant shifts in the Penetration score as schizophrenic patients recovered from acute disorganization. McConnell and Daston (1961) recorded meaningful changes in the Penetration score of pregnant women from pre- to post-delivery period. Reitman and Cleveland (1964) discovered the exciting fact that both Barrier and Penetration scores are altered in neurotic and schizophrenic patients during the course of a sensory-isolation experience. Furthermore, these alterations are accompanied by equivalent changes in light touch threshold and concept of one's body size. Here one sees boundary score changes to be correlated with such widely different phenomena as personality reorganization; the completion of the pregnancy process; and the impact of decreased sensory experience. It is actually more correct to say that the Penetration score is correlated with these phenomena, since the Barrier score was consistently related only to the sensory-isolation variable. This, by the way, is congruent with results from our earlier studies which indicated that the Barrier score was primarily an index of persisting attitudes rather than of short-term variations in state. The Penetration score, by contrast, seems to be much more sensitive to immediate situational conditions. Apparently, fluctuations in boundary attributes do offer promise as indicators of certain kinds of modification of the individual. At this point one can only conjecture whether boundary fluctuations represent initiating forces in change processes or whether they are subsidiary effects.

When the boundary concept was first formulated and described, there were skeptical reactions. This was especially true with regard to the multiple levels of behavior with which the Barrier score seemed to be linked. It was apparently correlated with personality traits, behavior in small groups, response to stress, physiological activation patterns, psychopathology, cultural patterns, sex differences, and so forth. There was surprise that one variable could be so pervasively involved in many aspects of behavior. As the present review indicates, this involvement is a reality. Indeed, new data have been obtained, which have not been considered here, indicating that the Barrier score has significant relationships with an even greater range of variables than had been previously suspected [e.g., clothing preferences (Compton, 1964); ability to discriminate color hues (Wertheimer and Bachelis, 1966); and hypnotic susceptibility (Fisher, 1963)]. The state of the individual's boundaries seems to be a fundamental modifier which plays a role in the entire continuum from physiological reactivity to social interaction.

While the research since 1958 has touched upon a considerable number of the formulations and issues originally presented, there are some which have received little or no attention. The relationships of the following variables to boundary definiteness have been relatively neglected:

(1) Interest patterns
(2) Occupational choice
(3) Ethnic and cultural roles
(4) Electroencephalographic measures (e.g., alpha)
(5) Attitudes towards one's parents
(6) Sensory thresholds for different modalities
(7) Reactivity of interior organs other than the heart

Perhaps the next ten years will see these areas more fully clarified.

APPENDIX

....

Rorschach Protocols

THE FOLLOWING Rorschach protocols are listed together with the indicated scoring for Barrier and Penetration responses in order to provide
an opportunity to study at first hand some of the typical problems encountered in scoring Rorschach records for body-image fantasies. These
records have been drawn from various subject groups studied. Thus typical records from arthritic, neurodermatitis, conversion, stomach ulcer,
schizophrenic, and normal college groups are represented. In selecting
these various groups for examination, our intent was not only to provide
examples of scoring problems but also to furnish the reader with Rorschach records representative of these various groups.

It is our feeling that many of the body-image characteristics of the
groups discussed in this volume are highlighted in these sample records.
For instance, the unusually high number of Barrier responses often found
in the psychosomatic groups with body-exterior symptoms will be noted
here in the arthritic, dermatitis, and conversion records. The schizophrenic
record illustrates well the unusual and rather bizarre Penetration responses found in schizophrenic groups. All the records which are listed
here, except two, are individual Rorschachs collected by the traditional
mode of administration. The two exceptions are the college records. These
college records were gathered in a large group setting. The ink blots,
prepared as 35-mm. slides, were flashed on a screen and the subjects
asked to give a specified number of responses to each. It is our feeling
that these group records compare favorably to individual records in respect to completeness, complexity, and richness of body-image fantasy
productions.

NORMAL COLLEGE MALE

A 23-year-old, single college student who was in his junior year and majoring in economics. This is a Rorschach record obtained in a group setting
and with the number of responses per card specified by the examiner in
order to result in a consistent total of 24 responses. No formal inquiry is
conducted; but each subject is asked to describe each response as fully

and in as much detail as he can. It will be noted that this record furnishes fantasies which are as rich, complex, and varied as those obtained in individual records.

RESPONSE

SCORING

I.

1. A decaying moth.

1. Penetration, because of the degeneration of the object.

2. A winged horse walking beside a reflection pool.

2. Score "pool" for Barrier as an enclosed space.

3. Skull bone of a prehistoric animal.

3. _____

II.

4. Two red-haired girls playing patty-cake.

4. _____

5. Two bloody animal skins.

5. Score for Penetration the "bloody skins" which indicate damage to the body wall.

6. A Douglas skyray about to fly into a cloud.

6. Not scored for Barrier as the object is not seen as covered or hidden, but only potentially so.

III.

7. Two gnomes stirring a kettle.

7. A Barrier response as a container.

8. Design on a Grecian vase.

8. Could be scored Barrier both for the decorative design as well as for container. But only one score given for any one response.

9. Fluoroscope of a whirlpool.

9. Score for Penetration, as all X-rays are so scored.

   The "whirlpool" would not be scored as Barrier because it does not clearly refer to an enclosed "pool" area.

IV.

10. A worm's-eye view of a gorilla.

10. _____

11. Two women leaning back to back against a post.

11. _____

V.

12. Two snails.

12. Score for Barrier as a hard-shell animal.

13. Two bearded men's heads leaning against each other.

13. Beards are not scored for Barrier.

VI.

14. A modernistic Christmas tree.

14. Not scored for Barrier as there is not enough detail. If the tree were described as decorated, then a Barrier score would be assigned.

15. A bear rug attached to a totem pole.

15. _____

VII.

16. Two women in 18th-century costumes back to back, looking over their shoulders at each other.

16. Score all costumes for Barrier.

17. Bust of Napoleon.

17. _____

VIII.

18. Form of some kind of shellfish.

18. Score all reference to shell for Barrier.

19. Portion of the human breastbone.

19. _____

20. Two seahorses back to back and upside down.

20. Not included in the list of animals to be scored Barrier.

IX.

21. Two pot-bellied gnomes or witches facing each other and laughing, shaking their fingers.

21. The incidental reference to "pot-bellied" is not scored as Barrier, despite the pot connotation of the reference.

22. An A-bomb test.

22. Simply explosions, or A-bomb, are not scored Penetration. If reference is made to something being broken or burst by the explosion, a scoring for Penetration would be indicated.

X.

23. Eiffel Tower.

23. Towers are not scored as Barrier.°

24. A cowboy wearing chaps.

24. Score "chaps" for Barrier as protective and decorative covering.

Total Barrier Score = 7
Total Penetration Score = 3

° Since 1958 all references to buildings and related structures are scored Barrier.

NORMAL COLLEGE FEMALE

A 19-year-old, single female, who was a college sophomore majoring in psychology. This is a record obtained in a group setting with the number of responses per card specified by the examiner so as to result in a consistent total of 24 responses. Note that although this girl complies and gives a full record of 24 responses, she obtains a Barrier score of only 2, placing her in the low-scoring group for Barrier. Obviously it is possible for a subject to give a full, complete, and complex record and yet to score low on Barrier.

RESPONSE	SCORING
I.	
1. A large butterfly, wings outspread.	1. _____
2. The middle top looks like a monster with upraised hands.	2. _____
3. An ice cream cone, or cone shaped.	3. Score for Barrier as a container.
II.	
4. Two men making a toast.	4. Not scored for Barrier simply because of "making a toast." The container must actually be referred to for such a scoring.
5. Two men with their legs and heads blown off.	5. Scored for Penetration because of the reference to violent mutilation of the body.
6. The heads of two lambs with their noses together.	6. Not scored for Barrier unless the entire animal is seen.
III.	
7. Two natives cooking somebody.	7. Not scored for Barrier unless the cooking container is actually described. Also not scored for Penetration because the people being cooked are actually not seen in the blot.
8. The red splotches on the sides look like the inside of a chicken.	8. Scored for Penetration because the body wall has been by-passed and a direct view of the interior referred to.
9. Two skinny people warming their hands.	9. _____

IV.

10. A dragon's head with bulging eyes.

10. Not scored for Penetration, as "bulging eyes" only suggests a potential "lesion" of the body wall.

11. Two snakes by a fountain.

11. _____

V.

12. Human legs, calves and feet.

12. _____

13. A young bat at rest.

13. _____

VI.

14. A man on top of a totem pole.

14. _____

15. A cowhide stretched out to dry.

15. _____

VII.

16. Profile of two women facing each other with identical hairdo.

16. _____

17. Six separate fish facing each other.

17. _____

VIII.

18. A beautiful colored butterfly.

18. _____

19. A flower, maybe an iris.

19. _____

20. Two little red bugs.

20. _____

IX.

21. The center part looks like a fountain with different-colored water.

21. _____

22. Some kind of deep-sea vegetation.

22. _____

X.

23. Two people (red) drinking some-
+ thing (green) with two bushes
24. on the side and the top is some kind of statue; there is an aisle leading to the statue.

23. Score for Penetration "people
+ drinking." Body orifices open for
24. intake or expulsion are so scored. Score the "aisle" as Barrier because it defines a spatial region bordered on both sides.

Total Barrier score = 2
Total Penetration score = 3

CONVERSION REACTION (TORTICOLLIS)

A 34-year-old, married white male who had had torticollis (wryneck) for about six months. He had a diagnosis of conversion reaction, and no organic disease was found.

FREE ASSOCIATION	INQUIRY	SCORING
I.		
1. Looks something like a butterfly.	1. Whole thing. Shape.	1. _____
2. And in the center like a beetle.	2. Little things like claws in the center.	2. _____
II.		
3. Looks like a camel's head.	3. A long thin nose and a skinny neck. Also see two humps.	3. Not scored for Barrier. Animals with unusual skin or covering are scored Barrier only when most of the animal and not merely the head region is seen.
4. A dog in here.	4. Really has the head of a calf, more than a dog.	4. _____
5. Also a cat in there.	5. Real fuzzy-looking like very thick, matted fur.	5. Score for Barrier because of the emphasis on the fuzzy surface quality.
III.		
6. Monkeys hanging by their tails.	6. Long tail makes them monkeys.	6. _____
7. Two natives stirring a pot.	7. Stooped over. Black Africans. Men or women.	7. Score "pot" for Barrier as a container.
8. Could be a fish.	8. More like an eel because of slim length.	8. _____

IV.

9. A little kid's draw-
   ing of a gorilla.
10. Head of a shrimp.
11. A man's head with
    beams of light
    shining out of his
    eyes.

9. Has a muscled-up
   look, a huge thing.
10. Two eyes and feel-
    ers.
11. Like "amazing sto-
    ries," science fic-
    tion.

9. _____

10. _____

11. Score for Penetra-
    tion because some-
    thing is coming out
    of a body opening.

V.

12. Picture of a man
    blowing wind.

13. Two cobra heads.

14. A devil's head.

12. Puffed cheeks and
    wind blown
    through lips.

13. Slim and sticking
    up.
14. Mostly the horns.

12. Score for Penetra-
    tion because some-
    thing is coming
    out of a body open-
    ing.

13. _____

14. _____

VI.

15. A hide tacked on
    the wall to dry.

16. A battleship.

15. Stretched out. Has
    a pattern of stripes
    on it.

16. See the guns stick
    out.

15. Score for Barrier,
    as the hide is given
    an unusual attri-
    bute of pattern and
    stripes.

16. Score for Barrier
    because it is a
    hard, protective,
    and containing ob-
    ject.
    Do not score
    "guns stick out" as
    Penetration, be-
    cause the emphasis
    is on location of
    the guns rather
    than the fact that
    they pierce the
    surface.

VII.

17. Lady's face with long black hair. Other side looks like a baby's face.

17. Side-view angle. She has wavy hair.

17. Not scored for Barrier. Human hair, unless specified as hiding or covering something, is not scored.

18. A castle way up on top of a hill.

18. Like in the old days, a fortress with walls and all.

18. Score for Barrier as a protective, containing enclosure.

VIII.

19. Face of a clown.

19. Like a mask all made up with make-up colors.

19. While masks are not scored for Barrier, in this instance a Barrier response would be indicated because of the additional reference to decorative covering ("all made up").

20. A camel's head.

20. Just the head.

20. ─────────

IX.

21. Heads of a bunch of evil creatures.

21. One is not too evil. More like Joe Palooka, a dumb country boy.

21. ─────────

22. Some weird animal, a goat.

22. Rough, shaggy coat.

22. Score for Barrier as an animal with special covering.

X.

23. Christ on the Cross.

23. Head is hanging down.

23. The Penetration implications of this response are not scored because there must be more explicit reference to the body wall being violated.

24. A drumstick. No, I mean wishbone.

24. Like you get in a turkey.

24. ─────────

Total Barrier Score = 7
Total Penetration Score = 2

RHEUMATOID ARTHRITIS

A 38-year-old, married white male with a tenth-grade education, who had been a welder for twelve years and who had Marie Strumpell type arthritis of eight years' duration. Note that although the record contains only 17 responses, a total Barrier score of 6 is obtained, placing the record in the high-scoring group for Barrier.

FREE ASSOCIATION	INQUIRY	SCORING
I.		
1. Looks like a bat that comes out of a cave.	1. One that flies out of a cave at night.	1. "Cave" here is not scored for Barrier, as it is not actually seen in the blot. Note, however, that the fantasy is present.
2. A map with a rugged coastline, bays and coves.	2. Any coastline.	2. Score "cove" · or "bay" for Barrier because they refer to enclosed spaces.
II.		
3. Hide of an animal.	3. Bearskin.	3. _____
4. Melted metal in a foundry, runs over the top of the mold.	4. Hot metal in a mold.	4. Double scoring. Score "mold" for Barrier as a container. Score also for Penetration, as the boundaries of the container are being by-passed ("metal runs over the top of the mold").
III.		
5. Sheep out in the cold weather, half-frozen to death.	5. Sheep are white, and have ice all over them.	5. Score once for Barrier "sheep with ice all over them." Actually this is a Barrier response on two counts. "Sheep" is scored

6. Bones of an old dinosaur, prehistoric animals.

6. I read they found 4,000 bones of squirrels inside of a hollow tree. These bones remind me of that.

for Barrier because of its skin quality. Also, any animal "covered with ice" would be scored for Barrier.

6. Not scored for Barrier as the "hollow tree" is not actually a response to the ink blot, but only a reminiscence. Note that the fantasy is present, however.

IV.

7. Bear hide.

7. Whole thing.

7. Not scored for Barrier, as this is a popular response with no special emphasis on the fuzziness, wooliness, or other properties of the surface.

8. Roots of a tree, like of a dead tree.

8. Just the lower part. Like a dead tree because you can see them.

8. _____

V.

9. Jet-propelled airplane.
10. A map.

9. Swept-back wings suggest a jet.
10. Coastline with various inlets and bays.

9. _____

10. Score "inlets and bays" for Barrier as they represent enclosed spaces.

VI.

11. An animal hide.

11. A bear or something.

11. Not scored for Barrier because this is not one of the types of skins which has been designated as having special surface connotations.

12. A map of Florida.

12. Because it looks like a peninsula, but that's all.

12. Not scored for Barrier, as no mention is made of the land being enclosed or surrounded by water.

VII.

13. A lake, water is thawing out. Ice on the outside and water in the middle.

13. A coating of ice around the water. Some of the ice may be melting.

13. Score the covering of ice as a Barrier response. This implies a hard, outer covering and container. Also, score the thawing and melting ice for Penetration, since some of the surface is in the process of dissolution.

VIII.

14. Like a historical diagram of different species of animals in a museum.

14. Prehistoric animals, because I have never seen them.

14. Not scored since this is an unspecified naming of animals with no particular attributes mentioned or inferred.

15. An old squirrel.

15. On the sides, I said old meaning prehistoric.

15. _____

IX.

16. A human stomach like you see in a research diagram.

16. Looks like it has all different kinds of stuff in it.

16. The response "stomach" seen separately is scored for Barrier. In this case the subject makes it very plain he means a container when he refers to stomach.

X.

| 17. Mad artist stuff. | 17. Just colors. Doesn't resemble anything, really. | 17. _____ |

Total Barrier Score = 6
Total Penetration Score = 2

NEURODERMATITIS DISSEMINATA

A 43-year-old white male with tenth-grade education who had had recurrent skin lesions over a period of ten years. He was an auto mechanic by trade.

FREE ASSOCIATION	INQUIRY	SCORING
I.		
1. A bat. What we call a leatherwing bat. In flight.	1. Looks like a wing and it is black.	1. Not scored for Barrier. Bats are not included as animals to be scored for Barrier. The term *leatherwing bat* is a Texas colloquialism referring to no special surface quality.
2. A cloud formation but not exactly like one.	2. Maybe a thunderstorm with dark, boiling and rolling clouds.	2. _____
3. An eagle with claws.	3. An emblem, body and wings, like on a shield.	3. Score for Barrier because of the reference to 'shield."
II.		
4. A butterfly.	4. Usual.	4. _____
5. Two witches in an argument clapping hands.	5. Riding on broomsticks—tall hats on.	5. Not scored for Barrier as there is not enough emphasis on the costume or clothing. Merely describing "tall hats" is not sufficient to score for Barrier.*

---

* Since 1958 *any* reference to clothing is scored Barrier.

III.

6. Two people pulling something apart or picking up something.

6. Pulling away from each other is what I meant.

6. Score for Penetration.

7. People are doing a dance, some motion to it.

7. Could be mummies; they are all wrapped up like you see in a museum.

7. Score for Barrier as this focuses on external covering and protection.

8. A bow tie.

8. In the center.

8. Not scored for Barrier in this particular instance, because we have excluded popular responses which have specific Barrier implications from our scoring scheme.

IV.

9. Weird-looking, maybe a squid.

9. Just a big blob.

9. ———————

10. Something standing on its feet, head between its legs.

10. Clown shoes, but it's not a clown, not human. An animal.

10. Not scored for Barrier as not enough specific description is given of any costume or disguise.*

11. Bat or bird, weird-looking, like you see in movie pictures or at night—black.

11. Like you see in old caves or mine shafts.

11. Not scored for Barrier, since a "cave" or "mine shaft" is not actually seen in the ink blot.

V.

12. A bat.

12. An evening bat because it is black.

12. ———————

13. Old big black bug. The kind that hangs around lights at night.

13. Lights attract this kind of bug.

13. ———————

VI.

14. Hide of a deer or a coon.

14. Just shaped like a hide.

14. Not scored for Barrier, as there is no emphasis on any features of the surface.

———————

* Since 1958 any references to clothing (including shoes) are scored Barrier.

15. A head of something, animal.

15. Could say it was a turtle, the whole thing. A big sea-turtle shell.

15. Score for Barrier, a hard-coated animal.

VII.

16. Two cloud formations.

16. Dark, black thunderheads, 3,000 feet up.

16. _____

17. Two Halloween costumes, heads up and hands stretch out.

17. Black gowns, frightening looking.

17. Score for Barrier because of the idea of "costume."

VIII.

18. Two animals, dogs, stepping across something.

18. Bob-tail dogs.

18. _____

IX.

19. Two eyes.

19. Eyes, mouth, not human, made to look bad to scare someone.

19. _____

20. A wine glass or goblet.

20. Shape of one.

20. Score for Barrier as a container.

X.

21. Head with a big hat, Carmen Miranda hat.

21. Black face and a lot of fruit on top of her hat.

21. Score for Barrier because of the unusual hat with decorative fruit.

22. Some little boogers, angry, want to fight.

22. Animals or weird things.

22. _____

Total Barrier Score = 6
Total Penetration Score = 1

DUODENAL ULCER

A 25-year-old, single, white male college student, who had had ulcers of five years' duration. Persistent nausea and vomiting were present as secondary symptoms.

FREE ASSOCIATION	INQUIRY	SCORING
I.		
1. Form of a woman.	1. Hips down.	1. _____
2. Head of a man.	2. Profile, has a hat on his head, a grass hat like Chinese coolies wear.	2. Score for Barrier an unusual article of clothing ("a grass hat").
3. Someone standing near the windows of a building.	3. Like a picture frame, a window.	3. Double scoring. A frame is an enclosed space and is scored for Barrier. A window is an opening and is scored for Penetration.
II.		
4. Two roosters fighting.	4. Red is feathers falling off.	4. Score for Penetration, because part of the body wall is falling apart.
5. Vagina.	5. See the lips and opening.	5. Penetration response, a body orifice.
6. Two people lying down, one a woman on one side, a man on the other.	6. Both asleep or dead.	6. _____
III.		
7. Two people trying to pull aside a chest of a person.	7. Pulling apart a chest.	7. Penetration, because part of the body is being split open.
8. Lungs.	8. They pulled the chest apart and there are the lungs.	8. _____

IV.

9. Hideous-looking thing, a booger man, a nightmare.

9. Grotesque head.

9. _____

10. Face, funny face, big mouth open wide.

10. Porky Pig.

10. Penetration: body opening.

11. Head and two eyes squinting.

11. Smoke coming out of the eyes.

11. Penetration, because something is coming out of a body opening.

V.

12. A bat.
13. Face of the devil.

12. Shape of one.
13. Horns.

12. _____
13. _____

VI.

14. A stream of water.

14. A river, a deep stream.

14. Score for Barrier: an enclosed space.

15. Beak of a reptile with open mouth.

15. Just the head.

15. Penetration: a body opening.

VII.

16. Vagina again.

16. See the slit.

16. Penetration: a body opening.

17. Another picture of the devil.

17. Horns.

17. _____

VIII.

18. Face of a Buddha.
19. Vertebra of a person.

18. Profile.
19. Ribs.

18. _____
19. _____

IX.

20. Ugly old face.

20. Deformed, crooked nose. Something dangles from his nose. Maybe he swallowed something.

20. Score for Penetration, because of the use of the term "deformed" and because there is a reference to something which is penetrating into the body via the nose.

21. Another man, no eyes, all sunk in where eyes should be.

21. A devil with no horns. The eyes are gone or sunk in.

21. Score for Penetration, surface of the body is broken and degenerated ("eyes gone").

X.

22. A grasshopper.	22. Green.	22. _____
23. Insects and two bees.	23. Yellow bees.	23. _____

Total Barrier Score = 3
Total Penetration Score = 10

ADULT MALE SCHIZOPHRENIC

A 25-year-old, white single male veteran who was diagnosed as a Schizophrenic Reaction, undifferentiated type. He manifested auditory hallucinations, ideas of reference, and outbursts of rage. He had also made several abortive suicide attempts.

FREE ASSOCIATION	INQUIRY	SCORING
I.		
1. One way it is a bear's head.	1. Mostly the nose, I guess.	1. _____
2. And a fellow might say it could remind you of a bat, a little bit, but I never did see a bat real close.	2. Wings, except they don't have straight lines like bat here.	2. _____
3. Dark spots. Could be shot.	3. Bat got shot and holes tore into him.	3. Score for Penetration: the body wall is injured and damaged.
II.		
4. Two bears without any head and their feet are burning up.	4. Maybe heads are bent down and they stepped in red paint or a fire is burning their feet.	4. Score for Penetration: the "burning feet" and body surface being detroyed.
5. An object lay flat on ground. If it had a shell it would be a turtle.	5. Claws there, but it lost its shell. Just see the body and no shell.	5. Score for Penetration. The outer protective covering, the "shell," is specifically referred to as missing. This denotes an open and vulnerable body. If the removed

shell were also seen
as part of the per-
cept, an additional
Barrier response
would be indicated.

6. Might be a rooster, but head is too big.

6. Some kind of fowl.

6. _____

III.

7. Two men with some kind of bundle, maybe a bundle of clothes.

7. The men are cut in two where their belt was.

7. Score the "bundle" for Barrier as a container concept. Score the "two men cut in two" for Penetration, as the body wall is radically injured.

8. A rat somebody throwed against the wall.

8. Splattered against the wall and that is blood.

8. Score for Penetration the "rat splattered against the wall."

9. Roots on a tree.

9. Don't see the tree, just roots.

9. _____

IV.

10. Eyes and ears like a grasshopper.

10. Just little points.

10. _____

11. Maybe some kind of beetle or bug.

11. Whole thing, eyes here.

11. _____

V.

12. A leg or something sticking out there.

12. Almost like a human leg.

12. _____

13. A snake sticking its tongue out.

13. Head of snake with his tongue out.

13. Score for Penetration, since the tongue is sticking out of a body opening.

14. A flying outfit. Wouldn't be a buzzard would it?

14. Wings and feet there. Part of it is kinda nipped off, the wings.

14. Score "nipped off" as Penetration.

VI.

15. An animal split down the middle.

15. Split open and spread out.

15. Score for Penetration. The body wall here is clearly opened up.

16. A picture somebody took of the ground.

16. Aerial view, trees and hills.

16. _____

VII.

17. A woman's parts, private parts.

17. Sex parts, can see the slit and all.

17. All body orifices are scored for Penetration.

18. May be ground all around and water here.

18. Like a harbor, water in there.

18. Score for Barrier because of the reference to an enclosed, protected space.

VIII.

19. Looks like a backbone, ribs and all.

19. Different parts of the body, ribs and maybe kidneys.

19. Not scored for Penetration. Only if some direct reference were made to the fact that the body had been opened permitting inside view of the organs would such a response be scored for Penetration.

20. Inside there might be a rotted tree.

20. Looks all rotted out.

20. Score for Penetration because of reference to the deterioration of the object.

IX.

21. Could be a rotting log.

21. Because it's lying down. I've seen a lot like that and they naturally rot. The limb blowed off or jerked off.

21. Score for Penetration the "rotting log" because of the degeneration and dissolution suggested.

22. And I guess that would be a green pasture.

22. Color mostly.

22. _____

X.

23. Meat cut off something and bleeding.

23. The red part might have been butchered and it's bloody.

23. Score for Penetration the opened and bleeding body.

Total Barrier Score = 2
Total Penetration Score = 12

BIBLIOGRAPHY

1. Abel, T. A.: Figure drawing and facial disfigurement. *Am. J. Orthopsych.*, 23:253–264 (1953)
2. Ackerly, W., W. Lhamon, and W. T. Fitts: Phantom breast. *J. Nerv. & Ment. Dis.*, 121:177–178 (1955)
3. Adler, A.: *Problems of Neurosis.* New York: Cosmopolitan Book, 1930
4. Adler, G.: Notes regarding the dynamics of the self. *Brit. J. Med. Psychol.*, 24:97–106 (1951)
5. Adorno, T. W., E. Frenkel-Brunswick, D. J. Levinson, and R. N. Sanford: *The Authoritarian Personality.* New York: Harper & Brothers, 1950
6. Alexander, F., and T. M. French: *Studies in Psychosomatic Medicine.* New York: The Ronald Press Company, 1948
7. Allport, F. H.: *Theories of Perception and the Concept of Structure.* New York: John Wiley & Sons, Inc., 1955
8. Alper, T. G.: Memory for completed and incompleted tasks as a function of personality: an analysis of group data. *J. Abnorm. Soc. Psychol.*, 41:403–420 (1946)
9. Ames, L. B., J. Learned, R. W. Métraux, and R. V. Walker: *Child Rorschach Responses.* New York: Paul B. Hoeber, Inc., 1952
10. Angyal, A.: Experiences of body self in schizophrenia. *Arch. Neurol. & Psychiat.*, 35:1629–1634 (1936)
11. Appleby, L.: The relationship of a Rorschach Barrier typology to other behavioral measures. Ph.D. dissertation, University of Houston, 1956
12. Aronson, E.: Symbolism and the need for achievement. Unpublished report
13. Atkinson, J. W.: Recall of successes and failures related to differences in *n* Achievement. (Paper delivered at the APA meeting, 1951)
14. Bacon, C. L., R. Renneker, and M. Cutler: A psychosomatic survey of cancer of the breast. *Psychosom. Med.*, 14:453–460 (1952)
15. Barron, F.: Complexity-simplicity as a personality dimension. *J. Abnorm. Soc. Psychol.*, 48:163–172 (1953)
16. Bartlett, F. C.: Review of Henry Head's *Aphasia and Kindred Disorders of Speech*, in *Brain*, 49:581–587 (1926)
17. Bass, B. M., et al.: Personality variables related to leaderless group discussion behavior. *J. Abnorm. Soc. Psychol.*, 48:120–128 (1953)
18. Beck, S. J.: *Rorschach's Test.* Vol. 1, *Basic Processes.* New York: Grune & Stratton, Inc., 1944
18A. Beck, S. J., et al.: The normal personality as projected in the Rorschach test. *J. Psychol.*, 30:241–298 (1950)
19. Becker, W. C.: Perceptual rigidity as measured by aniseikonic lenses. *J. Abnorm. Soc. Psychol.*, 49:419–422 (1954)

20. Bell, G. B., and R. L. French: Consistency of individual leadership position in small groups of varying memberships. *J. Abnorm. Soc. Psychol.*, 45:764–767 (1950)

21. Bender, L., and W. R. Keeler: The body image of schizophrenic children following electro-shock treatment. *Amer. J. Orthopsych.*, 22:335–355 (1952)

22. Bender, M. B.: *Disorders in Perception with Particular Reference to Extinction and Displacement.* (American Lecture Series in Neurology) Springfield, Ill.: Charles C Thomas, Publisher, 1952

23. Bender, M. B., and M. Fink: Tactile perceptual tests in the differential diagnosis of psychiatric disorders. *J. Hillside Hospital*, 1:21–31 (1952)

24. Bender, M. B., M. A. Green, and M. Fink: Patterns of perceptual organization with simultaneous stimuli. *Arch. Neurol. & Psychiat.*, 72:233–244 (1954)

25. Benedict, R.: *Patterns of Culture.* Boston: Houghton Mifflin Company, 1934

26. ————: *The Chrysanthemum and the Sword.* Boston: Houghton Mifflin Company, 1946

27. Benjamin, F. B., and A. C. Ivy: The threshold of skin flare in persons with and without malignant neoplastic disease. *J. Investigative Dermatology*, 19:467–488 (1952)

28. Bennett, G.: Structural factors related to the substitute value of activities in normal and schizophrenic persons: I. A technique for the investigation of central areas of the personality. II. An investigation of central areas of the personality. *Character and Pers.*, 10:42–50 (1941); 10:227–245 (1942)

29. Benton, A. L., J. F. Hutcheon, and E. Seymour: Arithmetic ability, finger localization capacity and right-left discrimination in normal and defective children. *Amer. J. Orthopsych.* 21:756–766 (1951)

30. Benton, A. L.: Right-left discrimination and finger localization in defective children. *A.M.A. Arch. Neurol. & Psychiat.*, 74:583–589 (1955)

31. Berdie, R. F.: Measurement of adult intelligence by drawings. *J. Clin. Psych.*, 1:288–295 (1945)

32. Berman, S., and J. Laffal: Body type and figure drawing. *J. Clin. Psych.*, 9:368–370 (1953)

33. Bettelheim, B.: *Love Is Not Enough.* Glencoe, Ill.: Free Press, 1950

34. Bills, R. E., E. L. Vance, and O. S. McLean: An index of adjustment and values. *J. Consult. Psych.*, 15:257–261 (1951)

35. Bills, R. E.: Self concepts and Rorschach signs of depression. *J. Consult. Psych.*, 18:135–137 (1954)

36. Bindman, A. J.: Self-esteem and stability of the self concept in personality adjustment. Ph.D. dissertation, Boston University, 1955

37. Blake, R. R., and J. S. Mouton: Personality factors associated with individual conduct in a training group situation. *Human Research Training Laboratory Monograph*, No. 1. Austin, Texas: University of Texas Press, 1956

38. Bleuler, E.: *Dementia Praecox, or, The Group of Schizophrenias.* New York: International Universities Press, 1950

39. Blumberg, E. M., P. M. West, and F. W. Ellis: A possible relationship between psychosomatic factors and human cancer. *Psychosom. Med.,* 16:277–286 (1954)

40. Boguslavsky, G. W., and E. R. Guthrie: The recall of completed and interrupted activities; an investigation of Zeigarnik's experiment. *Psych. Bull.,* 38:575–576 (1941)

41. Bollea, G.: Contributo sperimentale alla fisiopatologia del cosidetto schema corporeo, *Riv. Neurol.,* 18:337–342 (1948)

42. Bonnier, P. L.: Aschématie. *Rev. Neurol.,* 54:605–621 (1905)

43. Borgatta, E. F.: Analysis of social interaction and sociometric perception. *Sociometry,* 17:7–31 (1954)

44. Bourguignon, E. E.: Class structure and acculturation in Haiti. *Ohio J. Sci.,* 6:317–320 (1952)

45. Bovard, E. W., Jr.: Social norms and the individual. *J. Abnorm. Soc. Psych.,* 43:62–69 (1948)

46. Bray, D. W.: The prediction of behavior from two attitude scales. *J. Abnorm. Soc. Psych.,* 45:64–84 (1950)

47. Bressler, B., S. I. Cohen, and F. Magnussen: Bilateral breast phantom and breast phantom pain. *J. Nerv. & Ment. Dis.,* 122:315–320 (1955)

48. Bressler, B., S. I. Cohen, and F. Magnussen: The problem of phantom breast and phantom pain. *J. Nerv. & Ment. Dis.,* 123:181–187 (1956)

49. Brody, S.: *Patterns of Mothering.* New York: International Universities Press, Inc., 1956

50. Brogden, H. E.: The primary personal values measured by the Allport-Vernon Test: A study of values. *Psych. Monogr.,* 66, No. 16, 1952 (Whole No. 348)

51. Bromberg, W., and C. L. Tranter: Peyote intoxication. *J. Nerv. & Ment. Dis.,* 97:518–527 (1943)

52. Brown, E. T., and P. L. Goitein: The significance of body image for personality assay. *J. Nerv. & Ment. Dis.,* 97:401–408 (1943)

53. Bruner, J. S., and L. Postman: Symbolic value as an organizing factor in perception. *J. Soc. Psych.,* 27:203–208 (1948)

54. Bunzel, R.: Introduction to Zuni ceremonialism. *Bureau of American Ethnology Report* 47, Washington, 1929–1930

55. Burton, A. C., and O. G. Edholm: *Man in a Cold Environment.* London: Edward Arnold & Co., 1955

56. Bychowski, G.: Disorders in the body-image in the clinical pictures of psychoses. *J. Nerv. & Ment. Dis.,* 97:310–334 (1943)

57. Carlson, V. R., and R. S. Lazarus: A repetition of Meyer Williams' study of intellectual control under stress and associated Rorschach factors. *J. Consult. Psych.,* 17:247–253 (1953)

58. Cattell, R. B.: *Description and Measurement of Personality.* Yonkers, N. Y.: World Book Company, 1946

59. Caudill, W.: Japanese-American personality and acculturation. *Genet. Psych. Monogr.,* 45:1–102 (1952)

60. Cheatham, M. J.: Sheldon's somatotypes and the projective techniques. Ph.D. dissertation, Western Reserve University, 1953
61. Cleveland, S. E.: Three cases of self castration. *J. Nerv. & Ment. Dis.*, 123:386–391 (1956)
62. Cleveland, S. E., and S. Fisher: Behavior and unconscious fantasies of patients with rheumatoid arthritis. *Psychosom. Med.*, 16:327–333 (1954)
63. ———: Psychological factors in the neurodermatoses. *Psychosom. Med.*, 18:209–220 (1956)
64. ———: Body image and small group behavior. *Hum. Relat.*, 10:223–233 (1957)
65. Cobb, B., and J. B. Trunnell: Medical psychological study of stress in cancer of the thyroid. Paper read at Southwestern Psychological Association, Dallas, 1954
66. Cohen, R.: Role of "body image concept" in pattern of ipsilateral clinical extinction. *Arch. Neurol. Psychiat.*, 70:503–509 (1953)
67. Critchley, M.: The body image in neurology. *Lancet*, 1:335–340 (1950)
68. ———: *The Parietal Lobes.* London: Edward Arnold & Co., 1953
69. Cronholm, B.: Phantom limbs in amputees: Study of changes in integration of centripetal impulses with special reference to referred sensations. *Acta Psychiat. et Neurol. Scandinav.*, Supp. 72, 1951
70. Culler E., and F. A. Mettler: Conditioned behavior in a decorticate dog. *J. Exp. Psych.*, 18:291–303 (1934)
71. Curran, F. J., and J. Frosch: The body image in adolescent boys. *J. Genet. Psych.*, 60:37–60 (1942)
72. Curran, F. J., and M. Levine: A body image study of prostitutes. *J. Crim. Psychopath.*, 4:93–116 (1942)
73. Cushing, F. H.: My adventures in Zuni: I. *Century Magazine*, N.S. No. 3, 1882–1883
74. Cutner, M.: On the inclusion of certain "body experiments" in analysis. *Brit. J. Med. Psych.*, 26:262–277 (1953)
75. Darling, R. P.: Autonomic action in relation to personality traits of children. *J. Abnorm. Soc. Psych.*, 35:246–260 (1940)
76. Darrow, C. W.: Differences in the physiological reactions to sensory and ideational stimuli. *Psych. Bull.*, 26:180–201 (1929)
77. Darrow, C. W., and A. P. Solomon: Galvanic skin reflex and blood pressure in psychotic states. *Arch. Neurol. Psychiat. Chicago*, 32:273–299 (1934)
77A. Davis, A. D.: Test of a body exterior vs. body interior theory of physiological reactivity. Ph.D. dissertation, University of Texas, 1957
78. Davis, A., B. B. Gardner, and M. R. Gardner: *Deep South.* Chicago: University of Chicago Press, 1941
79. Davis, R. C., A. M. Buchwald, and R. W. Frankmann: Autonomic and muscular responses, and their relation to simple stimuli. *Psychol. Monogr.*, 69, No. 20, 1955 (Whole No. 302)
80. Deutsch, M. A.: A theory of cooperation and competition. *Hum. Relat.*, 2:129–152 (1949)
81. De Vos, G.: A comparison of the personality differences in two genera-

tions of Japanese-Americans by means of the Rorschach test. *Nagoya. J. Med. Sci.*, 17:153–265 (1954)

82. ———: A quantitative Rorschach assessment of maladjustment and rigidity in acculturating Japanese-Americans. *Genet. Psych. Monogr.*, 52: 51–87 (1955)

83. Dunlap, K.: Improved forms of steadiness tester and tapping plate. *J. Exp. Psych.*, 4:430–433 (1922)

84. Elkisch, P.: Significant relationship between the human figure and the machine in the drawings of boys. *Amer. J. Orthopsych.*, 22:379–385 (1952)

84A. Ellingson, R. J.: Brain waves and problems of psychology. *Psych. Bull.*, 53:1–34 (1956)

85. Embree, J. F.: *Suye Mura: A Japanese Village.* Chicago: University of Chicago Press, 1939

86. Ericson, M. C.: "Social status and child-rearing practices," in *Readings in Social Psychology* (Ed. T. M. Newcomb, and E. L. Hartley). New York: Henry Holt and Company, 1947

87. Eriksen, C. W.: Psychological defenses and "ego strength" in the recall of completed and incompleted tasks. *J. Abnorm. Soc. Psych.*, 49:45–50 (1954)

88. Erikson, E. H.: *Childhood and Society.* New York: W. W. Norton & Company, Inc., 1950

88A. ———: Sex differences in the play configurations of preadolescents. *Amer. J. Orthopsych.*, 21:667–692 (1951)

89. Eysenck, H. J., and W. D. Furneaux: Primary and secondary suggestibility: an experimental and statistical study. *J. Exp. Psych.*, 35:485–503 (1945)

90. ———: *Dimensions of Personality. London.* Kegan Paul, Trench, Trubner & Co., 1947

91. Federn, P.: Some variations in ego feeling. *Int. J. Psychoanal.*, 7:434–444 (1926)

92. Fenichel, O.: *The Psychoanalytic Theory of Neurosis.* New York: W. W. Norton & Company, 1945

93. Ferguson-Rayport, S. M., R. M. Griffith, and E. W. Straus: The psychiatric significance of tattoos. *Psych. Quart.*, 29:112–131 (1955)

94. Fine, H. J., S. C. Fulkerson, L. Phillips: Maladjustment and social attainment. *J. Abnorm. Soc. Psych.*, 50:33–35 (1955)

95. Fingert, H., J. R. Kagan, and P. Schilder: The Goodenough test in insulin and metrazol treatment of schizophrenia. *J. Gen. Psych.*, 21:349–355 (1939)

96. Fisher, R.: The effect of a disturbing situation upon the stability of various projective tests. Ph.D. dissertation, University of Chicago, 1956

97. Fisher, S.: Patterns of personality rigidity and some of their determinants. *Psych. Monogr.*, 64: No. 1, 1950 (Whole No. 307)

97A. ———: The organization of hostility controls in various personality structures. *Genet. Psych. Monogr.*, 44:3–68 (1951)

98. Fisher, S., and R. Fisher: Style of sexual adjustment in disturbed women and its expression in figure drawings. *J. Psych.*, 34:169–179 (1952)

99. Fisher, S., and S. E. Cleveland: The role of body image in psychosomatic symptom choice. *Psycho. Monogr.*, 69, No. 17, 1955 (Whole No. 402)

100. ———— and ————: Body-image boundaries and style of life. *J. Abnorm. Soc. Psych.*, 52:373–379 (1956)

101. ———— and ————: Relationship of body-image boundaries to memory for completed and incompleted tasks. *J. Psych.*, 42:35–41 (1956)

102. ———— and ————: Relationship of body-image to site of cancer. *Psychosom. Med.*, 18:304–309 (1956)

103. Fisher, S., and D. Mendell: The communication of neurotic patterns over two and three generations. *Psychiatry*, 19:41–46 (1956)

104. Fisher, S., and S. E. Cleveland: An approach to physiological reactivity in terms of body image schema. *Psych. Rev.*, 64:26–37 (1957)

105. Fisher, S., and R. B. Morton: Levels of prediction from the TAT. *J. Consult. Psych.*, 21:115–120 (1957)

106. Flescher, J.: On neurotic disorders of sensibility and body scheme. *Int. J. Psychoanal.*, 29:156–162 (1948)

107. Fordham, M.: Some observations on the self in childhood. *Brit. J. Med. Psych.*, 24:83–96 (1951)

108. Fouriezos, N. T., M. L. Hutt, and H. Guetzkow: Measurement of self-oriented needs in discussion groups. *J. Abnorm. Soc. Psychol.*, 45:682–690 (1950)

109. Freed, H., and J. R. Paster: Evaluation of the "Draw-A-Person" Test (modified) in thalamotomy with particular reference to the body-image. *J. Nerv. & Ment. Dis.*, 114:106–120 (1951)

110. Freeman, G. L.: Changes in tonus during completed and interrupted mental work. *J. Gen. Psych.*, 4:309–334 (1930)

111. Freud, S.: *The Ego and the Id.* London: Hogarth Press, Ltd., 1927

112. ————: *A General Introduction to Psychoanalysis.* New York: Garden City Publishing Company, Inc., 1943

113. ————: *Collected Papers.* London: Hogarth Press, Ltd., 1949

114. Friedman, E. L.: Level of aspiration and some criteria of adjustment in an aged population. Ph.D. dissertation, Duke University, 1956

115. Friedman, G. A.: A cross-cultural study of the relationship between independence training and *n* Achievement as revealed by mythology. Unpublished Honors thesis, Harvard University, 1950

116. Friedman, S. M.: An empirical study of the castration and oedipus complexes. *Gen. Psych. Monogr.*, 46:61–130 (1952)

117. Fromm, E.: *Escape from Freedom.* New York: Farrar and Rinehart, Inc., 1941

117A. Funkenstein, D. H., and S. H. King, and M. A. Drolette: The direction of anger during a laboratory stress-inducing situation. *Psychosom. Med.*, 16:404–413 (1954)

118. Galdston, I.: On the etiology of depersonalization. *J. Nerv. & Ment. Dis.*, 105:25–39 (1947)

119. Gallinek, A.: The phantom limb. *Amer. J. Psychiat.*, 96:497–500 (1939)
120. Gant, W. H.: *Experimental Basis for Neurotic Behavior.* New York: Paul B. Hoeber, Inc., 1944
121. Garma, A.: The origin of clothes. *Psychoan. Quart.*, 18:173–190 (1949)
121A. Garrett, H. E.: *Statistics in Psychology and Education.* New York: Longmans, Green, and Co., Inc., 1948
122. Gellhorn, E.: *Physiological Foundations of Neurology and Psychiatry.* Minneapolis, University of Minnesota Press, 1953
123. Gengerelli, J. A., and F. I. Kirkner: *The Psychological Variable in Human Cancer.* Berkeley: University of California Press, 1954
124. Gerstmann, J.: Fingeragnosie. Eine umschriebene Störung der Orientierung am eigenen Körper. *Wien klin. Wchnschr.* 37:1010–1023 (1924)
124A. ————: Problem of imperception of disease and of impaired body territories with organic lesions. Relation to body schema and its disorders. *Arch. Neurol. Psychiat.*, 48:890–913 (1942)
125. Gesell, A., and L. B. Ames: The development of directionality in drawing. *J. Genet. Psych.*, 68:45–61 (1946)
126. Gill, M.: *Hypnosis and Ego Boundaries.* Unpublished manuscript
127. Goldfrank, E.: Socialization, personality, and the structure of Pueblo society. *Amer. Anthropologist,* 47:516–539 (1945)
128. Goitein, P. L.: The subjective experience in asthma. *J. Nerv. & Ment. Dis.*, 96:173–183 (1942)
129. Goodenough, F. L., and D. B. Harris: Studies in the psychology of children's drawings: II. 1928–1949. *Psych. Bull.*, 47:369–433 (1950)
130. Greenacre, P.: The mutual adventures of Jonathan Swift and Lemuel Gulliver: A study in pathography. *Psychoan. Quart.*, 24:20–62 (1955)
131. Greene, W. A., Jr.: Psychological factors and reticuloendothelial disease. *Psychosom. Med.*, 16:220–230 (1954)
132. ————: Process in psychosomatic disorders. *Psychosom. Med.*, 18:150–158 (1956)
133. Greene, W. A., Jr., L. E. Young and S. N. Swisher: Psychological factors and reticuloendothelial disease. *Psychosom. Med.*, 18:284–303 (1956)
134. Grinker, R. R.: *Toward a Unified Theory of Human Behavior.* New York: Basic Books, Inc., 1956
135. Gunvald, G.: Reliability and validity of a new method for the study of the body image. Master's dissertation, University of Washington, 1951
136. Gutheil, E.: Depersonalization. *Psychoan. Rev.*, 17:261–270 (1930)
137. Haber, W. B.: Effects of loss of limb on sensory organization and phantom limb phenomena. Ph.D. dissertation, New York University, 1954
138. ————: Effects of loss of limb on sensory functions, *J. Psych.*, 40:115–123 (1955)
139. ————: Observations on phantom limb phenomena. *A.M.A. Arch. Neurol. Psychiat.*, 75:624–636 (1956)
140. Hall, G. S.: Some aspects of the early sense of self. *Am. J. Psych.*, 9:351–395 (1898)

422 *Bibliography*

141. Hallowell, A. I.: *Culture and Experience*. Philadelphia: University of Pennsylvania Press, 1955
142. Hare, P. A., E. F. Borgatta, and R. F. Bales: *Small Groups, Studies in Social Interaction*. New York: Alfred A. Knopf, Inc., 1955
143. Hartman, H., E. Kris, and R. M. Lowenstein: "Comments on the formation of psychic structure," in *The Psychoanalytic Study of the Child*, vol. 2. New York: International Universities Press, 1951
144. Haythorn, W.: The influence of individual members on the characteristics of small groups. *J. Abnorm. Soc. Psych.*, 48:276–294 (1953)
145. Head, H.: Sensory disturbance from cerebral lesions. *Brain*, 34:187–189 (1911)
146. ———: Studies in neurology, vol. 2. London: Hodder & Stoughton, Ltd., and Oxford University Press, 1920
147. ———: *Aphasia and Kindred Disorders of Speech*. London: Cambridge University Press, 1926
148. Hemphill, R. E.: Misinterpretation of mirror image of self in presenile cerebral atrophy. *J. Ment. Sci.*, 94:603–610 (1948)
149. Henry, J.: Symposium: projective testing in ethnography. *Amer. Anthropologist*, 57:245–270 (1955)
149A. Herring, F. H.: Response during anesthesia and surgery. *Psychosom. Med.*, 18:243–251 (1956)
150. Hoffer, W.: "The mutual influences in the development of ego and id: earliest stages," in *The Psychoanalytic Study of the Child*, vol. 3–4. New York: International Universities Press, 1952
151. ———: "Mouth, hand, and ego integration," in *The Psychoanalytic Study of the Child*, vol. 3–4. New York: International Universities Press, 1952
152. Hoffman, J.: Facial phantom phenomenon. *J. Nerv. & Ment. Dis.*, 122:143–151 (1955)
152A. Holtzman, W. H.: Progress report of research on the development of a new inkblot test. Unpublished manuscript
153. Holtzman, W. H., and M. E. Bitterman: A factorial study of adjustment to stress. *J. Abnorm. Soc. Psych.*, 52:179–185 (1956)
154. Hull, C. L.: Quantitative methods of investigating waking suggestion. *J. Abnorm. Soc. Psych.*, 24:153–169 (1929)
155. ———: *Hypnosis and Suggestibility*. New York: D. Appleton-Century Company, Inc., 1933
156. Johnson, L.: Body cathexis as a factor in somatic complaints. *J. Consult. Psych.*, 20:145–149 (1956)
157. Johnson, L. C., and J. A. Stern: Rigidity on the Rorschach and response to intermittent photic stimulation. *J. Consult. Psych.*, 19:311–317 (1955)
158. Jolles, I.: A study of the validity of some hypotheses for the qualitative interpretation of the H-T-P for children of elementary school age: I. Sexual identification. *J. Clin. Psych.*, 8:113–118 (1952)
159. Jourard, S. M.: Ego strength and the recall of tasks. *J. Abnorm. Soc. Psych.*, 49:51–58 (1954)

160. Jourard, S. M., and P. F. Secord: Body-cathexis and the ideal female figure. *J. Abnorm. Soc. Psych.*, 50:243–246 (1955)

161. Jung, C. G.: *Psychological Types*. London: Kegan Paul, Trench, Trubner & Co., Ltd., 1926

162. ————: *Psychology of the Unconscious*. New York: Dodd, Mead and Company, Inc., 1931

163. ————: *Psychology and Alchemy*. New York: Pantheon Books, 1944

164. Kaplan, B.: *Primary Records in Culture and Personality*, vol. 1. Madison, Wisconsin: Microcard Foundation, 1956

165. Karush, A., R. B. Hiatt, and G. E. Daniels: Psychophysiological correlations in ulcerative colitis. *Psychosom. Med.*, 17:36–56 (1955)

166. Katcher, A., and M. M. Levin: Children's conceptions of body size. *Child Develpm.*, 26:103–110 (1955)

167. Keiser, S.: Body ego during orgasm. *Psychoan. Quart.*, 21:153–166 (1952)

167A. Kelly, E. L., and D. W. Fiske: *The Prediction of Performance in Clinical Psychology*. Ann Arbor, Mich., University of Michigan Press, 1951

168. Kelman, H. C.: Effects of success and failure on "suggestibility" in the autokinetic situation. *J. Abnorm. Soc. Psych.*, 45:267–285 (1950)

169. Kepecs, J. G.: Patterns of somatic displacement. *Psychosom. Med.*, 15: 425–436 (1953)

170. Kepecs, J. G., and M. Robin Studies in itching. II. Some psychological implications of the interrelationships between the cutaneous pain and touch systems. *A.M.A. Arch. Neurol. and Psychiat.*, 76:325–340 (1956)

171. Kleitman, N.: *Sleep and Wakefulness as Alternating Phases in the Cycle of Existence*. Chicago: University of Chicago Press, 1939

172. Klemperer, E.: Changes of the body image in hypnoanalysis. *J. Clin. Exp. Hypnosis.*, 2:157–162 (1954)

173. Kluckhohn, C.: Anthropological field research in solution of a specific problem: participation in ceremonials in a Navaho community. *Amer. Anthropologist.*, 40:359–369 (1938)

174. ————: A Navaho personal document with a brief Paretian analysis. *Southwestern J. Anthropol.*, 1:260–283 (1945)

175. Kluckhohn, C., and D. C. Leighton: *The Navaho*. Cambridge, Mass.: Harvard University Press, 1946

176. Kluckhohn, C.: "Some aspects of Navaho infancy and early childhood," in *Psychoanalysis and the Social Sciences*. (Roheim, G., ed.) vol. 1. New York: International Universities Press, 1947

177. Kluver, H.: Mescal visions and eidetic vision. *Am. J. Psych.*, 37:502–509 (1926)

178. Koffka, K.: *Principles of Gestalt Psychology*. New York: Harcourt, Brace and Company, Inc., 1935

179. Kosseff, J. W.: A study of changes in body image during psychotherapy. Ph.D. dissertation, New York University, 1952

180. Kowal, S. J.: Emotions as a cause of cancer. *Psychoan. Rev.*, 42:217–227 (1955)

181. Kretschmer, E.: *Physique and Character.* New York: Harcourt, Brace and Company, Inc., 1923

182. Kubie, L. S.: The central representation of the symbolic process in psychosomatic disorders. *Psychosom. Med.,* 15:1–7 (1953)

183. Lacey, J. L.: Individual differences in somatic response patterns. *J. Comp. Physiol. Psych.,* 43:338–350 (1950)

184. Lacey, J. L., and R. Van Lehn: Differential emphasis in somatic response to stress. *Psychosom Med.,* 14:71–81 (1952)

185. Lacey, J. L.: The evaluation of autonomic responses: toward a general solution. *Annals of New York Academy of Sciences.* 67:123–164 (1956)

186. Lee, D.: Notes on the conception of self among the Wintu Indians. *J. Abnorm. Soc. Psych.,* 45:538–543 (1950)

187. Leighton, D. C., and C. Kluckhohn: *Children of the People.* Cambridge, Mass.: Harvard University Press, 1947

188. Le Shan, L., and R. Worthington: Some psychologic correlates of neoplastic disease: a preliminary report. *J. Clin. Exp. Psychopath.,* 16:281–288 (1955)

189. Le Shan, L., and R. E. Worthington: Personality as a factor in the pathogenesis of cancer: a review of the literature. *Brit. J. Med. Psych.,* 29:49–56 (1956)

190. Levin, M. M., and G. A. Gunwald: New technique for the study of the body image. (Abstr.) *Amer. Psychologist,* 6, 490 (1951)

191. Levy, P. M.: Body interest in children and hypochondriases. *Am. J. Psychiat.,* 12:296–315 (1932)

192. Levy, R. J.: The Rorschach pattern in neurodermatitis. *Psychosom. Med.,* 14:41–49 (1952)

193. Lewin, B. D.: The body as phallus. *Psychoan. Quart.,* 2:24–47 (1933)

194 Lewin, K.: *Dynamic Theory of Personality.* New York: McGraw-Hill Book Company, Inc., 1935

195. Lewinsohn, P. M.: Some individual differences in physiological reactivity to stress. Ph.D. dissertation, John Hopkins University, 1954

196. Lhermitte, J.: *L'image de notre corps.* Paris: Editions de la Nouvelle Revue Critique, 1935

197. ———: De l'image corporelle. *Rev. Neurol.,* 74:20–38 (1942)

198. Linn, L.: The discriminating function of the ego. *Psychoan. Quart.,* 23:38–47 (1954)

199. ———: Some developmental aspects of the body image. *Int. J. Psychoan.,* 36:36–42 (1955)

200. Little, K. B.: An investigation of autonomic balance in peptic ulcer patients. Ph.D. dissertation, University of California, 1950

201. Lorr, M., E. Rubenstein, and R. L. Jenkins: A factor analysis of personality ratings of out-patients in psychotherapy. *J. Abnorm. Soc. Psych.,* 48:507–514 (1953)

202. Lundin, W. H.: Projective Movement Sequences: motion patterns as a projective technique. *J. Consult. Psych.,* 13:407–411 (1949)

202A. Lurie, W. A.: A study of Spranger's value types by the method of factor analysis. *J. Soc. Psych.*, 8:17–37 (1937)

203. Machover, K.: *Personality Projection in the Drawing of the Human Figure.* Springfield, Ill.: Charles C Thomas, Publisher, 1949

204. ————: Human figure drawings of children. *J. Proj. Tech.*, 17:85–91 (1953)

205. Mahoney, C. G.: Treatment of painful phantom limb by removal of the postcentral cerebral cortex. *A.M.A. Arch. Neurol. and Psychiat.* 64:894–896 (1950)

206. Malmo, R. B., and C. Shagass: Physiologic studies of reaction to stress in anxiety and early schizophrenia. *Psychosom. Med.*, 11:9–24 (1949)

207. ————, and ————: Physiologic study of symptom mechanisms in psychiatric patients under stress. *Psychosom. Med.*, 11:29–39 (1949)

208. Margolin, S. G.: The behavior of the stomach during psychoanalysis. *Psychoan. Quart.*, 20:349–373 (1951)

209. Mayer-Gross, W.: On depersonalization. *Brit. J. Med. Psych.*, 15:103–109 (1935)

210. McCleary, R. A.: The nature of the galvanic skin response. *Psych. Bull.*, 47:97–117 (1950)

211. McClelland, D.: *Personality.* New York: The Dryden Press, Inc., 1951

212. McClelland, D., J. W. Atkinson, R. A. Clark, and E. L. Lowell: *The Achievement Motive.* New York: Appleton-Century-Crofts, Inc., 1953

213. McCurdy, H. G.: An experimental study of waking postural suggestion. *J. Exp. Psych.*, 38:250–256 (1948)

214. Mead, G. H.: *Mind, Self, and Society.* Chicago: University of Chicago Press, Chicago, 1934

215. Meerlo, J. A. M.: Psychological implications of malignant growth. *Brit. J. Med. Psych.*, 27:210–215 (1954)

216. Mendell, D., and S. Fisher: An approach to neurotic behavior in terms of a three generation family model. *J. Nerv. & Ment. Dis.*, 123:171–180 (1956)

217. Meyer, B. C., F. Brown, and A. Levine: Observations on the House-Tree-Person Drawing Test before and after surgery. *Psychosom. Med.*, 17:428–454 (1955)

218. Michael, D. N.: A cross-cultural investigation of closure. *J. Abnorm. Soc. Psych.*, 48:225–230 (1953)

219. Michel-Hutmacher, R.: Das Körperinnere in der Vorstellung der Kinder. *Schweiz. Z. Psychol. Anwend.*, 14:1–26 (1955)

220. Miles, J. E.: Phantom limb syndrome occurring during spinal anesthesia. *J. Nerv. & Ment. Dis.*, 123:365–368 (1956)

221. Moloney, J. C.: *The Magic Cloak.* Wakefield, Mass.: Montrose Press, 1949

222. Morris, C., and L. V. Jones: Value scales and dimensions. *J. Abnorm. Soc. Psych.*, 51:523–535 (1955)

222A. Moruzzi, G., and H. W. Magoun: Brain-stem reticular formation and activation of the EEG. *Electroencephalog. Clin. Neurophysiol.*, 1:445–473 (1949)

222B. Moses, L.: Psychodynamic and electroencephalographic factors in duodenal ulcer. *Psychosom. Med.*, 8:405–409 (1946)

223. Mowrer, O. H.: *Learning Theory and Personality Dynamics.* New York: Ronald Press Company, 1950

224. Mueller, A. D., and A. M. Lefkovits: Personality structure and dynam‑ics of patients with rheumatoid arthritis. *J. Clin. Psych.*, 12:143–147 (1956)

225. Mullahy, P.: *Oedipus Myth and Complex.* New York: Hermitage House, Inc., 1952

226. Nacht, S.: "Mutual influences in development of ego and id," in *The Psychoanalytic Study of the Child*, vol. 3–4. New York: International Universities Press, 1952

227. Nielsen, J. M.: Gerstmann syndrome: finger agnosia, agraphia, confusion of right and left, acalculia. Comparison of this syndrome with dis‑turbance of body scheme resulting from lesions of the right side of the brain. *Arch. Neurol. and Psychiat.*, 39:536–542 (1935)

228. Northway, M. L.: The concept of the "schema." *Brit. J. Psych.*, 30:316–326 (1940)

229. Oldfield, R. C., and O. L. Zangwill: I. Head's concept of the schema and its application in contemporary British psychology. II. Critical anal‑ysis of Head's theory. III. Bartlett's theory of memory. *Brit. J. Psych.*, 33:58–64, 113–129 (1942)

230. Orlansky, H.: Infant care and personality. *Psych. Bull.*, 46:1–48 (1949)

231. Owen, M.: Perception of simultaneous tactile stimuli in emotionally disturbed children and its relation to their body image concept. *J. Nerv. & Ment. Dis.*, 121:397–409 (1955)

232. Parsons, T., and R. F. Bales: *Family Socialization and Interaction Proc‑ess.* Glencoe, Ill.: Free Press, 1955

233. Penfield, W., and E. Boldrey: Somatic motor and sensory representation in the cerebral cortex of man as studied by electrical stimulation. *Brain*, 60:389–443 (1937)

234. Perry, J. W.: *The Self in Psychotic Process; Its Symbolization in Schizo‑phrenia.* Berkeley: University of California Press, 1953

235. Pick, A.: Störung der Orientierung am eigenen Körper, *Psychol. For‑schung.*, 1:303–315 (1922)

236. Rabinovitch, M. S.: Personal communication

237. Rank, O.: *The Trauma of Birth.* New York: Harcourt, Brace and Com‑pany, Inc., 1929

238. Reed, M. R.: A study of the masculinity-femininity dimension of per‑sonality in "normal" and "pathological groups": an investigation of differences in M-F test productions of hospitalized and nonhospitalized women. Ph.D. dissertation, Washington University, 1955

239. Reich, W.: *Character Analysis.* New York: Orgone Institute Press, 1949

240. Reymert, M. L. (ed.): *Feeling and Emotions.* New York: McGraw-Hill Book Company, Inc., 1950

241. Reznikoff, M.: Psychological factors in breast cancer: A preliminary

study of some personality trends in patients with cancer of the breast. *Psychosom. Med.*, 17:96–108 (1955)

242. Rickers-Ovsiankina, M.: Studies of the personality structure of schizophrenic individuals. I. The accessibility of schizophrenics to environmental influences. II. Reaction to interrupted tasks. *J. Gen. Psych.*, 16:153–178, 179–196 (1937)

243. Riddoch, G.: Phantom limbs and body shape. *Brain*, 64:197–222 (1941)

244. Riese, W., and G. Bruck: Les Membres fantômes chez l'enfant. *Rev. Neurol.*, 83:221–222 (1950)

245. Riesman, D.: *The Lonely Crowd.* New Haven, Conn.: Yale University Press, 1950

246. Roe, A.: Artists and their work. *J. Person.*, 15:1–40 (1946)

247. ————: A psychological study of eminent biologists. *Psych. Monogr.*, 65, No. 14, 1951 (Whole No. 331)

248. ————: A psychological study of eminent physical scientists. *Genet. Psych. Monogr.*, 43:121–239 (1951)

249. ————: Group Rorschachs of university faculties. *J. Consult. Psych.*, 16:18–22 (1952)

250. ————: A psychological study of eminent psychologists and anthropologists, and a comparison with biological and physical scientists. *Psych. Monogr.*, 67, No. 2, 1953 (Whole No. 352)

251. Roff, M.: Intra-family resemblances in personality characteristics. *J. Psych.*, 30:199–227 (1950)

252. Roman, R. A.: Comparative study of Northern and Southern ethnocentrism as related to the rigidity of personality structure. Ph.D. dissertation, University of Houston, 1953

253. Roseborough, M. E.: Experimental studies of small groups. *Psych. Bull.*, 50:275–303 (1953)

254. Rosenzweig, S.: An experimental study of "repression" with special reference to need-persistive and ego-defensive reactions to frustration. *J. Exp. Psych.*, 32:64–74 (1943)

255. Rosenzweig, S., and S. Saranson: An experimental study of the triadic hypothesis: reaction to frustration, ego defense, and hypnotizability. I. Correlational approach. *Character and Person.*, 11:1–20 (1942)

256. Rubin, S., and K. M. Bowman: Electroencephalographic and personality correlates in peptic ulcer. *Psychosom. Med.*, 4:309–318 (1942)

256A. Rubin, S., and L. Moses: Electroencephalographic studies in asthma with some personality correlates. *Psychosom. Med.*, 6:31–37 (1944)

257. Rust, R. M., and F. G. Ryan: The relationship of some Rorschach variables to academic behavior. *J. Person.*, 21:441–456 (1953)

258. Sandifer, P. H.: Unusual types of anosognosia and their relation to the body image. *J. Nerv. & Ment. Dis.*, 100:35–43 (1944)

259. Sandler, J., and B. Ackner: Rorschach content analysis: an experimental investigation. *Brit. J. Med. Psych.*, 24:180–200 (1951)

260. Sanford, N.: The dynamics of identification. *Psych. Rev.*, 62:106–118 (1955)

261. Sanford, R. N., M. M. Adkins, R. B. Muller, and E. Cobb: Physique, personality and scholarship. *Mon. Soc. Res. Child Dev.*, 7, Ser. No. 34 (1943)

262. Sanford, R. N., and J. Risser: Age as a factor in the recall of interrupted tasks. *Psych. Rev.*, 53:234–240 (1946)

263. Sarbin, T. R., and R. F. Berdie: Relation of measured interests to the Allport-Vernon Study of Values. *J. Appl. Psych.*, 24:287–296 (1940)

263A. Saul, L. J., H. Davis, and P. A. Davis: Psychologic correlations with the electroencephalogram. *Psychosom. Med.*, 11:361–368 (1949)

264. Savage, C.: Variations in ego feeling induced by D-lysergic acid diethylamide (L SD-25). *Psychoan. Rev.*, 42:1–16 (1955)

265. Scarborough, W. R., F. W. Davis, et al.: A ballistocardiographic study of 369 apparently normal persons. *Amer. Heart J.*, 45:161–189 (1953)

266. Schaffer, H. R.: Behavior under stress: a neurophysiological hypothesis. *Psych. Rev.*, 61:323–333 (1954)

267. Schilder, P.: Localization of the body image (postural model of the body). Localization of function in the cerebral cortex. *Res. Publ. Ass. Nerv. Ment. Dis.*, 13:466–585 (1934)

268. ———: *The Image and Appearance of the Human Body*. London: Kegan Paul, Trench, Trubner & Co., 1935

269. ———: *Goals and Desires of Man*. New York: Columbia University Press, 1942

270. Schneider, D. E.: The image of the heart and the synergic principle in psychoanalysis (psychosynergy). *Psychoan. Rev.*, 41:197–215 (1954)

271. Scott, R. D.: The psychology of the body image. *Brit. J. Med. Psych.*, 24:254–266 (1951)

272. Scott, W.: The "body scheme" in psychotherapy. *Brit. J. Med. Psych.*, 22:139–150 (1949)

273. Scott, W., and M. Clifford: Some embryological, neurological, psychiatric, and psychoanalytic implications of the body scheme. *Int. J. Psychoan.*, 29:141–155 (1948)

274. Searl, M. H.: Note on depersonalization. *Int. J. Psychoan.*, 13:345–351 (1932)

275. Sechehaye, M. A.: *Symbolic Realization*. New York: International Universities Press, 1951

276. Secord, P. F.: Objectification of word-association procedures by the use of homonyms: a measure of body cathexis. *J. Person.*, 21:479–495 (1953)

277. Seitz, P.: Experiments in the substitution of symptoms by hypnosis: II. *Psychosom. Med.*, 15:405–424 (1953)

278. Seward, G., and L. M. Morrison: Personality structure in a common form of colitis. *Psych. Monogr.*, 65, No. 1, 1951 (Whole No. 318)

279. Seymour, R. B.: Personality correlates of electrodermal resistance to response. Ph.D. dissertation, University of California, 1950

280. Sheldon, W. H., and S. S. Stevens: *The Varieties of Temperament*. New York: Harper and Brothers, 1942

281. Sherif, M.: A study of some social factors in suggestion. *Arch. Psych.*, No. 187, 1935

282. Silverberg, J. A.: A study in body concept. Ph.D. dissertation, University of Kentucky, 1949

283. Silverstein, A. B., and H. A. Robinson: The representation of orthopedic disability in children's figure drawings. *J. Consult. Psych.*, 20:333–341 (1956)

284. Simmel, M. L.: On phantom limbs. *Arch. Neurol. Psychiat.*, 75:637–647 (1956)

285. Simpson, G. E.: Sexual and familial institutions in Northern Haiti. *Amer. Anthropologist*, 44:655–674 (1942)

285A. Sisson, B. D., and R. J. Ellingson: On the relationship between "normal" EEG patterns and personality variables. *J. Nerv. & Ment. Dis.*, 121:353–358 (1955)

286. Smith, M. B., J. S. Bruner, and R. W. White: *Opinions and Personality.* New York: John Wiley and Sons, Inc., 1956

287. Snedecor, G. W.: *Statistical Methods.* Ames, Iowa: Iowa State College Press, 1946

288. Spillaine, J. D.: Disturbances of the body scheme. *Lancet.*, 242:42–44 (1942)

289. Stainbrook, E., and H. Lowenbach: Writing and drawing of psychotic individuals after electrically induced convulsions. *J. Nerv. & Ment. Dis.*, 99:382–388 (1944)

290. Stanton, J. B.: Investigation of Gerstmann's syndrome induced by hypnotic suggestion. *J. Ment. Sci.*, 100:961–964 (1954)

291. Steisel, I.: The Rorschach test and suggestibility. *J. Abnorm. Soc. Psych.*, 47:607–614 (1952)

292. Stephenson, J. H., and W. J. Grace: Life stress and cancer of the cervix. *Psychosom. Med.*, 16:287–294 (1954)

293. Sternberg, C.: Personality traits of college students majoring in different fields. *Psych. Monogr.*, 69, No. 18, 1955 (Whole No. 403)

294. Steuer, E. I.: Über das Nichterkennen des eigenen Spiegelbildes. *Mschr. Psychiat. Neurol.*, 106:294–310 (1942)

295. Strauss, A.: Finger agnosia in children. *Am. J. Psychiat.*, 95:1215–1225 (1939)

296. Strauss, A., and H. Werner: Deficiency in the finger scheme in relation to arithmetic disability. *Am. J. Orthopsych.*, 81:719–723 (1938)

297. Stratton, C. M.: Some preliminary experiments on vision without inversion of the retinal image. *Psych. Rev.*, 3:611–627 (1896)

298. ———: Vision without inversion of the retinal image. *Psych. Rev.*, 4:341–360, 463–481 (1897)

299. Streitfeld, H.: Specificity of peptic ulcer to intense oral conflicts. *Psychosom. Med.*, 16:313–326 (1954)

300. Strong, E. K.: *Manual for Vocational Interest Blank for Men.* Stanford, Calif.: Stanford University Press, 1938

301. ———: *Vocational Interests of Men and Women.* Stanford, Calif.: Stanford University Press, 1948

302. Sutherland, A. M., C. E. Orbach, R. B. Dyk, and M. Bard: The psychological impact of cancer and cancer surgery. I. Adaptation to colostomy; preliminary report and summary of findings. *Cancer*, 5:857–872 (1952)

303. Swensen, C. H.: Sexual differentiation on the Draw-A-Person Test. *J. Clin. Psych.*, 11:27–41 (1955)

304. Swensen, C. H., and K. R. Newton: The development of sexual differentiation on the Draw-A-Person Test. *J. Clin. Psych.*, 11:417–419 (1955)

305. Swift, J. W.: Rorschach responses of 82 preschool children. *Ror. Res. Exch.*, 9:74–84 (1944)

306. Tait, Jr., C. D., and R. C. Ascher: Inside-of-the-Body Test. *Psychosom. Med.*, 17:139–148 (1955)

307. Tarlau, M., and M. A. Smalheiser: Personality patterns in patients with malignant tumors of the breast and cervix. *Psychosom. Med.*, 13:117–121 (1951)

308. Tausk, V.: On the origin of the influencing machine in schizophrenia. *Psychoan. Quart.*, 2:519–556 (1933)

309. Teevan, R. C.: Personality correlates of undergraduate field of specialization. *J. Consult. Psych.*, 18:212–214 (1954)

310. Teicher, J.: Disorientation of body image. *J. Nerv. & Ment. Dis.*, 106:619–636 (1947)

311. Teitelbaum, H. A.: Psychogenic body image disturbances associated with psychogenic aphasia and agnosia. *J. Nerv. & Ment. Dis.*, 93:581–612 (1941)

312. Teuber, H. L., H. P. Krieger, and M. B. Bender: Reorganization of sensory function in amputation stumps: two-point discrimination. *Fed. Proc.*, 8:156 (1949)

313. Thetford, W., and G. Devos: A Rorschach study of clinical groups by means of Fisher's Maladjustment Scale (Unpublished paper, read at the Midwest Psychological Association Convention, 1951)

314. Thetford, W. N., H. B. Molish, and S. J. Beck: Developmental aspects of personality structure in young children. *J. Proj. Tech.*, 15:58–78 (1951)

314A. Thompson, C. M., and P. Mullahy: *Psychoanalysis: Evolution and Development.* New York: Hermitage House, Inc., 1950

315. Thompson, L.: Perception patterns in three Indian tribes. *Psychiatry*, 14:255–263 (1951)

316. Thurstone, L. L.: *Thurstone Interest Schedule (Manual).* New York: The Psychological Corporation, 1947

317. Todd, J., and K. Dewhurst: The double: its psychopathology and psychophysiology. *J. Nerv. & Ment. Dis.*, 122:47–55 (1955)

317A. Travis, L. E., and C. L. Bennett: The relationship between the electroencephalogram and scores in certain Rorschach categories. (Abstr.) *Electroencephalog. Clin. Neurophysiol.*, 5:474 (1953)

318. Trunnell, J. B.: *Second Report on Institutional Research Grants of the American Cancer Society.* New York: American Cancer Society, 1952

319. Underwood, F. W., and I. Honigmann: A comparison of socialization and personality in two simple societies. *Amer. Anthropologist,* 49:557–577 (1947)

320. Van der Valk, J. M., and J. Groen: Electrical resistance of the skin during induced emotional stress. *Psychosom. Med.,* 12:303–314 (1950)

321. Vollmer, H.: Psychosomatic significance of body orifices. *Amer. J. Orthopsych.,* 18:345–350 (1948)

322. Walker, D. E.: The relationship between creativity and test behaviors for chemists and mathematicians. Ph.D. dissertation, University of Chicago, 1956

323. Walker, H. M., and J. Lev: *Statistical Inference.* New York: Henry Holt and Company, Inc., 1953

324. Ware, K., S. Fisher, and S. E. Cleveland: Body image boundaries and adjustment to poliomyelitis. *J. Abnorm. Soc. Psych.,* 55:88–93 (1957)

325. Warner, W. L., and P. S. Lunt: *The Social Life of a Modern Community.* New Haven, Conn.: Yale University Press, 1941

326. Weber, E. H.: "Der Tastsinn und das Gemeingefühl," in R. Wagner's *Handwörterbuch der Physiologie,* vol. 3, Braunschweig: Vieweg, 1846

327. Weinstein, E. A., R. L. Kahn, S. Molitz, and J. Roganski: Delusional reduplication of parts of the body. *Brain,* 77:45–60 (1954)

328. Weinstein, E. A., S. Malitz, and W. J. Barker: Denial of the loss of a limb. *J. Nerv. & Ment. Dis.,* 120:27–30 (1954)

329. Weinstein, E. A., and R. L. Kahn: *Denial of Illness.* Springfield, Ill.: Charles C Thomas, Publisher, 1955

330. Wenger, M. A.: Measurement of individual differences in autonomic balance. *Psychosom. Med.,* 3:427–434 (1941)

331. ———: Stability of measurement of autonomic balance. *Psychosom. Med.,* 4:94–105 (1942)

332. Wenger, M. A., and M. Ellington: Measurement of autonomic balance in children: method and normative data. *Psychosom. Med.,* 5:241–253 (1943)

333. Wenger, M. A.: Preliminary study of the significance of measures of autonomic balance. *Psychosom. Med.,* 11:301–309 (1947)

334. ———: Studies of autonomic balance in Army Air Forces personnel. *Comp. Psych., Monogr.,* 19, No. 4, 1948 (Serial No. 101)

335. Werner, H.: *Comparative Psychology of Mental Development.* Chicago: Follett Publishing Co., 1948

336. Werner, H., and S. Wapner: Sensory-tonic field theory of perception. *J. Person.,* 18:88–107 (1949)

337. West, J.: *Plainville, U.S.A.* New York: Columbia University Press, 1945

338. Westrope, M. R.: Relations among Rorschach indices, manifest anxiety, and performance under stress. *J. Abnorm. Soc. Psych.,* 48:515–524 (1953)

339. Whiting, J. W. M., and I. L. Child: *Child Training and Personality.* New Haven, Conn.: Yale University Press, 1953

340. Wieder, A., and P. A. Noller: Objective studies of children's drawings of human figures. I. Sex awareness and socioeconomic level. *J. Clin.*

Psych., 6:319–325 (1950) II. Sex, age, and I.Q. *J. Clin. Psych.*, 9:20–23 (1953)

341. Wilcoxin, F.: *Some Rapid Approximate Statistical Procedures*. New York: American Cyanamid Co., 1949

342. Wille, W. S.: Figure drawings in amputees. *Psych. Quart. Suppl.*, 28:192–198 (1954)

343. Williams, M.: An experimental study of intellectual control under stress and associated Rorschach factors. *J. Consult. Psych.*, 11:21–29 (1947)

344. Winder, C. L.: On the personality structure of schizophrenics. *J. Abnorm. Soc. Psych.*, 47:86–100 (1952)

345. Winne, J. F.: A scale of neuroticism. An adaptation of the Minnesota Multiphasic Personality Inventory. *J. Clin. Psych.* 7:117–122 (1951)

346. Wischner, J.: Neurosis and tension; An exploratory study of the relationship of physiological and Rorschach measures. *J. Abnorm. Soc. Psych.*, 48:253–260 (1953)

347. ———: The concept of efficiency in psychological health and in psychopathology. *Psych. Rev.*, 62:69–80 (1955)

348. Witkin, H. A., H. B. Lewis, M. Hertzman, K. Machover, P. B. Meissner, and S. Wapner: *Personality through Perception*. New York: Harper and Brothers, 1954

349. Wittkower, E. D.: Studies of the personality of patients suffering from urticaria. *Psychosom. Med.*, 15:116–126 (1953)

350. Wittreich, W. J.: Aniseikonia and distortion of the self-image. (Abstr.) *Am. Psychol.* 8:457–458 (1953)

351. Wittreich, W. J., and M. Grace: Body image development. Unpublished progress report to Office of Naval Research

352. Wittreich, W. J.: Body image and psychopathology: A pilot study. Unpublished report to Office of Naval Research

353. Wittreich, W. J., and K. B. Radcliffe, Jr.: The influence of simulated mutilation upon the perception of the human figure. *J. Abnorm. Soc. Psych.*, 51:493–495 (1955)

354. Wolff, H. F.: *Life Stress and Bodily Disease*. Baltimore: The Williams & Wilkins Company, 1950

355. Wolff, W.: Gestaltidentität in der Characterologie. *Psychol. und Med.*, 4:32–44 (1929)

356. ———: *The Expression of Personality*. New York: Harper and Brothers, 1943

357. Woods, W. A., and W. E. Cook: Proficiency in drawing and placement of hands in drawings of the human figure. *J. Consult. Psych.*, 18:119–121 (1954)

358. Wortis, H., and B. Dattner: An analysis of a somatic delusion. *Psychosom. Med.*, 4:319–323 (1942)

359. Wright, G. H.: The names of the parts of the body. *Brain*, 79:188–210 (1956)

360. Zaidens, S. H.: The skin: psychodynamic and psychopathologic concepts. *J. Nerv. & Ment. Dis.*, 113:388–394 (1951)

361. Zeigarnik, B.: Über das Behalten von erledigten und unerledigten Handlungen. *Psychol. Forsch.*, 9:1–85 (1927)

References to Chapter 15*

Allardice, Barbara S., and A. A. Dole: Body image in Hansen's disease patients. *Journal of Projective Techniques and Personality Assessment,* 30:356-358 (1966)

Appleby, L.: The relationship of a Rorschach barrier typology to other behavioral measures. Doctoral dissertation, University of Houston, 1956

Armstrong, H.: The relationship between a dimension of body-image and two dimensions of conditioning. Doctoral dissertation, Syracuse University, 1964

Azima, D., and F. J. Cramer: Effects of the decrease in sensory variability on body scheme. *Canadian Journal of Psychiatry,* 1:59-72 (1956)

Bachelis, L. A.: Body-field perceptual differentiation as a variable in creative thinking. Doctoral dissertation, Yeshiva University, 1965

Barts, G. J.: The perception of body boundaries. Master's thesis, Ohio State University, 1959

Blake, R. R., and J. S. Mouton: Personality factors associated with individual conduct in a training group situation. *Human Research Training Laboratory Monograph No. 1.* Austin: University of Texas Press, 1956

Blum, G.: A study of the psychoanalytic theory of psychosexual development. *Genetic Psychology Monographs,* 39:3-99 (1949)

Brodie, C. W.: The prediction of qualitative characteristics of behavior in stress situations, using test-assessed personality constructs. Doctoral dissertation, University of Illinois, 1959

Brown, D. G.: Psychosomatic correlates in contact dermatitis: A pilot study. *Journal of Psychosomatic Research,* 4:132-139 (1959)

Brown, D. G., and A. J. Young: The effect of extraversion on susceptibility to disease: A validatory study on contact dermatitis. *Journal of Psychosomatic Research,* 8:421-429 (1965)

———— and ————: Body image and susceptibility to contact dermatitis. *British Journal of Medical Psychology,* 38:261-267 (1965)

Cassell, W. A.: A tachistoscopic index of body perception. *Journal of Projective Techniques,* 30:31-36

————: Body perception and symptom localization. *Psychosomatic Medicine,* 27:171-176 (1965)

————: A projective index of body-interior awareness. *Psychosomatic Medicine,* 26:172-177 (1964)

Cassell, W. A., and S. Fisher: Body-image boundaries and histamine flare reaction. *Psychosomatic Medicine,* 25:344-350 (1963)

Cleveland, S. E.: Body image changes associated with personality reorganization. *Journal of Consulting Psychology,* 24:256-261 (1960)

Cleveland, S. E., and S. Fisher: A comparison of psychological characteristics and physiological reactivity in ulcer and rheumatoid arthritis groups: I. Psychological measures. *Psychosomatic Medicine,* 22:283-289 (1960)

---

* An attempt has been made to list all publications and dissertations concerning boundary definiteness stimulated by our original work.

Cleveland, S. E., S. Fisher, E. E. Reitman and P. Rothaus: Perception of body size in schizophrenia. *Archives of General Psychiatry,* 7:277-285 (1962)

Cleveland, S. E., and D. C. Johnson: Personality patterns in young males with coronary diseases. *Psychosomatic Medicine,* 24:600-610 (1962)

Cleveland, S. E., and R. B. Morton: Group behavior and body image: A follow-up study. *Human Relations,* 15:77-85 (1962)

Cleveland, S. E., E. E. Reitman and E. J. Brewer, Jr.: Psychological factors in juvenile rheumatoid arthritis. *Arthritis and Rheumatism,* 8:1152-1158 (1965)

Cleveland, S. E., and M. P. Sikes: Body image in chronic alcoholics and non-alcoholic psychiatric patients. *Journal of Projective Techniques and Personality Assessment,* 30:265-269 (1966)

Cleveland, S. E., Rebecca Snyder, and R. L. Williams: Body image and site of psychosomatic symptoms. *Psychological Reports,* 16:851-852 (1965)

Compton, N.: Body image boundaries in relation to clothing fabric and design preferences of a group of hospitalized psychotic women. *Journal of Home Economics,* 56:40-45 (1964)

Conquest, R. A.: An investigation of body image variables in patients with the diagnosis of schizophrenic reaction. Doctoral dissertation, Western Reserve University, 1963

Cormack, P. H.: A study of the relationship between body image and the perception of physical disability. Doctoral dissertation, State University of New York, Buffalo, 1966

Darrow, C. W.: Differences in the physiological reactions to sensory and ideational stimuli. *Psychological Bulletin,* 26:185-201 (1929)

Daston, P. G., and O. L. McConnell: Stability of Rorschach penetration and barrier scores over time. *Journal of Consulting Psychology,* 26:104 (1962)

Davis, A. D.: Some physiological correlates of Rorschach body-image productions. *Journal of Abnormal and Social Psychology,* 60:432-436 (1960)

Davis, R. C.: Response patterns. *Transactions of the New York Academy of Science,* 19 (Series II): 731-739 (1957)

Dorsey, D. S.: A study of the relationship between independence of group pressures and selected measures of body image. Doctoral dissertation, University of California, Los Angeles, 1965

Eigenbrode, C. R., and W. G. Shipman: The body image barrier concept. *Journal of Abnormal and Social Psychology,* 60:450-452 (1960)

Fish, J. E.: An exploration of developmental aspects of body scheme and of ideas about adulthood in grade school children. Doctoral dissertation, University of Kansas, 1960

Fisher, Rhoda Lee: Body boundary and achievement behavior. *Journal of Projective Techniques and Personality Assessment,* 30:435-438 (1966)

————: Mother's hostility and changes in child's classroom behavior. *Perceptual and Motor Skills,* 23:153-154 (1966)

————: The social schema of normal and disturbed school children. *Journal of Educational Psychology* (in press)

————: Failure of the conceptual styles test to discriminate normal and highly impulsive children. *Journal of Abnormal Psychology* (in press)

Fisher, S.: Body image in neurotic and schizophrenic patients. *Archives of General Psychiatry*, 15:90-101 (1966)

————: Body boundary sensations and acquiescence. *Journal of Abnormal and Social Psychology*, 1:381-383 (1965)

————: The body image as a source of selective cognitive sets. *Journal of Personality*, 33:536-552 (1965)

————: Body sensation and perception of projective stimuli. *Journal of Consulting Psychology*, 29:135-138 (1965)

————: The body boundary and judged behavioral patterns in an interview situation. *Journal of Projective Techniques and Personality Assessment*, 28:181-184 (1964)

————: Body image and psychopathology. *Archives of General Psychiatry*, 10:519-529 (1964)

————: Sex differences in body perception. *Psychological Monographs*, 78:1-22 (1964)

————: Body image and hypnotic response. *International Journal of Clinical and Experimental Hypnosis*, 11:152-157 (1963)

————: A further appraisal of the body boundary concept. *Journal of Consulting Psychology*, 27:62-74 (1963)

————; Body image boundaries and hallucinations. In *Hallucinations* (ed. by J. West), New York: Grune and Stratton, 1962

————: Body image boundaries in the aged. *Journal of Psychology*, 48:315-318 (1959)

————: Prediction of body exterior vs. body interior reactivity from a body image scheme. *Journal of Personality*, 27:56-62 (1959)

Fisher, S., and S. E. Cleveland: Personality, body perception, and body boundary in *The Body Percept* (ed. by S. Wapner and H. Werner). New York: Random House, 1965

———— and ————: A comparison of psychological characteristics and physiological reactivity in ulcer and rheumatoid arthritis groups: II. Differences in physiological reactivity. *Journal of Psychosomatic Medicine*, 22:290-293 (1960)

———— and ————: Body image boundaries and sexual behavior. *Journal of Psychology*, 45:207-211 (1958)

Fisher, S., and Rhoda Lee Fisher: Body image boundaries and patterns of body perception. *Journal of Abnormal and Social Psychology*, 68:255-262 (1964)

Fisher, S., and O. D. Renik: Induction of body image boundary changes. *Journal of Projective Techniques and Personality Assessment*, 30:429-434 (1966)

Fitzgerald, W. E.: A psychological factor in Legg-Calve-Perthes disease. Doctoral dissertation, Harvard University, 1961

Gibby, R. G., H. B. Adams and R. N. Carrera: Therapeutic changes in psychiatric patients following partial sensory deprivation. *Archives of General Psychiatry*, 3:33-42 (1960)

Gordon, Gail: Developmental changes in responses on the Holtzman Ink Blot Technique. Master's thesis Univ   of Texas, 1964

Gorham, D. R.: Validity and reliability of a computer scoring system for inkblot responses. *Psychological Research Reports*, May, 1966, No. 5. Psychology Research, VA Hospital, Perry Point, Maryland

————: The development of a computer scoring system for inkblot responses. *Psychological Research Reports*, September, 1961, No. 1. Psychology Research, VA Hospital, Perry Point, Maryland

Hammerschlag, C. A., S. Fisher, J. DeCosse and E. Kaplan: Breast symptoms and patient delay: Psychological variables involved. *Cancer*, 17:1480-1485 (1964)

Hartley, R. B.: A homonym word association measure of the barrier variable and its comparison with the inkblot barrier measure. Doctoral dissertation, University of Washington, 1964

Herron, E. W.: Changes in inkblot perception with presentation of the Holtzman Inkblot Technique as an "intelligence test." *Journal of Projective Techniques and Personality Assessment*, 28:442-447 (1964)

————: Intellectual achievement-motivation: A study in construct clarification. Doctoral dissertation, University of Texas, 1962

Holtzman, W. H., D. R. Gorham and L. J. Moran: A factor-analytic study of schizophrenic thought processes. *Journal of Abnormal and Social Psychology*, 69:355-364 (1964)

Holtzman, W. H., J. S. Thorpe, J. D. Swartz, and E. W. Herron: *Inkblot perception and personality*. Austin: University of Texas Press, 1961

Jacobson, G. R.: The effects of sensory deprivation on body image and field dependence. Master's thesis, William and Mary College, 1965

Jaskar, R. O.: Assessment of body image organization of hospitalized and non-hospitalized subjects. Doctoral dissertation, University of Portland, 1962

Jaskar, R. O., and M. R. Reed: Assessment of body image organization of hospitalized and non-hospitalized subjects. *Journal of Projective Techniques and Personality Assessment*, 27:185-190 (1963)

Kissel, S.: The "paradoxical" response of schizophrenics to sensory deprivation: A psychoanalytic interpretation. *The Psychological Record*, 15:245-248 (1965)

Koschene, R. L.: Body image and boundary constancy in kidney transplant patients: A test of the Fisher-Cleveland hypotheses. Master's thesis, University of Colorado, 1965

Landau, M. F.: Body image in paraplegia as a variable in adjustment to physical handicap. Doctoral dissertation, Columbia University, 1960.

Leeds, D. P.: Personality patterns and modes of behavior of male adolescent narcotic addicts and their mothers. Doctoral dissertation, Yeshiva University, 1965

McConnell, O. L., and P. G. Daston: Body image changes in pregnancy. *Journal of Projective Techniques*, 25:451-456 (1961)

Malev, J. S.: Body image and physiological reactivity in children. Master's thesis, Baylor University, 1961

————: Body image and physiological reactivity in children. *Journal of Psychosomatic Research* (in press)

Masson, R. L.: An investigation of the relationship between body-image and attitudes expressed toward visibly disabled persons. Doctoral dissertation, State University of New York, Buffalo, 1963

Megargee, E. I.: Relation between barrier scores and aggressive behavior. *Journal of Abnormal Psychology*, 70:307-311 (1965)

Miner, H. M., and G. DeVos: *Oasis and Casbah: Algerian culture and personality in change*. Ann Arbor: University of Michigan Press, 1960

Morton, Joyce C.: The relationship between inkblot barrier scores and sociometric status in adolescents. Master's thesis, University of British Columbia, 1965

Nichols, D. C., and B. Tursky: Body image, anxiety, and tolerance for experimental pain. *Psychosomatic Medicine* (in press)

Ohzama, M.: The changes of body image boundary scores under condition of alcoholic intoxication. *Tohuku Psychol. Folia*, 22:100-107 (1964)

Ramer, J. C.: The Rorschach barrier score and social behavior. Doctoral dissertation, University of Washington, 1961

————: The Rorschach barrier score and social behavior. *Journal of Consulting Psychology*, 27:525-531 (1963)

Reitman, E. E.: Changes in body image following sensory deprivation in schizophrenic and control groups. Doctoral dissertation, University of Houston, 1962

Reitman, E. E., and S. E. Cleveland: Changes in body image following sensory deprivation in schizophrenic and control groups. *Journal of Abnormal and Social Psychology*, 68:168-176 (1964)

Rosenzweig, N., and L. Gardner: The role of input relevance in sensory isolation. *The American Journal of Psychiatry*, 122:920-928 (1966)

Rothschild, B.: Boundary definiteness and yielding. *Journal of Consulting Psychology* (in press)

Rubinstein, E. A., and M. B. Parloff: *Research in psychotherapy*. Washington, D. C.: American Psychological Association, 1959

Schiebel, D. R.: Tactile behavior in psychopathology. Doctoral dissertation, University of Michigan, 1965

Schilder, P.: *The image and appearance of the human body*. London: Kegan Paul, Trench, Trubner and Company, 1935

Schultz, T. D.: A comparison of the reactions and attitudes toward stress of two psychosomatic groups. Doctoral dissertation, Washington University, 1966

Secord, P. F.: Objectification of word association procedures by the use of homonyms: A measure of body cathexis. *Journal of Personality*, 21:479-495 (1953)

Sherick, I. G.: Body image, level of ego development and adequacy of ego functioning. Doctoral dissertation, Washington University, 1964

Shipman, W. G.: Personality traits associated with body-image boundary concern. Paper presented at American Psychological Association meeting, New York City, 1965

Shipman, W. G., D. Oken, R. R. Grinker, I. B. Goldstein and H. A. Heath: A study in the psychophysiology of muscle tension. II: Emotional factors. *Archives of General Psychiatry*, 11:330-345 (1964)

Sieracki, E. R.: Body-image as a variable in the acceptance of disability and vocation interests of the physically disabled. Doctoral dissertation, State University of New York, Buffalo, 1963

Twente, E. W.: Patterns of awakening. *The Clinical Counselor*, 1964 (Winter), 7-17

Wapner, S., and H. Werner (eds.): *The body percept.* New York: Random House, 1965

Wapner, S., H. Werner and P. E. Comalli: Effect of enhancement of head boundary on head size and shape. *Perceptual and Motor Skills*, 8:319-325 (1958)

Ware, K. S., S. Fisher and S. E. Cleveland: Body image boundaries and adjustment to poliomyelitis. *Journal of Abnormal and Social Psychology*, 55:88-93 (1957)

Wertheimer, Rita, and L. A. Bachelis: Individual differences in hue discrimination as a cognitive variable. Presented at American Psychological Association meeting, New York City, 1966

Williams, R. L.: The relationship of body image to some physiological reactivity patterns in psychosomatic patients. Doctoral dissertation, Washington University, 1962

Williams, R. L., and A. G. Krasnoff: Body image and physiological patterns in patients with peptic ulcer and rheumatoid arthritis. *Psychosomatic Medicine*, 26:701-709 (1964)

Wittreich, W. J., and K. B. Radcliffe, Jr.: The influence of simulated mutilation upon the perception of the human figure. *Journal of Abnormal and Social Psychology*, 51:493-495 (1955)

Zimny, G. H.: Body image and physiological responses. *Journal of Psychosomatic Research*, 9:185-188 (1965)

Subject Index

··

Name Index

Abel, T. A., 33
Ach, N., 40
Adams, H. B., 388
Adler, A., 42, 46, 48
Adler, G., 48
Allardice, B. S., 390
Allport, F. H., 39-41, 359-62
Allport, G. W., 153-60, 162, 164-65, 219
Alper, T. G., 125
Ames, L. B., 264
Appleby, L., 68-69, 103-04, 119-21, 124, 154-56, 158, 160-61, 163-65
Armstrong, H., 375
Ascher, R. C., 32-33
Atkinson, J. W., 151
Azima, D., 388

Bacon, C. L., 301-02
Bachelis, L. A., 390, 394
Bales, R. F., 207, 270, 349-50, 353
Bard, M., 305
Barron, F., 363
Bartlett, F. C., 5
Bass, B. M., 207
Beck, S. J., 129, 234, 264, 269, 279-80
Becker, W. C., 254
Bell, G. B., 207
Bender, L., 17
Bender, M. B., 13, 53
Benedict, R., 273-74, 291-92
Bennett, C. L., 338-40
Bennett, G., 125
Benton, A. L., 8
Berdie, R. F., 160
Berman, S., 35
Bernreuter, R. G., 253
Bettelheim, B., 239-40, 243
Bialos, D. S., 379
Bills, R. E., 112-13
Bindman, A. J., 254
Bitterman, M. E., 138-39, 149-50
Blake, R. R., 69, 217-25, 381
Bleuler, E., 230-32, 238
Blumberg, E. M., 302
Bollea, G., 7
Bonnier, P. L., 4, 6
Borgatta, E. F., 207
Bourguignon, E. E., 282, 284
Bovard, E. W., Jr., 129
Bowman, K. M., 338
Bray, D. W., 129
Brewer, E. J., 374
Brodie, C. W., 379-80

Brody, S., 284
Brogden, H. E., 153
Bromberg, W., 25-26
Brown, E. T., 32, 35
Brownfain, J. J., 254
Bruner, J. S., 171-205
Buchwald, A. M., 311-12
Burton, A. C., 314-15

Carlson, V. R., 142, 144-45
Carrera, R. N., 388
Cassell, W. A., 372, 376
Cattell, R. B., 207, 309-10, 320
Caudill, W., 274-75
Cheatham, M. J., 110-11, 280
Child, I. L., 284, 289, 293
Clemens, T. L., 302-03
Cleveland, S. E., 70, 146-47, 270, 373-74, 382-83, 385, 387-88, 393
Cobb, B., 302-03
Cohen, R., 14-15
Comalli, P. E., 388
Compton, N., 394
Conquest, R. A., 386
Cook, W. E., 35
Cormack, P. H., 378
Cramer, F. J., 388
Critchley, M., 3, 7-8
Curran, F. J., 29
Cushing, F. H., 290-91
Cutler, M., 301-02
Cutner, M., 243

Daniels, G. E., 318
Darrow, C. W., 309
Daston, P. G., 378-79, 390, 393
Davis, A., 284
Davis, A. D., 327-36, 373, 377
Davis, H., 338
Davis, P. A., 338
Davis, R. C., 311-12
Deutsch, M. A., 207
De Vos, G., 254, 271-75, 389
Dole, A. A., 390
Dorsey, D. S., 384-85, 390
Drolette, M. A., 132-33, 316-17, 324-26
Dunlap, K., 140

Edholm, O. G., 314-15
Edwards, A., 120
Eigenbrode, C. R., 374, 377, 390
Elkisch, P., 34-35
Ellingson, R. J., 339-40

445

A CATALOGUE OF SELECTED DOVER BOOKS
IN ALL FIELDS OF INTEREST

MODERN CHESS STRATEGY, Ludek Pachman. The use of the queen, the active king, exchanges, pawn play, the center, weak squares, etc. Section on rook alone worth price of the book. Stress on the moderns. Often considered the most important book on strategy. 314pp. 20290-9 Pa. $3.50

CHESS STRATEGY, Edward Lasker. One of half-dozen great theoretical works in chess, shows principles of action above and beyond moves. Acclaimed by Capablanca, Keres, etc. 282pp. USO 20528-2 Pa. $3.00

CHESS PRAXIS, THE PRAXIS OF MY SYSTEM, Aron Nimzovich. Founder of hypermodern chess explains his profound, influential theories that have dominated much of 20th century chess. 109 illustrative games. 369pp. 20296-8 Pa. $3.50

HOW TO PLAY THE CHESS OPENINGS, Eugene Znosko-Borovsky. Clear, profound examinations of just what each opening is intended to do and how opponent can counter. Many sample games, questions and answers. 147pp. 22795-2 Pa. $2.00

THE ART OF CHESS COMBINATION, Eugene Znosko-Borovsky. Modern explanation of principles, varieties, techniques and ideas behind them, illustrated with many examples from great players. 212pp. 20583-5 Pa. $2.50

COMBINATIONS: THE HEART OF CHESS, Irving Chernev. Step-by-step explanation of intricacies of combinative play. 356 combinations by Tarrasch, Botvinnik, Keres, Steinitz, Anderssen, Morphy, Marshall, Capablanca, others, all annotated. 245 pp. 21744-2 Pa. $3.00

HOW TO PLAY CHESS ENDINGS, Eugene Znosko-Borovsky. Thorough instruction manual by fine teacher analyzes each piece individually; many common endgame situations. Examines games by Steinitz, Alekhine, Lasker, others. Emphasis on understanding. 288pp. 21170-3 Pa. $2.75

MORPHY'S GAMES OF CHESS, Philip W. Sergeant. Romantic history, 54 games of greatest player of all time against Anderssen, Bird, Paulsen, Harrwitz; 52 games at odds; 52 blindfold; 100 consultation, informal, other games. Analyses by Anderssen, Steinitz, Morphy himself. 352pp. 20386-7 Pa. $4.00

500 MASTER GAMES OF CHESS, S. Tartakower, J. du Mont. Vast collection of great chess games from 1798-1938, with much material nowhere else readily available. Fully annotated, arranged by opening for easier study. 665pp. 23208-5 Pa. $6.00

THE SOVIET SCHOOL OF CHESS, Alexander Kotov and M. Yudovich. Authoritative work on modern Russian chess. History, conceptual background. 128 fully annotated games (most unavailable elsewhere) by Botvinnik, Keres, Smyslov, Tal, Petrosian, Spassky, more. 390pp. 20026-4 Pa. $3.95

WONDERS AND CURIOSITIES OF CHESS, Irving Chernev. A lifetime's accumulation of such wonders and curiosities as the longest won game, shortest game, chess problem with mate in 1220 moves, and much more unusual material —356 items in all, over 160 complete games. 146 diagrams. 203pp. 23007-4 Pa. $3.50

How to Solve Chess Problems, Kenneth S. Howard. Practical suggestions on problem solving for very beginners. 58 two-move problems, 46 3-movers, 8 4-movers for practice, plus hints. 171pp. 20748-X Pa. $2.00

A Guide to Fairy Chess, Anthony Dickins. 3-D chess, 4-D chess, chess on a cylindrical board, reflecting pieces that bounce off edges, cooperative chess, retrograde chess, maximummers, much more. Most based on work of great Dawson. Full handbook, 100 problems. 66pp. 7⅞ x 10¾. 22687-5 Pa. $2.00

Win at Backgammon, Millard Hopper. Best opening moves, running game, blocking game, back game, tables of odds, etc. Hopper makes the game clear enough for anyone to play, and win. 43 diagrams. 111pp. 22894-0 Pa. $1.50

Bidding a Bridge Hand, Terence Reese. Master player "thinks out loud" the binding of 75 hands that defy point count systems. Organized by bidding problem—no-fit situations, overbidding, underbidding, cueing your defense, etc. 254pp. EBE 22830-4 Pa. $3.00

The Precision Bidding System in Bridge, C.C. Wei, edited by Alan Truscott. Inventor of precision bidding presents average hands and hands from actual play, including games from 1969 Bermuda Bowl where system emerged. 114 exercises. 116pp. 21171-1 Pa. $1.75

Learn Magic, Henry Hay. 20 simple, easy-to-follow lessons on magic for the new magician: illusions, card tricks, silks, sleights of hand, coin manipulations, escapes, and more —all with a minimum amount of equipment. Final chapter explains the great stage illusions. 92 illustrations. 285pp. 21238-6 Pa. $2.95

The New Magician's Manual, Walter B. Gibson. Step-by-step instructions and clear illustrations guide the novice in mastering 36 tricks; much equipment supplied on 16 pages of cut-out materials. 36 additional tricks. 64 illustrations. 159pp. 6⅝ x 10. 23113-5 Pa. $3.00

Professional Magic for Amateurs, Walter B. Gibson. 50 easy, effective tricks used by professionals —cards, string, tumblers, handkerchiefs, mental magic, etc. 63 illustrations. 223pp. 23012-0 Pa. $2.50

Card Manipulations, Jean Hugard. Very rich collection of manipulations; has taught thousands of fine magicians tricks that are really workable, eye-catching. Easily followed, serious work. Over 200 illustrations. 163pp. 20539-8 Pa. $2.00

Abbott's Encyclopedia of Rope Tricks for Magicians, Stewart James. Complete reference book for amateur and professional magicians containing more than 150 tricks involving knots, penetrations, cut and restored rope, etc. 510 illustrations. Reprint of 3rd edition. 400pp. 23206-9 Pa. $3.50

The Secrets of Houdini, J.C. Cannell. Classic study of Houdini's incredible magic, exposing closely-kept professional secrets and revealing, in general terms, the whole art of stage magic. 67 illustrations. 279pp. 22913-0 Pa. $2.50

THE RED FAIRY BOOK, Andrew Lang. Lang's color fairy books have long been children's favorites. This volume includes Rapunzel, Jack and the Bean-stalk and 35 other stories, familiar and unfamiliar. 4 plates, 93 illustrations x + 367pp.
21673-X Paperbound $3.00

THE BLUE FAIRY BOOK, Andrew Lang. Lang's tales come from all countries and all times. Here are 37 tales from Grimm, the Arabian Nights, Greek Mythology, and other fascinating sources. 8 plates, 130 illustrations. xi + 390pp.
21437-0 Paperbound $3.50

HOUSEHOLD STORIES BY THE BROTHERS GRIMM. Classic English-language edition of the well-known tales — Rumpelstiltskin, Snow White, Hansel and Gretel, The Twelve Brothers, Faithful John, Rapunzel, Tom Thumb (52 stories in all). Translated into simple, straightforward English by Lucy Crane. Ornamented with headpieces, vignettes, elaborate decorative initials and a dozen full-page illustrations by Walter Crane. x + 269pp.
21080-4 Paperbound $3.00

THE MERRY ADVENTURES OF ROBIN HOOD, Howard Pyle. The finest modern versions of the traditional ballads and tales about the great English outlaw. Howard Pyle's complete prose version, with every word, every illustration of the first edition. Do not confuse this facsimile of the original (1883) with modern editions that change text or illustrations. 23 plates plus many page decorations. xxii + 296pp.
22043-5 Paperbound $4.00

THE STORY OF KING ARTHUR AND HIS KNIGHTS, Howard Pyle. The finest children's version of the life of King Arthur; brilliantly retold by Pyle, with 48 of his most imaginative illustrations. xviii + 313pp. 6⅛ x 9¼.
21445-1 Paperbound $3.50

THE WONDERFUL WIZARD OF OZ, L. Frank Baum. America's finest children's book in facsimile of first edition with all Denslow illustrations in full color. The edition a child should have. Introduction by Martin Gardner. 23 color plates, scores of drawings. iv + 267pp.
20691-2 Paperbound $3.00

THE MARVELOUS LAND OF OZ, L. Frank Baum. The second Oz book, every bit as imaginative as the Wizard. The hero is a boy named Tip, but the Scarecrow and the Tin Woodman are back, as is the Oz magic. 16 color plates, 120 drawings by John R. Neill. 287pp.
20692-0 Paperbound $3.00

THE MAGICAL MONARCH OF MO, L. Frank Baum. Remarkable adventures in a land even stranger than Oz. The best of Baum's books not in the Oz series. 15 color plates and dozens of drawings by Frank Verbeck. xviii + 237pp.
21892-9 Paperbound $2.95

THE BAD CHILD'S BOOK OF BEASTS, MORE BEASTS FOR WORSE CHILDREN, A MORAL ALPHABET, Hilaire Belloc. Three complete humor classics in one volume. Be kind to the frog, and do not call him names . . . and 28 other whimsical animals. Familiar favorites and some not so well known. Illustrated by Basil Blackwell. 156pp.
(USO) 20749-8 Paperbound $2.00

SLEEPING BEAUTY, illustrated by Arthur Rackham. Perhaps the fullest, most delightful version ever, told by C.S. Evans. Rackham's best work. 49 illustrations. 110pp. 7⅞ x 10¾. 22756-1 Pa. $2.00

THE WONDERFUL WIZARD OF OZ, L. Frank Baum. Facsimile in full color of America's finest children's classic. Introduction by Martin Gardner. 143 illustrations by W.W. Denslow. 267pp. 20691-2 Pa. $3.00

GOOPS AND HOW TO BE THEM, Gelett Burgess. Classic tongue-in-cheek masquerading as etiquette book. 87 verses, 170 cartoons as Goops demonstrate virtues of table manners, neatness, courtesy, more. 88pp. 6½ x 9¼. 22233-0 Pa. $2.00

THE BROWNIES, THEIR BOOK, Palmer Cox. Small as mice, cunning as foxes, exuberant, mischievous, Brownies go to zoo, toy shop, seashore, circus, more. 24 verse adventures. 266 illustrations. 144pp. 6⅝ x 9¼. 21265-3 Pa. $2.50

BILLY WHISKERS: THE AUTOBIOGRAPHY OF A GOAT, Frances Trego Montgomery. Escapades of that rambunctious goat. Favorite from turn of the century America. 24 illustrations. 259pp. 22345-0 Pa. $2.75

THE ROCKET BOOK, Peter Newell. Fritz, janitor's kid, sets off rocket in basement of apartment house; an ingenious hole punched through every page traces course of rocket. 22 duotone drawings, verses. 48pp. 6⅞ x 8⅜. 22044-3 Pa. $1.50

PECK'S BAD BOY AND HIS PA, George W. Peck. Complete double-volume of great American childhood classic. Hennery's ingenious pranks against outraged pomposity of pa and the grocery man. 97 illustrations. Introduction by E.F. Bleiler. 347pp. 20497-9 Pa. $2.50

THE TALE OF PETER RABBIT, Beatrix Potter. The inimitable Peter's terrifying adventure in Mr. McGregor's garden, with all 27 wonderful, full-color Potter illustrations. 55pp. 4¼ x 5½. USO 22827-4 Pa. $1.00

THE TALE OF MRS. TIGGY-WINKLE, Beatrix Potter. Your child will love this story about a very special hedgehog and all 27 wonderful, full-color Potter illustrations. 57pp. 4¼ x 5½. USO 20546-0 Pa. $1.00

THE TALE OF BENJAMIN BUNNY, Beatrix Potter. Peter Rabbit's cousin coaxes him back into Mr. McGregor's garden for a whole new set of adventures. A favorite with children. All 27 full-color illustrations. 59pp. 4¼ x 5½. USO 21102-9 Pa. $1.00

THE MERRY ADVENTURES OF ROBIN HOOD, Howard Pyle. Facsimile of original (1883) edition, finest modern version of English outlaw's adventures. 23 illustrations by Pyle. 296pp. 6½ x 9¼. 22043-5 Pa. $4.00

TWO LITTLE SAVAGES, Ernest Thompson Seton. Adventures of two boys who lived as Indians; explaining Indian ways, woodlore, pioneer methods. 293 illustrations. 286pp. 20985-7 Pa. $3.00

DECORATIVE ALPHABETS AND INITIALS, edited by Alexander Nesbitt. 91 complete alphabets (medieval to modern), 3924 decorative initials, including Victo_an novelty and Art Nouveau. 192pp. 7¾ x 10¾. 20544-4 Pa. $4.00

CALLIGRAPHY, Arthur Baker. Over 100 original alphabets from the hand of our greatest living calligrapher: simple, bold, fine-line, richly ornamented, etc. — all strikingly original and different, a fusion of many influences and styles. 155pp. 11⅜ x 8¼. 22895-9 Pa. $4.50

MONOGRAMS AND ALPHABETIC DEVICES, edited by Hayward and Blanche Cirker. Over 2500 combinations, names, crests in very varied styles: script engraving, ornate Victorian, simple Roman, and many others. 226pp. 8⅛ x 11. 22330-2 Pa. $5.00

THE BOOK OF SIGNS, Rudolf Koch. Famed German type designer renders 493 symbols: religious, alchemical, imperial, runes, property marks, etc. Timeless. 104pp. 6⅛ x 9¼. 20162-7 Pa. $1.75

200 DECORATIVE TITLE PAGES, edited by Alexander Nesbitt. 1478 to late 1920's. Baskerville, Dürer, Beardsley, W. Morris, Pyle, many others in most varied techniques. For posters, programs, other uses. 222pp. 8⅜ x 11¼. 21264-5 Pa. **$5.00**

DICTIONARY OF AMERICAN PORTRAITS, edited by Hayward and Blanche Cirker. 4000 important Americans, earliest times to 1905, mostly in clear line. Politicians, writers, soldiers, scientists, inventors, industrialists, Indians, Blacks, women, outlaws, etc. Identificatory information. 756pp. 9¼ x 12¾. 21823-6 Clothbd. $30.00

ART FORMS IN NATURE, Ernst Haeckel. Multitude of strangely beautiful natural forms: Radiolaria, Foraminifera, jellyfishes, fungi, turtles, bats, etc. All 100 plates of the 19th century evolutionist's Kunstformen der Natur (1904). 100pp. 9⅜ x 12¼. 22987-4 Pa. $4.00

DECOUPAGE: THE BIG PICTURE SOURCEBOOK, Eleanor Rawlings. Make hundreds of beautiful objects, over 550 florals, animals, letters, shells, period costumes, frames, etc. selected by foremost practitioner. Printed on one side of page. 8 color plates. Instructions. 176pp. 9³/₁₆ x 12¼. 23182-8 Pa. $5.00

AMERICAN FOLK DECORATION, Jean Lipman, Eve Meulendyke. Thorough coverage of all aspects of wood, tin, leather, paper, cloth decoration — scapes, humans, trees, flowers, geometrics — and how to make them. Full instructions. 233 illustrations, 5 in color. 163pp. 8⅜ x 11¼. 22217-9 Pa. $3.95

WHITTLING AND WOODCARVING, E.J. Tangerman. Best book on market; clear, full. If you can cut a potato, you can carve toys, puzzles, chains, caricatures, masks, patterns, frames, decorate surfaces, etc. Also covers serious wood sculpture. Over 200 photos. 293pp. 20965-2 Pa. $3.00

VISUAL ILLUSIONS: THEIR CAUSES, CHARACTERISTICS, AND APPLICATIONS, Matthew Luckiesh. Thorough description and discussion of optical illusion, geometric and perspective, particularly; size and shape distortions, illusions of color, of motion; natural illusions; use of illusion in art and magic, industry, etc. Most useful today with op art, also for classical art. Scores of effects illustrated. Introduction by William H. Ittleson. 100 illustrations. xxi + 252pp.

21530-X Paperbound $2.50

A HANDBOOK OF ANATOMY FOR ART STUDENTS, Arthur Thomson. Thorough, virtually exhaustive coverage of skeletal structure, musculature, etc. Full text, supplemented by anatomical diagrams and drawings and by photographs of undraped figures. Unique in its comparison of male and female forms, pointing out differences of contour, texture, form. 211 figures, 40 drawings, 86 photographs. xx + 459pp. 5⅜ x 8⅜.

21163-0 Paperbound $5.00

150 MASTERPIECES OF DRAWING, Selected by Anthony Toney. Full page reproductions of drawings from the early 16th to the end of the 18th century, all beautifully reproduced: Rembrandt, Michelangelo, Dürer, Fragonard, Urs, Graf, Wouwerman, many others. First-rate browsing book, model book for artists. xviii + 150pp. 8⅜ x 11¼.

21032-4 Paperbound' $4.00

THE LATER WORK OF AUBREY BEARDSLEY, Aubrey Beardsley. Exotic, erotic, ironic masterpieces in full maturity: Comedy Ballet, Venus and Tannhauser, Pierrot, Lysistrata, Rape of the Lock, Savoy material, Ali Baba, Volpone, etc. This material revolutionized the art world, and is still powerful, fresh, brilliant. With *The Early Work*, all Beardsley's finest work. 174 plates, 2 in color. xiv + 176pp. 8⅛ x 11.

21817-1 Paperbound $4.00

DRAWINGS OF REMBRANDT, Rembrandt van Rijn. Complete reproduction of fabulously rare edition by Lippmann and Hofstede de Groot, completely reedited, updated, improved by Prof. Seymour Slive, Fogg Museum. Portraits, Biblical sketches, landscapes, Oriental types, nudes, episodes from classical mythology—All Rembrandt's fertile genius. Also selection of drawings by his pupils and followers. "Stunning volumes," *Saturday Review*. 550 illustrations. lxxviii + 552pp. 9⅛ x 12¼.

21485-0, 21486-9 Two volumes, Paperbound $12.00

THE DISASTERS OF WAR, Francisco Goya. One of the masterpieces of Western civilization—83 etchings that record Goya's shattering, bitter reaction to the Napoleonic war that swept through Spain after the insurrection of 1808 and to war in general. Reprint of the first edition, with three additional plates from Boston's Museum of Fine Arts. All plates facsimile size. Introduction by Philip Hofer, Fogg Museum. v + 97pp. 9⅜ x 8¼.

21872-4 Paperbound $3.00

GRAPHIC WORKS OF ODILON REDON. Largest collection of Redon's graphic works ever assembled: 172 lithographs, 28 etchings and engravings, 9 drawings. These include some of his most famous works. All the plates from *Odilon Redon: oeuvre graphique complet,* plus additional plates. New introduction and caption translations by Alfred Werner. 209 illustrations. xxvii + 209pp. 9⅛ x 12¼.

21966-8 Paperbound $6.00

AUSTRIAN COOKING AND BAKING, Gretel Beer. Authentic thick soups, wiener schnitzel, veal goulash, more, plus dumplings, puff pastries, nut cakes, sacher tortes, other great Austrian desserts. 224pp. USO 23220-4 Pa. $2.50

CHEESES OF THE WORLD, U.S.D.A. Dictionary of cheeses containing descriptions of over 400 varieties of cheese from common Cheddar to exotic Surati. Up to two pages are given to important cheeses like Camembert, Cottage, Edam, etc. 151pp. 22831-2 Pa. $1.50

TRITTON'S GUIDE TO BETTER WINE AND BEER MAKING FOR BEGINNERS, S.M. Tritton. All you need to know to make family-sized quantities of over 100 types of grape, fruit, herb, vegetable wines; plus beers, mead, cider, more. 11 illustrations. 157pp. USO 22528-3 Pa. $2.25

DECORATIVE LABELS FOR HOME CANNING, PRESERVING, AND OTHER HOUSEHOLD AND GIFT USES, Theodore Menten. 128 gummed, perforated labels, beautifully printed in 2 colors. 12 versions in traditional, Art Nouveau, Art Deco styles. Adhere to metal, glass, wood, most plastics. 24pp. 8¼ x 11. 23219-0 Pa. $2.00

FIVE ACRES AND INDEPENDENCE, Maurice G. Kains. Great back-to-the-land classic explains basics of self-sufficient farming: economics, plants, crops, animals, orchards, soils, land selection, host of other necessary things. Do not confuse with skimpy faddist literature; Kains was one of America's greatest agriculturalists. 95 illustrations. 397pp. 20974-1 Pa. $3.00

GROWING VEGETABLES IN THE HOME GARDEN, U.S. Dept. of Agriculture. Basic information on site, soil conditions, selection of vegetables, planting, cultivation, gathering. Up-to-date, concise, authoritative. Covers 60 vegetables. 30 illustrations. 123pp. 23167-4 Pa. $1.35

FRUITS FOR THE HOME GARDEN, Dr. U.P. Hedrick. A chapter covering each type of garden fruit, advice on plant care, soils, grafting, pruning, sprays, transplanting, and much more! Very full. 53 illustrations. 175pp. 22944-0 Pa. $2.50

GARDENING ON SANDY SOIL IN NORTH TEMPERATE AREAS, Christine Kelway. Is your soil too light, too sandy? Improve your soil, select plants that survive under such conditions. Both vegetables and flowers. 42 photos. 148pp. USO 23199-2 Pa. $2.50

THE FRAGRANT GARDEN: A BOOK ABOUT SWEET SCENTED FLOWERS AND LEAVES, Louise Beebe Wilder. Fullest, best book on growing plants for their fragrances. Descriptions of hundreds of plants, both well-known and overlooked. 407pp. 23071-6 Pa. $4.00

EASY GARDENING WITH DROUGHT-RESISTANT PLANTS, Arno and Irene Nehrling. Authoritative guide to gardening with plants that require a minimum of water: seashore, desert, and rock gardens; house plants; annuals and perennials; much more. 190 illustrations. 320pp. 23230-1 Pa. $3.50

MANUAL OF THE TREES OF NORTH AMERICA, Charles S. Sargent. The basic survey of every native tree and tree-like shrub, 717 species in all. Extremely full descriptions, information on habitat, growth, locales, economics, etc. Necessary to every serious tree lover. Over 100 finding keys. 783 illustrations. Total of 986pp.
20277-1, 20278-X Pa., Two vol. set $9.00

BIRDS OF THE NEW YORK AREA, John Bull. Indispensable guide to more than 400 species within a hundred-mile radius of Manhattan. Information on range, status, breeding, migration, distribution trends, etc. Foreword by Roger Tory Peterson. 17 drawings; maps. 540pp. 23222-0 Pa. $6.00

THE SEA-BEACH AT EBB-TIDE, Augusta Foote Arnold. Identify hundreds of marine plants and animals: algae, seaweeds, squids, crabs, corals, etc. Descriptions cover food, life cycle, size, shape, habitat. Over 600 drawings. 490pp.
21949-6 Pa. $5.00

THE MOTH BOOK, William J. Holland. Identify more than 2,000 moths of North America. General information, precise species descriptions. 623 illustrations plus 48 color plates show almost all species, full size. 1968 edition. Still the basic book. Total of 551pp. 6½ x 9¼. 21948-8 Pa. $6.00

AN INTRODUCTION TO THE REPTILES AND AMPHIBIANS OF THE UNITED STATES, Percy A. Morris. All lizards, crocodiles, turtles, snakes, toads, frogs; life history, identification, habits, suitability as pets, etc. Non-technical, but sound and broad. 130 photos. 253pp. 22982-3 Pa. $3.00

OLD NEW YORK IN EARLY PHOTOGRAPHS, edited by Mary Black. Your only chance to see New York City as it was 1853-1906, through 196 wonderful photographs from N.Y. Historical Society. Great Blizzard, Lincoln's funeral procession, great buildings. 228pp. 9 x 12. 22907-6 Pa. $6.00

THE AMERICAN REVOLUTION, A PICTURE SOURCEBOOK, John Grafton. Wonderful Bicentennial picture source, with 411 illustrations (contemporary and 19th century) showing battles, personalities, maps, events, flags, posters, soldier's life, ships, etc. all captioned and explained. A wonderful browsing book, supplement to other historical reading. 160pp. 9 x 12. 23226-3 Pa. $4.00

PERSONAL NARRATIVE OF A PILGRIMAGE TO AL-MADINAH AND MECCAH, Richard Burton. Great travel classic by remarkably colorful personality. Burton, disguised as a Moroccan, visited sacred shrines of Islam, narrowly escaping death. Wonderful observations of Islamic life, customs, personalities. 47 illustrations. Total of 959pp. 21217-3, 21218-1 Pa., Two vol. set $10.00

INCIDENTS OF TRAVEL IN CENTRAL AMERICA, CHIAPAS, AND YUCATAN, John L. Stephens. Almost single-handed discovery of Maya culture; exploration of ruined cities, monuments, temples; customs of Indians. 115 drawings. 892pp.
22404-X, 22405-8 Pa., Two vol. set $8.00

COOKIES FROM MANY LANDS, Josephine Perry. Crullers, oatmeal cookies, chaux au chocolate, English tea cakes, mandel kuchen, Sacher torte, Danish puff pastry, Swedish cookies — a mouth-watering collection of 223 recipes. 157pp.
22832-0 Pa. $2.00

ROSE RECIPES, Eleanour S. Rohde. How to make sauces, jellies, tarts, salads, pot-pourris, sweet bags, pomanders, perfumes from garden roses; all exact recipes. Century old favorites. 95pp.
22957-2 Pa. $1.25

"OSCAR" OF THE WALDORF'S COOKBOOK, Oscar Tschirky. Famous American chef reveals 3455 recipes that made Waldorf great; cream of French, German, American cooking, in all categories. Full instructions, easy home use. 1896 edition. 907pp. $6\frac{5}{8}$ x $9\frac{3}{8}$.
20790-0 Clothbd. $15.00

JAMS AND JELLIES, May Byron. Over 500 old-time recipes for delicious jams, jellies, marmalades, preserves, and many other items. Probably the largest jam and jelly book in print. Originally titled May Byron's Jam Book. 276pp.
USO 23130-5 Pa. $3.00

MUSHROOM RECIPES, André L. Simon. 110 recipes for everyday and special cooking. Champignons a la grecque, sole bonne femme, chicken liver croustades, more; 9 basic sauces, 13 ways of cooking mushrooms. 54pp.
USO 20913-X Pa. $1.25

FAVORITE SWEDISH RECIPES, edited by Sam Widenfelt. Prepared in Sweden, offers wonderful, clearly explained Swedish dishes: appetizers, meats, pastry and cookies, other categories. Suitable for American kitchen. 90 photos. 157pp.
23156-9 Pa. $2.00

THE BUCKEYE COOKBOOK, Buckeye Publishing Company. Over 1,000 easy-to-follow, traditional recipes from the American Midwest: bread (100 recipes alone), meat, game, jam, candy, cake, ice cream, and many other categories of cooking. 64 illustrations. From 1883 enlarged edition. 416pp.
23218-2 Pa. $4.00

TWENTY-TWO AUTHENTIC BANQUETS FROM INDIA, Robert H. Christie. Complete, easy-to-do recipes for almost 200 authentic Indian dishes assembled in 22 banquets. Arranged by region. Selected from Banquets of the Nations. 192pp.
23200-X Pa. $2.50

Prices subject to change without notice.
Available at your book dealer or write for free catalogue to Dept. GI, Dover Publications, Inc., 180 Varick St., N.Y., N.Y. 10014. Dover publishes more than 150 books each year on science, elementary and advanced mathematics, biology, music, art, literary history, social sciences and other areas.